THE LIFE OF MY CHOICE

By the same author

Arabian Sands
The Marsh Arabs
Desert, Marsh and Mountain
Visions of a Nomad
The Life of my Choice
My Kenya Days
The Danakil Diary
Among the Mountains

THE LIFE
OF MY CHOICE

Wilfred Thesiger

HarperCollins*Publishers*

HarperCollins*Publishers*
77–85 Fulham Palace Road,
Hammersmith, London W6 8JB

www.**fire**and**water**.com

Published by HarperCollins*Publishers* 2000
1 3 5 7 9 8 6 4 2

First published in Great Britain by
Collins 1987

A catalogue record for this book
is available from the British Library

ISBN 0 00 216194 X

Set in Palatino

Printed and bound in Great Britain by
Clays Ltd, St Ives plc

To the memory of
His late Imperial Majesty
Haile Selassie

CONTENTS

List of Maps   9
List of Illustrations   11
Introduction   15

PART I   FAMILY AND ABYSSINIA 1910–33

           1 Arrival in Addis Ababa   23
           2 Abyssinia   31
           3 Revolution, 1916–17   43
           4 The Aftermath   57
           5 England and School   65
           6 Oxford   77
           7 Haile Selassie's Coronation   88
           8 Oxford and The Milebrook   97

PART II   AMONG THE DANAKIL 1933–4

           9 The Highlands of Arussi   109
          10 Into Danakil Country   119
          11 Bahdu and the Awash River   128
          12 Exploration in the Aussa Sultanate   144
          13 Journey to the Coast   158

PART III   THE NORTHERN SUDAN 1935–7

          14 The Sudan   171
          15 Service in Darfur   186
          16 Darfur: Herdsmen and Hunters   203
          17 The Italian Occupation of Abyssinia   220
          18 Last Year in Darfur   239

PART IV   THE SOUTHERN SUDAN 1938-40

19   The Western Nuer   257
20   A Journey to Tibesti   277
21   Return to the Swamps   297

PART V   WAR YEARS 1940-4

22   The Sudan Defence Force   311
23   The Invasion of Abyssinia, 1940-1   323
24   Victory under Wingate   341
25   The Druze   355
26   With the SAS in the Western Desert   369

PART VI   RETURN TO ABYSSINIA 1944-5;
AND LATER TRAVELS

27   With the Crown Prince at Dessie   393
28   Desert, Marsh and Mountain, 1945-58   397
29   Lalibela; and South
     to the Kenya Border   402
30   North to the Simien; and Magdala   412
31   Last Days of a Civilization   431

Epilogue   442
Glossary   445
Index   449

LIST OF MAPS

Abyssinia	18–21
Danakil Country, 1930–4	106–7
Anglo-Egyptian Sudan, 1935–40	170
Northern Darfur, 1935–7	188–9
The Invasion of Abyssinia, 1936	221
Upper Nile Province, 1937–40	260
Tibesti, 1938	280–1
Gojjam, 1940–1	324
Syria, 1942–3	356–7
Western Desert, 1939–42	370–1
Southern Abyssinia, 1959	406
Northern Abyssinia, 1960	413

LIST OF ILLUSTRATIONS

The Regent of Abyssinia, Ras Tafari, with the Duke of York
(*courtesy of David Duff*)
My father and mother
My father being escorted into Addis Ababa, 1910
The new Legation, now the British Embassy
Myself, aged four, holding the horns of a mountain nyala
The original British Legation in Addis Ababa
The Emperor Menelik
The Abyssinian delegation to King George V's coronation
Lij Yasu, heir designate to the Emperor Menelik
Ras Tafari as Regent, 1917
Scenes during the revolution of 1917
Captured generals at the victory parade after the battle of
Sagale
A Tigrean from Northern Abyssinia
A view of Ankober, Menelik's capital before Addis Ababa
My uncle, Lord Chelmsford, in his state robes as Viceroy of
India, 1918
An official gathering at Viceregal Lodge, 1917
The Milebrook, Radnorshire, our family home for more than
twenty years
Old Boys' Match, Eton, 1933
The blessing of the waters by the priests at Epiphany in
Addis Ababa
A market near Addis Ababa
Haile Selassie on the day of his coronation as Emperor
Members of my Danakil expedition, 1933–4
Watering camels at Bilen
A group of Danakil warriors
Crossing the Awash river
The Jira crater rising above the swamps of Southern Aussa
Abhebad, the lake where the Awash ended
Outside my house at Kutum, with my lion cubs

Idris, my personal retainer in the Sudan

A gathering of the Maidob in Northern Darfur

Idris and other Zaghawa with a lioness

Travelling with my porters in the Western Nuer District

The *Kereri*, the paddle steamer which was the Headquarters
of the Western Nuer District

My trophies, 1935

Wedderburn-Maxwell with two Nile perch he had caught

Nuba wrestling in the eastern jabals of Kordofan

The Nanamsena Gorge, near Aouzou, in Tibesti

The Mashakazy Gorge, on Emi Koussi, in Tibesti

My party on the Tibesti journey

Brigadier Dan Sandford (*courtesy of the Imperial War Museum*)

Colonel Orde Wingate (*courtesy of the Imperial War Museum*)

Dedjazmatch Mangasha

The Blue Nile Gorge at Shafartak

Prisoners who surrendered to me at Agibar

Faris Shahin and his grandfather

A Druze cavalryman

Druze elders

David Stirling and an SAS patrol (*courtesy of the Imperial War
Museum*)

Myself with Colonel Gigantes (*courtesy of the Imperial War
Museum*)

The mountains of Northern Abyssinia

My caravan in Northern Abyssinia

A church drum at Lalibela

A Fitaurari with his wife and family

The Tisisat Falls on the Blue Nile

The monolithic church of Medhane Alam at Lalibela

The cruciform rock-hewn church of Giorgis at Lalibela

The seventeenth-century palace built by Fasiladas in Gondar

The twelfth-century church of Imrahanna Krestos

Haile Selassie

INTRODUCTION

THIS BOOK centres on Abyssinia, the name I have used – except in the final chapter – for the country in which I was born and spent the first eight years of my life. Then and for many years to come it was known, not as Ethiopia, but as Abyssinia. When the Italians invaded it in 1935, the newspapers, the politicians and the public spoke of it as Abyssinia, and during the Second World War, when we liberated the country, we always referred to it as Abyssinia. I have continued to refer to Abyssinia when describing my journeys there in 1959–60, although the name Ethiopia was by then in current use. I have, however, conformed with modern usage in the final chapter which is chiefly concerned with the overthrow of the Emperor Haile Selassie, the famine relief organizations and the present Marxist government.

Similarly, until very recently the Afar were always called the Danakil, which is the name I have used for them in *The Life of My Choice*. Likewise, despite present-day popular usage, I never refer to Addis Ababa (which in Amharic means New Flower) as 'Addis'; this to me is as inappropriate as referring to New College at Oxford as 'New'.

For events in Abyssinia from 1910 to 1919, I have depended on my father's despatches to the Foreign Office, his demi-official letters, copies of which are in my possession, and the many letters he wrote to his mother. I kept a detailed diary during my exploration of the Danakil country in 1933–4 and during my journey in Tibesti in 1938. For the years I served in the Sudan and during the war, I have the long letters I wrote regularly to my mother, and diaries for the last two journeys in Abyssinia.

I have included a chapter about the Italian invasion of Abyssinia in 1935–6. Few people today will have any knowledge of that war which occurred fifty years ago in a remote African country. I took no part in it, but no other event has ever distressed me so profoundly. Without an appreciation of the atrocities committed by the Italians, it would be impossible to understand the hatred I felt for them, and my wartime dedication to the liberation of Abyssinia. For this chapter I have relied almost entirely on Thomas M. Coffey's *Lion by the Tail* (1974). This lucid and detailed book is the definitive account of the subject, and should certainly be read by anyone interested in that brutal and unprovoked aggression by Mussolini.

For my description, at second hand, of the establishment in Ethiopia of Colonel Mengistu's communist regime, I have relied on accounts published in *The Times*, and on discussions with Professor Edward Ullendorff. A distinguished scholar with a comprehensive knowledge of Abyssinia, he has also kindly checked my résumé of Abyssinian history in chapter 2, and my transliterations of Amharic names.

The transliteration of Arabic names into English always poses problems. I have retained the customary spelling for such well-known names as Khartoum and Hadendoa: I am grateful to Mark Allen who has advised me on the others.

The following have helped greatly with the writing of this book. Gillian Gibbins has always taken a keen interest in its progress, and given me incessant encouragement and assistance. Adrian House, my unofficial editor, has read through the typescript many times and given me much valuable advice, especially on the structure of the book. Above all, George Webb has made time, in the course of the very busy life he leads, to read the typescript with meticulous care, made many suggestions that have improved the flow of the material and ensured factual accuracy. Mollie Emtage, for forty years, welcomed me back from my travels and took care of me in my flat in Chelsea. Only I know how much this meant to me; in this haven I have written much of this book.

I have eaten your bread and salt,
I have drunk your water and wine,
The deaths ye died I have watched beside,
And the lives ye led were mine.

Was there aught that I did not share
In vigil or toil or ease —
One joy or woe that I did not know,
Dear hearts across the seas?

KIPLING

PART I

Family and Abyssinia
1910–33

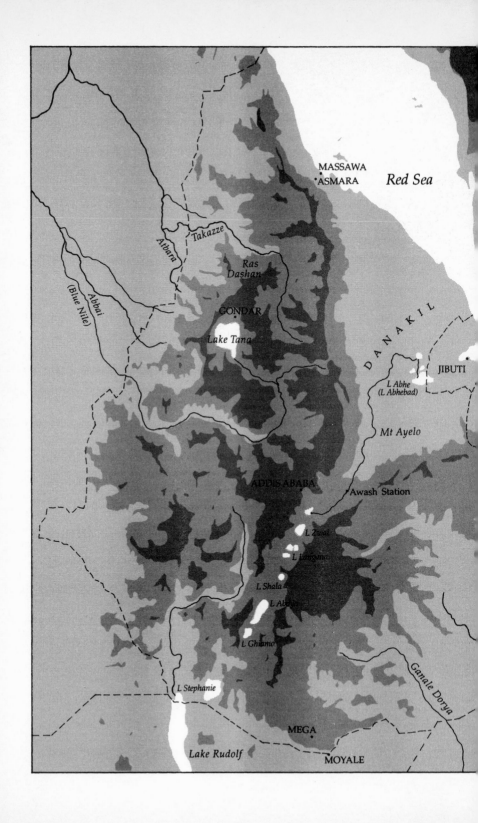

MASSAWA
ASMARA

Red Sea

Atbara

Takazze

Ras Dashan

GONDAR

(Blue Nile)

Abbai

Lake Tana

D A N A K I L

L Abhe (L Abhebad)

JIBUTI

Mt Ayelo

ADDIS ABABA

Awash Station

L Zwai

L Langana

L Shala

L Abiata

L Ghiamo

Ganale Dorya

L Stephanie

MEGA

Lake Rudolf

MOYALE

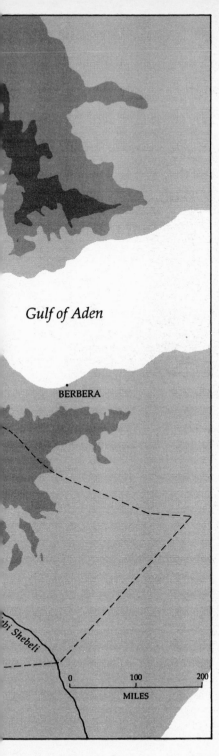

Gulf of Aden

BERBERA

bi Shebeli

0   100   200

MILES

Abyssinia

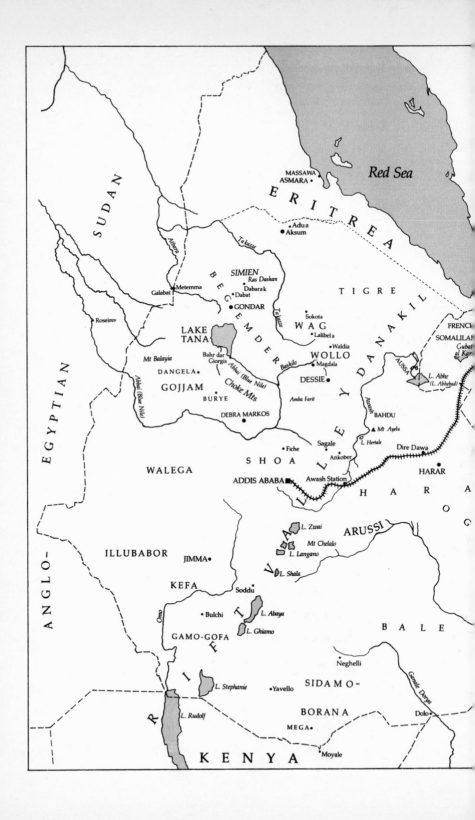

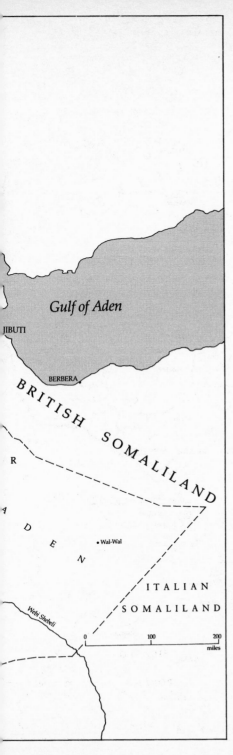

Gulf of Aden

JIBUTI

BERBERA

BRITISH SOMALILAND

R

A
D
E
N

• Wal-Wal

ITALIAN
SOMALILAND

Webi Shebeli

0   100   200
                miles

Abyssinia

CHAPTER 1

Arrival in Addis Ababa

IN THE SUMMER of 1924, during my first year at Eton, Ras Tafari, later to be Emperor Haile Selassie but at that time Regent, paid a State Visit to England and invited my mother and me to call on him in London. I had seen him on a number of occasions during my childhood in Abyssinia where my father had been British Minister at Addis Ababa, but this was the first time I spoke to him. Wearing a black, gold-embroidered silk cloak over a finely woven *shamma*, he came across the room to greet us, shook hands and with a smile and a gesture invited us to be seated. He was very small but even then to my mind his slight body and lack of height emphasized his distinction, drawing attention to the sensitive and finely moulded face.

My first and lasting impression was of dignity, a dignity entirely unassumed; then I was conscious of his kindness. In years to come I was to appreciate his inflexible will, his intense patience, his courage, his horror of cruelty, his dedication to his country and his deep religious faith.

We spoke in French, the foreign language in which he was fluent. He expressed at once his sorrow for my father's death. 'I shall never forget', he said, 'the support and help he gave me during the critical months of the revolution in 1916. He was a friend on whose advice I could always count. Such friends are few.'

My mother enquired after Ras Tafari's wife and family, especially after his eldest son, Asfa Wossen, who as a baby at the time of the battle of Sagale had sheltered with us in the Legation; then they spoke of mutual friends, and recalled events that had occurred while we were in Abyssinia. Meanwhile tea and cakes were brought in. Later, as we took our leave, I told Ras Tafari how I longed above all to return to his country.

'You will always be very welcome. One day you must come as my guest.'

When my father arrived in Abyssinia in mid-December 1909 to take up his post as British Minister in charge of the Legation, the

Emperor Menelik, the greatest ruler the country had known for centuries, was reported to be still alive; but no one knew for certain, and all men asked what would happen when he died.

For a year or more Menelik had lain in the palace, a living corpse, paralysed and speechless. He lived for another four years while his empire lapsed into chaos. He is said to have rallied before he died and to have whispered, 'My poor people', as the tears ran down his face. A few years earlier he had been the undisputed master of the empire: two hundred thousand of his warriors had paraded before him while a hundred thousand others guarded the marches of the north or fought the Somalis in the deserts to the east. He had founded Addis Ababa, 'the New Flower', below the Entoto mountains. Before his reign the site would have been on the southernmost borders of the empire; when he died it was at the empire's heart.

My father and mother had travelled by train from Jibuti, on the coast of French Somaliland, to Dire Dawa, the railhead in Abyssinia. There they were met by Wakeman, the Anglo-Indian doctor from the Legation whom Lord Herbert Hervey, the Consul, had sent to help them organize their onward journey. They had brought all that they would require in Abyssinia: provisions, clothes, books, pictures, furniture, tents, saddlery. There were scores of boxes and crates, all to be checked and loaded before they left Dire Dawa.

My mother had been married only a few months, and had never previously been further abroad than Italy. She was now faced with an arduous journey into a remote country where there might well be anarchy when Menelik died. It was enough to daunt most people, but she once told me that the only thing that dismayed her was sorting out their incredible mass of luggage, making sure that the right things went by the right route and that nothing was left behind. The heavier loads were being sent to Addis Ababa on camels by the desert route, where the Danakil, always dangerous, were said to be giving more trouble than usual. My parents, using mule transport, travelled to Addis Ababa through the Chercher mountains, by way of Harar, that ancient walled city which Burton had reached fifty-four years earlier.

There my father was anxious to meet Dedjazmatch Balcha, Governor of the Muslim city of Harar and one of the most powerful men in Abyssinia. Balcha was a Gurage by origin; as a boy he had been wounded and castrated in one of the many battles which Menelik had fought while subduing the southern tribes. When the fighting

24

was over Menelik noticed the boy and told his servants to tend him. Balcha recovered, grew up as a page in Menelik's household and later fought with distinction at Adua, where in 1896 the Abyssinians destroyed an Italian army. As Governor of Harar he had a well-merited reputation for ruthlessness, brutality and avarice, and was hated and feared by his subjects.

Two days after leaving Dire Dawa my parents camped in the highlands beside Haramaya Lake, a small stretch of water teeming with wildfowl, not far from Harar. Next day Balcha sent a force to escort my father to the town: my mother, who was pregnant and tired, remained in camp – and would regret it all her life. Now, for the first time, my father saw the barbaric splendour of the Abyssinian Empire. He described it in a letter to his mother:

> The Chiefs and notables were gorgeous in mantles of crimson, blue or green velvet, richly embroidered with gold thread, worn over silken shirts; some had lion- or leopard-skin capes draped about their shoulders. Many wore jewelled, gilded coronets fringed with lions' manes. Their shields were embossed with gold or silver; their long, curved swords were in richly decorated scabbards. The splendour of their robes was emphasized by the plain white clothes of their retainers.

The long, winding column of armed men, on horses, on mules and on foot, was an unforgettable sight as it moved across the plain in a haze of dust under a blazing sky. I wish my father had left a description of his encounter with Balcha but I can find none in his letters or despatches. That remarkable man was to play an important part in forthcoming events and twenty-six years later was killed fighting against the Italians once more.

A month later my parents were met on the open plain outside Addis Ababa by Lord Herbert Hervey and a deputation of Abyssinian notables who escorted them to the Legation, at some distance to the east of the town, in an extensive compound at the foot of the Entoto hills. The Legation consisted of connecting wattle-and-daub *tukuls*, each circular and thatched with grass. These buildings were comfortable and spacious, and had great charm. I was born in one of them in June 1910, the first British child born in Abyssinia. Not until the following year was the stone-built Legation completed, which houses the Embassy today.

In those days Great Britain was represented by an Ambassador in

Paris, Berlin, St Petersburg, Rome, Constantinople and Washington, but in most other countries by a Minister Plenipotentiary in a Legation.

When he arrived at the Legation my father's staff comprised the Consul, the doctor and an Abyssinian interpreter; there was also a Legation escort of five Sikhs from the Indian Army. Lord Herbert Hervey was transferred shortly afterwards and was replaced some months later by Colonel Doughty-Wylie. This outstanding man had been seconded from the Royal Welch Fusiliers to serve as Consul at Adana in Turkey, where he behaved with courage and firmness during the Armenian massacres, rescuing several hundred people before he himself was wounded as he rode round the town. He soon became a close friend of my parents and was later godfather to my brother Brian. In 1915 at Gallipoli Doughty-Wylie won a posthumous VC: at a critical moment in the landing he went ashore from the *River Clyde*, rallied the remnants of a battalion of the Hampshires, captured the heights above the beach, and there he was killed. I was too young to remember him, but later at intervals a number of remarkable men, among them Arnold Hodson, Hugh Dodds and Arthur Bentinck, served on my father's staff and were to remain our friends over the years.

A few days after his arrival my father was received in audience. In full diplomatic uniform he rode to the palace on a richly caparisoned mule sent to him by Menelik: in Abyssinia mules were more highly esteemed than horses. With him was my mother, the Consul and the mounted escort of Sikhs, and a small army even more colourful and far more numerous than the escort provided by Dedjazmatch Balcha. The palace was several miles from the Legation and every time they topped a rise my parents saw the whole procession spread out in front and behind.

By now Menelik was totally incapacitated and my father never met him. Instead he was greeted by Ras Tasamma, the Regent, and by Lij Yasu, the Emperor's fifteen-year-old grandson and heir. In another letter to his mother he described the day's events:

> At the main gate of the palace officials drove back the unauthorized with the unsparing use of long bamboos to clear a passageway. Inside the large first court musicians blew on long, straight trumpets and negroes with long flutes added to the din which was very thrilling and appropriate.

They rode through another crowded court and came to the inner court lined only by chiefs. There they dismounted and entered

> an enormous building, very dimly lit, with pillars of wood on either side; the floor was strewn with green rushes and a long carpet lay down the centre. Against the walls sat row behind row of chiefs, in all the glory of full dress.

Lij Yasu sat on a dais in front of the throne. At that first meeting my father can have had no idea of the troubles this boy would bring upon his country.

Such was my father's introduction to Abyssinia where, except for three periods of leave, he was to remain for the next ten years.

Already my father had had an interesting and varied career. Born in 1870, he had served during 1896–7 as honorary Vice-Consul at Van in Asia Minor, and was there during the Armenian massacres. Van in those days was remote from Constantinople and had been visited by few Europeans. Among the mountains around the lake, Kurdish tribes, in their distinctive and spectacular garb, lived as their ancestors had lived for centuries.

My father made a number of water-colour sketches of them that fascinated me as a boy but have since disappeared. At Van he was very conscious of a past greatness, when kings of Assyria ruled, fought and fell among these mountains; he could visualize the palaces in which they lived and the queens who shared their beds, and he wrote:

> Where are they now, with all their joys and cares?
> Scattered to dust and all their beauty fled.
> Only some grassy mounds and rock-hewn stairs
> Bear silent witness to the silent dead.
> And over these mounds the Kurdish shepherd strays,
> Watching the flocks that feed along the vale.
> What are to him these tales of ancient days
> Who never heard of Ashtaroth or Baal?
>
> (Van, 1896)

On his return to England my father was appointed to the Consular Service and posted to Taranto in southern Italy, where he served for two years. During the Boer War he joined the Imperial Yeomanry as a trooper, but was soon commissioned and later promoted to captain. He fought in South Africa from March 1900 until October 1901 and was awarded the DSO.

After the war he contemplated becoming a District Officer in Rhodesia but decided to rejoin the Consular Service. In 1902 he was sent as Vice-Consul to Belgrade, and was left in charge of the Legation, with the acting rank of Second Secretary, when the Minister was withdrawn in protest after King Alexander and Queen Draga had been butchered by members of the Black Hand. Among his papers I found a newspaper cutting, but with no indication of its source:

> Mr Thesiger held his post for three years in circumstances both irksome and perilous. During this period of voluntary ostracism from social contact with those around him, Mr Thesiger's fondness for out-of-doors sports and predilection for the simple life stood him in good stead. Horses, gun-dogs and books filled his day, and many a regicide glanced wrathfully at the nonchalant figure of the tall Englishman strolling unconcernedly in the highways and byways of Belgrade. They felt their power was being undermined ...

From Belgrade he was posted in 1906 to St Petersburg, and in 1907 to Boma in the Belgian Congo, soon after the Casement investigations into the Belgian atrocities. In 1909 he was appointed Minister in Addis Ababa. My father was thirty-eight, my mother twenty-nine when they married; a few months later they set off for Addis Ababa. A photograph of my mother at that time shows a beautiful, resolute face under waves of soft brown hair. There in the Legation, remote from family involvements and interference, she devoted herself to my father. His devotion to her is evident in the letters he wrote whenever they were separated. Years later she told me she could never remember an angry word between them.

My father was the grandson of Lord Chelmsford, the Lord Chancellor, and was the third son of General Lord Chelmsford. The latter, my grandfather, had served in the Crimea, in the Indian Mutiny, and in Abyssinia as Deputy Adjutant-General during the Magdala campaign; he then commanded the troops in South Africa during the Kaffir and Zulu wars. On retirement he was appointed ADC to Queen Victoria and Lieutenant of the Tower of London. He died at the age of eighty-one while playing billiards in the United Services Club.

My father was intensely and justifiably proud of his family, which in his own generation produced a viceroy, a general, an admiral, a Lord of Appeal, a High Court judge and a famous actor. Intelligent, sensitive and artistic, with a certain diffidence which added to his charm, he was above all a man of absolute integrity. He enjoyed sketching, writing verse and playing music. The faint sound of his cello, as I lay tucked up in bed, is woven into my childhood memories. He had an abiding love of the English countryside, and wrote of Beanley Moor:

Golden lights on the Cheviots, that flicker and change and fade
As the soft white clinging mist rack swirls down corry and glade,
Stretching down chilly fingers to the depths where the snow drifts
  lie
Or flinging on high its smoke rings to fade in the pale blue sky.
Pine trees, swayed by the north wind, whisper; the bracken sighs;
Like arras by fairies woven, dew-gemmed the gossamer lies
Outspread on the gorse beneath us, where the wild black moors
  begin.
And there from saddle we worship the goddess of moorland and
  whin.   18 May 1902

He loved horses and greatly enjoyed fox-hunting, the theme of several of his poems. With the Yeomanry in South Africa he had acquired much experience in horse management. In Addis Ababa he kept a large stable, trained the horses carefully, played polo with enthusiasm and won many races against the other legations.

He was a natural games player; he had been a notable cricketer like several of his family, and had captained the school XI at Cheltenham. He had always been drawn to the sea, as is also evinced by his poems; at Taranto he became a keen yachtsman. In the Congo he had hunted big game for the first time and in Abyssinia he took every opportunity to do so, and conveyed his enthusiasm to me when I was only a small boy. I was known as Billy, and was three when he wrote to his mother:

Billy goes out shooting every day but does not get much as his only weapons are a tennis bat and empty cartridge case which he hits at the birds. He says he can't get them flying but if they would only sit for him he is sure he could kill one. His sporting instincts are very strongly developed.

Kathleen Mary, my mother, was a Vigors from County Carlow

where her family had long been established at Burgage, their ancestral home. She was the second of four children, two boys and two girls. When she was seven her parents separated and her mother took the children to England. My maternal grandmother was an undemonstrative and rather prudish woman, whereas my grandfather was rather a rake, a confirmed gambler and obviously excellent company. My mother remembered him with affection all her life. As she grew up she often visited relations in Ireland and she developed a lifelong romantic passion for that country, originating in her childhood adoration of Burgage.

Naturally adventurous, she loved the life in Abyssinia, where nothing daunted her. She shared my father's love of horses and enjoyed to the full the constant riding. Like him, she was an enthusiastic and skilful gardener: from a bare hillside they created the garden which is today such a delightful feature of the British Embassy in Addis Ababa. Since she was utterly devoted to my father, her children inevitably took second place. In consequence in my childhood memories she does not feature as much as my father; only later did I fully appreciate her forceful yet lovable character.

The ten years my parents spent in Abyssinia were undoubtedly the happiest of their lives.

CHAPTER 2

Abyssinia

MY GRANDFATHER must have recounted to his children his own role in some of the exciting events of the Magdala campaign, when a British army set out to rescue their Consul imprisoned by the Emperor Theodore. Such stories would have made a lasting impression on my father and given him an early interest in Abyssinia. Going there in 1909, he took with him a number of books on the country, its inhabitants and history. Only with some knowledge of their history could he hope to deal with these singular people, who believed implicitly that their emperors were descended from Solomon and Sheba.

The Abyssinians could claim an uninterrupted succession going back more than two thousand years; in Africa, only Egypt had a more ancient civilization. From the sixth century to the third century BC, some of the Habashat, the Agazan and other tribes in South Arabia migrated across the Red Sea and settled in the northern highlands of present-day Abyssinia. There these Semites imposed their language, their customs and their institutions on the indigenous Hamitic population, with whom they interbred to produce the ancestors of modern Tigreans and Amhara. Only archaeological traces survive of their original civilization, which emerged in what became the unique Aksumite kingdom that lasted until the end of the tenth century AD.

Little is left today to bear witness to the past greatness of Aksum, other than some revealing inscriptions, the stone-wrought thrones of the kings and judges, and the giant monoliths. Elaborately and exactly carved to represent towers with as many as thirteen storeys, these monoliths were probably erected in the third and fourth centuries AD. One that is seventy feet high still stands; another, more than a hundred feet long, larger than any Egyptian obelisk, lies broken on the ground. Here, on one of these thrones, the emperors of Abyssinia were crowned, until the coronation of Menelik in Shoa at the end of the nineteenth century.

The earliest recorded mention of Aksum is in the *Periplus of the*

31

Erythrean Sea probably written in the second century AD. It states that Aksum was eight days' journey inland from Adulis, a port on the Red Sea established by Greek traders sent by the Ptolemys to bring back elephants to be trained for war. The *Periplus* also describes Zoscales, King of Aksum, as 'a covetous and grasping man but otherwise noble, and imbued with Greek learning'.

In the third century AD Afilas recorded in a Greek inscription how, among other conquests, he had subdued the tribes as far as the Egyptian frontier. He ended his inscription: 'When I had established peace in the lands subject to me, I came to Adulis and sacrificed to Zeus, Ares and Poseidon, on behalf of those who voyage on the sea.'

In the middle of the fourth century Ezana, son of Ella Amida, recorded that he was 'King of Aksum and of Himyar, Raidan and Saba in Arabia'. One of his inscriptions bears witness to his conversion to Christianity.

This all-important event was confirmed by Rufinus, a contemporary Roman historian. He gives the traditional account of how a merchant ship was pillaged in the Red Sea and its crew and passengers massacred except for two boys who were brought to Ella Amida in Aksum. There the boys grew up in the King's court. One of them, Frumentius, was appointed Regent during Ezana's childhood. A devout Christian, Frumentius visited Alexandria, where in about AD 330 he was consecrated Bishop by the Patriarch Athanasius. Returning to Abyssinia he converted Ezana and his people to Christianity. The Roman Emperor Constantine had only been converted in 312, and not till 433 did St Patrick go to Ireland.

In the sixth century the Emperor Justinian despatched an embassy to Aksum. The envoy was received by the King standing in a four-wheeled chariot overlaid with gold and drawn by four elephants. The King wore a great collar of gold, was robed in a linen garment embroidered with gold thread and decorated with pearls, and was armed with two gilded spears and a gilded shield.

The rise of Islam in the middle of the seventh century isolated Abyssinia from the rest of the Christian world. After Abyssinian pirates sacked Jidda in 702, the Caliph, in revenge, seized the ports from which they operated. Thereafter, in Gibbon's memorable phrase, 'encompassed on all sides by the enemies of their religion, the Aethiopians slept near a thousand years, forgetful of the world by whom they were forgotten'.

The death blow to the Aksumite kingdom came in the tenth century from unassimilated Agaw in the south. The Agaw were Hamites and had inhabited the highlands since time immemorial. In the north they had merged with the Semitic colonists from Arabia to produce the civilization of Aksum. In the south they were either pagan or more probably belonged to that archaic South Arabian form of Judaism which is still held by the Falashas. Under a formidable Queen, known to tradition as Judith, they ravaged the Aksumite kingdom, burnt the churches, overthrew the last King of Aksum and massacred the princes of the royal line whom they found, confined as custom decreed, on a mountain-top. Aksum had outlasted Jerusalem and Rome, going down in ruin only eighty years before the Norman conquest of Britain.

Despite their initial ferocity the victorious Agaw were eventually assimilated into the civilization they had sought to destroy, and were converted to Christianity. After a period of chaos a sequence of Agaw monarchs, known as the Zagwe dynasty, established themselves. One of them constructed the astounding rock-hewn churches at Lalibela. In the later years of the dynasty there was a growing belief that the Queen of Sheba had visited Solomon in Jerusalem, had been seduced by him and borne him a son named Menelik, who founded the Abyssinian royal line. It was also believed that Menelik visited his father Solomon, and on his departure contrived to substitute a copy of the Ark of the Covenant that his father had given him for the original, which he then carried off to Aksum.

In 1270 this usurping Agaw dynasty was overthrown by Yekuno Amlak, whose claim to be descended from the Aksumite princes was accepted. Thirty years later it was universally believed in Abyssinia that the Solomonic line had been re-established, a belief which endured until the overthrow of Haile Selassie and the establishment of the present Marxist republic.

Another tradition which grew up about Abyssinia was the European belief in the country's legendary priest-king, Prester John. At the time of the Crusades, Europe took comfort in the expectation that somewhere in the East there ruled a mighty Christian monarch, known as Prester John, who in due time would march on Jerusalem, destroy the infidel and liberate the Holy Places. The Prester was believed to have written to the Byzantine Emperor Manuel Comnenus, enumerating the wonders of his kingdom, and affirming that he ruled over the three Indies and over seventy kings, and that twenty bishops, twelve archbishops and a patriarch acknowledged his authority.

As early as 1177 Pope Alexander III wrote to 'John, the illustrious and magnificent King of the Indies' – a letter he almost certainly despatched to the King of Abyssinia, who was already being identified as the Prester John.

In 1487 King John of Portugal sent Pedro da Covilham to search for the kingdom of Prester John. He arrived in Abyssinia and was cordially received by the Emperor, but was never allowed to leave the country.

Some thirty years later, after Vasco da Gama had opened the sea route to India, a Portuguese mission under Rodrigo de Lima arrived at Massawa and travelled inland to the court of Lebna Dengel, the Negusa Nagast, King of Kings, or Emperor.

Lebna Dengel proved friendly to the Portuguese, although dissatisfied with the presents they had brought him and exasperated by their quarrels among themselves. Covilham was still alive, and his profound knowledge of the customs and languages of the country proved invaluable. The mission remained for six years in Abyssinia and after its return to Portugal the chaplain, Francisco Alvares, wrote his famous account of the country, *A true relation of the lands of the Prester John*. Throughout his narrative he refers to Lebna Dengel as the Prester or Prester John.

He describes Lebna Dengel's capital as being the size of a town but consisting entirely of tents. The Emperor's five tents were invariably pitched on a rise in the centre of the camp and the royal enclosure was surrounded by a wall of curtains with five entrances. All other tents were pitched in their allotted place. Nearby were the two churches of St Mary and the Holy Cross, and two other tents containing the royal treasure.

Also close at hand were the Queen's camp, the camp of the pages and the royal kitchens with, not far off, the great tent used for the court of justice, and the quarters of the two commanders-in-chief, of the Abuna or archbishop, of the state officials and the nobility.

Lebna Dengel conducted state business inside his great white tent, sitting on a platform, dressed in rich robes and with his face partly veiled with blue taffeta. Similar formality was observed when the court was on the move. The Emperor rode on a finely bedecked mule led by six pages, and was concealed behind red curtains carried on poles. Ahead of him marched twenty other pages following six saddled mules and six saddled horses, each led by four men. Four lions, held on strong chains, always went before him.

He was very preoccupied with religion and at any hour of day or night might summon Alvares for a religious discussion. The Abyssinian Church was Monophysite, believing in the 'single divine' nature of Christ. This was a fundamental difference from the Catholic belief, which regards Christ as having both human and divine natures. Alvares also found fault with many of the Abyssinian Church's customs, such as the observance of a Sabbath as well as a Sunday, and the universal practice of circumcision. He was, however, immensely impressed by the great number of monasteries and churches. Among many other observations, Alvares recorded the age-old custom of secluding all members of the royal line, other than the King's children, on an almost sheer-sided mountain. This effectively prevented them from interfering in matters of state, or fomenting rebellion. On one occasion while he was in Abyssinia, a letter from them was smuggled down but was intercepted, whereupon the guards responsible were flogged for days.

After the Portuguese mission left Abyssinia, Lebna Dengel found himself increasingly faced by the threat from the Muslim states of Ifat and of Adal, which included Harar, with which ever since the fourteenth century the Emperors of Abyssinia had been intermittently at war; these states were forever encroaching on the eastern borders of the empire in a war of raid and counter-raid. This Muslim threat had become more pronounced in the fifteenth century after Sultan Salim of Istanbul had conquered Egypt and received the submission of the Hejaz.

The arrival of the Turks in the Red Sea in 1517 proved disastrous for the Abyssinians. The Portuguese mission had barely left when Ahmad Ibrahim, the Adal leader, best known as Ahmad Granj or 'the left-handed', invaded the country. Armed with matchlocks supplied by the Turks, and supported by some two hundred Turkish soldiers, he scattered the armies opposed to him, overran the land, carried off its treasure, burnt every church he could locate, and massacred the royal princes on their mountain-top. The effect of relatively few firearms had been devastating against a warrior race with no previous experience of them.

Lebna Dengel, undaunted, found refuge among the mountains of the interior and there, with a small but faithful following, he fought on. He appealed to the Portuguese for help, but died and was succeeded by his only surviving son, Claudius, before a Portuguese force under Christopher, son of the famous Vasco da Gama, arrived.

Heavily outnumbered, but with a superiority in firearms, Christopher da Gama fought an inconclusive battle near Lake Ashangi. Before the next battle Ahmad Granj was strongly reinforced, especially with firearms; Christopher da Gama was killed and his force was routed. Claudius, despite the defeat of his allies, proved as resolute in adversity as his father. In 1542 he rallied the Abyssinian forces, reassembled the remaining Portuguese and surprised the Muslim army near Lake Tana. Ahmad Granj was killed early in the battle and his demoralized army broke and fled, to be remorselessly hunted down by the vengeful Abyssinians. Few of them got back to their own country.

For the first time for more than two thousand years Abyssinia had been invaded, though not conquered, by an alien race. The inhabitants of the country had been decimated, their land ravaged, much of their unique ecclesiastical heritage destroyed; but as a race they had not been mongrelized. The Abyssinians of today in Tigre, Begemder, Gojjam and in such areas as Manz in Shoa are the lineal descendants of a race that antedated the Roman Empire.

The incursion of pagan Galla tribes, who now seized the chance to profit from the chaos and disruption of the Muslim war, did, however, have a lasting effect on large areas. A Hamitic people, they established themselves over a great part of Shoa and even pushed northwards along the escarpment for some hundred and fifty miles beyond Dessie. From now on there was almost continuous warfare between them and the kings of Shoa. Some Galla became Christian and were assimilated by the Amhara; others, notably in Wollo, became Muslim; but many remained pagan.

The Church in Abyssinia had been rescued from extinction with the help of the Portuguese: without their intervention the Abyssinians might well have been absorbed into the adjacent Muslim world. But these Portuguese lived in an age when Christian burnt Christian to save souls, and their Jesuit missionaries now condemned the doctrine and ritual of the Church which the Portuguese troops had helped to save. The Abyssinians, as Monophysites, owed allegiance to the Patriarch of Alexandria; he alone could appoint the Abuna who was head of their Church. The Jesuit missionaries were men dedicated to the reform of the native Church, but their very zeal and intolerance defeated their aim and permanently alienated a people justifiably proud of their own Christian tradition.

The Jesuits did convert one king, whereupon the Abuna absolved his subjects from their allegiance; and in the subsequent rebellion the king was killed. Susenyos, his nephew, succeeded him; he too became a Catholic and the immediate result was further insurrection. Eventually, horrified at the unending slaughter, he capitulated:

> Hear Ye! Hear Ye! We gave you this faith believing it was good, but innumerable people have been slain – Julius, Gabriel, Takla Giorgis, Sarsa Kristos, and now these peasants. For which reason we restore to you the faith of your fathers . . . and do ye rejoice.

Susenyos died shortly afterwards and was succeeded by his son Fasiladas, who drove the Jesuits from the country and banished every recalcitrant native Catholic. A hundred years of missionary effort had failed utterly; its only effect had been to confirm the Abyssinians in their attachment to their ancient faith and to sow in them the seeds of xenophobia.

Fasiladas established his capital at Gondar, just north of Lake Tana, and there the hitherto peripatetic court remained for two hundred years. At Gondar, Fasiladas built the first of the remarkable stone palaces which still stand today. Yasu, his grandson, succeeded in 1680 and reigned for twenty years, the last effective Emperor at Gondar. His successors eventually lost all authority, even in the town, and survived merely as puppets in the hands of ruthless, ambitious nobles who fought to overthrow their rivals and to gain control of the disintegrating kingdom. At one moment six Emperors were said to be alive, each as impotent as the others. These chaotic times lasted for a hundred and fifty years.

James Bruce of Kinnaird arrived in Abyssinia in 1769, determined to discover the source of the Blue Nile. Though he was fortunate to secure the friendship of the ruthless Ras Mikael of Tigre, who at that time dominated Abyssinia, it was three and a half years before he could leave the country.

Bruce published in five volumes an account of his travels and described in horrifying detail the endless warfare, the wholesale slaughter, the torture and the executions when the streets of Gondar were littered with corpses bereft of hand and foot. He wrote: 'I at last scarce ever went out and nothing occupied my thought but how to escape from this bloody country.' Tragically, the monumental work written by this great traveller, the first from the British Isles to visit Abyssinia, was initially derided and discredited. Bruce died in 1794, an embittered man. I bought his *Travels to Discover the Source of the Nile* for ten shillings when I was a Lower boy at Eton; engrossed, I read through all five volumes.

Order was temporarily imposed on this chaos by the Emperor Theodore. Born in about 1819, the son of a minor chieftain in the district of Kwara in western Abyssinia, this outstanding man started his career as an outlaw with a small but devoted following; by 1854 he had subjugated Gondar and Gojjam and the following year, having defeated at Derasge in Simien his most formidable rival, the ruler of Tigre, he proclaimed himself Emperor and took the name of Theodore. Shoa submitted to him in 1858 and Menelik, the young Prince of Shoa, became a captive at his court.

Theodore was determined to break the power of the provincial Rases and unite the country under his sole control, administered by governors appointed by himself. He was also resolved to impose a number of reforms, including the abolition of slavery. At first he was assisted by two remarkable Englishmen. Walter Plowden, before Theodore's rise to power, had been sent to Abyssinia as Consul to negotiate a commercial treaty with the most powerful of the several Rases. He failed to achieve this but remained in the country with his friend John Bell. They became Theodore's trusted advisers. It was his misfortune that Plowden and Bell were killed by rebels and their restraining influence was removed.

Theodore was a fanatical Christian, convinced that he was 'The Awaited One' destined to lead his armies against the infidel and deliver Jerusalem. In 1862 he sent a letter to Queen Victoria, requesting her assistance against the Turks and offering to send her an envoy with presents. He received no reply; seldom can a mislaid letter have had so costly a sequel. Infuriated by this apparently deliberate slight, Theodore imprisoned Charles Cameron, the British Consul at Massawa, and a number of missionaries of various nationalities.

The British Government despatched Hormuzd Rassam, an official of Armenian descent at the Residency at Aden, to negotiate their release; he too was imprisoned. Finally in 1868 the British Government, at an eventual cost of ten million pounds, sent General Sir Robert Napier from India, with an army of sixteen thousand men including elephants to carry the guns, to release the captives. My grandfather was Napier's Deputy Adjutant-General. This formidable operation was well planned and ably conducted, but it was helped to a large extent by the widespread resentment which Theodore's policy had engendered.

His attempts to subject the traditional rulers of the provinces to his authority had resulted in constant warfare, and the extortions of his army, forever in the field, caused much discontent. Despite the terror which as a result of his ruthlessness, cruelty and ungovernable rages his name evoked, he had by the time of the British invasion lost effective control of his country except around his mountain fortress of Magdala.

Napier advanced methodically on Magdala, and below the mountain Theodore's army gave battle. The Abyssinians fought with outstanding courage but inflicted pathetically few casualties. After the battle Theodore absolved from their allegiance any of his followers who so desired, and despatched Cameron and the other European prisoners to Napier's camp.

Napier sent Theodore a letter demanding his surrender. Theodore's reply included the following passage: 'I had intended, if God so decreed, to conquer the world, and it was my desire to die if my purpose could not be fulfilled. Since the day of my birth no man dared to lay hands on me.' Then, almost alone, he awaited his fate, and as the British troops stormed through the gateway of his stronghold he shot himself with a pistol sent to him in happier days by Queen Victoria.

Napier fired the buildings and, his mission accomplished, withdrew to the coast. He took with him to England Theodore's son Alamayahu, who was sent to Rugby School and then to the Royal Military Academy at Sandhurst, where he fell ill and died, aged nineteen. Queen Victoria had a brass plaque put up in his memory in St George's Chapel at Windsor, where I searched for it and found it while I was at Eton.

*   *   *

The Ras of Tigre, who had greatly facilitated Napier's advance on Magdala, was suitably rewarded with firearms and cannon, with which during the troubled years that followed Theodore's death he was able to overcome his rivals. In 1872 he was crowned at Aksum as John IV. Like Theodore he was a brave and skilful general; unlike him he was patient, self-controlled and temperate in his habits.

Throughout his reign of seventeen years, John's empire was constantly threatened from beyond its borders. The Egyptians, who had succeeded the enfeebled Turkish presence in the Red Sea, invaded his country and in 1875 and 1876 were decisively defeated. Their withdrawal was followed in 1885 by Italy's occupation of the hot humid seaport of Massawa, from which the Italians cast covetous eyes on the cool uplands. One force that probed towards the plateau was destroyed, but the Italian threat remained.

Meanwhile John was menaced by the Dervish armies from the Sudan, who were massing on his frontier. He summoned his subject kings and princes to his assistance and they marched to join him, eating up the land as they came, for they numbered two hundred thousand men. But they too posed a threat, for there were few of his vassals whom he could trust.

Menelik was now King of Shoa. After nine years' captivity at Theodore's court he had escaped from Magdala and returned to his homeland. There he had been rapturously received by its inhabitants, over whom his house had ruled for generations. Profiting from the troubles in the north, he had extended his kingdom to the south and east but had temporarily forfeited his chance of becoming Emperor. His ambition, however, was unabated, and his intrigues against John were unceasing. He had already received thousands of rifles from the Italians in return for promises of assistance, a fact of which John was fully aware.

Takla Haymanot of Gojjam, another of John's powerful and ambitious subjects, was also motivated solely by self-interest. However his army, though estimated at a hundred thousand, was decisively defeated in 1888 by the Dervishes under the formidable ex-slave Abu Anga. They followed up their victory by sacking Gondar, burning numerous churches. When they eventually withdrew they took with them four thousand slaves and great herds of cattle.

The following year John advanced to the Sudanese frontier and attacked the Dervish position at Galabat. He was killed just when his victory seemed assured, and as news of his death spread his army disintegrated. The Dervishes did not follow up their victory, content to send John's body to the Khalifa at Omdurman, where the head was cut off, stuck on a pole, and paraded round the northern Sudan.

Menelik now achieved his ambition: in 1889, at Entoto just outside Addis Ababa, he was crowned Emperor. Meanwhile the Italians had taken advantage of John's death to occupy Asmara and Keren. Menelik accepted this and signed with them the Treaty of Uccialli. The Italians claimed that by this treaty Menelik had granted them a protectorate over Abyssinia. They based their claim on the Italian translation, but the Amharic version which Menelik had signed did not confirm this, and no agreement was reached. Menelik finally repudiated the treaty: war followed in 1895.

The Italians won an easy initial victory over a Tigrean force. After the battle a prisoner warned them: 'For the present you have been victorious because God willed it; but wait a month or two and you will see Menelik's soldiers. They are as many in number as locusts.' Over-confident, the Italians occupied parts of Tigre and pushed as far south as Amba Alagi. Then, outmanoeuvred and defeated in a number of engagements by Ras Makonnen, Menelik's cousin and ablest general, they were driven back beyond Makalle.

General Baratieri, hearing he was to be superseded in command of the Italian forces, advanced by night with three columns through the rocky hills and gorges near Adua to give battle to Menelik's army, which numbered a hundred thousand men. His columns lost touch and on 1 March 1896 were overwhelmed in turn. Out of a force of 17,700, of whom 10,600 were Italian and the rest native troops, over 6000 were killed, nearly 1500 were wounded and between 3000 and 4000 were taken prisoner. Abyssinian losses amounted to some 7000 killed and 10,000 wounded. They pursued the fugitives for about nine miles and then lit bonfires on the hill-tops to alert the local peasantry. Everywhere that night, over the battlefield and among the bivouacs, rose the victory chant:

> Mow, mow down the tender grass – Ebalgume! Ebalgume! The corn of Italy that was sown in Tigre has been reaped by Abba-Dagnaw and given to the birds.

41

The reference was to Menelik who rode his famous horse Dagnaw into battle.

Some 1500 native prisoners had their right hand and left foot cut off, the traditional punishment for fighting against their country: most of them died. Some were castrated, although this was against Menelik's express orders. Most of the Amhara had abandoned the custom of castrating their victims, traditionally based on David's treatment of the Philistines; but among the Galla tribes it was still customary to castrate the dead and dying, and that day there were many Galla in Menelik's army.

It is futile to judge by modern standards the Abyssinians' treatment of their prisoners: theirs were still the standards of the Middle Ages. They had just overwhelmingly repulsed an unprovoked attack by a European power, and their past history gave them little cause to regard Europeans with favour. After his victory Menelik showed marked restraint: he tacitly recognized the Italian claim to Eritrea, stipulating only that the frontier should be on the Mareb river. Forty years later the Italians, in another unprovoked attack, used poison gas to ensure victory and shot many of their prisoners out of hand.

CHAPTER 3

Revolution, 1916–17

WHEN MY FATHER arrived there, Addis Ababa consisted of a series of scattered villages grouped on hillsides with open, uncultivated spaces in between. Menelik's palace crowned the largest hill; nearby a jumble of thatched huts and some corrugated-iron-roofed shacks clustered round the large open market. Nowhere were there any proper roads. My father once wrote after he had been to the French Legation to dine: 'A forty-minute ride across two ravines and a swamp, then a shocking road up to the house on a moonless night is really no fun.'

Abyssinians of any standing travelled everywhere on muleback, followed by an armed mob of slaves and retainers, varying in number according to the importance of their master. Galla, Somali, Gurage, people from the subject kingdom of Kaffa, negroes from the west, mingled on the streets with their Amhara and Tigrean overlords; but it was these latter who dominated the scene, imposed their stamp upon the town and gave it its unique character. Wrapped in white toga-like *shammas* worn over long white shirts and jodhpurs, they set a fashion which over the years was copied by an increasing number of their subjects.

The clothes, the buildings, the pitch and intonation of voices speaking Amharic; the smell of rancid butter, of red peppers and burning cow dung that permeated the town; the packs of savage dogs that roamed the streets and whose howling rose and fell through the night; an occasional corpse hanging on the gallows-tree; beggars who had lost a hand or foot for theft; debtors and creditors wandering round chained together; strings of donkeys bringing in firewood; caravans of mules; the crowded market where men and women squatted on the ground, selling earthen pots, lengths of cloths, skins, cartridges, bars of salt, silver ornaments, heaps of grain, vegetables, beer – all this combined to create a scene and an atmosphere unlike any other in the world.

The Amharas and Tigreans, as opposed to the Galla and the other tribes they had incorporated into their empire, resembled no other

43

race in appearance or character. They regarded themselves, however fallaciously, as light-skinned; in their paintings they were invariably shown full face and almost white, whereas their enemies were always depicted in profile and black, unless they were Europeans.

Encircled by British, French and Italian territories, they were intensely proud of their age-old independence and very conscious that their forefathers had been among the earliest converts to Christianity. Consequently they were both arrogant and reactionary, while the past three hundred years had made them suspicious and obstructive in dealing with Europeans. As a race they had an inborn love of litigation and suffered from inherent avarice. Yet they were naturally courteous, often extremely intelligent and always courageous and enduring.

Conditions in Addis Ababa and in the country as a whole were already chaotic when my father arrived. They were soon to become very much worse. In and around Addis Ababa murder, brigandage and highway robbery increased alarmingly; in restoring order, public hangings, floggings and mutilations had little effect. The town was filled with disbanded soldiery from Menelik's army, and on the hills outside were camped the armies of the various contenders for power.

Before he was incapacitated, Menelik had won recognition for his conquests and acceptance of his new frontiers. He had incorporated into his empire the Ogaden, the town of Harar, the lands of the Galla tribes, the Gurage country, the ancient kingdom of Kaffa, and the Anuak and other tribes on the borders of the Sudan. By the rulers of the ancient provinces of Abyssinia and by the nobility as a whole he was universally accepted as Emperor.

In 1908, however, he suffered his first stroke. His last effective act was to proclaim his thirteen-year-old grandson, Lij Yasu, as his heir, with Ras Tasamma as Regent. Lij Yasu's father was the ruler of Wollo, Ras Mikael, who had been converted from Islam to Christianity during the reign of the Emperor John, and had later married Menelik's elder daughter, Shoaragad. A great man, one of the most formidable of his age, he was to be crowned Negus, or King, only to be destroyed by his loyalty to his worthless son.

Inside the palace the Empress Taitu, Menelik's wife, once a woman of outstanding beauty but now an obese hulk, schemed and intrigued to retain power. Menelik was her fifth husband; they had

44

no children, though Menelik had had a son and two daughters by previous marriages. His son had died young; the elder daughter, Shoaragad, was the mother of Lij Yasu. Since the younger daughter, Zauditu, had married Taitu's nephew, Ras Gugsa Wale of Begemder, Taitu was determined to put Zauditu instead of Lij Yasu on the throne when Menelik died, confident that she would then retain effective authority. However, the council of ministers, divided on every other issue, combined to thwart her.

In the north, old rivalries had broken out afresh: powerful Rases intrigued and fought for supremacy, struggled to suppress rebellion among their vassals, or marched on Addis Ababa. In the subject provinces of the south, governors and their armies of occupation pillaged the land and sold the inhabitants into slavery. 'The soldiers that leave a province sweep up all they can and those that enter take the rest,' was how my father described the situation. Meanwhile, the country was being flooded with rifles run in through French Somaliland with the connivance of French officials.

On 10 April 1911 Ras Tasamma, the Regent, died of a stroke. My father had judged him 'to stand for everything that was most corrupt in officialdom'. He had, however, possessed authority. As soon as the Rases heard of his death they congregated in Addis Ababa, which soon resembled an armed camp. All normal business came to a standstill. At this critical moment my father had to escort an Abyssinian Mission, headed by Ras Kassa, to England to attend King George V's coronation. Leaving Colonel Doughty-Wylie in charge of the Legation, he set off for Dire Dawa by caravan on 4 May and arrived in England on 15 June. The five Abyssinian notables, in their full regalia, created a stir in the Abbey.

In order to avoid the hot weather my mother had preceded my father to England, escorted as far as Jibuti by an official from the Sudan who was temporarily serving at the Legation. My father was due four months' leave and this they spent at Beachley, his attractive house near Chepstow at the mouth of the Severn. In the family album are some photographs of me on the lawn with Susannah, my Indian *ayah*, to whom I was devoted. I was then a year old and she was with us till I was nearly four. With her I could do no wrong. When my mother remonstrated she would answer, 'He one handsome Rajah – why for he no do what he want?' I apparently walked at an unusually early age but was slow learning to speak. My mother always maintained that the first words I said were 'Go yay,' which

45

meant 'Go away' and showed an independent spirit.

My brother Brian was born in October 1911, and my parents engaged Mary Buckle to look after us. She was eighteen and had never been out of England, yet she unhesitatingly set off for a remote and savage country in Africa. She gave us unfailing devotion and became an essential part of our family. As children we called her Minna, and she has been known to us and to our friends as Minna ever since. Now, after more than seventy years, she is still my cherished friend and confidante, the one person left with shared memories of those far-off days.

While my father was on his way to England, Lij Yasu, with the support of the Fitaurari Habta Giorgis, Menelik's commander-in-chief, seized the palace and assumed control of the country. He schemed to be proclaimed Emperor, but as long as Menelik was known to be alive this was impossible. Even after Menelik's death Lij Yasu was never crowned, possibly because he believed a prophecy that if he was crowned he would die. This omission certainly weakened his position during the struggle that lay ahead.

The situation in Abyssinia was becoming increasingly chaotic when my father returned there in January 1912. This was due in large part to the character of Lij Yasu. From the day he seized power in 1911 he thought of nothing but his own amusement and he was frequently absent from Addis Ababa, which he detested, for months on end. During his absence all government business, even the most trivial, came to a stop, since no minister was willing to make a decision while Lij Yasu was away.

On one occasion my father sent a runner to him in the Danakil country with an important letter. The man returned with the letter, having failed to deliver it. In a despatch to the Foreign Office my father wrote:

> Lij Yasu is camped out in the bush with only five Abyssinians in his retinue; while in the neighbouring villages are various messengers from the government and from provincial chiefs who dare not approach to deliver their letters for fear of the flogging with which anyone who disturbs him is threatened. Lij Yasu has his head shaved in the Danakil fashion and is living with the Danakil; what food or milk he requires he seizes from the nearest villages, and he is doing nothing but hunt occasionally.

Cruelty and arrogance predominated in his nature. He would watch an execution or a flogging with evident enjoyment. A story was even current that to prove his manhood he had killed and castrated a boy belonging to the palace. Soon after he came to power he personally led an expedition against the Shanqalla negroes on the Sudan border, and my father affirmed that the slaughter there must have satisfied for a time even his craving for blood.

In 1913, the year of Menelik's death, Lij Yasu wantonly attacked some Danakil encampments and massacred three hundred men, women and children. My father's explanation was that 'It was simply because he liked the sight of blood'. He had apparently adopted the Danakil custom of castrating the dead and dying. Count Colli, the Italian Minister, quoted one of Lij Yasu's officers as saying on his return from this expedition that Lij Yasu cut the breasts off a girl who had refused his advances, after he had watched her being raped by his soldiers.

By 1913 conditions on the boundary between Abyssinia and the British East Africa Protectorate, later known as Kenya, had become worse than usual, with frequent incursions by well-armed gangs of Abyssinians raiding for slaves and ivory. My father was therefore anxious to travel to Nairobi and discuss with the Governor measures to prevent these raids, as well as the possibility of delimiting the frontier and finding an answer to the demand by the Abyssinian Government for the return of the Boran and Gabbra tribesmen who had migrated in large numbers into East Africa after Menelik's conquest of their homelands.

In November 1913 he accompanied his family on their way to England as far as the railhead, which had now reached the Awash river, and then returned to Addis Ababa. From there he set off with a caravan of mules on a journey of some eight hundred miles to Nairobi. His letters evince the excitement he felt at undertaking this journey, one which few Europeans had as yet made, and his anticipation of getting plenty of big game hunting on the way.

My father travelled to Nairobi by way of Mega, Moyale, Marsabit, Laisamis and Nyeri, all places with which I was to be familiar some fifty-five years later. After several days in Nairobi he took the train to Mombasa where he caught a ship to England; there, soon after my brother Dermot was born, he rejoined my mother. He was still on leave in England when war was declared on 4 August 1914. An accomplished linguist, fluent in German and French, he was accepted by the Army, given an appointment as a captain in the Intelligence Branch, and sent to France, where he arrived on 23

47

September. This posting was a remarkable achievement, considering the number of regular officers trying desperately to get to the front, dreading that the war would be over before they could take part. He was attached to the 3rd Army Corps, and while serving in France he earned a mention in despatches. The Foreign Office had only given him permission to join the Army on the understanding that he would return to Abyssinia when his leave expired. He returned to Addis Ababa with his family in January 1915.

Susannah had gone back to India in 1913 when we sailed from Jibuti to England. I suspect that in the excitement of going on board I hardly realized she was leaving me for good. In England my parents engaged an elderly trained nurse to look after Dermot. We all called her Nanny; I never knew her name. She had charge of Dermot, and of Roderic, born a year later in the Legation. As far as I was concerned, she remained a vague figure in the background.

On his return to Addis Ababa my father was increasingly concerned by an evident predilection for Islam on the part of Lij Yasu, who was consorting more and more with the Muslims of his empire, and frequenting mosques. He was reputed to wear a turban, and to eat meat slaughtered according to Islamic observance.

Many Abyssinians were convinced that the Central Powers would win the war, a conviction strengthened by the British defeats by the Turks at Kut and the Dardanelles; they felt in consequence that it was prudent to keep on good terms with the Germans and Turks. But Lij Yasu's partiality for Islam was apparently more than a question of convenience. He had married the daughters of several important Muslim chiefs and was in frequent communication with the 'Mad Mullah' in Somaliland, supplying him with rifles and ammunition to help in his long-drawn-out war against the British. He evidently hoped to secure the Mullah's daughter as a bride; it was believed that he even aspired to marry the Caliph of Islam's daughter.

In June 1915 my father commented: 'I am coming to the conclusion that the heir to the throne of Solomon is at heart a Moslem and is entertaining dreams of one day putting himself at the head of the Mohammadan Abyssinians, and of producing a Moslem kingdom that will stretch far beyond the frontiers of his present Empire.'

In May 1916 on the anniversary of the Sultan's accession, Lij Yasu presented an Abyssinian flag to the Turkish Consul in Addis Ababa on which was embroidered the Turkish crescent and the Islamic declaration of faith. This created consternation in the town. In July he slipped away by train to Dire Dawa and my father wrote despondently to the Foreign Office: 'Lij Yasu, during his three months' stay in Addis Ababa, has succeeded in destroying even the semblance of central government, and is dragging down the prestige of individual ministers so that there is no authority to whom the Legation can appeal.'

In Dire Dawa Lij Yasu attended the Islamic festival of the Eid of Bairam, prayed publicly in the mosque and presented three camels and five bullocks to the Muslim community for the feast. He then went to Jig Jigga, where at a mass meeting of Somalis he swore on the Koran that he was a Muslim. He had circulated a document which professed to trace his descent, through his father, from the Prophet. In August, as the first step to setting up an Islamic government in Harar, he peremptorily recalled its Governor, Dedjazmatch Tafari. This was Tafari Makonnen, the future Emperor Haile Selassie, who had replaced the detested Dedjazmatch Balcha as Governor of Harar in 1911. As Ras Makonnen's son, he had been rapturously received by its inhabitants, and by his justice and humanity he soon merited this acclaim.

Menelik had occupied Harar in 1887 after a ferocious battle and had appointed Ras Makonnen, the ablest of his generals and his devoted friend and cousin, as Governor. Ras Makonnen governed Harar until his death in 1906 and there his son Tafari was born and grew up under the enlightened administration of his eminent father; he was thirteen when his father died. Had Ras Makonnen lived he would have assumed control of the country when Menelik was incapacitated, and as his cousin would undoubtedly have succeeded him. His son was now to take charge and lead the opposition to Lij Yasu.

In Addis Ababa Tafari did his best to unite the frightened and divided chiefs and to persuade them to take effective action. An attempted coup in August was frustrated by the timorous behaviour of the Abuna, who stayed away from a crucial meeting. At a later meeting of all the chiefs, in the palace, a proclamation was read out detailing the acts which had convinced the ministers that Lij Yasu had become a Muslim. The irresolute Abuna got to his feet and began, 'If these things are true . . .' He was shouted down.

My father wrote:

> A scene of indescribable confusion followed: a shot was fired and immediately the excited crowd of soldiers began to fire their rifles in all directions, without knowing why or wherefor. In the congested space few bullets could have missed their mark and the slaughter would probably have continued but for the presence of mind of the officer in charge of the war drums, who ordered them to beat the signal for silence, when the madness ceased as soon as it had arisen. Many were found to be dead and the total casualties were reported to be about a hundred.
>
> In the silence that followed most of the chiefs were seen to be in tears and the council was dissolved until the afternoon. At a second meeting it was decided that Waizero Zauditu, daughter of Emperor Menelik, should be proclaimed Empress, and Dedjazmatch Tafari be made Ras and heir to the throne. The town remained absolutely quiet, the population receiving the news with satisfaction and relief. . . .

Now that the Abuna had absolved the inhabitants of the empire from their allegiance to Lij Yasu, Ras Tafari was the obvious choice for Emperor. He was resolute, outstandingly able, just, patient and merciful. He was of royal blood, the great-grandson of King Sahle Selassie, a second cousin to Menelik and son of the famous Ras Makonnen. Yet he was mistrusted by many. It was suspected that he wished to abolish slavery, to found schools, to build roads and to modernize the country. His peers, indeed the country as a whole, wanted none of these innovations. In consequence, instead of being proclaimed Emperor he was appointed Regent. For the next fourteen frustrating and hazardous years he survived, far-sighted and unembittered, until he finally achieved his ambition.

Lij Yasu remained for a while round Harar. His apostasy had cost him his empire. The Somali tribes, with whom he had identified himself, might well have rallied to his cause had he in this decisive hour shown himself a leader. Instead he thought only of his personal safety, and as the army from Addis Ababa under the formidable Dedjazmatch Balcha drew near he fled into the Danakil desert. Balcha entered Harar and his troops massacred such Muslims as they could find within the walls. Hugh Dodds, then Consul in Harar, reported that the smell of corpses pervaded the town for days.

Negus Mikael, Lij Yasu's father, being now a devout Christian, had condemned his son's affiliation to Islam, but when he heard that Lij Yasu had been deposed family pride was outraged. He gathered his troops and prepared to march on Addis Ababa. His entire force of some eighty thousand men could be mobilized within fifty miles of his capital, Dessie, whereas Ras Tafari's forces were very dispersed, some being stationed more than two hundred miles from Addis Ababa. My father reported that the Shoan leaders estimated their troops at a hundred and twelve thousand, but he warned the Foreign Office that they tended to count the number at a chief's disposal rather than how many he could effectively assemble.

These were anxious days for my father. Lij Yasu's restoration would at the least constitute a considerable propaganda success for Turkey; it might even bring Abyssinia into the war on the side of our enemies, at a time when we were fighting the Germans in East Africa, the Turks in Sinai, Mesopotamia and the Aden Protectorate; and the Dervishes in Somaliland.

On 10 October 1916 he wrote in a despatch:

> Previous to the Revolution Ras Tafari expected daily that he would be imprisoned which, in his opinion, would have been the equivalent of a death sentence; and accordingly he confided his will and all his available money to me in order that I should arrange for its transmission to the Bank of England in trust for his children. He has now given me a further, and most embarrassing proof of his confidence by asking me to take charge of his son and heir, aged two-and-a-half months, for a short time. Both the Ras and his wife appear to have been very anxious and nervous about the child, and I feel that it would be impossible for me to refuse without risking his friendship which will be of the utmost importance to us in the future ...

I watched Tafari's son, Asfa Wossen, being carried up the Legation steps in a red cradle hung round the neck of his servant, while a large escort of armed retainers dispersed down the drive. My mother's only stipulation had been that not more than two servants should remain with the child. She did not want a small army camping indefinitely among her flowerbeds and rose bushes. I remember the names of the two servants were Abatahun and Astakakalij, the wet nurse.

My father made arrangements for three hundred Europeans, Indians and Arabs to take refuge in the Legation grounds if Negus Mikael defeated the Shoan armies. He believed in that case the main danger would come from Wollo soldiery pursuing the Shoans into the town, and passing close to the Legation. He was determined to disarm any refugees who came into the grounds, and so prevent anyone from starting trouble there.

He managed to buy enough flour, grain, cattle and sheep to feed these potential refugees, despite the fact that the market in Addis Ababa was closed. He also collected sandbags and wood to barricade the Legation buildings. I watched with interest as rifles were brought up from the cellar and sandbags were filled. Many of the Legation servants wanted to go off and fight, but it was essential that they should stay and help. A few, however, did leave and at least one was killed in the war.

As late as 13 October the Shoan leaders continued to believe that Negus Mikael was still at Dessie. They were dismayed when news came that he was as close as Manz, less than a hundred miles from Addis Ababa, harrying the district with a vast army. They immediately ordered Ras Lul Seged, who had eight thousand men, to fall back and join Fitaurari Gelli, stationed with a further six thousand at Ankober. As yet Fitaurari Habta Giorgis, who commanded the Shoan armies, had with him only twenty thousand men, and Ras Kassa a further ten thousand. It remained to be seen whether these four armies could be united before Negus Mikael could blockade Ras Lul Seged and Fitaurari Gelli in Ankober and advance into the plain of Debra Berhan where the first battle was expected to take place. My father wrote, 'The roads from Addis Ababa to the north are crowded with bands of soldiers moving up to join their various commands, and every day's delay thus adds strength to the Fitaurari's forces.'

My brother Brian and I watched the Shoan armies as they went north to give battle to Negus Mikael and his Wollo hordes. For days they passed across the plain below the Legation. Sometimes there was a dense mass of men, sometimes only a trickle hurrying to catch up with the main body. Barefoot men jogged past, close-packed about their leaders on their colourfully bedecked, trippling mules; groups of horsemen, mostly Galla, cantered past or were engulfed among yet more men on foot. All were armed – some with rifles, others with spears, while nearly all wore swords and carried shields. Scattered among them were the camp followers: women and young boys driving loaded mules and donkeys. This was the chivalry of Abyssinia going forth to war, unchanged as yet from the armies of the past. It was an enthralling, unforgettable sight for a small, romantically minded boy.

Time, however, for the Shoans was running out. Negus Mikael surprised Fitaurari Gelli before Ras Lul Seged could reinforce him, and on 19 October wiped out his force and took Ankober. He then surrounded and annihilated Ras Lul Seged's army, and the Ras was among those killed.

When news of this double disaster reached Addis Ababa the town was panic-stricken, with the German and Turkish Legations spreading rumours and adding to the confusion. Such chiefs as had yet arrived from the south were accompanied only by their bodyguards, the rest of their troops being still on the road. Ras Tafari left next day for the front; he had with him barely four thousand men. By the evening of 21 October, however, all the Shoan forces were assembled, with the ruthless Dedjazmatch Balcha left in charge of Addis Ababa.

Brian and I were out riding one morning when we suddenly heard heavy firing ahead of us. We turned our ponies and galloped back to the Legation, where we learnt that news had just come in of a great victory for the Shoan army. The firing in the town was in celebration.

On 27 October 1916 the armies of the north and south had joined battle on the plain of Sagale, sixty miles north of Addis Ababa, and there they fought hand-to-hand throughout the day. Finally Negus Mikael was captured, and his army was routed and largely destroyed. Forty-four years later I visited the battlefield and saw skulls and bones in crevices on the rocky hillock where Negus Mikael had made his final stand.

My father reported:

> It is difficult to get a consecutive account of the battle. All agree that it was fought with the greatest bravery on both sides and that the victory was by no means an easy one for Shoa. The slaughter appears to have been very great and the Shoan losses are estimated at twelve thousand killed, to which must be added twelve to fourteen thousand killed in the two previous fights when Fitaurari Gelli's and Ras Lul Seged's forces were annihilated.
>
> From this it is evident that if Negus Mikael had advanced immediately after seizing Ankober, when the army of Fitaurari Habta Giorgis was still far from complete, he would have stood a very good chance of entering Addis Ababa, in which case the whole

course of events would have been altered. As it is, however, his army has been annihilated and the fugitives will probably be slaughtered by peasants before they can reach a place of safety.

A few days later the victorious army entered Addis Ababa and paraded before the Empress Zauditu on Jan Meda, that great open space where Menelik had reviewed his troops.

Early that morning my father and mother, with Brian and me, preceded by the Legation escort with their red and white pennoned lances, rode down the wide lane between Balcha's troops to the royal pavilion. The war drums throbbed, a muffled, far-carrying, never-ceasing sound that thrilled me to the core; the five-foot trumpets brayed. Above the lines of waiting troops a host of banners fluttered in the breeze. My father described this scene in a letter to his mother:

> Huge tents, open-fronted, had been put up and the Empress came in state with all her ladies, veiled to the eyes, and took her place on the throne. We were presented and Billy and Brian shook hands. All the local army was ranged up on either side and in front, the chiefs a mass of colour, with their gold-embroidered robes and jewelled crowns and shields, the lesser chiefs in lion- or leopard-skins or sheep-skins dyed in brilliant colours.
>
> About 10.30 a.m. the army began to march past. First came the minstrels, yelling war songs, and when they had finished they tore off their mantles and threw them down before the Empress, saying now that they had fought for her such clothes were no longer worthy of them and would she give them new ones? On these occasions every freedom of speech is allowed. The advance guard of men on mules and horses came up in regular lines but as soon as they got near they dashed up at full gallop, shouting and brandishing their weapons, each man shrieking out how many men he had killed; and then they wheeled round to make room for others.
>
> Men and horses were decorated with green, yellow and red silks and shields covered with gold and silverwork; and round the horses' necks were hung the bloodstained cloaks and trophies of the men each rider had killed.
>
> It was a wonderful sight. The foot soldiers came up in rows, yelling and dancing and it was a marvel they were not ridden down, as the cavalry seemed to dash right into them. Each big chief was preceded by some twenty slaves on mules banging away on kettle drums, with war horns and huge flutes blaring away all the time. The chiefs of each detachment galloped up to the tent, dismounted

and bowed to the ground before taking their places in the Empress's circle, which grew larger every moment, a brilliant mass of gold and colour.

Perhaps the most impressive sight was the remainder of Ras Lul Seged's army, which had been almost annihilated in a furious battle and the Ras himself killed. Only a hundred and fifty marched past out of the original six or eight thousand, headed by the Ras's son, who had escaped. They still wore the clothes they had fought in, with no decorations or marks of triumph, and filed past in dead silence, the Ras's son coming in to sit in his stained clothes among all the gloriously dressed chiefs, a very silent but dignified figure.

Ras Tafari's army came in and he received a great ovation; in his army were the captured guns and chiefs. The Abuna, Petros, the head of the church, rode on a mule with his throne carried before him. He dismounted and was received into the royal tent. After him came more chiefs and then banners and icons of the two principal churches which had sent their Arks to be present at the battle.

When they had passed by they wheeled and formed a huge square lined by all the officers and flags, and then Negus Mikael was brought in. He came on foot and in chains, an old, fine-looking man dressed in the usual black silk cloak with a white cloth wound round his head, stern and very dignified, to bow before the Empress before being led away. One felt sorry for him; he had fought like a man, leading the charge of his troops, for a worthless son who had not even the courage to risk death in supporting the father who had thrown away everything for his sake. Only a month before Mikael had been the proudest chief in Abyssinia and it must have been a bitter moment for him to be led in triumph before the hated Shoans.

More cavalry came by and then his three principal generals, in chains and dressed like the Negus, but each carrying on his shoulder a large stone as a mark of servitude. They came before the tent and prostrated themselves on the ground before following their chief to prison. We then went to say goodbye to the Empress and to shake hands and congratulate Ras Tafari and his chiefs; and the review was over.

It was the most wonderful sight I have ever seen, wild and barbaric to the last degree and the whole thing so wonderfully staged and orderly. Billy and Brian were thrilled and should never forget it. They have been in the middle of war and think nothing of hearing shooting all round them. We had an alarm the other day ... We have been living in exciting times and it has needed a strong hand to keep order in the town, where all the disorderly elements tried to take advantage of the situation. Now each of the main bridges and principal crossroads is decorated with a gallows and the dangling body of such robbers as have been caught red-handed.

James Bruce had no doubt witnessed similar scenes in the 1760s when victorious armies returned in triumph to Gondar. Few other Europeans have seen the like; certainly never before had two small English boys watched such a spectacle in Abyssinia. Even now, nearly seventy years later, I can recall almost every detail: the embroidered caps of the drummers decorated with cowries; a man falling off his horse as he charged by; a small boy carried past in triumph – he had killed two men though he seemed little older than myself; the face of Ras Lul Seged's young son, and the sheepskin over his shoulder. I had been reading *Tales from the Iliad*. Now, in boyish fancy, I watched the likes of Achilles, Ajax and Ulysses pass in triumph with aged Priam, proud even in defeat. I believe that day implanted in me a life-long craving for barbaric splendour, for savagery and colour and the throb of drums, and that it gave me a lasting veneration for long-established custom and ritual, from which would derive later a deep-seated resentment of Western innovations in other lands, and a distaste for the drab uniformity of the modern world.

CHAPTER 4

The Aftermath

WITH LIJ YASU a fugitive and his father a captive, Empress Taitu, Menelik's widow, emerged from seclusion. She and Zauditu and Ras Gugsa Wale, Zauditu's husband, plotted to eliminate Ras Tafari, but they underestimated his intelligence and resolution, a mistake many were to make in the years to come. In the event, Zauditu was crowned on 11 February 1917, but only after she had divorced Ras Gugsa. Taitu was banished.

The country remained in a disturbed state. My father reported that Zauditu's coronation ceremonies were barely over when the provinces of Simien, Walkait, Wojju and Wogara revolted. The Wollo Muslims, who were being persecuted by the Shoan army, had attacked Dessie and, though defeated, were still raiding at large. The Arussi, and Muslim and pagan tribes from Ginir to Dolo, had risen and a revolution in Tigre was generally expected. Since the soldiery could only live by looting, the peasantry were rising out of sheer desperation. The council of ministers were intriguing for their own gains. Meanwhile Ras Tafari stood alone, shouldering full responsibility without real power, and uncertain whom he could trust.

Lij Yasu, after observing his father's defeat at Sagale from a safe distance, had fled back into the Danakil desert. He now emerged and joined Ras Yemer, whose lands had been pillaged by the Shoan forces. Ras Yemer had been renowned as one of Negus Mikael's foremost captains. Together he and Lij Yasu now raised an army and occupied Magdala, where they were besieged on the almost impregnable mountain-top. The Shoan leaders had little inclination to assault it, but when the redoubtable Fitaurari Habta Giorgis arrived from Addis Ababa with reinforcements, Ras Yemer, accompanied by Lij Yasu and several thousand men, escaped through the Shoan lines. The surrounding country then rallied to him, and he wiped out a detachment of Ras Kassa's troops; three hundred prisoners were mutilated and died. Then, on 27 August 1917, between Dessie and Ankober, he gave battle to Fitaurari Habta Giorgis.

My father wrote:

> Lij Yasu's forces were defeated with tremendous losses. Ras
> Yemer was killed. Fitaurari Sera Bezu (his second-in-command)
> was seriously wounded. The casualties were great. I am told that
> there are ten thousand dead and wounded on the battlefield. Most
> of the prisoners have been mutilated, with the loss of a hand or
> foot, for having fought again after having been pardoned for
> fighting with Negus Mikael.

Lij Yasu escaped once more into the Danakil country. Meanwhile
Ras Tafari thwarted another plot hatched by the banished Empress
Taitu and designed to coincide with Lij Yasu's attack from the north.
Four months later Taitu, mischievous to the end, died of a heart
attack.

By December 1917 my father badly needed leave. The altitude of
Addis Ababa, at eight thousand feet, was affecting his heart. He had
been short-handed, overworked and under considerable strain as a
result of the events leading to the Revolution, well aware of the
importance of its success to the Allied cause, and the danger to his
family if the Revolution failed. On being granted leave, he decided
to take us to India and visit his brother, Lord Chelmsford, the
Viceroy.

By now the railway had reached Addis Ababa so we were able to
travel all the way to Jibuti by train. From Jibuti my father crossed to
Aden and then went to Cairo to confer with Sir Reginald Wingate,
the High Commissioner, while we went to Berbera to stay with
Geoffrey Archer, the Commissioner in British Somaliland; he and
his wife had stayed with us at the Legation for Zauditu's coronation
in February.

Although my father was six foot two, Geoffrey Archer seemed a
real giant; he must have been six foot four and broad in proportion,
but he was a kind giant, having an instinctive sympathy with small
boys. He was an authority on the birds of Somaliland and seeing I
was interested he showed me his collection. Several times he lent
Brian and me a .410 shotgun and took us shooting along the shore,
and when we got back told his skinner to stuff the birds we had shot;
I was thrilled by these expeditions. He also sent us out to a dhow in
the harbour to fish; we had never before been on a vessel that rode
so close to the water.

Everything at Berbera was unfamiliar and exciting: the barren, burnt-up countryside, so very different from the highlands of Abyssinia; the camel herds at the wells; the gaunt, half-naked Somalis with great mops of hair, leaning on their spears and talking a harsh incomprehensible language; the bugle calls; the uniformed troops drilling on their parade ground, and especially an evening when they staged for us a realistic attack with blank ammunition on a position 'held' by tribesmen. I frequently heard reference to the 'Mad Mullah', whose forces still occupied half the country; and I listened enthralled to descriptions by officers in the Somali Camel Corps of fights against his Dervishes.

My father arrived back from Cairo in time to spend Christmas with us. On his way there the frigate taking him to Suez had called at Jidda to enable him to meet Sharif Husain, the father of Amir Faisal who was leading the Arab Revolt. My father described the Sharif as 'a delightful old man with a decided sense of humour'.

We sailed together from Berbera to Aden in HMS *Minto*. It was an appalling journey; the sea was very rough and the frigate pitched and rolled throughout the night. We were all desperately seasick. At Aden we stayed in the Residency as guests of General Stewart. The Turks had invaded the Aden Protectorate from the Yemen and were fighting the British forces not far away at Lahej. The general took my father on a visit to the trenches: Brian and I went with him and there we watched British shellfire on the Turkish lines. On our way back to Aden we attended a gathering of Arab sheikhs, who presented my father with a magnificent dagger. I would have liked to wear it thirty years later when I travelled in the deserts of southern Arabia, but by then it had been lost.

For me, the highlight of these memorable months was our time in India. At Viceregal Lodge we were housed in palatial tents luxuriously carpeted and furnished, and were looked after by a host of servants. There were rows of similar tents on the lawns, for the accommodation in the Lodge itself was limited. The Government of India had only moved to Delhi from Calcutta in 1911, and the magnificent Lutyens buildings which today dominate New Delhi were still being built.

From the moment I arrived I was immensely impressed by the pomp and the ceremony which surrounded my uncle as Viceroy, fascinated by the splendour of the bodyguard, and the varied liveries and elaborate turbans of the doorkeepers, messengers, coachmen, household servants and other functionaries.

Edwin Montagu, Secretary of State for India, had arrived in Delhi for the discussions which resulted in the Montagu-Chelmsford Reforms, the first concession to Indian nationalism. The Princes, the Governors of the Provinces, their staffs and many other officials were in Delhi; in consequence my uncle was very busy. I had never met him before. I saw him once in his State robes; then, to his highly impressionable nephew, he seemed more than human. On another occasion Brian and I were invited to have tea with him and our aunt Francie. I felt overawed. They both tried, no doubt, to put us at our ease, but I do not think either had much understanding of small children. It was ten years before Uncle Fred really took an interest in me.

I had grown up in Addis Ababa where there were few permanent buildings other than the Legations. I had only the vaguest recollections of England. I therefore associated towns with tin roofs and thatched huts; in Jibuti, Berbera and Aden I had seen no memorable buildings. I was totally unprepared for Delhi, yet old enough to understand what I saw. The Moghul tombs, the Red Fort, the towering minarets of the Jami Masjid, made me aware for the first time of the significance of civilization, and the meaning of history.

One afternoon we were taken to the Ridge above Delhi where British troops had held out against constant attacks during the Mutiny. We were shown a bullet-ridden orb, lying on the ground, that had once decorated the church spire. My father described to me how the Guides had arrived and gone straight into action after marching day and night from the Punjab; how Nicholson had been killed leading the troops as they stormed the ramparts of Delhi. He told me that my grandfather had fought in the Mutiny, and that Mrs Inglis, daughter of my great-grandfather Chelmsford, had been in Lucknow through the siege, where her husband commanded the troops.

My parents went to visit the Rajput States while we boys continued to go for rides in the mornings and picnics in the afternoons. Perhaps a fortnight later Brian and I were sent with Minna to join them at Jaipur, where they were guests of the Maharajah. We travelled there by train; I remember herds of blackbuck grazing near the line and bullock-carts lumbering along in clouds of dust.

When we arrived at Jaipur my father told us that he had sent for us so that we could go with him tiger-shooting. I could hardly believe what I heard. I do not remember how long we stayed at Jaipur but every day was packed with excitement. From the backs of elephants we watched pig-sticking, and went out after blackbuck in a bullock-cart; my father shot two, each with a good head. Then the great day dawned.

Soon after breakfast we set off into the jungle. We saw some wild boar which paid little attention to our passing elephants, and we saw several magnificent peacock and a number of monkeys; to me the monkeys were *bandar log*, straight out of Kipling's *Jungle Book*. It must have taken a couple of hours or more to reach the *machan*, a platform raised on poles. We climbed up on to it; someone blew a horn and the beat started. After a time I could hear distant shouts. I sat very still, hardly daring to move my head. A peacock flew past. Then my father slowly raised his rifle and there was the tiger, padding towards us along a narrow game trail, his head moving from side to side. I still remember him as I saw him then. He was magnificent, larger even than I had expected, looking almost red against the pale dry grass.

My father fired. I saw the tiger stagger. He roared, bounded off and disappeared into the jungle. He was never found, though they searched for him on elephants while we returned to the palace. I was very conscious of my father's intense disappointment. Two days later we went on another beat, this time for panther, but the panther broke back and we never saw it. However, a great sambhur stag did gallop past the *machan*. Scenes such as this remained most vividly in my memory.

As guests of a Maharajah in one of the great Indian Native States, we were surrounded by an opulence and splendour little changed since the time of Akbar. At the time I accepted it as a marvellous background for the all-important hunting, though too young really to appreciate this privileged glimpse of Indian court life. I do remember my first sight of the Palace of the Winds, a seemingly immense building, reddish in colour, its front pierced by row above row of latticed windows. Otherwise I have only confused memories of large rooms, the marbled walls ornately inlaid, of men in gorgeous robes, of others more humbly dressed, of rows of shackled elephants, and of wild animals fighting in an amphitheatre for our entertainment.

At the end of March we left Bombay in a P and O liner to Aden, and from there crossed to Jibuti in HMS *Juno*, flagship of the East

Indies Squadron. This was a very different crossing from our night-mare voyage in the *Minto*: the sea was calm and the great ship was steady as the land. The officers made much of us children: the Marine band played on deck and the captain fired off one of the guns, after we had been given cotton wool to stuff in our ears.

At the Legation we were welcomed back by the servants and reverted happily to our accustomed way of life. We had learnt to ride by the time we were four, and we rode everywhere; no one went for walks in those days. Our ponies with Habta Wold, the *syce* who accompanied us, were always waiting for us as we finished breakfast.

Brian and I usually rode up the steep hillside at the back of the house to where, at 8500 feet, there was a grotto, crudely cut out of the rock below ground level. From here we had immense views, northwards across Ras Kassa's province of Salale towards the Blue Nile gorge, or southwards to the distant Arussi mountains.

Some mornings we galloped over the open plain below the Lega-tion; at that hour the tracks were threaded with groups of villagers on their way to market in Addis Ababa. In the afternoons we either rode or tried to shoot birds with our air rifles. For children of our age we were allowed a remarkable degree of freedom; only the town was out of bounds.

Had it not been for the First World War I might have been sent to school in England, separated indefinitely from my parents, as was the fate of so many English children whose fathers served in India or elsewhere in the East. I must have had some lessons at the Legation, though I have no recollection of them, for I learnt to read and write. My father read to me in the evening, something I looked forward to enormously. I grew up on *Jock of the Bushveld*, that marvellous book by Sir Percy Fitzpatrick about hunting in South Africa. The other books I remember were Keary and Keary's *Heroes of Asgard*, Kipl-ing's *Jungle Books* and *Puck of Pook's Hill*, and, particularly, *A Sporting Trip Through Abyssinia* by Powell-Cotton.

Always gentle, patient and understanding, my father gave a young boy, who no doubt was often tiresome and demanding, a happy sense of comradeship. He always explained things but never talked down to me. I still have a letter written in pencil from his camp at Laisamis on his way to Nairobi in 1914. It is illustrated with drawings of buffalo, giraffe, warthog and camp scenes, and describes a rhino hunt. It could have been written to a boy of seven; I was only half that age.

Inevitably in Addis Ababa he was busy for most of the day, writing his despatches, interviewing people or visiting his colleagues in the other Legations. However, during our visit to India he had been constantly with us, and in Jaipur I had experienced a gratifying sense of shared adventure; but it was perhaps in the camp where we went each year from the Legation for an eagerly awaited ten days that I remember him most vividly. I can picture him now, a tall lean figure in a helmet, smoking his pipe as he watched the horses being saddled or inspected them while they were being fed; I can see him cleaning his rifle in the verandah of his tent, or sitting chatting with my mother by the fire in the evening.

Our camp was an enchanted spot, tucked away in the Entoto hills. A stream tumbled down the cliff opposite our tents, then flowed through a jumble of rocks among a grove of trees. Here were all sorts of birds: top-heavy hornbills, touracos with crimson wings, brilliant bee-eaters, sun-birds, paradise flycatchers, hoopoes, golden weaver birds and many others. My father knew them all and taught me their names.

Vultures nested in the cliffs and circled in slow spirals above the camp. I used to watch them through his field glasses, and the baboons that processed along the cliff tops, the babies clinging to their mothers' backs. At night we sometimes heard their frenzied barking when a leopard disturbed them. Several times I went up the valley with my father in the evening and sat with him behind a rock, hoping he would get a shot at the leopard. I remember once a large white-tailed mongoose scuttled past within a few feet of us.

In August 1918 my father was recalled to London to report to the Foreign Office and he did not get back until mid-December. In September the epidemic of Spanish influenza that devastated Europe, and killed more people than the war, reached Abyssinia; there it killed three of the five doctors in the country and incapacitated a fourth. Dermot and I caught it. My mother was reading to me from *A Sporting Trip Through Abyssinia*, and I can remember exactly where she had got to in the book when, thinking I looked feverish, she took my temperature and put me to bed. There were seventy cases among the servants and their dependants in the small village in the Legation grounds. More than ten thousand people died in the town. They were buried in mass graves, the corpses piled one on top of the other under a few inches of soil. Inevitably the hyenas and pi-dogs dug them up. Ras Tafari sickened. His present-day detractors might well ponder what would have happened to the country had he died.

After ten years of duty in Abyssinia my father's spell there had come to an end. We went to England early in 1919, travelling by train to Jibuti and then by a Union Castle boat to Marseilles. Until almost the last day I could not believe that we were really leaving Abyssinia for good, that we should not be coming back.

CHAPTER 5

England and School

C HILDREN ARE certainly adaptable, but England was an entirely different world from Abyssinia. I had once asked my father if there were hyenas in England. What? No hyenas, no kudu, no oryx; only a few eagles in a place called Scotland and, unbelievably, hardly any kites. I thought what a dull place it must be.

My father's house at Beachley had been requisitioned by the Navy during the war, so now we had no home. We went to Ireland for the summer and our visit there was great fun; Brian and I drove about in a donkey-cart, fished for eels, and shot rabbits with a .410. I spent much of my time with my father, watching him sketch, or fish for salmon in the Slaney. It was a happy interlude before Brian and I, dressed conventionally like the other boys in suits and bowler hats, were sent to St Aubyn's, a boarding school at Rottingdean, near Brighton.

In January 1920 at the beginning of our second term at school, my father died. He was only forty-eight. He collapsed suddenly while he was shaving, murmured, 'It's all right, my dear,' and died in my mother's arms. His death was a devastating shock for her. They were living in lodgings at Brighton at the time, so as to be near our school. Now, utterly desolate, my mother was without a home, and, as a result of my father's death, short of money. When a kind and affluent sister-in-law offered to buy her a house in the suburbs of London, she asked, 'What will my boys do there?' The reply was, 'We'll get them bicycles and they can learn to ride them.'

Instead my mother went to Radnorshire (now Powys), and at first took rooms in a farmhouse at Titley. The accommodation was cramped and the conditions were primitive. For transport she used the farmer's pony and trap: the pony was so decrepit that we called it the dead pony. For my mother it must have been a sad comedown from the Legation, but we boys enjoyed ourselves. Minna was with us and the local gentry were kind. A Colonel Drage, for instance, who lived at The Rodd near Presteigne, would sometimes invite

Brian and me over for a night. He would call us by candlelight and in the dawn take us round his wood after rabbits. Any time would have done, but he realized the excitement for us of such early awakenings. We looked forward immensely to these visits.

A year or so later in 1922 my mother leased The Milebrook, a charming house near Knighton, where Radnorshire borders Shropshire. She had fallen in love with the house as soon as she saw it, and knew that this was where her family should grow up. Here she gave us a happy home for the next twenty years. Our landlord was C. C. C. Rogers, Lord Lieutenant of Radnorshire and elderly owner of a large and beautiful estate, Stanage Park. Charlie Rogers and, later, his son, Guy, were very good to us, allowing us to treat their estate as our own, to ride all over it and to wander where we would with our dogs. Not far away was the great sweep of the Radnor Forest, and beyond it the Elan valley where peregrines nested, the Towy valley with the last kites in Britain, and Tregaron Bog where wild geese came in winter. During holidays at The Milebrook I found once again the freedom I had known in Abyssinia, but now for only three months in the year.

Before Brian and I went to school we had hardly met any other English boys; I remember only one, Standish Roche, who lived nearby while we were in Ireland. Gerald Campbell, Consul in Addis Ababa during our last years there, had two children, a little younger than me, but they were girls and had no part in our lives. There had been no other English children in Abyssinia, none in Somaliland, none at Aden, and in Delhi I can only remember meeting girls.

Suddenly at St Aubyn's we found ourselves in a crowd of seventy boys, nearly all older. There was no privacy anywhere; we were always among others, whether in classrooms, dining room or gymnasium, on the playing fields or in the dormitory at night. Schoolboys are very conventional and quick to gang up on any boy who in behaviour or dress does not conform. With our extraordinary background, Brian and I lacked the ability to cope with our contemporaries; as English boys who had barely heard of cricket we were natural targets.

Soon after we arrived I was interrogated about my parents and our home life. At first I was a friendly, forthcoming little boy, very ready to talk, perhaps to boast about journeys I had made and things I had seen. My stories, however, were greeted with disbelief and derision, and I felt increasingly rejected. As a result I withdrew into myself, treated overtures of friendship with mistrust, and was easily provoked. I made few friends, but once I adapted to this life I do not think I was particularly unhappy. I could comfort myself, especially at night, by recalling the sights and scenery of Abyssinia, far more real to me than the cold bleak English downs behind the school.

St Aubyn's had a good reputation when my father decided to send us there. Unfortunately, just before we arrived, a new head-master, R. C. V. Lang, took over. He was unmarried; his sister looked after him. He was a large, imposing man who had been a noted athlete and I am sure he created a favourable impression on my parents. In fact he was a sadist, and after my father's death both Brian and I were among his victims. The school motto was 'Quit you like men: be strong', an exhortation not without relevance to some of us boys. He beat me on a number of occasions, often for some trivial offence. Sent up early to the dormitory, I had to kneel naked by the side of my bed. I remember crying out the first time, 'It hurts!' and Lang saying grimly, 'It's meant to.'

For two or three days after each beating, I was called to his study so that he could see I was healing properly. Though I had never been hurt like this before, strangely enough I bore him no resentment for these beatings, accepting them as the penalty for what I had done. It never occurred to me how disproportionate was the punishment to the offence.

After we had been at school for about three years Arnold Hodson, who had been Consul in Southern Abyssinia, was staying with us at the beginning of the holidays. One evening he said jokingly, 'I don't suppose you get beaten at school nowadays, not like we were in my time.' Neither Brian nor I had told our mother about these beatings but now, incensed, I pulled up my shorts and showed him some half-healed scars. Years later I learnt that Hodson went down to Sussex and told the headmaster that if he beat either of us again he would have him taken to court.

There was another punishment I dreaded. Each day the school was drilled by a retired sergeant living in the village, and on special occasions we paraded with the school band. These parades were taken seriously and in the afternoon, while the rest of the school played games, defaulters had to run endlessly round an asphalt yard. On a hot summer's day this was a punishment more suited to the Foreign Legion than to an English preparatory school.

Recently I went back to St Aubyn's to give a lecture, and I spent the night there. Time seemed to have stood still. The boys wore the same grey shorts and jerseys; the band was practising, marching and counter-marching on the playing field. I attended morning chapel, and neither the seating nor the service had altered. In the dormitories I identified the beds in which I had slept, with the same trays beneath them for dirty clothes and the same chairs beside them. In the dining room, team photographs were ranged along the wall: I recognized Brian in one of them; I myself had never made the grade. In sixty years the school had hardly changed in outward appearance; what was profoundly different was the relationship of headmaster and boys. Between them I sensed affection, confidence and trust. I had heard that St Aubyn's was now one of the best preparatory schools in the country, with a distinguished academic record. Having stayed with the headmaster and talked to the boys, I know this to be true.

Several of my family, including my grandfather, had been at Eton; he, however, sent his sons, other than my father, to Winchester. My father for some reason went to Cheltenham, where he was happy; but he decided to send us to Eton. When my father died, his brother Percy generously undertook to pay for the education of Brian and myself. Had he not done so I could not have gone to Eton, and should have been deprived of one of the most formative influences in my life.

I was an unreceptive boy to teach, disinclined to concentrate on any subject that bored me. I certainly learnt next to nothing at St Aubyn's and when I took the Common Entrance examination for Eton I failed so ignominiously that the authorities wrote to my mother that it would be futile for me to try again. Undismayed, she sent me to a first-class crammer for two terms, and Brian to another preparatory school. At my next attempt I passed into Eton a whole form from the bottom of the school.

Early in September 1923 I arrived at Windsor Station with my mother, and from there we drove in a horse-drawn cab past the Castle and across the Thames into Eton. There were twenty-four houses at Eton, each with about forty-five boys who were known as Oppidans and were distinct from the seventy Scholars who lived apart in College. Each house was run by a senior master and was known by his name. My housemaster was A. M. McNeile. We had tea with him and his wife and met the three other new boys and their parents: Harry Phillimore, small, dark-haired and bespectacled;

Ronnie Chance, slim, blond and diffident; and Desmond Parsons, a tall, good-looking boy.

Every boy had his own room from the day he arrived at Eton. Mine was very small, with hardly space for a fold-up bed, washstand, bureau, padded chest for clothes, and easy chair; but that did not matter. What mattered was that it was my own, with the inestimable sense of privacy which this conferred. Before she went back to London my mother and I went into town and bought a carpet, and pictures by Caldwell of African big game to hang on my walls. In the course of time I moved into other, larger rooms; the last had a splendid view of Windsor Castle.

At Eton the different houses and classrooms were spread over a large area, and in the next day or two I had somehow to find out where and when which masters were teaching me what subjects. There was also the anxiety of discovering where I was to sit in chapel; then I had to learn the names and whereabouts of the different houses and of the scattered playing fields.

McNeile's house, like the others, was run by four or five boys who were known as 'the Library' – the equivalent of house prefects. Except for the head of the house, who was chosen by the housemaster, the Library elected its own members. A curious system prevailed whereby the Library could beat offenders but the housemaster could not: he had to refer the matter to his Library or, for really serious offences, to the Headmaster or Lower Master. Similarly the Eton Society known as Pop, the equivalent of school prefects, elected its own members with the exception of a few who belonged *ex officio*.

The school was divided into Upper and Lower boys, and the Lower boys in each house fagged for members of the Library: they cooked their tea, ran errands for them, being sent perhaps as far as Windsor to fetch a cake from Fuller's teashop, and they had to come at once when someone in the Library shouted 'Boy!', the last arrival being given the job. Anyone who failed to answer the summons was liable to be beaten. New boys were excused fagging for a fortnight until they had found their feet. I believe that both fagging and beating by the Library have now been done away with. I accepted them quite cheerfully.

Every evening I had tea with the friend or two with whom I had arranged to mess for the 'half', as a term was known at Eton. Tea was a substantial meal of eggs, bacon, sausages, even chops, provided by ourselves and cooked over a gas ring in the passage. At McNeile's we should otherwise have fared ill, since neither breakfast, lunch nor supper was inviting.

I messed at first with Harry Phillimore, who was to become a lifelong friend. Scholarly and intensely hard-working, his otherwise serious nature was lightened by a streak of mischief. We were an unruly lot of Lower boys at McNeile's and it was usually Harry Phillimore who instigated the disturbances we caused. He died in 1974, a Lord Justice of Appeal. Listening once to him on the Bench I recalled an occasion when the aged and formidable boys' maid who looked after our rooms had stood with arms akimbo accusing him of some peccadillo, and ended her tirade: 'Mr Phillimore, don't you stand there lying like Ananias!'

Our worst enormity was when we flushed Desmond Parsons out of his room with the fire hydrant and, having turned it on, could not turn it off. Water was soon cascading down the stairs from the top storey. Eventually McNeile appeared, holding his trousers above his knees, and muttering, 'Hooligans, damned hooligans,' he turned it off. That was one of the many occasions when we were sent for after supper and beaten by the Library.

Only once did I bear resentment after being beaten. I had been selected in my second year at Eton, while I was still a Lower boy, to box against the Eton Mission from Hackney Wick in the East End of London. I was giving tea to my opponent who, though the same weight, was probably two years older, when I was sent for by Julian Hall, my fag master. He was head of the house, in the sixth form, captain of the Oppidans and in consequence in Pop.

'Why have you not turned up to cook my tea?' he demanded.

'I'm sorry,' I replied, 'I forgot to tell you I'm boxing against the Eton Mission tonight and am giving tea in my room to the boy I'm boxing.'

'I'll teach you to forget. Bend over,' he said, and gave me six with his Pop cane, a stiff, knotted bamboo. I have often wondered what my guest would have thought when I got back if I had told him I had just been beaten. I never forgave Hall. Anyone else would have said, 'Good luck. Be sure to beat him.' It was an unfortunate evening for me: I was knocked out in the second round, the only time I was knocked out, either at Eton or at Oxford.

It is winter evenings at Eton that I remember most vividly: talking and arguing about anything and everything with friends in front of a coal fire; sitting in my armchair with my feet up, reading a story by Buchan, Kipling or Conrad, or something by one of the African big-game hunters whose books I was already collecting. There was a civilized comfort about these winter evenings that gained by contrast with the hardships of daytime.

Many people assume that Eton is a luxurious school. When I was there it was one of the most spartan in the country. The Thames Valley is often bitterly cold and damp. The classrooms were heated in winter, but in the houses there was no form of heating until we lit fires in our rooms at six in the evening. We were given a lot of work to prepare in our spare time and I remember trying to keep warm in the daytime in an overcoat and scarf while I wrote an essay or struggled with Latin composition. After a hard frost the passage walls sweated and water trickled down the corridors. In McNeile's there were no changing rooms or showers, only foot baths in which we could wash after games, and only two baths and five lavatories for forty-seven of us. Except for the Library, who could bath at any time, a boy was allocated two baths a week. It never occurred to us to criticize these conditions, which we accepted as a part of Eton life, like the tailcoats and top hats we wore.

Archie McNeile, as he was known to the boys, was a wiry, upright figure with an alert, intelligent face. He had not been at Eton himself but when he played for the masters his volleying in the Field Game – the Eton form of football – was long remembered. At Oxford he had gained a First in Greats, for which, according to a contemporary, he had worked as if he were taking a chartered accountancy exam. At Eton he taught mathematics. Years later I discovered that he had been a talented musician, yet he never revealed this, not even to music-loving boys in his house. Modest, self-contained and abstemious, he kept aloof from the fellowship of other masters, and his dry, sarcastic wit, and inability to unbend, prevented his establishing a warm relationship with the boys in his house. I accepted this as natural; it never occurred to me at the time that a housemaster could also be a friend.

When a boy arrived at Eton he was allocated to a 'classical tutor' who oversaw his work and gave him special tuition. Many Eton masters, such as C. H. K. Martin, the historian who later tutored Princess Elizabeth and Princess Margaret, and especially George Lyttelton, whose published letters to Rupert Hart-Davis have given pleasure to many, were inspired teachers. For one rewarding half I was taught by Lyttelton. He came into the room once, said, 'Put away your books,' and read us *The Lemnian*, Buchan's story about Thermopylae. Not a boy stirred while he read it. However, it was my misfortune that McNeile selected C. O. Bevan as my classical tutor. A stolid, red-faced clergyman without wit or humour, he contrived to make any and every subject dull. I was interested in history, and enjoyed writing essays, consciously modelling my style on Buchan's. Cob Bevan made me loathe Latin, and as a result of his tuition Latin verse remained incomprehensible to me. Bored stiff by him, I paid little attention: he retaliated by having me birched for idleness on three occasions, but these attempts to drive Latin into me from the wrong end proved equally unproductive.

As a Lower boy at the time I came before the Lower Master. Ramsey, pompous, rubicund and white-haired, put on his mortarboard as he pronounced sentence and then, wrapped in his gown, swept into the adjoining room where the block, dating back some two hundred years, was kept. As I followed him through the doorway the porter whispered, 'Get your braces undone, sir, don't keep him waiting.'

On either side of the block stood a *praepostor* from the sixth form, there to see that sentence was carried out decently and to order. The junior *praepostor* bowed and handed the birch to the senior *praepostor*, who handed it with a bow to the Lower Master. The whole proceeding was reminiscent of a beheading on Tower Hill. After a birching twelve shillings and sixpence for 'school medicine' was reputedly put on the school bill – I presume for a new birch, but I never verified this.

Though barely moderate scholastically, I was just good enough at games to become Captain of Games in an athletically undistinguished house. This meant that I got into the Library. I was never popular and I had few friends, but such friendships as I made were mostly lasting. Eton, however, meant far more to me than my relationships with others, or the learning I acquired or the games I played. I was conscious that here I belonged to a community with roots in the distant past and a distinguished place in British history.

Every day I passed the weathered statue of Henry VI in the middle of School Yard. He had founded the College during the Middle Ages, even before Columbus discovered the New World. The arms granted to his chosen foundation were the *fleur-de-lis* of France and the royal lion of England, above the three lilies of the Virgin

Mary. They were displayed on the Eton flag and stamped on school documents.

One side of School Yard was dominated by College Chapel. Henry VI had intended this building to be one of the largest churches in the land. When he was murdered during the Wars of the Roses only the choir had been built; later the ante-chapel was added and together they formed College Chapel. Lower School was opposite the Chapel and here, under the dark oaken beams and arches, I was taught in a classroom that had been in continuous use as such since 1443. In Upper School every inch of the panelling was scored with the names of generations of boys. Many had become illustrious; some, like Wellington, world-famous, a few notorious: Sir Francis Verney had become a Barbary pirate, Greenhall had been hanged as a highwayman.

Along the colonnade under Upper School were recorded 1157 names of Old Etonians killed in the First World War (748 others, including my brother Dermot's, were added to them after the Second World War). No wonder that in this setting, during those impressionable years, I acquired lasting respect for tradition and veneration for the past. Here, too, from masters and boys alike, I learnt responsibility, the decencies of life, and standards of civilized behaviour.

Brian came to McNeile's the year after me: I was glad he was there with me. When I left in December 1928 he succeeded me in the house as Captain of Games. He gained his school colours for rugger and was unlucky not to get them for the Field Game and the Wall Game – another game confined to Eton. Dermot and Roderic also went to McNeile's: we missed by only one half all being there together.

I have many memories of Eton: services in College Chapel, especially in winter when the lights were lit and I listened to the massed singing of a favourite hymn; the Headmaster, Dr Alington, an Olympian figure in scarlet gown, taking 'absence' on the chapel steps; the Fourth of June, a festival peculiar to Eton, and fireworks bursting over the river; the Field Game on winter afternoons while mist crept across the grounds; the lamps in the High Street and crowds of boys hurrying back to their houses before 'lock-up'.

*   *   *

We spent our holidays at The Milebrook. I remember my excitement when I had arrived there for the first time from St Aubyn's. It was an attractive creeper-covered house in a beautiful setting. From the lawn was a spacious view across the valley of the Teme to Stowe Hill, where in summer the heather up to the skyline showed purple above hanging oak woods. The house was just the right size for us; downstairs, an entrance hall, four rooms, a kitchen and a servants' hall; upstairs, six bedrooms and an attic.

Below my bedroom window lay the garden, made very beautiful by my mother over the years. Beyond were the orchard, stables, a marshy field where peewits called and snipe drummed in spring, and distant woods. In the morning the sun came in at the window and woke me. I always think of The Milebrook as a happy, sunlit house, with butterflies fluttering among the stocks outside the drawing room windows.

Here we grew up in a close-knit, self-sufficient family. We did not often have other boys to stay, almost never a girl, and we seldom went away on visits. London we passed through, on our way to and from school, but except during the half-term 'long leave' from Eton we rarely spent a night there. In the immediate neighbourhood of The Milebrook were few families except for the local farmers, and for the first four years there we had no transport other than bicycles and a pony cart. Then, in 1924, our grandmother, Lady Chelmsford, died and the money my mother inherited made us reasonably well off. She bought a car, which widened the range of our activities but made little other difference to the lives of us boys. For years we had no telephone, and the house was lit in our time by acetylene gas which we made each evening in the pigsty.

During the first few winter holidays I went out on our pony with the Teme Valley, the local pack of hounds that hunted the rough hill country on the Welsh border. In those days the field was small and consisted mostly of farmers. The pony, though fast and a good jumper, had a mouth of iron and was almost impossible to control. Despite this I had a lot of fun, until my mother replaced him with another pony that Brian could manage, and I gave up hunting. I never shared my family's passion for horses. I was, however, devoted to the three dogs I owned while I was at The Milebrook. The first was a golden spaniel pup. He died of distemper while I was away at St Aubyn's; the news overwhelmed me with a child's grief. The next was a black cocker spaniel, and the third a springer spaniel which I trained to retrieve and took with me whenever I went away to shoot. Each of them slept in my room.

When I was fifteen we rented a rough shoot of about a thousand acres on Stowe Hill, part of the Stanage estate; Guy Rogers let us have it for a fiver. There we shot grouse, partridge, pheasant, occasional duck, snipe and woodcock and innumerable rabbits, more than earning whatever we shot by the amount of exercise we took to get it. Stanage had one of the country's finest pheasant shoots, renowned for its high birds. During my last two years at Eton, and my years at Oxford, Guy Rogers invited me to his covert shoots. I was a good shot and held my own among his guests. Though my brothers too enjoyed shooting, they preferred hunting, and my mother, who had hunted in Ireland before she went to Abyssinia, now took it up again. All my brothers rode in point-to-points and Dermot rode his own horse in the National Hunt Cup at Cheltenham: his ambition was to ride in the Grand National.

Thinking back to those days, I realize how different I should be today had I grown up in the suburban house in London, suggested to my mother. At the time I accepted without question all that The Milebrook offered. Only later did I appreciate what sacrifices my mother made to give it to us, and how lonely she must often have been when we were all away at school; after our father's death she became almost possessively devoted to us.

She was a sociable person with a remarkable gift for friendship and an immediate understanding of others, especially the young. In Abyssinia the limited social life had not mattered to her, since she had her husband. When he died, after their long absences abroad, she was left with few friends in England. Nor was it easy for her at first to make new ones at The Milebrook, having only a pony and cart and her nearest neighbours being two, four and five miles away.

Though not intellectual, my mother was intelligent, and she now acquired a wide range of new interests. She loved the countryside round The Milebrook and was never happier than when riding over the hills. She was generous by nature and had an Irish sense of hospitality, and combined great pride with high standards and absolute loyalty. She had instinctive good taste, especially in her dress, and whatever the setting she always looked right. Above all, my mother was fun to be with.

At Eton I had passed School Certificate, but without the credit in

Latin which was indispensable for getting to Oxford. I therefore went for a term to a crammer, secured the necessary credit and was accepted by Magdalen College.

Before going up to Oxford I spent three months of the summer of 1929 in France to improve my French. For the first two months I lived with a French family in Fontainebleau and studied with a Commandant Lettauré, who was coaching fifteen other young Englishmen. I visited Paris and Versailles, and Lettauré took me to a Joan of Arc festival at Orléans. I enjoyed my time at Fontainebleau, especially wandering in the forest, hoping to see a wild boar.

The third month I spent in Brittany at Sable d'Or; there I made friends with an elderly, bearded fisherman called Pierre. Like the other Breton fishermen, he had been a *pêcheur d'Islande*. Every morning, before it was light, I crossed the mile-long sands to the cove where the fishermen kept their boats, while curlew, disturbed by my approach, called around me in the darkness. It would be getting light as I arrived. Some men would already be at the boats, others coming down the steep path from the village. There Pierre and his thirteen-year-old *mousse*, or assistant, would join me – Pierre in sea-boots, jacket and cap, the *mousse* bare-headed and barefoot, in a ragged sweater, with his trousers rolled up about his knees. We would push out the boat, hoist the sail and visit the lobster pots and conger lines. We hauled up the pots, removed the lobsters and crabs and dropped the pots back in the sea. The congers were ugly-looking brutes, some of them three feet or more in length; Pierre warned me they could bite through a sea-boot.

We trolled for mackerel, passing up and down the coast. Sometimes we got into a shoal of them and pulled them in as fast as we could handle the lines; sometimes we failed to find any. Then we lowered the sail and sat in the sun, and Pierre spoke of the lot he and his fellow villagers had been born to, the weeks at sea, the gales, the great hauls of fish, the hardships and achievements of a Breton fisherman's life, while we ate the food he had brought with him, and drank his rough cider.

CHAPTER 6

Oxford

I WENT UP to Magdalen College, Oxford, in the autumn of 1929 and was there four years. Most of my Eton contemporaries at Oxford were at Christ Church, Trinity, Balliol or New College, and it was with them I spent much of my time. Nevertheless, I was always thankful that I was at Magdalen, perhaps the most beautiful of Oxford colleges. Though small it was spacious, with its deer park and Addison's Walk along the bank of the Cherwell. My memories of Oxford, unlike my memories of Eton, are summer ones: the tranquil beauty of the High Street in the early morning before the traffic; May morning and the choirboys singing on Magdalen Tower; reading in a punt on the river beneath overhanging willows; the water meadows beyond Parsons' Pleasure, and the sound of corn-crakes; sailing with Robin Campbell on Port Meadow and then tea together at the Trout Inn; dinner parties in my rooms, with evening light on the College buildings and the scent of wallflowers from the President's garden.

George Gordon was President of Magdalen; he was a liberal-minded man of distinction and charm, always friendly and interested in my doings. He died in 1942 and it is my lasting regret that after I left Oxford I did not see him again; I still have the letters he wrote me when I was in the Sudan.

My uncle Fred, whom we had stayed with as Viceroy of India, was a Fellow of All Souls, the only college without undergraduates, and was its Warden for two terms before he died in 1933. Several times while I was at Magdalen he had me to dine at All Souls with its distinguished Fellows. He had had a varied and an outstanding career. He had been a scholar at Winchester and at Magdalen, where he gained a First in Law and got his Blue for cricket. Later he became President of the MCC. He had been Governor of Queensland and of New South Wales, Viceroy of India, First Lord of the Admiralty, an Honorary Fellow of Magdalen, Warden of Winchester and, finally, Warden of All Souls. Uncle Fred was an austere and impressive figure, whom some people found forbidding. Until I was seventeen, only occasionally and briefly meeting him, I thought of him as the rather alarming head of the family. Then, unexpectedly, he invited Brian and me to stay in Northumberland where he had taken a grouse moor for the summer; thereafter we went each year until he died, first to Otterburn and then to Wark. He could not have been kinder nor taken more trouble to see that we enjoyed ourselves. He was an enthusiastic fisherman, and taught me to fish: I shall never forget his excitement when I caught a salmon. We had had a long wet day on the moors but in the late afternoon the weather cleared. He was sixty-four now, and no doubt tired, but as soon as we had finished tea he said, 'We'll go down to the river and you can try for a salmon.' The keeper said resignedly, 'Anyway it will be good practice for your casting.' With a fast-rising river, conditions certainly appeared hopeless.

I had fished for half an hour when I felt the line tighten.

'Damn,' I thought, 'I'm caught up.' Then, unbelievably, I saw the line move up the river.

'By God, he's into one!' shouted the keeper, and my uncle kept repeating desperately, 'Keep your rod point up! Keep your rod point up!'

It was a fresh-run fifteen-pound salmon, the first caught there that year. No excitement in my life has ever quite equalled the tense fifteen minutes during which I was connected to that fish.

I always looked forward to the fortnights we spent in Northumberland. The shooting and fishing I enjoyed, but I soon looked forward even more to being with my uncle. I had always admired him, ever since as a small boy I had seen him in his State robes in India. I thought of him as a patrician in the Roman tradition, cultured, erudite, civilized, governed above all by his sense of duty. Now realizing that he was more approachable and understanding than I had supposed, I felt an affection for him which increased each time I met him. His elder son had been killed in Mesopotamia in the Great War and with his younger son he had little in common. I think he hoped I might eventually add distinction to the family name, of which he was intensely proud, and his initial interest in me also developed into affection. But he demanded high standards and as a classical scholar was exasperated by my inability to cope with Latin.

* * *

In Magdalen's communal life I took little part. I did not drink, and for such festivities as Bump Suppers celebrating success on the river by the College eight I had no taste. At Eton I had enjoyed the Field Game but loathed cricket, and had not played soccer or rugger since my preparatory school. As a result I took no part in organized college sport, though despite lack of skill I enjoyed an occasional game of squash. I did, however, box for Oxford for four years, winning against Cambridge three times, and this gave me a certain standing in the College.

I had been successful as a boxer at Eton and in my first term at Oxford I was selected to box against the Army. My opponent was Lieutenant Black of the Green Howards. When I got into the ring I was fortunately unaware that he was a Services champion. I was not a skilful boxer but I did have a knock-out punch, which connected early in the first round and won me the fight.

Finding it difficult to get down to middleweight, I decided to fight as a light-heavy in the University trials. I won and was selected for Oxford against Cambridge. My opponent was much the same height, build and temperament; we stood toe to toe and swapped blow for blow. I remember thinking, 'This can't last.' I was lucky enough to knock him out in the first round.

Brian, who went to New College the following year, lacked my knock-out punch but was a more skilful boxer. It was always inspiring to watch him fight; from the first bell, regardless of punishment, he attacked relentlessly. He was unlucky to have been in the University team only during his last year, when he easily gained a place.

During my last year, when I was captain, we won the Hospitals and Universities Championship, won against the Army and beat Cambridge 4–3. On that occasion I had the hardest fight of my career and my prominent nose was badly broken before I won on points.

Boxing was the only sport I was any good at, but I often wondered, sitting with gloves on waiting for the fight before mine to end, why on earth I did it. Yet, once I had started, I felt a savage satisfaction in fighting. I was never conscious of pain, even with a torn ear, a broken nose and split lips, but I do remember occasions of desperate tiredness, and of effort to keep my hands up or stay on my feet.

Arthur Bentinck, who had been on my father's staff in Addis Ababa, often came to watch me box. He had been appointed Military Attaché to my father in 1917 after being badly wounded in

France. One day at the Legation he had produced boxing gloves, and instructed Brian and me to put them on. He always maintained that our later success was due to his initial coaching. He alarmed us as children: he had a gruff manner, a game leg and a pronounced cast in one eye. Later he became a close family friend and I envied and admired him, for he got to one remote and interesting place after another – Somaliland, Abyssinia, Kurdistan, Burma and China.

I read history at Oxford and was fortunate to have J. M. Thompson, an authority on the French Revolution, as my history tutor at Magdalen. His tutorials were always stimulating and ranged over a variety of subjects. But little of the necessary reading for 'Schools' interested me: I had little interest in constitutional development, political theory or economic growth, none at all in the Industrial Revolution and the technical and scientific achievements that ushered in the modern age. I had a romantic, not an objective, conception of history; Alexander the Great was foremost among my heroes, Montrose was the leader I would most gladly have followed, John Knox was my particular aversion.

As a child I had watched history being made. I had seen the march of feudal armies, the victors returning in triumph, captive princes led past in chains. In The Milebrook were *assegais* and other trophies brought back by my grandfather after he had shattered the Zulu army at Ulundi in 1879 – but I never begrudged those peerless warriors their earlier, annihilating victory over a British force on the slopes of Isandhlwana. I had been thrilled by Rider Haggard's stories about the Zulus, especially *Nada the Lily* in which Mbopo, the blind witchdoctor, tells of the rise and death of Chaka whom he helped to murder.

At Eton I had read every book I could lay hands on about the Zulus, about Abyssinia and about the rise and fall of the Dervish empire in the Sudan. At Oxford I was increasingly interested by the mass movement of peoples who, from the dawn of recorded knowledge, had devastated the world from the Pacific to the Atlantic, with incalculable effects on the history of mankind. I could visualize the first restless stirring among tribes on the steppes of Central Asia, then the terrifying eruption of hordes of unknown people: lurching, creaking wagons, unkempt women and children, squat, slit-eyed men in padded garments, innumerable horses, felt tents, troops of mounted archers forever on the move. I saw them as a people honed by sun and wind to essential flesh and bone, accustomed since childhood to hardship, possessed of extraordinary mobility and genius for war.

Under Attila, and later under Genghis Khan and Timur Leng, armies ruthlessly welded from a variety of warring tribes swept out of Asia in transient conquests of unparalleled scope and ferocity. At their approach tribe pressed on tribe, nation upon nation, leaving an ever-widening swathe of destruction as each sought to escape from the terror behind; one far-flung ripple had driven the Saxons across the North Sea into Britain.

Other nomads erupted from the deserts of Arabia in the seventh century; within a hundred years their armies had reached the shores of the Atlantic and the borders of China but, in fascinating contrast to the Huns and Mongols, the Arabs created a new and enduring civilization and founded a faith which today numbers six hundred million adherents. Then, under the banner of Islam, descendants of Turkish shepherd tribes stormed Constantinople, fought under the walls of Vienna, subjugated the Balkans and held sway over the Hejaz, Egypt and Algiers.

All this I found enthralling, but unfortunately it fell outside the scope of Oxford's history school. I would have liked to take the Crusades as my special subject, but my inadequacy in Latin deterred me. Instead I read military history, a rewarding experience under C. T. Atkinson. An untidy man, with frequent egg stains down his waistcoat, he always brought his smelly little dog in with him, and would tolerate no women undergraduates in his class.

The cities I had seen in England and France left me unmoved; their crowds had no interest for me: they lacked the colour and variety for which I craved. I still had memories of Delhi and Jaipur, of massive forts, Moghul tombs, of streets alive with turbanned figures, crowded with lumbering ox-carts and pungent with the smell of spices. I remembered the *muezzin*'s call to prayer, heard in the stillness of the dawn. I had read *Eothen* and other tales of Eastern travel and my imagination endowed Constantinople with all the magic of the East. Samarkand, Merv and Bokhara were inaccessible but Constantinople was within my reach. I went there during my first summer vacation from Oxford, working my passage in a tramp steamer bound for the Black Sea.

On 28 June 1930 in the East India Docks I climbed the gangway of the *Sorrento* and set foot on her rusty iron deck. I was thrilled at the prospect ahead of me but diffident and embarrassed at joining a community so totally unfamiliar. I need not have worried; the officers and men were welcoming and friendly. The crew consisted of the captain, first, second and third mates, chief and second engineer, wireless operator, bosun, carpenter and eighteen other hands. On board was a Maltese deck passenger who boasted he had been in nine different prisons in England; after we had sailed a friend of his was discovered stowed away in the chain locker.

I found I had the best of both worlds. I worked regular hours as an ordinary member of the crew but fed with the officers; the food was substantial and good. I was given the bosun's cabin to sleep in. I apologized to him for this but he said, 'I'm glad to be out of it. Wait till you see the cockroaches.' These were the only things on the *Sorrento* that got me down; at night they sallied from every crack and crevice and nibbled dead skin on the soles of my feet. I have loathed cockroaches ever since.

Soon after I came on board we finished loading. Two hours later we weighed anchor, drew out into the dirty, oil-stained river and moved slowly downstream along London's crowded waterfront, passing other ships, docks, warehouses, cranes, wagons and lorries, and all the come and go of men associated with the sea. We sailed down the reaches of the Thames and, standing in the bows, I saw the river through the eyes of Marlow in Conrad's *Heart of Darkness*, as 'a waterway leading to the uttermost ends of the earth ... crowded with memories of men and ships it had borne to the rest of home or to the battles of the sea'.

Next day we passed Beachy Head and the Isle of Wight and in the evening saw a windjammer. Mr Harper, the mate, watched as she surged past with all her sails drawing, and then turning to me said: 'You're damned lucky to have seen her. There are so few of them left. She's a fine sight, isn't she?' To me she represented all that I had imagined of the bygone days of sail. Two days later in the Bay of Biscay we saw a whale blowing a jet of spray high in the air, and I thought of Moby Dick.

During the next four weeks we steamed from one port to another, unloading and loading a variety of cargoes. I was doing my four hours on and eight off, and as a supernumerary was given a variety of jobs. Most of the time I worked in the bunkers, trying to keep the stoker supplied with enough coal to fire the furnaces; he would rattle his shovel in the hatch if I fell behind. This was hard, hot, dirty, choking work. At other times I chipped rust off the deck, painted the boats and, in harbour, helped to repaint the ship's side or check the discharge of cargo. Sometimes during the mate's watch I took the wheel and learnt to steer. The first time or two he exclaimed, 'For God's sake, man, keep her steady. It'd break a snake's back to follow your course.' As I grew more proficient he leaned on the rail, sucked at his long clay pipe and reminisced about his days in sail or his experiences in ports from Aden to Hong Kong. Massive, grizzled and elderly, he had been in ships since he was a boy, and he wanted no other life.

Mr Jackson, the captain, was a small man, sparse, rather finicky and of solitary disposition; he fed alone in his cabin. In one port, I think Piraeus, where the water was particularly filthy, he forbade the crew to bathe, but the cook's lad slipped over the side. As he climbed back on deck the skipper was waiting. He handed the boy a mug filled with 'black draught', a foul-tasting and powerful purgative. 'Here, lad, drink this up, all of it!' And to me he added, 'That'll keep him on the run.'

When we were in port he let me off work and allowed me to go ashore for as long as I wanted: 'After all, you're here to see these places. Don't worry, we'll get along without you, but if you're late back we'll have sailed.' I always slept on board. I enjoyed sitting on the hatch in the twilight with the crew, listening to their talk, a combination of profanity and sense. They were a decent lot and I was glad that they accepted me despite my anomalous position. One of them had been blown up four times, minesweeping during the First World War, and in consequence had a chronic twitch. He had been in trawlers and, when he found I was interested, told me a lot about fishing off Iceland and Spitzbergen.

'If you want to go in a trawler, go in summer,' he advised me. 'Don't go in winter: then it really is hell.'

We called briefly at Gibraltar where I just had time to walk up the Rock and see the apes. We then sailed along the African coast. The Rif mountains were clearly visible; somewhere among them Abd al Karim and his fellow tribesmen had destroyed a Spanish army of sixteen thousand men in 1921. They had then invaded French Morocco and, after desperate fighting, had threatened Fez. At Eton I had gone each day to Spottiswoode's bookshop to follow the course of this war in *The Times*. I remember my despondency in 1926 when Abd al Karim was forced to surrender to the French.

At Malta a battle cruiser, an aircraft carrier and three destroyers were anchored in the inner harbour. We were only there for twenty-four hours, working throughout the night. Our next port of call was Piraeus, which I thought a dirty, uninteresting place. In the distance I could see the rock-girt Acropolis crowned by the ruins of the Parthenon. Without any great enthusiasm I visited Athens. The weather was hot and I felt little interest in ruins; but the Parthenon proved to have a matchless beauty for which I was quite unprepared.

We were four days in Piraeus and every day I went back to the Acropolis. At that time few tourists went to Greece during the summer; some goats wandered among the fallen pillars, the goatherd dozed in the shade, otherwise I had the place to myself. It was utterly peaceful, sitting there in the hot sun with the scent of thyme around me and a view of distant Hymettos over the tiled roofs of Athens. Only a murmur rose from the town below me. Two lesser kestrels the first I had ever seen, flew to and fro above my head.

We left for Salonika on 17 July, arrived next morning, and stayed two days, which gave me time to explore the older part of the town. From the ramparts I had a view across the bay to green marshes and, far above them, rising above a swathe of cloud, the snow-covered summit of Olympus, infinitely remote.

We sailed across the Aegean to Izmir, which till recently had been called Smyrna; and the captain told me how, a few years earlier, as he entered the port, his ship had nosed her way through the floating corpses of Greeks massacred by the Turks. The town had been largely burnt and rebuilt; it looked uninteresting and, as there was a lot of work to be done on board, I did not go ashore.

Our next port of call would be Constantinople – or, as it had just been renamed, Istanbul. We passed Lesbos, Lemnos and other Greek islands floating in the haze on a calm sea, each more beautiful than the last. Then we sailed through the Dardanelles, past beaches and rocky scrub-covered hills, once the scene of so much unavailing gallantry and sacrifice. Somewhere there on a hillside was Doughty-Wylie's grave.

On the other side of the straits was Asia and the site of Troy. The sun was setting as we anchored off Constantinople; in the twilight a crescent moon hung low above a silhouette of domes and minarets. I could hardly wait to land.

In the morning I went ashore with the captain in a bumboat, passing a variety of small craft that plied to and fro across the straits. At the ship's office I was informed that Sir George Clerk, the British Ambassador, had sent a message that as soon as I landed I was to call on him at the Embassy. I knew he had been a colleague of my father; I wondered how he knew I was on the *Sorrento*.

I felt embarrassed at the prospect of meeting him. I am conventional enough to dislike appearing anywhere in unsuitable clothes. Here I was wearing a shirt and an old pair of grey flannel trousers; they were clean, for I had washed them, but they were certainly not suitable for calling on an ambassador. However, I had nothing better on board and could not ignore his summons.

I had some difficulty in securing admission to the Embassy, past a *kavas* in a spectacular scarlet uniform. A secretary showed me into an ornately furnished drawing room and a few minutes later Sir George came in. He had a distinguished air, was formally dressed in a tailcoat, and was precisely my idea of an ambassador. He accepted my apologies for my appearance and quickly put me at ease, saying he had been a close friend of my father and was delighted to meet his son.

I told him that ever since listening to my father's vivid descriptions of Constantinople I had always wanted to visit the city, but that I had been sadly disillusioned by the Turks I had seen on my way to the Embassy; they had looked so incongruous in second-hand European clothes. Sir George agreed that the place was very different now from my father's time. The Sultan had since abdicated, the Caliphate had been abolished, the Dervish orders had been suppressed and most traditional ceremonies and pageantry had been done away with. But in spite of the changes, Sir George insisted that Constantinople was still a fascinating city, superbly sited, full of interest, and worth visiting just to see Hagia Sophia.

The *Sorrento* remained four days at Constantinople. In that time I followed the course of the massive city walls which over the centuries had sustained so many assaults before falling at last to the Turkish onslaught. I wandered among turbanned headstones in the Muslim cemetery, mingled with the crowds on the Galata Bridge over the Golden Horn, and ate Turkish food in unpretentious eating-houses on the waterfront. I visited the underground cisterns, spent hours in the covered bazaar and a whole morning among the treasures of the Seraglio. But most of my time I spent in the many and varied mosques, and each day I went back to Hagia Sophia, sometimes remaining for hours. Built by Justinian as the centre of Christian worship, this miraculous embodiment of space had been converted by the victorious Turks, with only minor modifications, into their foremost mosque and had been taken as the prototype for others which they built. None, however, rivalled it. The Blue Mosque and the Mosque of Suleiman the Magnificent were more impressive from outside; but inside them I was conscious of confinement.

On a Friday I witnessed the midday prayers in Hagia Sophia. Now that religious observance was officially discouraged only a few hundred worshippers were present. A few years previously thousands would have attended. This was the first time I saw an Islamic service and I was impressed by the unhurried, synchronized movements of the worshippers and by the sonorous rhythm of their prayers.

Still, the high expectations I had arrived with had been disappointed. Constantinople I found depressing, soulless, with drab crowds, deserted mosques, and palaces preserved as showpieces of a dead past. Six years later, revisiting Hagia Sophia, I had to buy a ticket to enter. The superb frescoes, concealed from sight by Muslim prejudice for nearly five hundred years, were again on view, but they did not compensate for a profound sense of desecration. For fourteen hundred years Hagia Sophia had been a place of worship: it was now debased into an ancient monument, open to the public for a fee.

On 28 July 1930 I disembarked from the *Sorrento* at Constanza in the Black Sea. I was touched by the good wishes of the crew when I went ashore. I had enjoyed every minute of the past month. No luxury cruise around the Mediterranean could have been half as rewarding; I should have been fed up at sea and embarrassed ashore, always conscious of the intrusion of our party as we were shown the sights. From Constanza I returned to England, travelling third class across Europe, by train to Bucharest and Budapest, by boat up the Danube to Vienna, and thence by train to Prague, Berlin and Ostend.

*   *   *

Back at The Milebrook I found two letters waiting for me. One was an invitation from Ras Tafari to attend his coronation as the Emperor Haile Selassie. The other was a notification from the Foreign Office that I had been appointed Honorary Attaché to HRH the Duke of Gloucester who would attend the coronation as the representative of his father, King George V.

CHAPTER 7

Haile Selassie's Coronation

WHEN RAS TAFARI had paid his State Visit to London in 1924 he had brought with him several important chiefs, among them Ras Hailu of Gojjam and Ras Seyum of Tigre, the grandson of the Emperor John, all of whom he suspected might make trouble if he left them behind. Two years later the aged and uncompromising Fitaurari Habta Giorgis and the Abuna Mattewos both died. Their deaths removed from the scene two powerful and reactionary figures, but Ras Tafari was still confronted by many others.

In 1928 Ras Tafari instructed Dedjazmatch Balcha, then Governor of Sidamo, to report to him in Addis Ababa. Balcha ignored the summons. He received another, more peremptory, order and eventually came to Addis Ababa with ten thousand men. He camped a few miles outside the town and there remained, determined to outface Ras Tafari, whom he discounted as astute but weak.

Ras Tafari invited him to a banquet at the palace and guaranteed his personal safety. Balcha only accepted after Tafari suggested he should bring with him as many men as he pleased. He arrived with six hundred. When he returned to his camp in the evening he found it deserted: while he had been feasting, Tafari's agents had persuaded his troops to return home. Balcha now had no alternative but to surrender to Ras Tafari who, with characteristic magnanimity, spared his life; as to whether he ordered Balcha to enter a monastery or banished him to his estates in the Gurage country, accounts differ. But seven years later in 1935, on the eve of the Italian invasion, while the war drums were beating outside the palace to summon the nation to war, an old man presented himself before the Emperor. 'I am Balcha. I fought the Italians at Adua. Now I have come to fight them again.' He was eventually killed, still fighting, after the Italians had occupied Addis Ababa.

In September 1928, at the instigation of the diehards, the Empress was involved in yet another attempt to overthrow Ras Tafari; her soldiers were ordered to arrest him while he was at the palace. He overawed them and calmly walked out through the palace gates. Having rejoined his own troops he insisted that the Empress should proclaim him Negus. She had to comply and soon afterwards he was crowned: as the crown was placed on his head his retainers, to a man, drew their swords with a rasp of steel and brandished them in the air. As Negus, Tafari now felt powerful enough to press ahead with the reforms he had set his heart on; but as he did so opposition intensified.

Early in 1930 Ras Gugsa Wale, the former husband of the Empress, marched south with his army, calling on the country to rise and overthrow the man who sought to corrupt their religion and, with his modern innovations, destroy their ancient heritage. It seemed probable that Ras Hailu and Ras Seyum would join him, and that all Tigre, Begemder, Gojjam and Wollo would rise in revolt. Undismayed, Tafari summoned his armies from Harar, from Sidamo and the other provinces of the south and sent them north under the grim old warrior Ras Mulugeta.

On 31 March at Zebit on the border of Begemder the armies of the north and south once again joined battle. Ras Gugsa was killed and his army routed. The Empress, who had been seriously ill, died of diabetes soon afterwards.

On 3 April Tafari was proclaimed Negusa Nagast, and invited Great Britain, France, Italy, Germany, the United States, Japan, Turkey, and a number of other states, to send representatives in November to his coronation as the Emperor Haile Selassie.

The Duke of Gloucester, the Earl of Airlie and the five other members of his staff, including myself, left Victoria by the boat train on 16 October 1930. Happily in those days there was no air travel to take us in a few hours to Addis Ababa and bring us back a few days later. We joined the P and O *Rampura* at Marseilles and sailed for Aden.

Accompanying us was the delegation from the Sudan, led by Sir John Maffey, the Governor-General; he was six foot three and impressive in appearance, with natural charm and a spontaneous interest in others. He had been Private Secretary to my uncle when he was Viceroy, and later Chief Commissioner of the North-West Frontier of India before he went to the Sudan. I had recently stayed with him in Scotland: knowing him was a help, for I felt out of my milieu. Lord Airlie also went out of his way to help me find my feet.

Another imposing figure, at the State banquet in Addis Ababa he wore the full dress of a Highland chief and looked magnificent.

But it was the natural kindness of the Duke that helped me most. He was an enthusiastic but, I suspect, an indifferent bridge player. When he asked me if I played I admitted that I had done so but insisted that I really was very bad. 'Never mind. Now we will get a four,' and I was roped in to play each evening. Harold MacMichael, who was Civil Secretary in the Sudan, was, I am sure, a brilliant player; he was also long-suffering. Once he did protest, 'Why on earth did you trump my ace?' Those games certainly helped to break the ice.

From Aden we crossed to Jibuti in HMS *Effingham*, flagship of the East Indies Squadron, and Admiral Fullerton joined our party with his Flag Lieutenant and another officer. At Jibuti we were met by Sir Sidney Barton, British Minister from Addis Ababa, by Sir Stewart Symes from Aden and Sir Harold Kittermaster from British Somaliland, and we travelled together in a special train to Addis Ababa.

The journey took only two nights and a day; previously it had always taken three days, since the train stopped for the night at Dire Dawa and the Awash Station. I felt thrilled to be back in Abyssinia and stared entranced at the arid landscape of the Danakil desert. I saw occasional Danakil with their camels and flocks of goats. But it was the vultures that fascinated me. I had forgotten how large they were; they seemed enormous, and there were so many of them, circling overhead, clustered in a tree or hopping about as they squabbled over carrion.

We arrived at Addis Ababa at midday on 28 October and were received at the railway station by the Emperor. The Duke of Gloucester and four of his staff were taken to one of the palaces, while the rest of us were accommodated in tents in the spacious Legation grounds. The town was much as I remembered it in 1919. The roads had certainly been widened and improved; there were more ramshackle buildings of European design along the main streets and everywhere more corrugated iron roofs; but outside the centre of the town grass-roofed *tukuls* still predominated, surrounded now by eucalyptus trees.

The great increase in the number and size of these trees was the most striking difference in the town's appearance. When Menelik founded Addis Ababa in 1889 the countryside had been forested with juniper and wild olive, but these had soon been cut down for firewood and building material, whereupon Menelik announced that he was going to move his capital for the third time. The newly established Legations protested and the introduction of the fast-growing eucalyptus obviated the necessity. By 1930 Addis Ababa was in a vast wood that spread up the slopes of the Entoto hills.

During the ensuing days every Ras and chieftain in the country must have been camped in and around Addis Ababa. They had travelled, in many cases for weeks, from all parts of the empire, from Tigre and Begemder, Gojjam, Wollo, Harar and Walega, from the furthest provinces of the south and west, on the borders of Kenya and the Sudan, to be present when their Emperor was crowned. Each vied with others in the number of his retainers, the magnificence of his robes and accoutrements.

This was the last time that the age-old splendour of Abyssinia was to be on view. Already it was slightly tarnished round the edges by innovations copied from the West: the bodyguard now wore khaki, some of the palace secretaries were in tailcoats and top hats. There were cars in the streets and brash, noisy journalists crowded round hotel bars competing for sensational stories to wire to their papers. On ceremonial occasions they thrust themselves forward with their cameras.

However, immensely moved by sights reminiscent of my childhood, I ignored what I had no desire to see. Each day I listened, enthralled, to the slow steady throb of war drums in the palace, where the *gebers* were being held. My parents had attended such feasts when thousands, entering in relays, gorged on raw meat, hacked in turn from the bleeding carcases of oxen carried on poles past rows of squatting men. Now, out of regard for their susceptibilities, Europeans were no longer invited, indeed were forbidden to attend.

It has always seemed to me a pity that Evelyn Waugh, the one person present with a gift for writing, was blind to the historical significance of the occasion, impercipient of this last manifestation of Abyssinia's traditional pageantry. He had come to Addis Ababa as correspondent for the *Graphic* and he later made use of the occasion to parody what he had seen in *Black Mischief* and other books. In *Remote People* he dwelt on 'The Great Flea Scandal', the underwear of the Emperor's European housekeeper and the remarks of an American professor during the coronation service, to the exclusion of more significant observations. He ridiculed the ceremonies in impeccable prose, and disparaged the British Minister and his family, who had not invited him to lunch.

Previously I had never heard of Waugh, nor of *Decline and Fall* and *Vile Bodies*, novels with which he had made his name. Now I met him at one of the numerous receptions. I disapproved of his grey suede shoes, his floppy bow tie and the excessive width of his trousers: he struck me as flaccid and petulant and I disliked him on sight. Later he asked, at second-hand, if he could accompany me into the Danakil country, where I planned to travel. I refused. Had he come, I suspect only one of us would have returned.

Haile Selassie was crowned on 2 November in St George's Cathedral. We left the Legation as the sun rose and our cars were constantly brought to a standstill in the crowded streets. At least a hundred thousand people surrounded the cathedral where the chiefs in all their finery were massed in serried ranks. Assembled in the church were a great number of turbanned priests, holding silver crosses, and deacons wearing coloured vestments and silver crowns. The air was heavy with incense from the many swinging censers.

Inside the sanctuary the Emperor and Empress still kept their all-night vigil to continuous chanting and the beat of the church drums. Attached to the church was a large canvas annexe to accommodate the Abyssinian notables and the foreign dignitaries, and it was here that the crowning took place.

The Emperor emerged from the cathedral itself at half past seven, escorted by the Abuna, the Patriarch of Alexandria and the Etchege, the senior monk of the realm who ranked second to the Abuna in the hierarchy of the Ethiopian Church. Haile Selassie seated himself on a crimson throne, and shortly afterwards the Empress took her place on a smaller throne.

Then the lengthy service began, conducted in Ge'ez, the ancient language of the Ethiopian Church, and accompanied by a Coptic choir from Alexandria. It lasted for three hours or more. Many complained afterwards of its inordinate length. I was not conscious of this – it could have lasted twice as long as far as I was concerned. The Etchege presented the Emperor with the robe, sword, sceptre, ring and two spears, each of which had been blessed by the Abuna. Then the Abuna approached the throne, anointed Haile Selassie with sacred oil and placed the crown upon his head.

Even as a boy Haile Selassie had believed in his imperial destiny;

for nearly twenty years he had survived conspiracies, wars and revolutions, and his resolution had never faltered. The crown settled on his brow. This was his supreme moment; yet his delicate face and sombre eyes remained impassive, showed no vestige of emotion. As the guns thundered their salute, the great Rases and chieftains led by Asfa Wossen, his eldest son, came forward to do him homage: Ras Kassa, his faithful kinsman, Ras Seyum of Tigre, Ras Hailu of Gojjam, Ras Imru, Ras Mulugeta and others. The Empress was crowned, and then the Emperor and Empress entered the cathedral to take communion. They came out at last and Haile Selassie went forward under a crimson canopy to show himself to his people.

That night there was a State banquet. When it ended we moved out on to the palace balcony to watch a display of fireworks, the first to be given in the country; but after two rockets had been fired something went wrong and the rest blew up. This must have been a bitter moment for Haile Selassie, but once again he gave no indication of his feelings. He stood for a while, watching the pyrotechnic chaos in the yard below, then moved slowly back into the banqueting hall.

Two days later he granted me a private audience, a remarkable consideration during those eventful days to his youngest and least important guest. He received me with grave courtesy and enquired after my family. When I expressed my appreciation of the honour he had done me by inviting me to his coronation, he replied that as the eldest son of his trusted friend, to whom he owed so much, it was proper that I should be present.

I told him how happy I was to be back in his country.

'It is your country. You were born here. You have lived here for half of your life. I hope you will spend many more years with us,' was his answer. As he spoke I was very conscious of the smile which transformed his usually impassive face. It was twenty minutes before he terminated the interview. That evening I received two elephant tusks, a heavy, ornate gold cigarette case, a large, colourful carpet and the third class of the Star of Ethiopia.

I had brought a rifle with me to Abyssinia, determined to achieve my dream of hunting big game. I had read and re-read books by Selous, Gordon Cumming, Baldwin, Newman, Powell-Cotton and many other African hunters. Whenever I had been in London I had visited the Natural History Museum and Rowland Ward's taxidermist shop in Piccadilly, where there was always a fascinating collection of heads, skins and mounted specimens. I was well versed in Rowland Ward's *Records of Big Game*.

I now decided that before going back to Oxford I would spend a month in the Danakil country. It was easily accessible from the Awash railway station and was one of the few areas in Abyssinia where wild animals survived in any number. The Danakil did not hunt and the Abyssinians, who had wiped out most of the game elsewhere, were afraid to venture into their country, since among the Danakil a man's standing depended on the number of men he had killed and castrated. Muslims of Hamitic origin, they were akin to the Somalis, though their language was distinct.

Much of the Danakil country was still unexplored, including the remote Aussa Sultanate where the Awash river was reputed to terminate. This considerable river rose in the highlands near Addis Ababa, flowed down into the Danakil desert but never reached the sea. My intention, however, was not to explore but to hunt, and I did not intend to penetrate far into the Danakil country. Even so, it was a challenging undertaking for a young man of twenty with no previous experience.

Sir Sidney Barton was apprehensive for my safety and suggested I should join him and Lord Airlie on a short hunting trip near the Awash Station. I explained that I wanted the experience of running my own expedition and, after some discussion, he withdrew his objections but warned me not to go further than Bilen.

I discussed my plans with Colonel Sandford; he had travelled across Abyssinia to the Sudan in 1907 and served under my father in the Legation in 1913, returning to Abyssinia with Christine, his wife, after the First World War in which he had fought with distinction. Since then he had been farming at Mullu, some fifteen miles outside Addis Ababa. He gave me every encouragement, lent me camp equipment, provided me with a Somali called Ali as my headman and helped me collect the necessary servants.

The month that followed was decisive in my life. I was among a savage, good-looking people with a dangerous reputation. I was travelling with camels in hot, arid country under testing conditions where, if things went wrong, I could get no help and where men's lives depended on my judgement.

I hunted buffalo in the swamps at Bilen; it was exciting following them through the dense reed beds. With more success I hunted greater and lesser kudu, oryx, waterbuck and gazelle. My aim was to secure a good head of each species and, in consequence, except when I shot for meat, I shot selectively and seldom.

I followed the Awash as far as Bilen and then turned eastwards across the desert to Afdam on the railway. The Danakil around Bilen were friendly, but were apprehensive of their formidable neighbours in Bahdu, who had raided them recently and inflicted many casualties.

Near Afdam I hunted greater kudu in the broken bush-covered country round Afdub, a volcanic mountain rising to seven thousand feet. One day I disturbed three separate males and was feeling thoroughly frustrated and incompetent when I saw a magnificent bull, silhouetted on a ridge against the setting sun, a graceful, powerful body with a great sweep of spiralling horns. It was an easy shot, but as I heard the bullet strike he bounded away. I thought despairingly, 'I've only wounded him and now I'll never find him in the dark.' I scrambled up the ridge and there he lay dead, a dozen yards away. It was a superb head, a veritable trophy of trophies, and a marvellous ending to the trip.

During this month I led the life for which I had always yearned, hunting big game on my own in the wilds of Africa; but now I realized that this expedition had meant more to me than just the excitement of hunting. I had been on the borders of a virtually unexplored land inhabited by dangerous, untouched tribes. Before I had turned back from Bilen I had watched the Awash flowing towards its unknown destination. I had felt the lure of the unexplored, the compulsion to go where others had not been.

From Afdam I took the train to Dire Dawa and from there rode to Harar, through mountains that were beautiful and green after recent rain, following the route my parents had taken in 1909. Harar could hardly have changed since my father had visited Dedjazmatch Balcha. The five gates still guarded the only entrances through the mud walls, inside which, among the warren of alleyways and flat-roofed mud houses, Balcha's soldiers had in 1916 massacred the Muslim population.

I had always wanted to see Harar, which had been Burton's objective in 1855. I fancied that except for a few corrugated iron roofs it still looked the same as when he had been here. The town lacked architectural distinction but the colour of the women's clothes, predominantly red, yellow and orange, was unforgettable, especially when large numbers were assembled at the wells or in the marketplace. Most of them were light-skinned and many were beautiful.

I stayed with Plowman, the Consul, and his wife: they had been in Addis Ababa for the coronation and had invited me to visit them at Harar. I was with them a week and they were kind to me. I explored the town and rode into the surrounding countryside, often towards Kondoro, the flat-topped Mountain of Refuge. I remember it as I saw it one evening, lit by the setting sun against a background of threatening clouds. I also remember the hyenas. They swarmed round the town at night and came close to the tent in which I slept in the consulate compound. I have never hated hyenas: their occasional maniacal laughter and their eerie whooping cries are among my earliest memories. More than any other sound, more even than the grunting roar of a lion, their howling evokes for me the African night.

I rode back to Dire Dawa, past Haramaya Lake where my parents had camped, took the train to Jibuti and then a Messageries Maritimes boat to Marseilles, third-class among a draft of the Foreign Legion; an interesting contrast with the Mission's journey to Aden first-class on a P and O with a deck reserved to ourselves.

CHAPTER 8

Oxford and The Milebrook

I WAS BACK in England in time for the Easter term of 1931 and resumed my university life, but during the next three years I thought incessantly of that slow-flowing muddy river, of the arid, scrub-covered plains and volcanic mountains, the herds of oryx and gazelle, the mat-roofed encampments, the slender, graceful figures in loincloths, attractive, armed and unpredictable. I was determined to return as soon as I had taken my degree, to follow the Awash river into the fabulous Sultanate of Aussa and discover how and where it ended. The challenge presented by the murderous company of the Danakil and the physical difficulties of the journey was irresistible. With this in mind, the first thing I did was to join the Oxford Exploration Club. John Buchan was President and I wrote to him asking for his advice.

For years, I had been reading and re-reading his novels, ever since I had come across *Prester John* at my prep school. This story of Laputa, the Zulu leader who died tragically and dramatically while attempting to free his people, made an indelible impression on me. Buchan was living at Elsfield Manor near Oxford and invited me to come and see him: no one could have been more helpful and encouraging. I went there several times. I can still picture him as I knew him, his sensitive, ascetic face etched with lines of pain but lit by his innate kindliness, his lean body in comfortable country tweeds. Although a man of many and varied accomplishments, he remained a countryman at heart, with an abiding love of the Scottish lowlands.

T. E. Lawrence was a friend of Buchan. I would have given much to meet him at Elsfield during one of his fleeting visits: indeed there was no one I would have been more interested to meet. I had read *Revolt in the Desert* while I was at Eton, and I later read *Seven Pillars of Wisdom* as soon as it was published after his death. Today it has become fashionable to disparage Lawrence and his achievements, but Churchill, Allenby, Wavell, men of action and men of letters and humble aircraftmen who knew him, paid tribute to him in *T. E. Lawrence by His Friends.*

On the strength of my boxing I was elected to Vincent's, a club consisting of Blues and other notable athletes. I seldom went there; instead I frequented the Gridiron, to which most of my friends belonged. I was getting over the feeling of rejection instilled into me at St Aubyn's, which by making me aggressive had deprived me of so much that Eton had to offer. At Oxford I discovered that most people were only too willing to be friendly if I gave them a chance.

I was also elected to the Raleigh Club, which met periodically in Rhodes House. Its interests were imperial and its speakers were always men of distinction: members of the Cabinet, colonial Governors and the like. Ramsay MacDonald, while he was Prime Minister, spoke at the annual dinner, and Gandhi accepted an invitation while he was in England for the Round Table Conference in 1933. I went to this meeting feeling prejudiced against him. Wrapped in his white cotton sheet, perched on a chair and peering at us over his steel-rimmed spectacles, he looked a frail, incongruous figure. It seemed to me extraordinary that this man should have such immense authority in caste-ridden India; yet no one has questioned his greatness. I do not remember any of the questions or answers, but I came away captivated by his personality, amazed by the endearing quality he radiated, a humour and charm utterly unexpected.

During my second long vacation from Oxford in the summer of 1931, I joined a Hull trawler which fished off Iceland. As a boy I had read a lot of sea stories and indulged in fancies of rounding the Horn in a windjammer. Talking to Pierre as we fished off the coast of Brittany had first given me the idea of working on a trawler.

The crew greeted my arrival on board with facetious comments: 'Anyone going trawling for pleasure should go to Hell for a pastime,' was one of them. But I was an extra hand and they were glad to have my help. I shared the skipper's cabin immediately below the wheelhouse. A taciturn man of medium height and powerful build, with a square, weather-beaten face, he was reputed to be one of the best skippers sailing out of Hull.

On our way to the fishing grounds off Iceland we passed close to the Faroes. They were an awe-inspiring sight, with the sea thundering against great black precipices and hurling shattered sheets of spray high up the face of the rock; above this turmoil a host of wheeling, screeching sea birds showed white against the cliffs. We fished off the southern coast of Iceland but never in sight of the mainland; all we saw of land was the Hvalsbakur or Whale's Back, a single forbidding rock sixteen feet high, visible from ten miles away in clear weather.

We were divided into watches but this was largely meaningless. Every three or four hours the trawl was winched alongside and we battled to pass a rope round the 'cod end' which held the fish, using the roll of the boat to help us. The cod end was then winched above deck, the bag was opened and the fish cascaded into the pens that divided the deck. Then for hours we gutted the living, flapping fish and threw them into baskets to be carried below and put on ice. It was back-breaking work. There were cod, haddock, coley and a variety of other fish, some of considerable size. We chucked their livers into a large barrel fastened to the mast; these were sold for cod-liver oil and the money they fetched was the perquisite of the crew.

Gradually the piles of fish would grow smaller; we had nearly cleared the pens. I hoped desperately that we should soon have a respite, however short, but the trawl would be alongside once more and the pens filled up again. So it went on day after day, night after night; we were out for a month. I remember the brief darkness at midnight when the arc lamps lit the decks; the interminable hours of daylight; the unceasing work with men too tired to talk; the hurried meals; the luxury of sleep when we were moving from one fishing ground to another.

This was summer. I could hardly conceive what it must be like in winter: the incessant darkness; the piercing cold when the spray froze as it hit the deck and formed great blocks of ice at the bows; howling gales and never-ending work; then a few days in port and out to sea again, week after week, month after month. Though they seemed very ordinary, with little to talk about except their families, their girlfriends, the football teams they supported and the films they had seen, these men represented the incomparable seamen of Britain.

There was fog as we came through the Pentland Firth on our way back to Hull. I was sitting talking to the skipper in his cabin when we heard the wheel go hard over. In one bound he had left his seat and was half way up the ladder; I was close behind. Right alongside were the bows of a ship; they seemed enormous and so close that I thought the bilge water would splash on our deck. Someone muttered 'Christ', and then the ship was gone. 'The bloody bastards. They'd have gone right over us and not even known they'd hit us.'

We docked in the evening. The crew went off to their homes. I found a large hotel and looked forward to a good dinner. I was disappointed; I'd eaten better food on board. I got back to The Milebrook next day.

During 1931 my mother, who was then fifty-one, married Reggie Astley, a widower with no children who was considerably older than her. They were very attached to each other and I hoped that my mother could now look forward to a happy old age. I knew how she dreaded a recurrence of loneliness when the four of us eventually left The Milebrook and went our various ways.

Reggie was an endearing, kindly man who had led a leisurely, unadventurous life as a country gentleman. Too old to fight, he had served as a special constable during the war. Now, though he was seventy, he was still robust and active, and there was nothing he enjoyed more than a day's shooting. I remember how indefatigably he mowed the lawn, even on a hot summer's day. Though he had few intellectual interests, he was fascinated by the lineage of ancient families, such as his own, even of those that had long lapsed into obscurity. We thought this rather a joke but his concern was academic, not snobbish. He was also well versed about historic homes, in many of which he had stayed, an interest he shared with Roddy, who even as a boy had been fascinated by pictures and architecture.

Reggie had owned the Weir House near Alresford, an attractive place where a well-stocked trout stream ran past the cedars on the lawn. He had some notable furniture and possessions, most of which he sold with the house when he moved into The Milebrook. We did not appreciate at the time what a wrench leaving the Weir House must have been for him, nor the difficulty he had in adjusting himself to four assertive stepsons he hardly knew.

My brothers and I grew up with very different interests and aspirations and we were to lead very different lives. I had always longed to get back to Abyssinia. As a child at the Legation I had met officers from the Sudan, Kenya and Somaliland, who were serving as Consuls in the border areas of Abyssinia. I had been enthralled by their stories of savage tribes, frontier raids and lion hunts. This, I felt, was the life for me. As a first step to achieving it I made up my mind, even before I went to Eton, to join the Sudan Political Service.

Brian, who had shared my experiences as a child in Abyssinia, had no desire to return there. More conventional by nature, he always intended to join the Army. When he went down from Oxford he was commissioned into the Royal Welch Fusiliers, his godfather's regiment, and took the name of Doughty-Wylie. Mrs Doughty-Wylie had constituted herself his godmother after her husband had been killed in Gallipoli and she induced him to change his name and join this regiment. During the war he served in the Italian campaign, won an MC at Anzio, and ended the war in Burma.

Dermot joined me at Magdalen for my fourth year at Oxford; Roddy did not go up to Oxford until the year after I had left. Dermot and I had been together at Eton but then Dermot was one of the Lower boys who came when I shouted 'Boy'. Now we were grown up and the difference in our ages was immaterial. I could discuss my plans for my proposed exploration of the Danakil country with him, take him to a meeting of the Raleigh Club or to Elsfield to have tea with John Buchan.

Dermot was devoted to England and always maintained that he never went abroad if he could avoid it. Witty, ambitious and idealistic, his ambition was to be elected to Parliament, his dream to become Prime Minister. He was called to the Bar when he left Oxford. While he was there he learnt to fly with the University Air Squadron, and was in despair when, on the outbreak of war, the RAF initially turned him down on medical grounds. Over six feet in height with no spare flesh, he did look gaunt. After he had been accepted he trained in South Africa, and was then posted as a Flight Sergeant to Coastal Command. His ineptitude at mathematics delayed his commission, which was finally granted on the day he was killed on an operational flight. He was, however, happy in the ranks, where his sociable and unassuming character and ability to mix with all sorts made him free of its easy comradeship. When he was killed Vincent Massey, the High Commissioner for Canada, and Mr Justice Lawrence, the High Court Judge for whom Dermot had marshalled, wrote appreciations of him in *The Times*, a remarkable tribute in this time of war to an unknown young man.

*　　*　　*

Reggie owned the Villa Cipressi on Lake Como in Italy and there I spent an unforgettable fortnight during the summer of 1932 with seven Oxford friends, including Harry Phillimore and Robin Campbell. This charming villa was spacious and comfortably furnished with a well-stocked library; the large garden ran down to the lake where there was both a motor boat and a sailing boat. We swam in the lake and sunned ourselves on the lawn among the flowering magnolias. We sailed, we climbed the precipice behind the villa, walked among the chestnut woods on the mountain slopes and came back to eat delicious Italian food cooked by the voluble old peasant woman who looked after the villa.

After dinner we would sit looking out over the three arms of the lake and talk until, drowsy with sun, swimming, food and wine, we went off to bed. Previously I had never heard a nightingale; here they sang throughout the night beneath our windows. I thought Italy astoundingly beautiful and liked the Italians I met in Varenna, a quiet, peaceful village just up the road from the Cipressi. It never occurred to me that within three years I should hate the Italians with an unrelenting hatred.

During my last year at Oxford I had applied to join the Sudan Political Service. The Anglo-Egyptian Sudan was a vast country, some 1300 miles from north to south and 900 from east to west, inhabited by a great diversity of tribes and races, ranging from camel-owning nomads in the north to naked pagans in the equatorial swamps of the south, and former cannibals in the forests bordering the Congo. But from my point of view what mattered most was that it bordered Abyssinia, where I hoped one day to be posted. I had become interested in the Sudan itself after reading Samuel Baker's books, but at first my interest was largely in the wild life and the big-game hunting in the Southern Sudan; then at Eton I chanced on *The River War*, Winston Churchill's vivid account of Kitchener's campaign to reconquer the Sudan from the Khalifa. After that I read every book I could find about the rise and fall of the Dervish Empire.

I was interviewed by the Sudan Agent in London who gave me lunch at his club, and told me I would be called before a selection board when I came down from Oxford. I explained that I was planning, as soon as I left Oxford, to go to Abyssinia for a year, to explore the Danakil country. He said this would be all right since on my return I should still be within the age limit for joining the Political Service.

Some months earlier I had written to Sir Sidney Barton who, fortunately for me, was still British Minister in Addis Ababa, asking him to obtain the Emperor's permission for me to follow the Awash river through the Danakil country to discover where and how it ended. I had recently heard from the Foreign Office that the Emperor had agreed to my undertaking this journey. I immediately wrote to Colonel Sandford asking for his help in collecting my caravan, and he promised to do whatever he could. I was now busy raising the necessary money. The Royal Geographical Society approved my plans and made me a grant, as did the Percy Sladen Trust of the Linnean Society. The Natural History Museum undertook to buy any suitable specimens which I brought back, and most firms I approached agreed to provide rations, ammunition, films, medicine and other requirements for the expedition, either free or at a considerable discount.

I had often discussed my plans with my uncle who, as Warden, now lived in the Warden's Lodge at All Souls, where he and his wife encouraged me to visit them and always made me welcome. Then, suddenly and unexpectedly, in the spring of 1933 my uncle collapsed and died while walking in a friend's garden. His death left me with a sense of desolation. Some months later his wife told me he had intended to contribute to the cost of my expedition and she insisted on my receiving from his estate the amount he had meant to give me.

I was quite prepared to do this journey alone, but my mother, who had given me every encouragement although well aware of the risks I was running, insisted I should take a companion. Surprisingly, I had difficulty in finding one until David Haig-Thomas, whom I had known slightly at Eton, offered to come with me. He had been at Cambridge, where he got his Blue for rowing.

On the last day of term I met the President and dons to say goodbye. I was aware how much I owed to their unobtrusive help; several of them were my friends. I had been happy at Magdalen and this was a moving occasion. The President wished me well on my expedition and then, quite unexpectedly, announced that the College had decided to make a contribution to its cost. Nearly fifty years later Magdalen did me the signal honour of electing me an Honorary Fellow.

PART II

Among the Danakil

1933–4

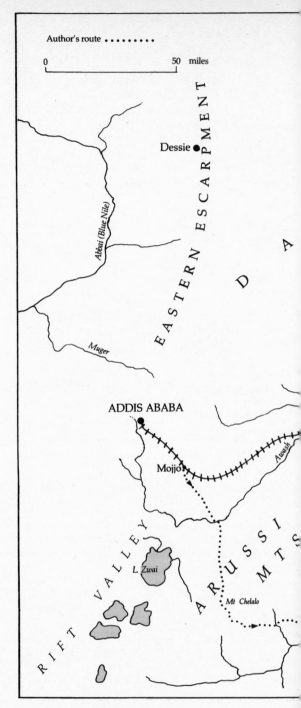

Danakil Country 1930–4

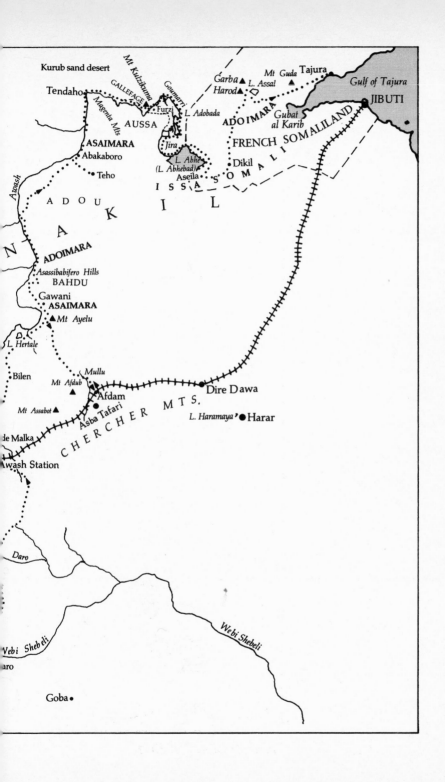

CHAPTER 9

The Highlands of Arussi

HAIG-THOMAS and I arrived in Addis Ababa on 8 September 1933 and stayed with Dan and Chris Sandford on their farm at Mullu. The house overlooked the sheer two-thousand-foot gorge of the Muger river and had a magnificent view down the valley towards the distant canyon of the Blue Nile. Primitive their house certainly was, with its earthen floor, mud walls, thatched roof and rude furniture; but it was imbued by those two remarkable and lovable people with a warmth that few homes can ever have equalled. The Sandfords kept open house for anyone who rode the fifteen miles from Addis Ababa, and it was a rewarding experience to stay with them, for their knowledge of the country and of its people was outstanding.

They told us of exciting events that had taken place in the valley below their house the previous year, the result of an attempted coup by Ras Hailu, the hereditary ruler of Gojjam. Autocratic, powerful and ambitious, he had long been jealous of the Emperor and had aspired to be made a Negus. This would have conflicted with Haile Selassie's intention of curtailing the power of the feudal Rases and centralizing the administration. Threatened now by a diminution of his semi-regal status, Ras Hailu decided to rebel and reinstate his son-in-law, Lij Yasu, as Emperor.

For the past fourteen years Lij Yasu had been held by Ras Kassa in comfortable detention at Fiche. Ras Hailu planned to free him and to raise the north in his name. For all his faults, Lij Yasu was remembered by many as a more comprehensible ruler than Haile Selassie, who failed to conform to the popular image of an Abyssinian monarch. The plot, however, miscarried. Lij Yasu escaped prematurely and Ras Hailu was arrested before he had organized the rebellion.

Almost any ruler other than Haile Selassie would have confirmed the sentence of death passed on him for treason by the high court, but the Emperor was content to fine him heavily and imprison him. Lij Yasu was arrested four days later near the Sandfords' farm; he

109

had been wandering in the Muger valley with a few retainers, hungry and terrified. Missing his women and his comforts, he had been more than ready to give himself up. He was imprisoned near Harar and died three years later, a physical wreck at thirty-seven.

Dan Sandford had met us at the railway station in Addis Ababa and had brought with him Omar, our prospective headman, to clear our baggage through customs and deal with the other formalities. Unlike most Somalis, Omar was large, stout and jovial. He impressed me at once, for he was obviously authoritative and efficient. He had been with Sandford since he was a boy and spoke adequate English. In those days many Europeans, especially in Kenya, relied on Somalis as their headmen; in turn, these Somalis identified themselves with their masters and gave them devoted service. Omar was in this tradition. They are all gone now and have no successors.

During the next nine months Omar more than justified Sandford's strong recommendation. Thanks to him there was never any trouble among my followers, though they included Amhara, Galla, Gurages, Somalis and Danakils; all of them, whether Christian or Muslim, accepted his authority without question. Omar was a devout Muslim and like the best Somalis was proud and fearless, though he proved to be remarkably tactful and forbearing whenever I was impatient or angry, and always upheld my authority even when I made a mistake. It was largely due to him that I managed to negotiate successfully with government officials and tribal chiefs during the months that followed.

Sandford had sent him, before our arrival, to the Awash Station on the edge of the Danakil country to buy us eighteen camels. These were now waiting there with the six Somalis Omar had engaged as our camelmen. Sandford, however, urged us to defer going down there for at least two months: the rains had only recently ended and after the rains a virulent type of malaria was prevalent in the Awash valley. He suggested that in the meantime we should visit the Arussi mountains; this would enable us to assess our men and, if necessary, change some before we committed ourselves to the Danakil country. Omar assured us that the Somalis he had engaged would wait contentedly with the camels until we turned up.

We had undertaken to collect birds and mammals for the Natural History Museum in London and we soon collected several specimens of blue-winged goose near the Sandfords' farm; the museum authorities had asked us specially to look out for this bird since they only had one specimen, collected in 1868 during Napier's Magdala expedition. We expected to get a variety of other interesting specimens in the highlands of Arussi, where Ivor Buxton had discovered the mountain nyala in 1910; this large buck, resembling a greater kudu, was known only from the highlands of Arussi and Bale. My father had shot one, as had the Duke of Gloucester during a hunting safari he made to Chelalo in the Arussi mountains after Haile Selassie's coronation; otherwise, few Europeans had even seen a mountain nyala, so it was a prize that both Haig-Thomas and I were keen to secure. We also hoped to obtain a specimen of the cuberow, the so-called Abyssinian wolf, an animal like a large fox which was confined to some of the higher mountains in Abyssinia. The more I thought about it, the more I looked forward to seeing this little known mountainous region, and I had every intention of penetrating at least as far as the Webi Shebeli river.

The first thing was to select the men to go with us. The Sandfords provided us with an elderly Amhara called Habta Mariam as cook. I liked him as soon as I met him and came to do so even more over the ensuing months. At first I was doubtful about taking him, for he did not look strong; but the Sandfords assured us that he had stood up to several long treks with them, invariably producing good meals even under the most unfavourable conditions, that he never interfered with other people, and was always ready to lend a hand at any job.

Omar produced two Somalis as gunbearers. Abdullahi was a small, slender, restless man with quick, vigilant eyes and an engagingly ugly face. Said Munge was short, stocky and usually impassive, though like all Somalis he could on occasion get worked up. Both fully lived up to Omar's recommendation.

We were fortunate to secure as head *syce* a middle-aged Amhara called Kassimi. Bearded, with natural dignity and quiet authority, this reserved man soon earned the position of second headman. Despite their racial and religious divergence, he and Omar worked closely together running the caravan. We were also lucky enough to find Goutama, whom I remembered as a young *syce* in the Legation stables when I was a boy; he had accompanied my father on his long trek to Nairobi in 1914. He was of slave origin, very black, cheerful, indefatigable and good with animals. Like Kassimi, he was a devout Christian. We engaged a third *syce* called Makonnen; he turned out

111

to be a quarrelsome intriguer and we eventually got rid of him. As our personal servants we had Birru, a Christian Galla, and Said, known as Said Boy, a Muslim Gurage. They were in their early twenties, were quietly efficient and worked well together.

Since we needed someone to skin and look after the specimens we collected, we eventually employed a lanky youth called Yusuf German who had worked for a Greek taxidermist in the town. He spoke a little French and was plausible, but he looked unreliable and indeed proved to be. Omar had a young servant called Demise, and there was another fifteen-year-old lad called Yusuf Nico, who Omar said would make himself useful doing odd jobs. We also employed three *zabanias* or guards.

Haig-Thomas and I each bought a pony and a riding mule, and three more riding mules for Omar, Kassimi and Habta Mariam. Omar had arranged for Beyyene, a *negadi* or muleteer, to meet us at Mojjo Station, sixty miles down the line, with his men and twenty pack mules, and we sent Kassimi, Goutama and Makonnen ahead with our own animals to join him there. The rest of us left Addis Ababa by train on the morning of 1 October 1933, arriving three hours later at Mojjo, which consisted of a few sheds and huts.

We eventually got away from the station and camped two hours later near a marsh, where we shot some duck for dinner, and two lily-trotters for our collection. As Haig-Thomas and I returned to camp, the summits of the Arussi mountains far in the distance glowed in the last of the setting sun. The tents were up; the fires were lit; everyone sounded cheerful, happy to be off at last. The stars came out and several hyenas howled round the camp. Eventually Birru brought us the ducks that Habta Mariam had cooked. They tasted delicious, a happy augury for future meals. I went to bed utterly content; ahead of me were weeks of hunting and travel in remote mountains, and later the excitement of exploring the Danakil desert.

During the next day's march there was a sudden commotion at the back of our straggling caravan. A *shifta* or brigand had stepped out of the bush, clubbed one of the men and made off with his rifle. I went in pursuit with Abdullahi and eventually saw the man on a hillside. I put a bullet close to his head and he dived for cover.

Very much on the alert, we followed him into thick bush. Luckily he had no ammunition for the rifle and gave himself up after Omar, who had caught up with us, put two more shots over his head. We tied his arms behind his back and handed him over to the next village headman we encountered. A few days later we passed the desiccated corpse of another brigand hanging on a gibbet beside the track. Hyenas had torn off his legs.

Three days after leaving Mojjo we crossed the Awash river by a rickety bridge; a large crocodile basked on the river bank and there were tracks of many hippopotamus. For the rest of the day we skirted a large swamp; that night the mosquitoes were particularly bad. Beyond the Awash we passed a number of Arussi graves, some with figures crudely incised on upright stones.

We reached Chelalo on the Arussi mountains in the afternoon of 5 October; it was here that we expected to find nyala. We had made an early start that morning and after a long stiff climb up a bare hillside entered a forest of wild olives and massive juniper trees resembling cedars, many of them festooned with lichen. I had never been in such a forest and found it fascinating. We camped on the edge of the moorland among magnificent red-tasselled hagenia trees and clumps of yellow flowering St John's wort; above us the mountain was covered with giant heath ten feet and more in height. Only the high tops, at thirteen thousand feet, were bare; there, tussocky grass, patches of everlastings and a scattering of giant lobelia were interspersed among crags of weathered rock.

It turned very cold in the evening, with the summit of the mountain periodically hidden in mist, but as the sun set we had a magnificent view. We could just see Lake Zwai and beyond it a wall of mountains on the far side of the Rift Valley.

Each morning we set off to hunt soon after dawn. It was always clear but perishingly cold at that early hour; later the mists came down and in the afternoon there were often storms of rain and sometimes hail. I took Abdullahi with me, while Said Munge accompanied Haig-Thomas. We both employed local Arussi as trackers, some of whom were very skilful and all of whom were tireless. Every day on Chelalo Haig-Thomas or I saw nyala, usually in small parties of cows and immature males; I once counted a dozen together. Several times I saw a big bull, sometimes even two together. It was easy enough to spot them in the distance if they were in a clearing on the mountainside, but extremely difficult to detect them as Abdullahi and I approached through a tangle of giant heath that rose far above our heads. Sometimes I saw nyala on the bare mountain-tops but never in the forest. Returning to camp in the evenings, I occasionally hunted for bushbuck in the forest. It was a test of skill to move silently among the trees with every sense alert, trying to spot one before it took fright and vanished. The males were dark, almost black, in colour, and difficult to make out among the shadows.

On the fourth day we moved our camp a few miles to the east, where our trackers maintained we should find the nyala more numerous; this proved to be the case. But it was a cold, dank place beside a stream in a shallow valley. There were no trees here, only heath to burn, and we missed the large fires at our previous camp.

We saw several cuberow, usually in pairs, while hunting for nyala. They were attractive-looking animals and they often allowed us to get quite close. Once I heard two calling to each other across a valley, a weird sound, vaguely resembling a baboon's bark. Judging from their droppings, they were plentiful. I shot one for the museum. Klipspringer were numerous on the cliffs at the top of the mountain, and there, above a thousand-foot precipice, I found among a mass of tumbled rocks the fresh tracks of leopard.

Haig-Thomas had shot two nyala, both with disappointingly small horns. Determined to shoot one with a really fine head, I decided to spend a night near the mountain-top so that I could hunt for them in the early morning before they lay up for the day. I therefore took with us Ergay, one of our *zabanias*, selected a place to sleep under an overhanging rock and sent him back to camp to bring Birru in the evening with a mule, blankets and food.

Even with the blankets it was very chilly, and in the morning the ground was white with frost. Abdullahi soon spotted a cow and three young bulls grazing in the open above the heathline. A little later we saw another cow and then through my glasses I picked up a bull lying down in the distance. He stood up while we watched and I realized he had magnificent horns, far longer than any I had yet seen. He was right out in the open and the wind was blowing towards us.

Crawling on our stomachs, making use of every scrap of cover or depression, however slight, and remaining motionless whenever he looked in our direction, Abdullahi and I eventually reached the shelter of a low ridge. The rest was easy and I got to within a hundred yards. He dropped to the shot. The horns measured forty-nine inches along the curve, longer than any listed in Rowland Ward's *Records of Big Game*. My triumph was enhanced by the hard work of the past week; on occasions even the Arussi trackers had confessed they were exhausted.

I believe that most men have an inborn desire to hunt and kill and that even today this primitive urge has only been eradicated in a small minority of the human race. Nowadays many people condemn big-game hunting, and rightly so, with the wildlife which they watch on television threatened with extinction. Fifty years ago this was not the case; there was then no apparent threat to any but a few species. I grew up as a child with a longing to hunt big game, and from 1930 to 1940 I took every opportunity to do so; for this I have no regrets. Inevitably I shot many animals to feed myself and my retainers, but the memorable occasions were when I hunted dangerous game or tried to secure a really fine head of a rare or elusive animal, like this mountain nyala. I have often been asked why I was not content to photograph instead of kill them. For me, the sound of the bullet striking home and a clean kill, with the animal dropping where it stood, was the climax of the hunt, all the more rewarding if it followed upon days and even weeks of testing and arduous hunting, or a really difficult stalk. With photography, and the uncertainty of whether the picture would be a success, there could be no such climax.

We struck camp next day and set off down the mountain on our way to the Webi Shebeli. It was 12 October. One of our baggage mules had died during the night and several others were sick. During the next few days we lost my pony, two of our riding mules and five more baggage mules. They were usually listless for a few days before they collapsed, breathing with evident difficulty and, in a few cases, discharging a white frothy liquid from their nostrils. We passed a merchant's caravan which was stranded; forty out of their fifty mules were dead. Though we continued to lose animals, we managed to replace them with ponies bought from the Arussi. On one occasion we bought two from a toothless ancient, whose family claimed he was a hundred and twenty years old and boasted that he had killed a hundred and forty men in his day. At intervals while we were negotiating with him, he screeched his battle songs and war cries. Omar was infinitely patient, humouring the rambling dotard with handfuls of salt, sugar and empty tins.

At first we travelled through magnificent stretches of forest, where we saw occasional bushbuck and many black-and-white colobus monkeys. Lower down we emerged on to a more open country of grass-covered hills, with delphiniums, gladioli and other flowers growing along the banks of the many streams. During these days there were brief, heavy storms in the afternoons, with more persistent rain at night. Fuel was difficult to come by after we left the forest, and when we reached the plains that stretched to the Webi Shebeli we had to make do with dry cattle dung. Despite the lack of firewood, the generally damp conditions and intermittent fever, Habta Mariam, squatting in the open beside his fire with his pots resting on stones, cooked us a good meal every evening.

We now passed great herds of cattle guarded by naked boys, and encountered frequent parties of mounted Arussi, all armed with spears. Their womenfolk were dressed in tanned skins with beads woven into their hair. I was impressed by these untamed people. They had been conquered by Menelik but among them the Abyssinian imprint was as yet barely discernible, for which I was thankful. I have always resented the imposition of an alien culture, whether European or otherwise, on the indigenous inhabitants. Once we passed a single telephone line, dangling on rickety poles, connecting Addis Ababa to some government post; I remember resenting even this slender evidence of outside interference.

We forded the Webi Shebeli on 17 October and camped near an Arussi village. On this side of the Webi, undulating grasslands rose to distant hills, and strips of woodland bordered numerous streams. We were unaware that having crossed the Webi we were now in Bale. Our passes were only valid for Arussi; consequently, when we reached Haro, a small administrative post further down the banks of the Webi, we were held up by Abyssinian officials and a mob of their compatriots. It was a feast day, and they were all drunk, and just as aggressive and unpleasant as drunken Abyssinians can be. They detained us, refusing even to allow us to re-cross the river and continue our journey on the other side. I sent Kassimi with a letter to the Governor at Goba, and a few days later we received an apology for our treatment and permission to continue our journey.

Meanwhile we had sent Muhammad Dankali, another of our *zabanias*, to tell Ahmad, the Somali in charge of our camels, to bring them to the Daro river at the foot of the escarpment. Omar believed we would do better in this lowland country if we used camels rather than mules.

For the next week we travelled across rolling, well-cultivated country intersected by steep ravines that developed into spectacular gorges at the edge of the plateau. Bohor reedbuck abounded on these uplands, generally in groups of four to seven; once I saw as many as eighty scattered over a hillside. Then, on 6 November, we descended the steep and difficult escarpment to the Daro river, where we found a pleasant camp site under some large fig trees.

The river was fast-flowing, crystal-clear and swarming with catfish and barbel; we had plenty of hooks and line and caught sixty in one day. We were here for six days before the camels arrived, but were reassured by hearing news of them from some of the many pilgrims who passed through our camp on their way to a famous shrine of Sheikh Husain; all carried peeled, forked wands as an emblem of their pilgrimage.

We left the Daro river next day and arrived at the Awash a fortnight later. Omar's information that the country below the escarpment would be suitable for camels could not have been more misleading. At first we travelled under the escarpment, which involved crossing a succession of spurs. In most places the track over these ridges was impassable for loaded camels until we had widened and levelled it. Omar was splendid, labouring indefatigably with the sweat pouring off him, while Kassimi, Birru, the two Saids, Abdullahi, Habta Mariam and the others worked without a stop.

The weather did not help. Almost every day there were downpours of rain and it often poured throughout the night, making the ground so slippery that the camels found it difficult to keep on their feet. I was compensated to some extent by the magnificent scenery. All around us were mountains; they were often half-smothered in cloud, but in the evenings this lifted and then the crests loomed over us, rain-washed, clear-cut and splendid.

Haig-Thomas had developed an infected throat and several nasty ulcers on his legs. Four days after we had left the Daro he decided to push on ahead with Kassimi, on our two best mules, in order to catch a train from the Awash Station to Addis Ababa for medical treatment. Soon after Haig-Thomas had left us we passed a shrine to Sheikh Husain; the white-washed dome with four turrets had been built to commemorate a place where the saint had lived alone for years, praying and fasting. Just beyond it we struggled over a particularly difficult pass and arrived next day on the Mana river. All

117

this lowland country was covered in thick bush, and large trees bordered the river and streams. We reached the Awash Station on 25 November.

Haig-Thomas was at the railway rest house. He had returned from Addis Ababa two days before, apparently cured, but his throat had now flared up again and when I arrived he could hardly speak. He caught the next train back to Addis Ababa and the following day sent me a wire: 'Cannot come.'

I was content to be on my own, glad that I should have no need to accommodate myself to a fellow-countryman, that any decisions in the days ahead would be entirely mine. Haig-Thomas had been cheerful and good-natured, and never once had we quarrelled. No one, indeed, could have been more easy-going; but we never got on close terms or found much in common during the four months we had been together since leaving England. He seldom read a book and this limited the range of his interests and the scope of his conversation. I did not feel I should miss his company, and the fact that I should have no fellow-countryman with me to take charge if I fell sick or was wounded did not worry me, since I had every confidence in Omar. In any case I have never, during more than fifty years of travel, anticipated falling ill. I have in fact only once been incapacitated, on that occasion by a severe attack of malaria.

The journey I had just completed in the Arussi had been the first I had undertaken in the highlands of Abyssinia. I had travelled through remote and spectacular country among exciting, barely administered tribes, and had secured the record head of a much-prized quarry. I had enjoyed the last two months greatly but the journey, though arduous, had involved no real danger. I knew conditions would be different once we crossed the railway and entered Danakil country.

CHAPTER 10

Into Danakil Country

T HE AUTHORITIES in Addis Ababa had undertaken to provide me with an escort of ten soldiers while I was among the Danakil. I found fifteen waiting for me when I arrived at the Awash Station, all thoroughly unhappy at the prospect ahead.

I was aware that the risks were considerable: had it been otherwise the Danakil country would already have been thoroughly explored. I had learnt during my journey in 1930 that the Danakil, or Afar as they called themselves, were divided into the Asaimara or Red Men, who comprised the tribes of noble descent, and the Adoimara or White Men. I had been told that the Asaimara inhabited Bahdu and Aussa while the Adoimara occupied the rest of the country. During that journey I had only travelled among the Adoimara, and at Bilen they had given me alarming accounts of the ferocity of the Asaimara in Bahdu. It had been evident that while both sections of the Danakil were murderously inclined, the Asaimara were the more formidable.

At Bilen I had often asked what happened to the Awash, curious to find out why this large river never reached the sea, and I had been told that it ended in a great lake at the foot of a mighty mountain called Goumarri in Aussa, where apparently there were many lakes, great forests and some cultivation. My informants stood in great awe of the Sultan, known as the Amoita, who ruled Aussa, and insisted that he hated all Europeans. Years later, when I was with Sandford in the Second World War, he told me that people in Addis Ababa had been saying that I would not have one chance in ten of survival if I entered Aussa.

I myself felt, however, that we would probably run our greatest risk in Bahdu. Omar was inclined to agree. He said the Danakil had killed some Greek traders who had ventured into Bahdu the previous year. After I had returned to Oxford from Abyssinia at the beginning of 1931, I had read Nesbitt's account of his journey, in the *Geographical Journal* for October 1930. From his account Bahdu was where he had been in most danger.

Nesbitt and his two Italian companions had evidently been fortunate to get away from Bahdu; it was here that the first of their servants was murdered; two others were killed in the course of the journey. The party had been more fortunate than their predecessors. During my researches in the library of the Royal Geographical Society I learnt that in 1875 an Egyptian army commanded by Munzinger, a Swiss mercenary who had served under Gordon in Equatoria, had set out to invade Abyssinia from Tajura, and been exterminated by the Danakil before they reached Aussa. Then in 1881 an expedition led by Giulietti, accompanied by thirteen other Italians, had been massacred somewhere to the north of Aussa, as was another expedition under Bianchi three years later in much the same area.

Nesbitt had met the Sultan on the outskirts of Aussa and been given permission to continue northwards across the lava desert to Eritrea, but was forbidden to enter Aussa, which remained unexplored. He had, however, confirmed that the Awash entered Aussa.

My immediate anxiety was that the authorities might forbid my journey, since the Asaimara of Bahdu had recently renounced their allegiance to the Government and refused to send tribute to Asba Tafari.

On 1 December, as we were preparing to start, an official did telephone from Asba Tafari, headquarters of Chercher Province which nominally included Bahdu. He said fierce fighting was taking place near Bahdu and insisted I would need at least a hundred soldiers if I went there. He refused to take the responsibility of letting me go with only fifteen, and intended to recall his men.

I told him I had twenty-two men with me, armed with fourteen rifles, as well as my own three rifles and shotgun. If, in addition, I were accompanied by his fifteen soldiers I believed we should be too strong a party to invite attack, while not so strong as to alarm and provoke the tribes. He would not agree. I therefore reminded him that the Emperor had authorized my journey, and told him that whether his soldiers came with me or not I was leaving that afternoon. Reluctantly he ordered them to accompany me. I was now in a fever to be off before someone else, perhaps from Addis Ababa, rang up to forbid my departure. Omar had bribed the telephone operator to leave his office, but I did not trust him to stay away. We finally set out in the evening. My eighteen camels were all heavily loaded, as we could expect no supplies from the Danakil but meat and milk until we reached Aussa.

The soldiers had four camels, but were hopelessly incompetent at loading them and I had got more and more exasperated at the delay. Only when the station buildings disappeared from sight did I feel safe from further intervention. Now, for good or bad, we were on our own. This was what I wanted.

There was a full moon and we marched until midnight, the camels tied head to tail in groups of three or four. That night many hyenas howled round our camp. We arrived next day at the hot springs of Sade Malka; these were surrounded by dom palms, odd-looking forked trees with clusters of hard nuts. I knew I had camped here with my parents in 1915 on our way back to Addis Ababa, but the place brought back no recollections.

We had with us a Danakil from the Awash Station, not only as guide but also as hostage, and would not be releasing him until he found a replacement from the next tribe. Each night at intervals he shouted a warning that anyone who approached would be shot. We now made a practice, as soon as we camped, of building a perimeter round the camp with loads and camel saddles, and, if there were sufficient bushes available, added a thorn fence or *zariba*. I always posted two sentries at night, more if the situation warranted it, and Omar or I checked at intervals to make sure they were awake.

Three days later we reached Bilen, after travelling across an extensive plain cut up by dry water-courses and marked by low rocky ridges. It was sparsely covered with acacia scrub, interspersed with thickets of sansevieria with formidable bayonet-like leaves. Here I saw several herds of beisa oryx, Soemering's gazelle, and occasional lesser kudu and gerenuk. I had come across a small herd of Swayne's hartebeeste near Awash Station, the only hartebeeste I saw during the journey.

Intermittent tamarisk jungle grew along the banks of the Awash and in this I saw several herds of waterbuck, many warthog and an occasional bushbuck. I stayed at Bilen for four days. I had tried to shoot buffalo there in 1930; now I tried again. A small herd inhabited a reedbed formed by the overflow from a large pool fed by hot springs, leaving its shelter only after dark and returning to it before light. Each day I followed their tracks and several times got close before they snorted and crashed off; but the reeds were so dense I never got a glimpse.

Groups of Danakil watered their camels and cattle at the overflow. Most of them were darkish-brown with fine features under mops of hair in which several had stuck an ostrich feather or a wooden comb. Many carried Fusil Gras rifles, usually resting on a shoulder and held by the barrel, or horizontally across the back of the neck supporting both arms. These single-shot service weapons, dating from the mid-nineteenth century and firing a lead bullet which inflicted appalling wounds, had been exported to Abyssinia in great numbers by the French.

Every man wore, strapped across his stomach, a formidable curved dagger known as a *jile*, with a sixteen-inch blade sharp on each side. Nearly all these daggers had one or more brass-bound leather thongs dangling from the scabbard, each thong denoting a man killed.

I thought the Danakil an attractive-looking people, and despite their murderous reputation they appeared to manifest a genuine friendliness. I was prepared to accept the fact that they would kill a man or boy with as little compunction as I would shoot a buck. Their motive would be much the same as that of an English sportsman who visited Africa to shoot a lion and, like him, they preferred to take their quarry unawares.

The Danakil invariably castrated any man or boy whom they killed or wounded, removing both the penis and the scrotum. An obvious trophy, it afforded irrefutable proof that the victim was male, and obtaining it gave the additional satisfaction of dishonouring the corpse. Nesbitt stated in *Desert and Forest* that 'the Danakil wore the testicles of their victims round their wrists ...' I never came across an instance of this, though I encountered a number of individuals who had just killed someone, including a complacent fourteen-year-old near Bilen. The boy's hair was plastered with ghee, or clarified butter, as evidence of his achievement.

All that mattered to these people was to kill; how they did so had little significance. Nesbitt described how one of his servants, accompanied by the Danakil guide, went to bathe in the river. He put his rifle down and entered the water. The guide picked up the rifle, shot and castrated him, and made off. It is impossible to exaggerate the importance that the Danakil attached to this practice, rating as they did a man's prowess by the number of his kills; many raids were undertaken principally for this purpose. On returning from a raid, any who had never killed were often ragged by their more competent companions, their clothes dirtied and cow dung, instead of ghee, rubbed in their hair.

If a man had been repeatedly unsuccessful he would go to the river, dive to the bottom and bring up a lump of clay with which he would mark his forehead, taking care to be unobserved, otherwise the spell lost its efficacy. I noticed that children often marked themselves like this in play. Most youths and even small boys wore a strip of hide around their wrists or ankles: this had been given them with appropriate blessing to bring them success when they became warriors.

In time I learnt to tell at a glance, from the decorations he wore, how often a man had killed, just as I might tell from his campaign medals where a British soldier had served. An ostrich feather or comb in the hair, slit ears, a coloured loin-cloth, an iron or ivory bracelet, a dagger and sheath decorated with brass or silver: each of these and other decorations had its special significance. When a famous warrior died he was commemorated by a monument known as a *das* in front of which upright stones indicated the number of his victims.

We left Bilen on the morning of 9 December and camped five hours later in thick bush on the edge of a swamp that extended out of sight along the river. Here we were in a dangerous border area, and our campsite was virtually indefensible, but we could find none better. The soldiers needed no encouragement to build a thick *zariba* round the camp. The mosquitoes here were particularly bad and kept most of us awake.

The following evening, after a slogging nine-hour march over volcanic hills that threw up waves of heat, making me irritable and all of us tired and thirsty, we toiled up yet another rise and suddenly saw Lake Hertale below us. It was an almost unbelievable sight in this desolate landscape, a long stretch of vivid blue water fringed by green reedbeds.

We camped on a terrace above the lake and had a splendid bathe, swimming and splashing in the fresh clear water. Swarms of bats appeared over our camp at sunset, and hippos grunted like pigs at intervals throughout the night. The Danakil guide we had acquired at Bilen had tried to bolt on the march, so I detailed two soldiers to guard him till dawn. I knew we should be in trouble if he got away.

In the morning we had difficulty getting the camels down to the lake; we then followed the stream that flowed out of it and after a short march camped not far from an Adoimara village. The previous day four men from this village had been surprised and killed by Asaimara from Bahdu, less than two hundred yards from where we camped. We were shown the place; there was dried blood on the rocks and sand. The funeral feast was under way and we were given a quantity of meat. These Adoimara Danakil were glad to have us with them, for they were expecting yet another raid by the Asaim-ara. Apparently it had been near here, not in Bahdu, that the Greek merchants had been killed the year before.

I had to stay in camp next day as there was strong opposition to my going out shooting. I noted in my diary: 'Incessant talk of the Asaimara. Extremely difficult to judge how great the danger really is.' That evening I bought two sheep which the Somalis slaughtered; they then gave the blood to some of the camels.

The following day we reached the Asaimara frontier. The head-man of a nearby village had saved the life of one of the Greeks and been rewarded by the Government. We now demanded that he should escort us into Bahdu. Obviously unwilling, he asked for an absurd sum for doing so, but eventually Omar settled with him for a reasonable amount. He then presented me with three sheep, after which all his family and relations asked for presents. It now remained to be seen whether this headman would be able to hand us over to another in Bahdu. Two and a half months earlier Dedjaz-match Abashum had come here with a large force to collect the tribute which the Asaimara were withholding, but he had been afraid to enter Bahdu and had withdrawn. The Asaimara were thereby convinced they could successfully defy the Government. This, of course, added considerably to the danger before us.

From our camp, Mount Ayelu dominated the countryside. Its massive cone rose five thousand feet above the Bahdu plain and a chain of foothills stretched south-west parallel with the Awash. The only track into Bahdu from the south, feasible for loaded camels, skirted a marsh at the foot of these hills. It took us over an hour the following morning to get through this pass, a notorious place for ambushes. Some of my men picketed the high ground while we passed underneath, constantly urged by the headman and his fol-lowers not to straggle.

When at last we emerged into the open we found ourselves on a plain, perhaps a mile wide, lying between the hills and the river. This was by far the most fertile area I had as yet seen in the Danakil country, and it was dotted with small villages of mat-covered huts. Large herds of cattle, flocks of sheep and goats, and a number of ponies and donkeys grazed on rich grass round patches of shallow water, and clusters of giant fig trees grew along the river bank.

About two hundred warriors were squatting under some of these trees and more were hurrying to join them. We halted the camels when we drew near and Omar and the Adoimara headman and I went over. We greeted them but no one returned our salutations; instead, as we approached, they shuffled round and turned their backs on us. I returned to my men and told them to unload under some fig trees on the steep river bank. Meanwhile our Adoimara headman was trying to identify his local counterpart. When at last he succeeded the man was sullen and uncooperative, repeatedly demanding why we had come to Bahdu.

An increasing number of Danakil gathered round our camp. We had constructed a perimeter and we now tried to keep them outside it without provoking them. I felt they were looking for any excuse to start a fight. Some of them, hearing my camelmen speaking Somali, became increasingly threatening, asserting that they were from the Issa, a Somali tribe with whom they were then, as always, at war. Ergay, who understood their language, warned Omar that they were planning to attack us after dark. To discourage them, we pretended that my rifle case contained a machine-gun, a weapon for which they had considerable respect, having occasionally encountered one when fighting Government troops.

The tension, however, eased after Omar managed to get hold of some elders. Over many cups of tea, he succeeded in convincing some of them that I was an English traveller on my way to visit the Amoita in Aussa. He persuaded them that I was not employed by the Government, explaining that I was under the Emperor's personal protection, which accounted for my escort of soldiers. Even so, I felt by no means certain that the elders would be able to prevent their refractory warriors from attacking us after dark. We spent an apprehensive night. At intervals I wandered round the camp, flashing my powerful torch into the darkness. I doubt if anyone slept.

Next morning we were taken to a small village nearby, on a patch of dry ground in the middle of a bog, and on this uninviting spot the chief, an aged, autocratic savage called Afleodham, instructed us to camp. Having heard that he was much respected and had great influence in these parts, I felt it was as well to do as he told us. Omar learnt that he was related to the Sultan, and we hoped that we might persuade him to provide us with a guide to Aussa.

Omar and I had a tiring discussion with him, beset by clouds of flies. Afleodham was rather deaf; every word had to be repeated and every argument gone over time and time again, all this using three languages. Finally he agreed to provide us with an escort to Aussa. Triumphant but exhausted, I went and lay down in my tent.

Just before sunset I heard a hubbub outside where a crowd had collected. A letter had arrived from Asba Tafari addressed to the head of my escort; it had been passed from chief to chief. It ordered me to return at once and in no circumstances to try to enter Bahdu. Should I refuse to do so, the soldiers themselves were to return after announcing to the Danakil that the authorities took no further responsibility for my safety. The soldiers made no attempt to conceal their delight.

I went back to my tent and discussed the situation with Omar. He said he thought some of my men would follow me if I decided to go on. I realized, however, that to do so after we had been deprived of half our rifles and whatever security the protection of the Government afforded us would be to invite almost certain massacre. For four years I had been planning this journey, and the thought of exploring Aussa and discovering what happened to the Awash had seldom been out of my mind. I had hoped we were now beyond reach of Government interference. We had managed to enter Bahdu, had been accepted, and the road to Aussa lay open. Now everything was wrecked.

I decided I must go up to Addis Ababa and try to get permission to start again, but I had little hope of succeeding. To save time, I determined to cut straight across the desert to Afdam instead of returning by the longer route we had come by. That evening my men, led by Kassimi, came to my tent and expressed regret that we had been recalled, which I felt was the genuine sentiment of most of them.

Next morning while we were loading, Omar brought a young but responsible-looking man over to me who had just arrived from Asba Tafari. His name was Ali Wali and he was the nephew and adopted son of Miriam Muhammad, the Hangadaala or spiritual head of Bahdu. He and his uncle had visited the Governor in Asba Tafari and there they had been detained as hostages for the good behaviour of the Asaimara; his uncle's refusal to guarantee my safety in Bahdu had led to my recall. I was impressed by Ali Wali and told him I hoped to get permission to return. Omar expressed anxiety that we might be attacked as we withdrew from Bahdu, but Ali Wali guaranteed our safety.

Two days later we arrived at a well in the dry water-course of the Mullu river. During the morning we had passed the remains of an Adoimara village which the Asaimara had obliterated a month earlier, killing sixty-one people, including women and children. The background was that these Asaimara had sent seven old men to the village to discuss a long-standing pasture dispute. The Adoimara had feasted the deputation and then, while they slept, had killed them all except one, who escaped with a shattered arm and numerous wounds.

We reached Afdam Station on 19 December, four days after leaving Bahdu, and from there I went up next day by train to Addis Ababa.

CHAPTER 11

Bahdu
and the Awash River

I WAS IN Addis Ababa for a month. Shortly after my arrival Sir Sydney Barton returned from leave, which was fortunate for me: he had approved my plans and obtained the initial permission for me to undertake the journey and now his persistence eventually obtained the permission for me to resume it. He insisted that Dr Martin, Governor of Chercher Province, should be summoned to Addis Ababa from Asba Tafari to discuss the matter.

Dr Martin was an Abyssinian who had led an extraordinary life. As a small boy he had attached himself to an officer on the Magdala Expedition as it returned to the coast in 1868. The officer took him to India, educated him and gave him a medical training. Martin served for a time as a doctor in northern Burma before eventually returning to his homeland, where his European background made him easier than most Abyssinian officials for foreigners to deal with.

At a meeting with Dr Martin, Sir Sidney pressed for me to be allowed to resume my journey; he also suggested that my escort should be increased but I opposed this, still sure that too large a force would risk provoking hostility. Dr Martin eventually agreed to sanction my return, but insisted that I first gave him the following letter:

> 20 January 1934
> Addis Ababa
>
> Dear Martin
>
> With reference to the permission given to me by the Ethiopian Government to travel along the Awash river to the place where it disappears in the Aussa Sultanate, I agree that the provision of an escort of fifteen men, to accompany me and remain with me until I return to the Awash Station or leave Ethiopian territory at the French frontier in Aussa together with letters recommending me to the tribal chiefs *en-route*, will constitute a discharge of the Ethio-

128

pian Government's responsibility for taking reasonable measures
to ensure my safety on my expedition.

Yours sincerely,
Wilfred Thesiger

His Excellency Dr Martin
Governor of Chercher Province
at Addis Ababa

I returned to Afdam on 22 January and was given a great reception
by my men, who performed a war dance in the evening. I was
impressed with how Omar had kept control and not let them get
demoralized, though nearly all, including Omar, had suffered badly
from malaria and some were still unfit. Unfortunately these
included Habta Mariam; he now looked so desperately frail that
despite his protests I sent him back to Addis Ababa. I engaged a
Galla called Adam who declared he could cook; he soon proved he
couldn't and Birru took over. Ahmad, the head camelman, was still
very feverish, so I paid him off and promoted in his place Badi, the
most reliable of the other camelmen. On Omar's advice I changed
two of the other six; he had already dismissed Muhammad Dankali
for making trouble. But most of the old guard, including Kassimi,
Goutama, Abdullahi, Birru and the two Saids, were still with me.

Ali Wali had turned up at Afdam from Bahdu while I was in Addis
Ababa, and Omar, realizing how useful he might be, had looked
after him. Ali Wali now suggested that I should ask Dr Martin to
release his uncle, Miriam Muhammad, who was still in detention at
Asba Tafari; he maintained that his uncle's return with us to Bahdu
would ensure us a friendly reception. I telephoned Martin, who
agreed to this. Martin also told me he was sending another important Danakil headman called Ahamado with our soldiers; both
Ahamado and Ali Wali had orders to accompany me to Aussa.

The escort were due to arrive on 1 February but, not unexpectedly, did not do so until the 5th and then without their camels.
Meanwhile Miriam Muhammad arrived with a dozen retainers. He
was an elderly, sparsely built man, rather smaller than most
Danakil. I noticed that he commanded great respect both among his
followers and the local tribesmen. Having expected to be detained
indefinitely at Asba Tafari, he came to my tent soon after his arrival
and solemnly and impressively blessed me for securing his release. I
liked and trusted him on sight, and agreed with Omar that we
should now be in good hands when we returned to Bahdu.

Our rations being almost exhausted I ordered thirteen sacks of maize flour, seven of *taff* flour, two of rice, as well as two sacks of barley for the four riding mules, to be sent by train from Addis Ababa, and bought locally a large tin of ghee. Omar reckoned this would suffice for our twenty-four men until we reached Aussa. On his advice I also bought a large sack of coffee beans as a present for the Sultan. By now our camels were well rested and in good condition, but to lighten their loads I bought an extra camel.

During the days I spent at Afdam I was never bored. I had trained an intelligent young Somali, Abdi, to skin birds, in place of the unsatisfactory Yusuf German, who had run away to avoid returning to Bahdu, and between us we collected many birds round the camp, and a number of small rodents.

During the mornings or afternoons I hunted for greater kudu round Mount Afdub, where I had shot a fine specimen in 1930. I was never sure whether I preferred to hunt in the freshness of the dawn, with the sun just lighting the hills and all around us the varied songs of awakening birds, or in the evening when the shadows lengthened and wildlife was on the move after the heat of the day; but I was content at any time to follow Abdullahi through the stillness of the bush, absorbed by a primitive zest for hunting.

When my escort eventually arrived by train from Asba Tafari I was not impressed. All but one were new. They were ill-equipped, and had brought inadequate rations and no waterskins; the latter I bought for them. More seriously, they were short of ammunition: some had only fifteen rounds. Ato Shona, their commander, struck me as ineffective, as indeed he proved to be; from the start he was overawed by one of his soldiers, a large, aggressive ex-slave who was to cause trouble. Their camels arrived two days later with two more armed men, which made them seventeen in all. With them was Ahamado, the Danakil headman who was to accompany me to Aussa, a thick-set, middle-aged, uncommunicative man.

We left Afdam on 8 February and camped next day at the waterholes in the dry bed of the Mullu river; as one of the women accompanying Miriam Muhammad was feverish, we remained there the following day. I had camped here in December. Then I had sat in my tent, too depressed to take an interest in anything. It was the same camp site, dusty and swarming with flies; but now I was happy to collect birds with Abdi, or watch the Danakil watering their animals at the ten-foot wells.

From the Mullu we marched for eight and a half hours across a stony plain dotted with occasional thorn bushes. Mount Afdub dropped behind and the great cone of Ayelu, the sacred mountain, once more dominated the landscape. Another march and we arrived in Bahdu, camping near the village from which we had turned back on 15 December. Everything had turned out for the best; now, under the aegis of Miriam Muhammad, we had a far better chance than we would have had in December of reaching Aussa and being received by the Sultan.

The day after our arrival in Bahdu the Asaimara performed a special ceremony to celebrate the return of their Hangadaala. Some twenty men formed up shoulder to shoulder; then, chanting in time to the clapping of their hands, they invoked a *janili* or soothsayer, who was seated nearby. He rose and entered the circle, where he stood on a sheepskin, covered to the eyes with a cloth. The chanting grew louder, the clapping faster, but none moved their feet although all bent further and further forward. Suddenly the *janili* spoke. The others immediately straightened and listened, then chanted back his words. In turn they asked questions, and everyone listened intently to the answers, for they had an implicit belief in his power of divination.

I watched this ceremony on three occasions, the most impressive under a full moon, when the *janili* was a woman. Among the Danakil a *janili* appeared to have no special standing, but was merely an individual with the gift of prophecy. Twelve years later in southern Arabia I watched a rather similar performance when the soothsayer was a young man unexpectedly possessed by a *zar*.

I found Ali Wali cooperative, ready to volunteer any information he thought would interest me. He described, for instance, the ceremony when Miriam Muhammad had been installed as Hangadaala. Robed in a red and white cloth and anointed with ghee, he had been enthroned on a special chair and then carried for some two hundred yards towards the rising sun, and back. Once seated he might not set foot on the ground again until the ceremony was over. The right to robe the Hangadaala, as well as the right to carry the chair, was hereditary.

Earth from the summit of Ayelu was rubbed on his hands, earth from beneath a large fig tree on his feet, and clay from the bottom of the Awash river on his forehead. More ghee was poured over him. A red goat and a white goat and two bulls, one red and one white, were then led forward. Ali Wali described how the Masara clan lifted the red bull above the Hangadaala and cut its throat so that the blood ran over him. I questioned if this was possible, but Ali Wali insisted that the bull's throat was cut while it was held aloft. It must have been a small animal. Some of the Asoda then did the same to the red goat and smeared themselves with its blood. Ali Wali, as Miriam Muhammad's nearest male relative, slaughtered the white bull and the white goat. For a week the Hangadaala was prohibited from drinking water or bathing. The ceremony was followed by a feast with great quantities of meat and milk, and the Danakil delicacy of milk mixed with ghee and spiced with red pepper.

The Hangadaala was credited with the power of making rain, and Ali Wali told me it had rained on the day of his uncle's installation. Among other duties, the Hangadaala presided over the annual sacrifice on Mount Ayelu, governed tribal movements in search of grazing and authorized large-scale raids, which were, however, commanded by a recognized war leader.

Accompanied by Ali Wali and several of my men, I climbed Mount Ayelu, setting off at dawn up a rough track over crumbling lava partly concealed by dried grass. I saw a few oryx on the lower slopes and three great kudu cows among some isolated acacia near the summit. On the very top of the mountain, which we reached after five strenuous hours, I found a rectangular enclosure, twenty yards long by ten across; the two-foot walls had largely tumbled down. Ali Wali informed me that as soon as the rains were over, Danakil from as far as Aussa made the pilgrimage to the summit of this mountain, where they sacrificed sheep inside the enclosure and prayed for good health, prosperity, an increase of their herds and success in war. He said there was another sacred mountain in the north-west of Aussa to which the Danakil also made a pilgrimage.

We remained in Bahdu for a fortnight, moving a short distance downstream every two or three days and usually camping under another clump of fig trees on the steep river bank. The country was populous, the villages, though small, being numerous. The circular huts were made of matting fastened over a framework of sticks; a whole settlement could easily be pulled down and transferred elsewhere, as was done during the rains when everyone moved up on to the slopes of Ayelu.

I was more than ever impressed by the fertility of Bahdu. The cattle, sheep and goats, and the horses used for raiding, seemed even more numerous than I had realized on my first visit; the pastures, interspersed with patches of open water carpeted with white water lilies, even more luxuriant.

The Danakil crowded round our camp throughout the day; we found it impossible to keep them out. I could only secure some privacy inside my tent, and even there they constantly pushed their heads in to look at me. Though frequently exasperated, I accepted this harassment as the price I paid to be there. The women kept apart in small groups but did not object when I approached and photographed them; they continued to behave naturally, none appearing shy, coy or embarrassed. In general, they had delicate features and some of the elderly women looked remarkably distinguished, but it was the younger ones who fascinated me. Many of them were really lovely, with surprisingly gentle expressions. They wore long skirts, dyed brown with the bark of acacia, and all were naked above the waist. Though unattractive in the old, this semi-nudity revealed the supple beauty of the young bodies. They all wore necklaces of coloured beads, very effective against their dark skins. Married women covered their heads with a shiny black cloth called *shash*.

According to Ali Wali, adultery was not a serious offence. The injured husband would lead the offender, bound round the neck with a woman's *shash*, before the headman, who would sentence him to a fine or, for repeated offences, to a ducking in the river. In that case the culprit was tied up, thrown into a pool and only pulled out when half-drowned: he must have felt he was being offered to the crocodiles. On the other hand, to beget a child on an unmarried girl was a serious crime: the offender became an outcast and if the girl died in childbirth he was killed: the child was always buried alive. I once passed a heap of stones where such a child had been buried. Each Danakil with me threw a stone on the pile, exclaiming, 'Hass! Hass!' In one notorious case the child had been the offspring of a brother and sister.

Among the Danakil it was customary for a man to marry his father's sister's daughter or, in default, his father's brother's daughter. This interbreeding appeared to have no ill effects, possibly because only the healthy survived childhood. Among the Asaimara, a girl might be given temporarily to someone else if her intended husband was too young to marry; when the marriage eventually took place the temporary incumbent paid the husband a number of cows for every child he had fathered.

One evening Ali Wali described a marriage he had witnessed among the Adoimara near the coast. The suitor paid three Maria Theresa dollars to the girl's father, who then told him where the girl was herding sheep. He went there. She, forewarned, had collected her girlfriends and had taken up a position on a hill-top where they defended her with sticks and stones. The man, bruised and cut, eventually carried her off to his hut where he kept her for seven days before he allowed her to return to her father. The suitor was then told to bring a camel, and word went round that so-and-so's daughter had received a camel. This camel had to be rutting, otherwise they believed any children of the marriage would be feeble and useless.

A crowd collected, and the girl, dressed in all her finery, was roped on to the camel's back and led three times round her father's hut; since the rutting camel was almost uncontrollable, the girl was much shaken. She was next laid on a decorated mat and swung to and fro by four women, who sang while they swung her. Then, covered up so that no one could see her face, she was taken by two women to a hut some distance from the village, in the direction of the rising sun, where she remained secluded with her husband for seven more days, while the young men danced and feasted outside. She then returned to her father's house from which she was finally fetched by her husband a few days later.

Each evening while I was in Bahdu I went for a stroll along the river, accompanied by a number of tribesmen. There was no game here but crocodiles were very common. I disliked these malevolent-looking reptiles and used them as targets, to impress the Danakil with my marksmanship. It never occurred to me that within fifty years crocodiles would be facing extinction over much of Africa.

At one camp my companions were particularly anxious for me to shoot a crocodile that had taken several people. There was no sign of it until someone made a sort of barking noise. Then a large crocodile appeared, swimming towards us across the river, and I shot it. It was about twelve feet long. Everyone was pleased, convinced that this was the culprit. These crocodiles lived largely on the catfish that abounded in the river: several times I saw a crocodile crawl up on to a sandbank to eat its catch.

Hippo were numerous in the river, still more so in the lagoons, in one of which I counted thirty-four. The Danakil dragged one, which I had shot the previous day and which had now floated to the surface, on to the bank. There they cut it up and went off with the meat. My Somalis, more conventional in their religious observance, disapproved, since the animal had not had its throat cut while still alive. To have done so, I suggested, would have presented a problem.

The night before we reached Miriam Muhammad's village of Gawani, the old man walked out of Omar's tent where he slept, and fell off the bank into a deep pool. Fortunately the sentries heard the splash and hauled him out. Had he been taken by a crocodile, his unaccountable disappearance while in our camp would have been catastrophic for us.

We camped close to Gawani and stayed there for four days. Ever since we had arrived in Bahdu we had been provided with sheep and skins full of milk by the village headmen. Miriam Muhammad now gave us nine sheep, and next day twelve more. This enabled me to reduce the flour ration, though some of the Somalis grumbled: Omar dealt with them. My Abyssinians never complained, but were cheerful and hard-working and showed no apparent fear of the Danakil. The Abyssinian soldiers, on the other hand, were windy and quarrelsome. The ex-slave was the troublemaker, refusing to take his turn as sentry when Ato Shona told him to do so. With the approval of the other soldiers I threatened to flog him unless he mended his ways: after that he gave us less trouble.

At Gawani a young chief called Hamdo Ouga visited our camp. He looked about eighteen, with a ready, friendly smile and considerable charm. His father, a renowned warrior and influential chief, had died a month or two earlier. Some of the tribe had objected to Hamdo Ouga succeeding him, since he had killed only one man: to win his spurs, Hamdo Ouga had gone down to Issa territory with some friends. He had just returned, with four trophies; no one any longer questioned his right to be chief. He now sported a wooden comb in his hair, which was liberally dressed with ghee, and five leather thongs dangled from his dagger. He struck me as the Danakil equivalent of a nice, rather self-conscious Etonian who had just won his school colours for cricket. When we arrived, his village was celebrating his achievement and he brought us over a quantity of roasted meat and a present of seven sheep. While we were at Gawani he spent a lot of time in our camp, and became a general favourite.

Miriam Muhammad accompanied us when we left his village. Beyond here the grass plain gave place to an extensive swamp bordered by an acacia forest, flooded during a part of the year. It had evidently been raining in the highlands, for the Awash was thick with mud and dotted with floating water cabbages displaced by the rising water. We spent the night at Kadabahdu, the village of Ahamado of the Bogale, a heavily built, unprepossessing man with unusually coarse features for a Danakil. He was related by marriage to the Sultan of Aussa and had considerable influence, his father having been the previous Hangadaala. It was customary for the chiefs of the Bogale and of the Ashura, two sections of the Madima tribe, to succeed alternately in this capacity. Miriam Muhammad belonged to the Ashura. Ahamado was obviously jealous of Ali Wali and tried to prejudice Omar against him. I took a strong dislike to the man and was glad when we left his village, although our next camp was on a shallow pool churned to liquid manure by the large numbers of cattle watering there. Even disguised as tea it tasted singularly unpleasant.

We reached the Asassibabifero hills on 24 February. This sandstone range was fantastically streaked with mauve, orange, brick red, yellow and white. There were many small villages on its western slopes, all of them surrounded by stone walls, while the various defiles were defended by crude breastworks, for these hills formed the border between the Asaimara of Bahdu and the Adoimara of Borharamala.

That evening we heard that Hamdo Ouga had been killed two days before, resisting an Adoimara raid from across the Awash. His death made me realize how precarious were the lives of these Danakil. Yet they were a cheerful, happy people, despite this incessant killing, and certainly were not affected by the boredom which weighs so heavily today on our urban civilization, driving many of the young to join the equivalent of tribal groups and to take part in versions of tribal warfare, which manifests itself as hooliganism at football matches.

Miriam Muhammad went back to Gawani the next day. I had grown attached to the old man and was sorry to see him leave. He had always been cheerful and friendly and had helped us in many ways; to ensure our safety he had slept each night in our camp rather than with his retainers. Omar told me that Miriam Muhammad had repeatedly assured his tribesman that I was their friend and that I had spoken well of them to the Government in Addis Ababa. Before leaving, he urged us to be on the alert, saying the border country ahead was particularly dangerous. The soldiers then declared they would go no further unless he went with us. I told them that in that case they could find their own way back to Afdam – and that was the end of that. Ali Wali and Ahamado were accompanying us to Aussa. I had confidence in Ali Wali, but ever since the start of the journey Ahamado had remained enigmatic, silent and unforthcoming.

For the next nine days we followed the Awash; here thick forest often made it difficult to camp on the river bank. We did short marches and on three occasions spent a day in camp, for I was in no particular hurry, and was anxious to collect birds in the forest. When we had left Asassibabifero we still had twenty sheep from the presents given to us; now, to vary my diet, I shot guineafowl and sandgrouse, both of which were plentiful.

At first the Danakil in Borharamala kept away from our camp, though they stole one of the soldiers' camels and tried to make off with one of mine, abandoning it only when the camelmen opened fire. Following Miriam Muhammad's advice, we kept well closed up on the march, the rear guard always blowing a trumpet if a camel had to be reloaded. Eventually Ali Wali made contact with the local Adoimara and told them I would treat any who were sick. I had doctored many in Bahdu, most of them with fever, infected eyes, or wounds, some of which, inflicted by the large lead bullets of the Fusil Gras, were appalling. I found many suffered from deep, suppurating ulcers, which I now think may have been caused by *bajal*, an infectious, non-venereal syphilis.

Eventually, a series of ravines forced us to leave the river and enter the desert to the east, known to the Danakil as Adou or 'the place of thirst'; here low gravel hills were sparsely covered with 'wait-a-bit' thorn. Five days later we rejoined the Awash at Abakaboro. We had in fact camped by wells every day except one. Most of them were about ten feet deep, the water in them clear and sweet, pleasant to drink after the muddy Awash. At the last of these wells

137

we encountered a caravan of thirty camels carrying salt from beyond Aussa, to trade in the highlands of Abyssinia. The bars of salt, wrapped in matting, were two feet long and four inches across.

At Abakaboro we camped under trees beside the river, an agreeably green spot in a desolation of black hills devoid of any apparent vegetation. The steep hills opposite our camp were fortified with breastworks. It was here, four years earlier, that a large band of Wagerat had destroyed a force sent against them by the Sultan of Aussa. The Wagerat were Galla and lived far off in Tigre on the edge of the escarpment. They were formidable fighters and made constant raids on the lowland tribes; one of their raids had penetrated as far as the railway line near the frontier of French Somaliland. We were told that some of them were even now raiding the Adoimara to the north of us; but they made off before we got down there.

From our camp we could see a high range of mountains called Magenta some thirty miles to the north-east. Beyond it was Aussa. I decided to send Ali Wali and two other Danakil to the Sultan with the Government letter and await their return at Abakaboro. Ahamado refused to go with them, saying he was involved in a feud with the local Adoimara. I noticed he never left our camp.

The only snag to this camp was the mosquitoes that swarmed out of the sedges along the river as it grew dark. I was giving everyone ten grains of quinine daily and we had had no further cases of malaria after leaving Afdam. The only game animals here were a few small gazelle, which at first I could not identify and hoped might be a new species. I shot several and, with the help of Lydaker's *Game Animals of Africa*, finally identified them by their curious inflatable noses as Speke's gazelle. I enquired about other animals, especially zebra, which existed on the plains south of Bahdu where I had found their tracks. No one here had ever seen or heard of them. They told me, however, that there were wild ass at some hot springs called Teho. At Teho, about twelve miles away, were some small pools of boiling water and patches of bubbling mud. On the way there we saw six wild ass, well proportioned animals, alert and fast-moving, with little resemblance to domestic donkeys.

We got back to Abakaboro after dark. Omar told me that three Danakil had come to inspect the camp and had asked Ahamado a lot of questions, especially whether we had a machine-gun with us. They had left just before sunset. Omar thought they had been sent by the Sultan to look us over.

Next day Ali Wali returned from Aussa; he had been away for eight days. He had seen the Sultan and spent the greater part of a day with him, during which time the Sultan had questioned him at length about my motives for making this journey. He had told Ali Wali that seven years earlier he had met three Europeans at Gallefage on the edge of Aussa and given them permission to continue their journey across the desert to the north; but he had then requested the Abyssinian Government never to authorize any other Europeans to visit his land. He said he would only permit me to skirt Aussa on the south on my way to French territory. Ali Wali had finally persuaded him to allow me to follow the Awash as far as Gallefage, but the Sultan insisted that in no circumstance would he allow me to enter Aussa itself.

I knew that the Sultan, like his father before him, feared and detested all Europeans, whom in any case he regarded as infidels. Sixty years earlier Munzinger's Egyptian army had been wiped out on the borders of Aussa; since then the French and the Italians had occupied all the arid coastline. Not unnaturally, the Sultan suspected the Europeans of having designs on his Sultanate, designs which he believed would be strengthened if he let them observe its fertility. His fears were to be realized two years later when the Italians, making use of information provided by Nesbitt and his two Italian companions, invaded Aussa during their war with Abyssinia.

Next day soon after sunrise we left Abakaboro and travelled for five tedious hours across a dust-blown plain devoid of vegetation. Even though it was overcast, the glare was trying. Parallel with our march we could just discern a line of trees that marked the course of the river. Once we were deceived by a mirage; we saw them frequently but this one was extraordinarily realistic, exactly like a small lake with trees reflected in the water. The only living things we saw were five ostriches, which made off with their high-stepping gait.

We eventually camped close to a Danakil village beside the river. It consisted of cramped shelters built with stacked tree trunks, affording an interesting contrast to three *das*, memorial monuments, that we had passed on the bare earthern plain. These had been neatly constructed with logs brought from a distance of several miles, and were the only *das* I saw not built with stones. A *das* would be erected by the tribe or family in a conspicuous spot, generally beside a well-used track, to commemorate a famous man. The site usually bore no relation to where he had died or been buried: what mattered was for as many people as possible to see it.

All the other *das* I saw were circular. They varied from a ring of stones ten or fifteen feet in diameter, with two piles of stones marking the entrance, to meticulously constructed stone circles five feet high and fifteen across, decorated with turrets. The walls of these were usually built with stone blocks carefully fitted to present a smooth surface. A line of upright stones was placed before the entrance, the first denoting the man himself, the others the men he had killed; a stone laid flat would represent a lion or elephant. Two or more brothers, or famous warriors killed in the same fight, might be commemorated by the same *das*, but each would have a separate entrance and line of stones denoting his kills. There were also family monuments, with each successive *das* linked to the original.

A *das* would be built a month or even a year after the celebrity had died. Cattle were then slaughtered and their meat was placed on a stone platform inside the *das* before being cooked on piles of heated stones. Two hundred and twenty cows had been butchered to commemorate the previous Hangadaala of Bahdu.

On this last stage of our journey to Aussa we were again in Asaimara territory, and on the next morning we had travelled only a short distance when we met two elderly men sent by the Sultan.

They said they had come fast and far and were weary, and they pressed us to camp nearby, which we did in a pleasant shady spot beside some rapids, the only ones I saw on the Awash. One of the envoys carried a staff decorated with silver bands. It was a renowned emblem, and irrefutable proof that we were under the Sultan's protection; with it in our camp we no longer ran the risk of casual murder by trophy-hunting Danakil. The two of them now tried to convince me that the only practicable route to French Somaliland lay south of Aussa through the Galatu Pass: they maintained that loaded camels would never be able to follow the river. I insisted, however, on going to Gallefage, and the discussion, eased by many cups of tea and a box of sweet biscuits, remained amicable.

Our route now lay on the other side of the Awash, but at dawn with no warning the river came down in a six-foot wall of water, almost drowning one of the Somalis saying his morning prayers under the bank. When the flood subsided we crossed the river amid the roars of protesting camels. Two loads got soaked but luckily they contained tents and bedding and not our dwindling rations, nor my collection of bird skins.

For the next three days we followed the river northwards towards Tendaho through a desolate region of black rocks. The track was relatively easy but the heat off the rocks was considerable. A sick camel finally collapsed, and I had to shoot it. In the morning of 23 March we reached Tendaho where the river passed through a defile before turning abruptly south-east towards Aussa. The sun-scorched hills on either side of the gorge were fortified with breast-works built by Ras Yemer, Negus Mikael's redoubtable general; he had routed the Wagerat, subjected the local Danakil and even come to terms with the Sultan of Aussa.

When that Sultan had died, his sons fought among themselves until Yaio mastered the others. Yaio then attacked Ras Yemer's troops at Tendaho and inflicted heavy casualties, but was eventually betrayed, captured, taken to Dessie, and later banished to Jimma. There he remained until the Government reinstated him in Aussa, and it was his son, Mohammed Yaio, who now ruled as Sultan.

Beyond Tendaho we camped on the edge of the Kurub plain, which, shimmering with mirages, stretched northwards to the horizon. To the south was the barren Magenta range; to the east I could vaguely discern another range, but heat haze, blown sand and dust largely obscured the view. Luckily the weather was overcast; otherwise it would have been extremely hot.

Nesbitt, after escaping from Bahdu, had eventually rejoined the Awash near Tendaho, and had then met the Sultan at Gallefage, where I hoped to arrive next day. We expected a long march and started before sunrise, but after an hour or two a local headman stopped us, with orders from the Sultan to camp there. I had hoped to buy provisions that day at Gallefage, for the soldiers' rations were now finished and ours were low, and there was nothing to shoot here. I spoke to the bearer of the silver staff and he ordered the headman to produce an ox and three goats. Typically, the soldiers grumbled that they wanted flour, not meat.

Next day we followed the edge of a forest which bordered the river. Ahead of us was the massif of Kulzikuma, its base and the range behind it partly obscured by smoke from an extensive grass fire; north of us was flat, empty desert. After five hours we turned aside into the forest to camp. The trees were large and the grass was green: it was an idyllic spot.

Goutama and Birru cut a gap through the bushes in front of my tent which gave me an outlook down the river. There I sat contentedly, watching the vervet monkeys playing at the water's edge and kingfishers flashing by, and I was more than happy to remain there next day, the Id al Adha, the Muslim festival of sacrifice marking the culmination of the pilgrimage to Mecca.

The Somalis put on their best clothes and the Danakil, many of whom had assembled, fired rifles in celebration. The Danakil asked Omar to lead the midday prayers, which pleased him greatly: they also presented my Muslims with an ox for the feast.

In the afternoon they played a game called *kossa*. Someone would throw a hard leather ball into the crowd, whereupon everyone would struggle to get hold of it and escape far enough to bounce it and catch it on the back of his hand, his pursuers uttering loud, trilling cries. The game was rough but good-natured, and the movement of the players' bodies was graceful. Some boys played a similar game but were careful to keep out of the way of their elders. Meanwhile women danced on the edge of the clearing; facing each other in two rows, they jumped up and down together, clapped their hands and sang a monotonous song; this went on for hours and was extraordinarily dull to watch.

From here I sent one of the Sultan's envoys to his residence at Furzi to convey my respects and announce my arrival at Gallefage – which turned out to be not a specific place but the general name for the area. The Sultan sent the man straight back to announce that his *wazir* and another important official would arrive the following day with presents at my camp.

However, it was nearly sunset next day and I had given up expecting the *wazir*, and was looking for crocodiles near the camp, when he arrived on a fine mule, with thirty men; some of these were driving three bulls and six sheep ahead of him, while the others marched in two ranks behind him. His bodyguard looked impressive; all had rifles, full bandoliers and the customary daggers; their loincloths and the cloths draped over their shoulders were spotlessly white. The *wazir*, whose name was Yaio, was a close relation of the Sultan and second to him in importance in Aussa. The Abyssinian Government had given him the rank of Kenyazmatch while the Sultan was a Dedjazmatch.

After we had drunk tea we inspected the bulls and sheep the Sultan had sent. Yaio then said he and his men would sleep in a nearby village and return next day to take me towards Furzi. He suggested we should leave in the afternoon, which would give us the morning to slaughter and cook some of the animals. He knew we had been short of food, he said, adding with a smile that we deserved a feast after our long journey. He was a middle-aged, sparsely built man with a frank, open face and very observant eyes, and I took to him at once.

That night hyenas, drawn by the smell of blood, whooped and chuckled round the camp where the Abyssinians and Somalis, in their separate groups, replenished the fires, roasted great chunks of meat, and chattered till nearly dawn.

When I went to my tent Omar said, 'I think Yaio will help us; he seems friendly. Now, God willing, the Sultan will allow us to travel through Aussa.'

CHAPTER 12

Exploration
in the Aussa Sultanate

T HE NEXT MORNING I had a discussion with Yaio, and indeed
found him friendly and easy to talk to. He told me that the
Sultan had been well informed of my movements ever since I
had left the Awash Station in November, and assured me I had
acquired a good name in Bahdu and elsewhere.

On the other hand he was very bitter about the French from
French Somaliland who, he declared, had recently appropriated
part of their land. I had heard in Addis Ababa that there had been a
confrontation with the Sultan's forces when French troops had
moved into hitherto unoccupied territory, claiming it was on their
side of the frontier; shortly after this, they had inflicted heavy losses
on a raiding party from Bahdu. These two incidents had augmented
the hatred and resentment which the Sultan and his people felt for
them. Unfortunately, the Danakil in general made no distinction
between the French and other Europeans; Yaio also mentioned that
a fortnight previously the Issa had murdered a German who was
working for the Abyssinian Government on the French Somali
frontier, not far from the railway.

We travelled only five miles that afternoon before camping under
a rocky hill covered with *waidellas*, the tumuli in which the Danakil
entomb their dead. South of Tendaho, the *waidellas* had consisted of
mounds of stones piled over the corpse chambers; there were many
of these grave mounds which, placed deliberately in prominent
positions, were a conspicuous feature of the countryside. In Aussa,
the *waidellas* were especially numerous and noticeable, and were far
more elaborate and of varying design. In some, there was a smooth,
circular platform some three and a half feet in height, instead of the
original mound. In others, a cone, three to four feet high, was
erected on the platform; this I think derived from the slab of rock
often placed over a grave mound to scare away hyenas. A man who
had avenged the killing of his brother signified this by setting up

two stones on the *waidella*: I saw such stones decorating the tops of several cones. Women and children were also buried in *waidellas*, and the same *waidella* might be used again and again.

Next day, 29 March, we went a further six miles downriver and camped at a place called Gurumudli in a forest clearing where the ground was carpeted with a clover-like vegetation with a heavy scent: it gave me pleasure to watch the camels and the four mules gorging themselves on it. In the late afternoon a messenger arrived to inform me that the Amoita was on his way to visit me.

We prepared camp to receive him and, as the sun set, we heard the sound of distant trumpets. The soldiers and my men had turne'd out to form a guard of honour when a second messenger ran up. He gave me to understand that the Amoita had too many men with him to enter my camp; instead he invited me to meet him nearby. I left two men in camp and, with Omar, Yaio and all the others, followed the messenger into the forest.

The brief twilight was almost gone but a full moon had risen, affording an uncertain light among the trees. We had gone some distance, further than I had expected, when I sensed rather than saw that the forest on either side of the track was alive with people. A little further and we emerged into a large clearing. With a shock, I saw some four hundred armed men drawn up in a line, motionless and silent, their loincloths very white in the moonlight against the dark forest background. In front of them the Sultan was seated on a chair, his household slaves grouped behind him, all with rifles in crimson silk covers.

He rose to greet me. My men bowed low and, except for Omar, withdrew; the Sultan then ordered everyone else other than Yaio and Talahun, his own interpreter, out of earshot. He looked round repeatedly to make sure no one had approached and two or three times waved away groups already at a distance. Omar had had the forethought to bring a chair for me; I should have been at a disadvantage standing.

The Sultan was bare-headed and dressed entirely in white, in narrow Abyssinian-type trousers, long shirt and finely woven *shamma*. He wore a superb, silver-mounted dagger, which had probably belonged to his father or grandfather, and held a black, silver-topped stick. Though he was darker, he reminded me at once

145

of Haile Selassie: like him he was small and gracefully built, with a bearded oval face, finely moulded features and shapely hands. His expression was sensitive and proud. I was aware that his authority was absolute, that his slightest word was law. I was certain that he could be ruthless, having heard tales of his appalling prison – men said it was better to be dead than shut up there; yet he gave me no impression of wilful cruelty.

As I looked round the clearing at the ranks of squatting warriors and the small isolated group of my own men, I knew that this moonlight meeting in unknown Africa with a savage potentate who hated Europeans was the realization of my boyhood dreams. I had come here in search of adventure: the mapping, the collecting of animals and birds were all incidental. The knowledge that somewhere in this neighbourhood three previous expeditions had been exterminated, that we were far beyond any hope of assistance, that even our whereabouts were unknown, I found wholly satisfying.

The Sultan made the customary enquiries about my health, speaking in Arabic to Omar who translated to me. He then asked at some length about my journey, the route I had followed, how long it had taken me and whom I had met, mentioning several names. I realized he knew the answers to these questions. There were frequent pauses during which he eyed me intently, stroking his beard and fingering his prayer beads. The night was very still, despite the large number of men gathered around us; if they spoke at all it must have been in whispers. I remember hearing a hyena howl in the distance, probably near our camp, and the purring of nightjars as they flew overhead.

The Sultan finally asked me where I wished to go. I told him. There was another long pause while he appeared to ponder, then he said abruptly that we would meet again in the morning in the same place. Yaio and a large number of Danakil escorted me back to my camp, where Yaio pointed out twelve large skins of milk and two of clarified butter, further presents from the Sultan.

Omar seemed to think things had gone well: I hoped so. Everything, even our survival, depended on the impression I had created.

In the morning I sent Omar and some of my men with an open-sided tent, chairs and a carpet to make arrangements for the meeting. At nine o'clock I followed them.

146

I found the Sultan seated under a tree; his troops, possibly even more than the previous night, formed three sides of a square. I escorted him to the tent, where Omar served coffee, tea and biscuits, all of which I tasted first. Yaio refused to sit down, and he and Talahun, the interpreter, screened us with their cloths while we ate and drank. I knew that Talahun was also the Sultan's trusted adviser: unlike Yaio, he did not inspire me with confidence.

The Sultan's first question was whether I worked for the Abyssinian Government. Why, if not, was I accompanied by Government soldiers? Was I concerned with the boundary dispute with the French? Had the German who had been killed by the Issa been employed by the Government? Did I know him? Did I know the French? Why had I come to Aussa unless I was working for the Government? What was the purpose of my journey? Why should I risk my life in Bahdu just to follow a river? What reason could I have for tracing the Awash? What good could it do me to reach its end? There were animals to hunt and plenty to shoot elsewhere in Abyssinia: I should be safe there, so why come to Aussa?

At intervals he turned to Omar and questioned him, often at length, no doubt seeking confirmation of my answers. I assured him that I did not work for the Government, and had no concern with the frontier except to cross it on my way to Tajura on the coast. The Emperor was a personal friend; three years earlier he had invited me from England to his coronation and he had now sent soldiers with me to ensure my safety as far as Aussa. I was a young man who sought adventure and enjoyed travelling in little-known lands. No European knew where or how the Awash ended; I had set out to discover this. It was important to me to succeed, and I had risked my life, as he knew, to come here. If I succeeded, I told him, I should acquire renown in my own country.

Eventually he asked me what route I wished to follow to get to Tajura. I told him I had permission from the French to enter their territory north of Lake Abhe, or Abhebad, as the Danakil called it, and had been instructed to report my arrival at their fort at Dikil.

The Sultan retorted that the French frontier was far away and that he knew of no lake called Abhebad. He now sent Yaio ostensibly to make enquiries; when Yaio came back he confirmed that no one had heard of Abhebad. The Sultan said he would make further enquiries about this; but he did at least agree to send me to Tajura.

I then produced the sack of coffee beans, which was too heavy for one man to carry, and four large pots of sweet jelly. I said I was ashamed to give him such insignificant presents after all his kindness, but I was far from my country. I tasted each pot of jelly and I spilt one. The Sultan said this signified good luck. Until then, he had taken only a sip of coffee; now he drank two cups and finished the biscuits. Yaio, Talahun and Omar then drank the tea. Four bulls were then driven past before being taken to my camp.

The Sultan now bade me farewell and moved off, surrounded by his soldiers. These were an impressive body of men, all armed with modern rifles and many wearing the decorations that signified prowess as warriors.

Awaiting me in camp was one of the Sultan's slaves, whom he had asked me to treat because he had been bitten on the finger by a snake and his whole arm was swollen and suppurating. This slave, it turned out, had been with Lij Yasu when the latter had taken refuge in Danakil country in 1916 after Negus Mikael's defeat at Sagale. He was one of many who now came to me for medicine. I did what I could and wished I could have done more, since they had pathetic faith in my power to cure even hopeless cases. I remember in particular one living skeleton who was carried into the camp and laid before my tent.

In the afternoon the Sultan sent for Omar, Ato Shona, Ali Wali and Ahamado. Though his residence at Furzi was nearby in the open country across the Awash, he met them in the forest on the near side of the river. He had no intention that Omar or Ato Shona should see Furzi, mistrusting them as much as he did me. He kept them a long time and asked many searching questions to confirm what I had told him, evidently still suspecting that I worked for the Abyssinian Government. However, when Yaio visited me in the evening, he told me that the Sultan had given permission for me to follow the Awash to its end, which was a lake not far away.

I discussed with Yaio what route to take after reaching the river's end. He pressed me to go directly to Tajura on the coast. However, the French authorities in Jibuti had only given me permission to cross the frontier provided I went to Dikil, and had not yet given permission to go to Tajura, though I hoped that once I reached Dikil they would do so. Yaio insisted that the route to Dikil was not feasible: Dikil was far off, with a difficult mountain to cross and with little water on the way. He reasoned that our camels were worn out and if they collapsed we should die of thirst; only small parties with fresh camels ever went that way, whereas the route to Tajura was easy, with adequate water and grazing.

The real reason, I suspected, was that the Sultan did not wish me to investigate the disputed area near Dikil. I was in his hands, but I could foresee trouble with the French if I went straight to Tajura; they were likely to be especially angered by the unauthorized passage of eighteen Abyssinian soldiers through their colony. I was also aware that these soldiers' presence might provoke hostility from the tribes across the border. Yet I could not possibly leave them in Aussa; they would never get back to Afdam on their own, especially now that they were quarrelling among themselves.

A third alternative, but one which I never seriously considered, was to cross the desert to the railway near the frontier. This would take me through the territory of the Issa, who were perpetually at war with the Danakil. We should have no guide and no means of making friendly contact with them. The Government, I was sure, had provided the German with guides and with what they considered an adequate escort, but this had not saved him from the Issa.

We stayed another two days at Gurumudli, where I collected more birds, several of which I had not previously seen. Abdi shot a vulture which was snapped up by a crocodile as it fell in the river. The river had risen again and was now very dirty. Before we left Gurumudli the Sultan sent me two large sacks of maize, one of which I gave to the soldiers.

Since the forest immediately ahead was impassable by camels, and we were forbidden to traverse the open country across the Awash, we were taken round under Kulzikuma, a short but difficult march among piles of boulders. The ill-defined track passed between two small lakes; in the larger, called Gallefagibad, were several hippo. Near the camp I found fresh tracks of a leopard and that night sat up for it over a goat. However, all that came near was a hyena, which I drove off with a handful of gravel. The mosquitoes were appalling.

In the morning Yaio, Abdullahi and I climbed to one of the summits above the smaller lake, and from there I looked out over a luxuriant plain, roughly square and about twenty miles across, ringed by barren mountains. I was thrilled, for as far as I knew no other European had as yet seen this legendary land. It was Aussa, heartland of the Sultan's domain. Below me I could see where the Awash, bordered by the thick forest where I had met the Sultan, entered through a gap between the Magenta and Kulzikuma mountains. The river then divided, the smaller branch bisecting Aussa while the main river bore north-east under Kulzikuma towards Goumarri, celebrated in Danakil songs as the mighty mountain that halted the Awash.

At the foot of the Goumarri precipice, the river entered Adobada or the White Water, a long narrow lake that extended southwards under this great wall of rock to the south-eastern corner of Aussa; I noted that the river appeared to emerge from the southern end of the lake and continue westwards towards a break in the mountains. The southern half of the Aussa looked like a grass-covered plain, whereas much of the northern part was under forest.

Three miles away in an extensive clearing in the forest, I could make out through my field glasses the Sultan's residence at Furzi. It appeared to comprise three large mat-roofed houses in a compound. Yaio, who spoke Amharic, some of which I remembered from my childhood, explained that during the rainy season when much of Aussa was flooded the Danakil moved with their herds into the mountains. As we had climbed this mountain, we had passed several encampments, and the sites of others. Some of these shelters were mats over a stick framework, others were built of rocks; the heat in those at midday must have been stifling.

There was a welcome stretch of grassland between the forest and the Kulzikuma range, the lower slopes of which were marked by a great many *waidellas*. Next morning we marched across this plain until the mountains closed in on the river. We forded it and then followed a well-marked track through dense forest; in occasional clearings the grass grew as high as six feet. Eventually we came to an open space where we camped. In the evening Yaio and I went out to look for bushbuck but I soon gave up, for it was almost impossible to leave the track except on hands and knees.

The following day we reached open country, with several villages and large herds of cattle which were humped, most of them black with half-moon horns sweeping backward and inward. Unlike in Bahdu, I saw no horses in Aussa. In one place we had difficulty getting the camels across a lava flow, with upthrust ridges separated by deep crevices between. Beyond it, the river flowed through beds of high, tufted reeds across an open plain. We camped near a large village by the river.

The village headman was someone of importance, who had the

present Sultan's confidence, having been a friend of his father. He entertained us royally, presenting me with two oxen, three fat sheep and three goats, and nine skins of milk mixed with ghee and red pepper. Yaio gave a skin full of ghee to Omar and another to the Abyssinian soldiers, who proceeded to have an unseemly row while dividing it up. By now they were split into three mutually hostile groups; Ato Shona had lost all control over them and slept at night in Omar's tent for safety.

We waded the river in the morning by a deep ford that gave the camels some trouble, and then crossed a treeless plain to the northern end of the Goumarri escarpment, and camped there. Several small villages nestled among the debris at the foot of the precipice. This unbroken wall of rock, some twenty miles long, was most impressive, especially when lit by the evening sun. In the morning we loaded what wood we could find and headed south for Adobada, intending to follow its western shore; but this proved impossible since the Awash flowed into the lake across an expanse of soft mud. I therefore decided instead to follow its eastern edge, only taking with me Kassimi, Abdullahi and Said Munge. Omar would find a camp site for the others on the Awash.

We started at dawn, accompanied by Yaio carrying the Sultan's staff, with two of his retainers, and taking two mules to carry food, cooking pots and blankets. We soon reached the lake. In most places the water lapped among the fallen rocks, and marks on the cliff indicated that in the past the lake had been perhaps twelve feet deeper; it must then have flooded much of Aussa. Even recently the level had fluctuated considerably. Yaio remembered a year when the Awash ran dry before it reached Gallefage; Adobada had then shrunk to two separate lakes, and the other lakes had dried up.

The water's edge was littered with the remains of catfish and marked with quantities of small white shells. Everywhere were tracks of hippo. I could hear them grunting far out in the lake but I only saw one. On the other hand I did see innumerable crocodiles, either cruising in the lake or basking on the shore, and I once inadvertently found myself between a large crocodile and the water. It rushed at me with open jaws and I wasted no time getting out of the way. The largest I saw were about twelve feet long. Yaio said they were dangerous, unusual for crocodiles in lakes with abundant fish. Some of them certainly swam purposefully towards us when we approached the water's edge.

151

It took us six hours to reach the southern end of the lake, where we stopped for the night. Yaio insisted that the Awash ended in this lake and that it had no exit. I doubted this, after what I had seen of Aussa from Kulzikuma and more especially as the lake water was fresh; so in the morning, despite his vigorous protests, I climbed a small hill to settle the question. As I expected, the Awash flowed out of Adobada; it then passed through three small lakes and entered a large swamp. I was unable to see if the river continued beyond the swamp, but I could see a suggestive-looking gap in the mountains.

I had a bathe before we started back. When I put on my shorts a scorpion inside stung me twice before I could rip them off again. We got back to the main camp next morning.

Omar had chosen a pleasant site under some trees near the Awash. While I had been away he had made discreet enquiries, and learned that the Awash flowed down to the border of the Issa country where it finally ended in a large salt lake. I therefore told Yaio I intended to take a small party down the west side of the lake to verify that the river really ended in the swamp I had seen. This made him very indignant: he said I had seen all I had asked to see, and warned me that the Danakil in Aussa were becoming restive as a result of my prolonged stay in their country. They expected me to leave next day: if I stayed longer or went off again in another direction they might well make trouble.

I had noticed that even Ali Wali was keeping away from me, not wishing to be compromised. I told Yaio, however, that I was prepared to risk trouble. Having come so far I had to reach the end of the river, otherwise my whole journey would have been in vain: I should feel ashamed to confess to my people that I had failed. The Sultan, after all his help and hospitality, would surely not thwart me now. Yaio eventually said he would send a man to the Sultan for instructions.

For the next two days while I waited for news I collected more birds with Abdi. We found several pythons in the reedbeds by the river; I shot and skinned one that measured sixteen feet. Then Talahun, the interpreter, arrived with a letter. I was given the choice of leaving at once for Tajura, or of following the river to its end with all my men, and then going straight on to Dikil.

Yaio, Talahun and others of the Sultan's people urged me to leave next day for Tajura. They assured me that they now regarded me as their friend, reiterated the difficulties of the Dikil road, and said they did not wish me to risk my life by going that way.

I was admittedly alarmed by their description of this route. However, as they would not agree to my returning here from the end of the river to take the easier Tajura road, I told them I would go to Dikil.

They went off for yet another discussion among themselves. When they came back they said that as I insisted on going to the end of the river they would take me there. They now confessed that the Awash did end in a large bitter-tasting lake called Abhebad, within a day's march of Dikil. The difficulty would be getting to Abhebad; after that the road was easy.

When I suggested travelling on the west side of Adobada, they insisted that I must follow my previous route, along its eastern shore. I agreed to this without demur, more than satisfied to have obtained permission to go to Abhebad, 'the evil-smelling lake'. It sounded like a sodium lake, which convinced me that the Awash really did end there. Yaio then went off to inform the Sultan of my decision, but promised to meet me at the far end of Adobada.

We broke camp and started next morning, 13 April, escorted by Talahun and his men. The camels found the rock-strewn lake edge hard going, so we stopped three hours later at a spring near the shore. The lake water was surprisingly dirty, whereas this spring was clean and sweet; we had not drunk the like since entering Danakil country. Personally, I would forgo any other comfort to drink clean water.

It took us two more days to reach the end of the lake, where Yaio was waiting as he had promised. He had brought with him five more oxen from the Sultan and twelve skins of milk. I felt overwhelmed by this generosity. Everywhere, in Bahdu and elsewhere, the Danakil had been lavish with gifts of meat and milk. They might be a murderously inclined race, but no one could call them inhospitable. We now had a friendly discussion about our route while in the distance a spectacular thunderstorm raged over Kulzikuma. Yaio warned me that the only way ahead was up the mountain under which we were camped, and then back down again on the same side but further on. From the top, he said, we should see Abhebad.

The following afternoon we climbed, pushing and hauling the reluctant camels until we eventually reached a plateau and found a

153

place where we could clear enough boulders for them to kneel and be unloaded. Nothing grew among these rocks but an occasional leafless thornbush, but the view was immense. Below us, far nearer than I had expected, set in a limitless waste of volcanic rock, lay a great expanse of water, sombre under threatening storm clouds.

That was where the Awash ended. I had come far and risked much to see this desolate scene, a striking contrast to the marshes, pastures and forests of Aussa. Sitting on a rock, I checked the sketch maps I had made and took more bearings on the surrounding mountains and prominent peaks; in the distance I could just discern the black hills around Tendaho.

We had difficulty in the morning getting the camels back down the mountain to the first of the three small lakes beyond Adobada. This lake, framed by green reedbeds, was vivid blue, its water crystal clear. A series of rock crests, stained white from frequent submersions and the droppings of numerous herons and darters, ran out into the lake. It was an enchanting place and I resolved to stay for a day or two. When Yaio and Talahun suggested that we resume our march in the afternoon, I insisted that we must rest the camels: the last few days had tried them sorely and Yaio himself had warned me of bad marches ahead.

Yaio, who never bore malice when we disagreed, came out with me in the evening. Before sunset great numbers of duck flew from the marshes to Abhebad and I shot several brown tree duck, a welcome change of food. I spent the following day agreeably in camp, bathing in the lake and pottering about the reedbeds. My Somalis, Abyssinians and the soldiers each slaughtered an ox. Neither the Christians nor the Muslims would eat the meat of an animal whose throat had been cut by a member of another religion: this caused difficulties when we had only one animal. Large numbers of vultures and ungainly marabou storks circled over the camp and fought clumsily for the discarded offal.

During the day three headmen with thirteen followers arrived with orders from the Sultan to escort me to Dikil: Yaio and Talahun were to return to Furzi. These headmen were nominally responsible to the Sultan for the country ahead, but Yaio warned me that the Danakil on the frontier of Aussa were savage and difficult to control. He said we should now be entering a no-man's-land between Aussa, Bahdu and the territory of Adi Faro Matal, a great Issa chief who recognized neither the Abyssinian nor the French Governments. He lived on the far side of Abhebad, and Yaio advised me to keep out of his reach.

We agreed that I should follow the course of the Awash with a few of my men, two of the headmen and some of their followers, while Omar took the rest of my caravan straight to Abhebad and waited there.

In the morning Yaio handed over the silver staff to the senior of the three headmen. I was sorry to part from Yaio, for I liked and respected him and was well aware of all that he had done for me. Without his good offices I should never have been given permission to travel in Aussa. I presented him with a rifle and assured him once again that I would never do anything to harm the Sultan or his people. He said he had realized this: it was why he had helped me.

After Yaio and Talahun had departed, I set off with Kassimi, Abdullahi, Said and such Danakil as were to accompany me, taking three mules with us. We skirted the swamp, making our way across the lava fields which had flowed down from a succession of craters on the Jira massif; in places the fissures were very deep and we spent a lot of time finding a way round them for the mules. Eventually we reached the last of the three small lakes through which the Awash flowed after leaving Adobada; we followed its shore to where the river emerged, and camped three miles downstream.

A band of baboons had scampered ahead of us into the rock-built shelters of an abandoned settlement: they appeared so much at home they might have built the place themselves. From this camp, a gap in the reeds allowed us to approach the river which was wide, deep and slow-flowing, the water very clear. Some Danakil were using a sodden raft of reeds; those who could not swim sat on it while the others pushed it across. They were as wild-looking as their cousins in Bahdu; most of them wore decorations showing the tally of men they had killed.

The day had been intensely hot; the barrel of my rifle was almost unbearable to the touch. Since we had entered Aussa my thermometers had been giving readings of between 98 and 103 degrees in the shade, but now both of them ceased to function. It was my fault for carrying them in a metal box which had got overheated in the sun. We were plagued during the night by mosquitoes and sandflies.

Next day we followed the course of the river which swung southwards round the western edge of Jira, where the reeds grew to the
edge of the lava. We stopped during the hottest hours and tried to
shelter from the sun under some rocks; when we camped we were
within a mile or two of Abhebad. In a vain attempt to get away from
the mosquitoes we chose a spot at a distance from the river. It was 20
April, twenty-three days since I had met the Sultan in Gallefage.

The Awash entered Abhebad across a wide expanse of unstable
black mud where reefs, encrusted with a hard white sediment, ran
out into the lake. The remains of many dead trees, some of them in
the lake, were similarly encrusted, as were the rocks for as much as a
mile inland, the effect of previous inundations by the caustic water.

We followed the lakeside for some fifteen miles before we reached
the camp Omar had set up near one of several fresh-water springs.
Here were patches of rushes, a few trees, the dead trunks of others,
plenty of grass for the mules and enough browse for the camels. The
place was indeed a small oasis. The only snag was clouds of small
hard-bodied midges, especially prevalent near the springs. My men
had built themselves shelters thatched with rushes but the Sultan's
men preferred to climb the ridges behind the camp and squat there
throughout the day, shifting occasionally from one rock to another.

From the camp the lake looked an attractive blue, but its water,
soapy to the touch, was in fact a dirty green, covered in places with
large patches of red algae. Groups of flamingos stalked about in the
shallows, sieving up the algae in their curious-shaped bills. There
were many other birds: Egyptian geese and duck of various kinds,
herons, avocets, storks and flocks of small waders. I was surprised
to see crocodiles in the lake, though the few I saw were all small.
Several jackal prowled round the camp and we found the tracks of
hyena. I also found the quill of a porcupine.

We stayed here four days. One evening we were hit by a sandstorm. We watched it coming towards us across the lake, a yellow
cloud blotting out each headland in turn. It lasted for twenty
minutes and was extremely unpleasant, but when it was over the air
was surprisingly cool and fresh. The following day there was
another storm, even more violent. Though it lasted a shorter time, it
blew down the tents in spite of every effort to hold them upright.
Two headmen arrived in our camp from a nearby village; with
typical Danakil hospitality they brought us a goat and forty pieces of
millet bread which came from Aussa. Equally typical of this country,

they brought news of a raid: the Issa had just killed two Danakil nearby.

On 25 April we moved our camp ten miles further down Abhebad and the Sultan's escort showed us where their fathers had destroyed an army of 'Turks' and thrown their cannon into the lake. This must have been where the Danakil had wiped out Munzinger's force.

Munzinger's attack on Aussa in 1875 had been part of a disastrous three-pronged attempt by the Egyptians to invade Abyssinia. Here, beside the bitter waters of the lake, where the black rocks shimmered under the scorching sun, it was easy to picture the confusion, the panic and the massacre as the Danakil closed in on the mob of unwilling conscripts. The Danakil wanted their trophies; not a man would have been spared and with nowhere to go, not a man would have escaped.

From our next camp I could see a number of odd-looking pinnacles sticking up along the lake's south-eastern shore. I fancied they were associated with hot springs and decided to investigate; by now I was convinced that if the lake had an outlet it could only be in that corner. I started off at first light with Abdullahi, Said and Goutama, and some reluctant Danakil. There was a seepage of hot water along the edge of the lake, with jets of steam in several places. The Sultan's men soon got hot and cross, grumbling that it was a long way and we should find no fresh water; when we did, they complained they had no food with them. The others, as always, were cheerful and enthusiastic.

It took us six hours to reach the pinnacles, as there were inlets and quicksands to circumvent. These sinter formations were very numerous; some were in the water, others on land, extending for about three miles along the edge of the lake. The tallest were as much as thirty feet in height, covered with the most delicate tracery. We got back to camp at sunset. I had found no outlet to the lake, and it was satisfactory to have established conclusively that the Awash did end in Abhebad.

CHAPTER 13

Journey to the Coast

OUR GUIDE maintained that if we marched for three hours in the afternoon, we could reach the French post at Aseila on the Gobad plain the following morning. On that understanding we set off that afternoon. The going proved to be uphill nearly all the way, over a surface littered with large chunks of rock: difficult enough for a man on foot, hardly possible for loaded camels. Anyway, when we found somewhere to unload and make camp late in the evening, the guide then told me that we could not possibly get to Aseila next day.

In the belief that we should arrive at Aseila in the morning, we had brought little water so as to lighten the loads. Now, after the intense heat, everyone was thirsty. The Danakil assured us we would find water next day, but I insisted that they should go at once and fetch us a skinful as evidence, or else I would return to our previous camp. After arguments that went on till ten o'clock, by which time I was more than ready for some soup, they set off, and before dawn they came back with some water. Next day they took us to a large pool of rainwater where a few acacias provided our camels with some food. To reach Aseila, however, was apparently going to take two more days. As the moon was almost full and the going had improved, I decided to travel by night.

We started at midnight; unluckily clouds had built up by now, so visibility was poor. However, we managed to cross another range, though with some difficulty on the descent, and we then went on till three hours after sunrise. When we camped we were on the Gobad plain, with water just under the surface in a river-bed; the valley smelt of aromatic grass and strongly scented shrubs, and the scattered trees were in leaf. Unfortunately on the previous day, after struggling on until they could go no further, two of the camels had collapsed. Had they only reached here I could have left them to recover; as it was I had to shoot them. During the night a gale blew, followed by heavy rain which brought a short-lived torrent racing down the dry river-bed. In the past week we had seen several storms in the distance: the rains, though delayed, had at last broken.

As soon as we had reached the Gobad plain I had sent a man to the French post at Aseila, with a letter warning them of my arrival, since I did not want to arrive unheralded. In the morning we went there. The outpost was only five miles away and was dug in on high ground with a good field of fire; it was surrounded by a thick belt of barbed wire and had emplacements for three machine-guns. The garrison consisted of sixty Somalis, most of them recruited from British Somaliland, and was commanded by a French sergeant.

He was a Corsican called Antoniali who proved welcoming, evidently glad to have a fellow European to talk to in this lonely place. He had planted a garden and was encouraging the local Adoimara to grow vegetables. I enjoyed his vegetables more than the red wine that he pressed on me.

His cook turned out to have previously been Henri de Monfreid's cabin boy. I had bought de Monfreid's *Les Secrets de la mer rouge* and *Aventures de mer* in Addis Ababa, and had just finished reading them. I had found his account of a wild and lawless life fascinating. He had come to Jibuti in 1910 as a clerk in a commercial firm, but soon found he had nothing in common with the *petit bourgeois* mentality of his fellow Frenchmen. The Danakil, however, appealed to his romantic nature, and he learned their language and spent all his spare time consorting with them. This scandalized the French community: he was sent for by the Governor and reprimanded. He paid no attention; he threw up his job and became a Muslim and virtually a Danakil. He bought a dhow, enlisted a crew, fished for pearls off the Farsan Islands and ran guns into Abyssinia through Tajura, to the fury of the long-established French gun-runners who traded more or less officially. When his dhow was wrecked he built himself another, which he named the *Altair*. Antoniali's cook, an alert and attractive lad, had obviously been devoted to him.

When I asked the sergeant how he liked being here, he said he preferred it to service in Algeria, Tunisia or Senegal: after all, digging trenches and posting sentries here made sense. The Gobad plain, which possessed the best grazing in the colony, was claimed alike by Asaimara, Adoimara and Issa, and until the French had recently occupied it, had been the scene of constant fighting. The previous year he and his troops, while on patrol, had been attacked by a large force from Bahdu, whom they had driven off with heavy loss. Nevertheless one of his soldiers confided to Omar that if the

159

Asaimara had kept up the attack after the machine-gun had jammed they would have been overrun.

Suitably rewarded, the three headmen and the Sultan's *askaris* set off cheerfully back to Aussa, accompanied by Ahamado and Ali Wali. I had never got anywhere with Ahamado, though his very presence in our camp had increased our security, but I had become attached to Ali Wali and was grateful for all the help and information he had given me. In Aussa he had been understandably reluctant to be seen talking to me, but Omar said he had been of great assistance during discussions with the Sultan. I gave Ali Wali a rifle and Ahamado a mule, and sent my greetings to Miriam Muhammad.

I remained at Aseila for three restful days before leaving for Dikil. Then on the second day we camped within sight of its fort among acacias that were very green after the recent rain. Just after we had pitched the tents there was another heavy storm. As soon as it was over I went up to the fort which was recently built and looked impregnable. Its walls, with a tower and machine-gun at each of two opposite corners, were twenty feet high and topped with broken glass. Surrounding them was a wide belt of wire which enclosed a large area containing a permanent well.

The Commandant du Cercle was a Captain Bernard, who lived in the fort with his wife and child, a French wireless operator and his *adjudant*, who corresponded to a British sergeant-major. His soldiers were Somalis, again almost all from British Somaliland: the French evidently had little confidence in the loyalty of the Issa or Danakil. I liked Captain Bernard; he was young, enthusiastic and well read. He insisted on my staying with him in the fort, though I would sooner have stayed in my own camp, finding it difficult after months in a tent to sleep in a small, hot room.

Bernard wirelessed the Governor for permission for me to cross from Dikil to Tajura, and it was granted a few hours later. I now arranged to send my Abyssinian soldiers by lorry to Alisabiet, a station on the railway line. They were happy to have reached here in safety and to be on their way back to Asba Tafari: unlike my own men, they had not come with me from choice, and they had often been troublesome. I had felt sorry for Ato Shona: a nice but utterly ineffective man, who in consequence had had an unhappy time. Now, letting bygones be bygones, I sent them off with a handsome

The Regent of Abyssinia, Ras Tafari, later Emperor Haile Selassie, with the Duke of York, later King George VI, who welcomed him on his State visit to London in 1924.

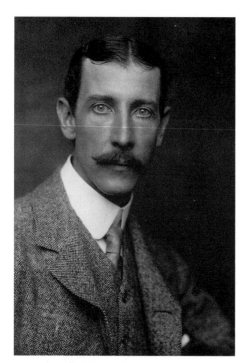

My father and my mother.

BELOW My father being escorted into Addis Ababa to present his credentials to Lij Yasu, the heir designate to the Emperor Menelik.

The new Legation, in which I grew up, now the British Embassy.

Aged four, I am holding the horns of a mountain nyala shot by my father.

BELOW The original British Legation in Addis Ababa, in which I was born.

ABOVE The Emperor
Menelik.

RIGHT The Abyssinian
delegation to King
George V's coronation,
led by Ras Kassa, (third
from right).

TOP LEFT Lij Yasu in traditional Abyssinian dress, and LEFT as a Muslim in Danakil dress.

ABOVE Ras Tafari as Regent, 1917.

ABOVE AND RIGHT
Scenes during the
revolution of 1917.

BELOW Negus Mikael's
captured generals
being led past at the
victory parade after
the battle of Sagale.

OPPOSITE A Tigrean
from Northern
Abyssinia.

OVERLEAF A view of
Ankober. Menelik's
palace was on the hill-
top (centre right)
before he moved his
capital to Addis Ababa.

My uncle, Lord Chelmsford, in his Viceregal robes, 1918.

BELOW An official gathering at Viceregal Lodge, 1917. On my uncle's left is the Secretary of State, Edwin Montagu, next to whom is my mother. Brian and are seated on the ground to the left. My father is immediately behind us in the second row.

OPPOSITE ABOVE The Milebrook, Radnorshire, our family home for more than twenty years.

OPPOSITE BELOW Old Boys' Match, Eton, 1933. My classical tutor, C. O. Bevan, in a cap, is next to my Housemaster, A. M. McNeile. Myself, second from right, back row, Brian, far right middle row; Roddy, second from left, front row, Dermot, third from right, front row.

ABOVE The blessing of the water by the priest at Epiphany in Addis Ababa.

BELOW A typical outdoor market near Addis Ababa.

OPPOSITE Haile Selassie on the day of his coronation as Emperor.

Journeying into Danakil country, 1933–34:
ABOVE Members of my expedition; Omar is in the centre with Kassimi on his right.
LEFT Watering camels at Bilen.
BELOW A group of warriors.

OPPOSITE The Awash:
ABOVE A crossing.
CENTRE The Jira crater rising above the swamps of Southern Aussa.
BELOW Abhebad, the lake where the Awash ended.

Outside my house at Kutum, with my lion cubs.

RIGHT Idris, my personal retainer in the Sudan, at Galabat during the war.

present of money and bought their two remaining camels for a good price. They departed singing my praises.

As to my route, Captain Bernard could give me no information. As far as he knew, no Europeans had travelled from Dikil to Lake Assal, which we would pass on our way to the coast. Ali Wali had told me that the lake was one of the places where the Danakil dug the bars of salt that passed as currency in the markets of Abyssinia. I was naturally excited to learn that the country ahead of me was unexplored, which was something quite unexpected. The officials in French Somaliland appeared to have shown a surprising lack of enterprise, in contrast to the outstanding exploration carried out by French officers in the Sahara.

Captain Bernard undertook to find reliable guides who were familiar with the tribes ahead of us, and said he intended to send with me Dongradi, his *adjudant*, with twelve soldiers, their own camels and a machine-gun: this, I felt, should more than ensure our safety. During my few days at Dikil there were heavy storms, and Omar, who was making enquiries, was assured we should now find plenty of water on the way to Tajura. On 9 May I said goodbye to Captain Bernard and his wife: they had been friendly and hospitable and I had enjoyed their excellent French food. Eight months later, Bernard went to the assistance of some Issa who were being attacked by a force of Asaimara later officially estimated at twelve hundred. On 18 January 1935 his entire force of twenty-one soldiers and numerous partisans were overwhelmed; all were killed and castrated.

I went to my camp, loaded up, and in the afternoon joined Dongradi at our rendezvous by a large pool of water. From there it took five days to reach Lake Assal. We lost several camels on the way; not because we ever did a long march, for they were no longer up to it, but because we hardly found any grazing – an occasional acacia among the scattered palms in the larger water-courses, but nothing among the black rocks on the broken hillsides.

On the third day we followed the Kuri river-bed to the Gagada plain, where the guides had assured us we should find abundant grazing. In fact we found virtually none, though part of the plain was under water; all the Adoimara normally living there had moved elsewhere. The guides now warned us that for the next three days, to Lake Assal and beyond, we should have difficulty finding wood for fires, let alone anything for the camels. I wondered desperately how many would survive, for they were in a sorry state. Still, we had been lucky with the rains, and every day we camped near water, usually large pools among the rocks; I remember one that was twenty-five feet across.

Soon after leaving the Gagada plain we entered the valley of the Aluli, and four hours later came on two small acacia trees in leaf, which we cut down for the camels; but by now they were almost too exhausted to eat. We found some shelter from the sun under overhanging rocks but none from the scorching wind and driving sand.

In the late afternoon we did another two hours, following the valley, which became progressively more striking. At first there was a string of pools in the river-bed, fed by water just under the surface, and some groves of dom palms. Then the mountains closed in and the valley became a succession of sheer-sided gorges. On both sides, the rock walls, sometimes a bare twelve yards apart, rose tier upon tier for hundreds of feet. Each gorge turned and twisted and every hundred yards revealed a different aspect. The rock was sandstone, the colouring fantastic. Red was the prevailing hue but there were varying shades of orange and purple, green and blue-grey, umber and cinnamon.

We camped beside a deep pool at the entrance to yet another gorge that looked sinister in the light of the setting sun, with mountains on either side rising against the darkening sky. Here Abdullahi found the tracks of hyena; an appropriate animal in this forbidding place. We loaded by the light of the waning moon and set off at dawn, passing some nearly boiling springs. I was anxious to be out of these gorges, knowing that if it rained behind us we could be swept away by a wall of water as much as thirty feet high.

An hour later we emerged from the last shadow-filled gorge and looked across the Assal depression. The lake, five hundred feet below sea-level, was sapphire in the light of the rising sun; it was set in a dazzling expanse of salt, a smooth plain two miles across, white as snow, hard as rock. All around, rising out of black hills and crumbling lava, were jagged mountains, topped by the peaks of Garba and Harod. Nowhere was any sign of life, no shrub nor wisp of vegetation, no bird in the sky, not even a lizard among the rocks.

We crossed the salt flat on a crust four or five inches thick with sludge underneath, entered the hills on the far side and made our way across broken ground to a string of small pools, where we camped. Here were a few acacia bushes and some knife-edged grass, the first vegetation I had seen that day. I hoped it would suffice for the camels. We had left one behind that morning but later they brought him in, and I was relieved to see him eat; like the others, he was not ill but collapsing from starvation and weakness. We decided to remain here until the following afternoon, and Omar set the men to cut what grass they could find for the camels to eat during the night.

Dongradi, as always, camped slightly apart, after positioning his men to defend our camp. I had been apprehensive that he might expect to take charge, but he accepted without question that this was my expedition and though he was helpful when I asked his advice he left decisions to me. I saw little of him, since he preferred to feed on his own and spent most of his time with his soldiers, who obviously had great respect for him. A dark, tough, undemonstrative Corsican, he confessed he was fed up with the colony and hoped shortly for a transfer to Algeria. He had been maddened by the constant interference to which they were subjected at Dikil, from officials in Jibuti who never ventured outside the town.

In the morning I explored the lake. It was bordered on one side by a sandstone cliff topped with lava, at the foot of which several hot springs gushed into its waters. From encrustations on the rocks I estimated that the lake had once been twenty feet higher. It was now summer and here, far below sea level, the heat in the afternoon was intense. Once again I regretted that my thermometers no longer worked, for the Assal depression may well be the hottest place on earth; it would have been interesting to register the temperature.

Before we left in the late afternoon I discarded my bed, table and chair, and everything else that was not essential. Fortunately, my collection of bird skins (which finally numbered 872, comprising 192 species and subspecies) weighed very little. Dongradi helped by carrying water for us on his camels.

Ahead were more escarpments. Omar as always was indefatigable, as indeed were they all, Somalis and Abyssinians alike. Short of food, thirsty in the blistering heat, they never complained as they unloaded the camels and themselves carried the loads over the worst stretches. Once when I suggested they should rest Abdullahi shouted back, 'We are men! We don't tire!' That evening Dongradi expressed his admiration for them.

The following day we found an encampment of Danakil on a permanent water hole called Dafarai, and induced them to hire us two camels. From now on the going was easier, but even so most of my few remaining camels, unable to go further, collapsed. Despite all our efforts to help them we had been losing camels every day since leaving Dikil; in the end, only four out of the nineteen with which I had started from Afdam reached Tajura. It was heartbreaking, for I knew them all so well; among others little Farur, Elmi, Hansiya and great-hearted Nagadras, who had always led the caravan.

The next morning we saw in the distance the sea, a narrow, almost land-locked stretch of water forming the western extremity of the Gulf of Tajura – the Gubat al Karib, reputed stronghold of the King of Devils.

We stopped that day at another water hole with brackish and scanty water. Here the Danakil were truculent; they belonged to the Sugha Guda, a tribe that had long defied the French. Some years earlier they had turned back a French officer who aimed to reach Lake Assal, and killed three of his Somali soldiers. On another occasion they had fired on the administrator from Tajura when he attempted to visit Mount Guda. This was a mountain I had heard of while I was in Aussa; the Danakil there had described its forests and perennial streams. From here, intervening foothills prevented us from seeing it properly. Only from Tajura, which we reached on 20 May, did it dominate the landscape.

The previous evening, I had suggested as a joke to Kassimi, Abdullahi and the others that, instead of crossing by sea to Jibuti, we should turn north across the lava desert to Massawa. Taking me seriously, one of them said, 'Give us three days in Tajura first.' I only wished it had been possible. I had no desire to return to civilization. It was six months since we had left the Awash Station to explore the Danakil country. Now I would happily have done the journey over again.

I was young, highly impressionable and incurably romantic, and Tajura was a marvellous place to end my journey. For me it belonged to that authentic Eastern world of which Conrad wrote, a world remote, beautiful, untamed. Its palm-fringed beach and sparkling green and blue sea; the sombre outline of mountains across the bay; dhows at anchor offshore, with dugouts passing to and fro; white mosques among the palms; narrow passageways between crowded mat-roofed dwellings; Somali and Arab merchants, stately in ankle-length robes, embroidered sleeveless jackets and coloured turbans; Danakil from the desert, shock-headed, half-naked, armed and unpredictable; groups of women in colourful dresses, who as I passed covered all but their eyes; harsh Somali voices; the sound of a stringed instrument, the throb of a drum; long-drawn, sonorous calls to prayer, taken up from one minaret to the next; the distant roaring of refractory camels at the wells; the sound of surf on the beach; the smells of dried shark's meat, clarified butter, wood smoke and spices.

The French, who had been on the Somali coast since 1862, had settled first at Obock; later they built Jibuti on a salt flat, and a squalid native quarter had grown up round the modern town, with its offices, fly-blown hotels, cafés, bars and brothels. Jibuti was an unromantic seaport in an uninviting landscape.

Tajura, a short distance across the bay, was as yet totally unaffected by the products and influence of the modern Western world. I wondered if in the distant past Greek sailors, exploring the Erythraean sea, had landed here; if Portuguese in their quest for Prester John had put in here for water, or careened their caravels on the beach; perhaps Turkish musketeers, on their way to support Ahmad Granj, had set out from here, as Munzinger had done on his ill-fated expedition against Aussa. Until recently slave-traders had loaded human cargoes here in dhows for passage to Arabia, and I suspected that an occasional consignment still went this way, the token presence of a French administrator being of little consequence.

When I arrived, a French sergeant came down from the flat-topped hill on the outskirts of the town, where the commandant confined himself behind his barbed wire entanglements. He pressed me for safety's sake to camp at the foot of the hill. I made the excuse that the ground was filthy, as indeed it was, and camped under some trees on the plain outside the town.

I was invited to lunch next day with the commandant. He was a fat little gourmet, with an embarrassing lack of self-assurance but an assertive manner. He had only recently arrived, hated Tajura and craved for the café-life of Jibuti. He assured me that Tajura was dangerous and warned me not to enter it unless escorted by his

165

soldiers. When I said I would like to visit Jabal Guda, he became excited and forbade me to leave Tajura. I then suggested I should visit Obock by dhow, but he said there were pirates on the coast and it was far too dangerous. Dongradi, who was staying with him, remained silent throughout the meal, but once or twice I caught his eye. In the evening he left by dhow for Jibuti with his soldiers. I hope he got his transfer to Algeria.

The Sultan of Tajura had asked to meet me, so at five o'clock I came back to the commandant's house. The Sultan, a good-looking young man in an immaculate white robe and closely wound white turban, had a quiet-spoken dignity, unlike our host, who waved his hands about, lit one cigarette from another, and hardly stopped talking – mostly about the advantages of a refrigerator. I invited the Sultan to visit my camp, which next day he did.

He asked many questions about my journey, and seemed especially interested that I had met the Sultan of Aussa and been allowed to travel through his territory. He asked if I had had a large force of Abyssinian soldiers with me. I knew that Omar had already heard that before my arrival wild rumours had been afloat in the town: I was said to be accompanied by an Abyssinian army that intended to seize Lij Yasu's son. I had never heard of this son, but it was not improbable that among the Danakil the lecherous Lij Yasu had produced several. The Sultan was non-committal about the French administration, though he did mention that the commandant had not left his house since arrival, and that his predecessor had never ventured outside Tajura.

On my last night in Tajura we held a feast in our camp, followed by tribal dancing. Many townsmen turned up to watch, and a few joined in. Some of the dancing was spectacular, and it went on till the early hours of the morning. I had asked the commandant's permission to fire off our rifles, and to my surprise he had given it; but when we did so he sent a Somali sergeant in a hurry to tell us to stop. Not unnaturally, the commandant was afraid the Danakil would assume the post was being attacked, but he might have thought of that earlier.

I chartered a dhow to take us to Jibuti and we left in the evening of 23 May. A storm was threatening but luckily passed over the land, for we were on an open deck without shelter. Tajura vanished into the distance and the sun set behind Guda. As night fell, the moon lit the sea. With small waves breaking against the bows the boat rolled slightly, her long raking yard dipping and rising against the stars above the much-patched lateen sail. My party lay about the deck, some already seasick.

Omar was talking to the sailors, one of whom came from Berbera. A young Dankali with very white teeth was cooking over his fire; later he brought us grilled fish, discs of unleavened bread, and tea flavoured with ginger. I was very content, travelling like this across a sea which de Monfreid had made his own. It was easy to picture the lawless life he had led, to understand the craving for freedom and adventure that inspired him, the comradeship that bound him to his savage crew.

We arrived in Jibuti next morning and there among the native craft was de Monfreid's *Altair*: he was now in France and the boat was for sale. I later went on board and met some of his crew, whose names I already knew from his books, and I was half-tempted to buy the boat and see if I could make a livelihood trading and pearling in the Red Sea. De Monfreid had bridged the gap between himself and his crew, identifying himself with them to the extent of becoming one of them. He had been rewarded by their acceptance, and I envied him his achievement. However, he had also become a Muslim, something I could never have done: not religious conviction but pride in my family background would have forbidden it.

During my journey of shared hardship and danger I had been kept apart from my followers partly by inability to communicate. My Amharic was basic, the Arabic I had learnt was rudimentary: I had relied on Omar to translate anything of importance. Yet even for Omar I had felt no authentic friendship, regarding him rather as a trusted subordinate. He in turn expected me to distance myself from my followers, which he accepted as proper for an Englishman. For instance, he would have been upset if I had shared a meal with the camelmen.

As a child at the Legation I had never known the intimate relationship with *ayahs* and bearers which many children in India had experienced. I had grown up accepting our servants as subordinates, distinct in colour, custom and behaviour. I undoubtedly had a feeling of superiority, since my father was the British Minister and I was his son. This feeling, however, certainly did not include colour prejudice, which is something I have never felt. Aesthetically, I regard white as the least attractive colour for skin.

167

In Jibuti I spent three days waiting for a boat to Marseilles, and I did not find a congenial soul in the town. Chapon Baisac, the Governor, summoned me for an interview. After I had been kept waiting a long time I was shown into his office, where I had hardly sat down before he asked me abruptly why I had brought Abyssinian soldiers into French territory, and why I had not handed over my weapons before leaving Dikil for Tajura. He barely listened to my explanations, which I should have thought self-evident, and during the half-hour I spent with him never spoke a gracious word. This corpulent, pompous and short-tempered little man was certainly not one I would have wished to serve under.

My men were anxious to return to their homes and families, and on the evening of our second day at Jibuti all but Omar and his servant left on the train. I went to the station to see them off, and the parting with them deepened my depression. Kassimi and Goutama, Birru and Said, Abdullahi, Said Munge, Abdi, Bedi and his fellow camelmen, and the rest: they were twenty-two in all, and some had been with me since I left Addis Ababa with Haig-Thomas for the Arussi mountains eight months before. All had proved utterly reliable, often under conditions of hardship and danger. None had ever questioned my decisions, however seemingly risky, and I had never doubted their loyalty. Despite their fundamental religious and racial differences as Amharas, Gallas and Somalis, they had never quarrelled or intrigued among themselves, but had worked side by side throughout.

I was glad to leave Jibuti next day, even third-class in a Messageries Maritimes boat returning from French Indo-China to Marseilles. Omar accompanied me on board and there we parted. As I watched him descend the gangway I was more conscious than ever how much of my success was due to him. He had ensured the loyalty of my men, accurate information, and the successful outcome of negotiations with tribal chiefs and with the Sultan himself, and his imperturbability had given me the assurance that I had sometimes needed. He and he alone had made possible my seemingly unattainable goal.

PART III

The Northern Sudan
1935–7

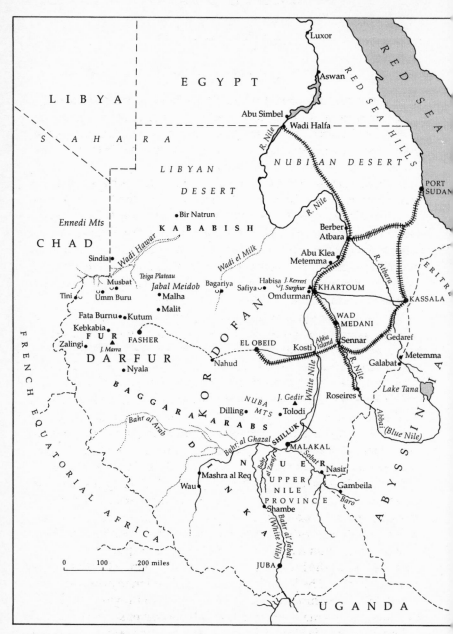

Anglo-Egyptian Sudan, 1935–40

CHAPTER 14

The Sudan

THOUGH HAPPY to be back at The Milebrook with my family, I inevitably suffered from a feeling of anticlimax. For four years I had been planning and then carrying out my Danakil expedition. Now that it was over it seemed impossible that the future would afford me a comparable experience.

In the summer of 1934, after my return from Abyssinia, I was instructed to appear before a Selection Board for the Sudan Political Service. There was no written examination for this service; a number of previously selected applicants were interviewed by six senior officials from the Sudan and were assessed on their academic record and athletic prowess at the university, the recommendations of their schoolmasters, university tutors and heads of colleges, and by the impression they made at the interview.

My own selection may have been partly due to four turn-over articles, just published in *The Times*, in which I had described my exploration in the Danakil country. Having been accepted, I was sent to the School of Oriental and African Studies in London on a four-month Arabic course. Unfortunately, a lecture on my expedition that I was invited to give at the Royal Geographical Society fell in the middle of this course. Not surprisingly, I spent most of my spare time working on my maps and preparing the paper I was to read, instead of concentrating on my studies. I have always regretted this missed opportunity to become proficient in classical Arabic.

In those days, a lecture at the Geographical Society was a formal occasion, with the President, Council and lecturer in white tie and tailcoat, and the audience in dinner jackets. The lecture was preceded by a dinner with the Society's dining club. Sir Percy Cox, an awe-inspiring man renowned for his ability to keep silent in a dozen languages, was the President, and I sat next to him. After checking a few facts with me he lapsed into silence, while I in my confusion ate a plateful of mushrooms, even though on two previous occasions mushrooms had made me violently ill. I had never spoken in public before and was feeling sick with apprehension anyway: now, I thought, I really will be sick in the middle of my lecture. However, all went well, and when he closed the meeting Sir Percy was complimentary about my journey.

John Hamilton, the Sudan Agent in Cairo, who was on leave in England and had read my articles in *The Times*, asked me to lunch. I gladly accepted his invitation to stay with him in Cairo in December on my way to Khartoum, and go on from there up the Nile, instead of going by sea to Port Sudan. A few days later he invited me to the theatre. His other guests were officials from the Sudan with their wives, among them Lady Gillan, wife of Sir Angus, the Civil Secretary and head of the Sudan Political Service; he himself, however, was not there. After the play we went on to a well-known nightclub, the 400. When the others got up and danced I was left at the table with Lady Gillan, who struck me as formidable. I apologized for not asking her to dance, and explained that I did not know how to dance.

'Nonsense, of course you know how to. Come on,' she said, and got up.

We circled the small, crowded floor and, opposite our table again, she stepped back, said, 'I think you're right,' and sat down. I now found her unexpectedly easy to talk to.

I was at The Milebrook when I read in the papers that on 5 December 1934 Italian and Abyssinian forces had clashed on the wells at Walwal near the border of Italian Somaliland. As she read this my mother said: 'I hope this won't lead to another world war.' Indirectly her foreboding proved all too correct. The skirmish at Walwal provided Mussolini with his ostensible reason for invading and annexing Abyssinia; and his success, more than any other event, encouraged Hitler on his fatal course of territorial aggression.

For some years it had been evident that Mussolini was looking for an excuse to invade and incorporate Abyssinia with Eritrea and Italian Somaliland as a part of his new Roman Empire. He was convinced that war with Abyssinia would have for the Italian people the emotional appeal of avenging Italy's humiliating defeat at Adua in 1896. Walwal gave him his pretext. Knowing that the Emperor would never consent, he immediately demanded abject apologies, a large indemnity and concessions from the Abyssinian Government. Haile Selassie appealed to the League of Nations.

Many of my generation were to be passionately concerned with the Spanish Civil War. I felt no such involvement: I detested the anarchists and communists on the Government side, and hated the Italians with whom Franco had allied himself. But with the Abyssinian cause I identified myself completely, and was emotionally drained by the ensuing tragedy.

I went to Cairo at the end of 1934 on my way to the Sudan, and spent a week with John Hamilton in his comfortable flat in Zamalek, the large and fashionable island on the Nile. The Gezira Sporting Club was nearby and we went there in the afternoons; its extensive and well-kept grounds contained a polo ground, a golf course and tennis courts.

Since Hamilton was popular with the large British community, and had many friends among the Egyptian aristocracy, we dined out most nights and I met many interesting people. He had served with distinction as a District Commissioner in the Sudan, but was now chiefly concerned with the effect on the Sudan of the Italian threat to Abyssinia, and with the increasing resentment in the Arab world at Jewish immigration into Palestine.

In those days modern Cairo was still an attractive town, not yet defaced by shoddy, high-rise buildings: compared with today there was little traffic, with almost as many donkey-carts as cars. It fascinated me to see the great river flow past, still brown with residual silt washed down by rain in the highlands of Abyssinia, and to watch feluccas glide slowly and silently upstream under their lateen sails. Many of them were moored along the river banks, where happy, naked little boys bathed off the steps without hindrance from the police.

Hamilton sent me each morning with one of his native staff to see the sights, and I paid my duty call on the pyramids: having seen innumerable photographs of them I expected to be bored, but in fact was enormously impressed by the size and symmetry of these colossal tombs, which in those days stood apart in their desert setting. I spent another morning in the museum, looking at the Tutankhamun exhibition: much of this was of outstanding beauty, but it was the calm perfection of that youthful face that moved me most. I was taken to see some of the mosques, the Mouski or bazaar, and the Citadel, garrisoned at that time by the Grenadier Guards;

173

several of the young officers had been my contemporaries at Eton.

Spread out in view below the Citadel was medieval Cairo, a great eastern city. Minarets, domes of mosques and tombs, roofs of caravanserais, remnants of massive walls and arched gateways rose above a patchwork of flat, earthen roof-tops, courts and alleys. In the clear air and bright sunlight every detail was distinct: wisps of smoke, a distant kite twisting and diving at another, a woman hanging washing on a roof. I could distinguish voices, shouts, the bray of a donkey, the sound of hammering, a hint of music, among the rise and fall of other, indefinable noises.

For centuries Cairo had crumbled in this rainless climate, its buildings had been patched and new ones built. The city was dilapidated, dusty, infested with flies and smelt of ordure and urine; it was packed with people, many destitute and living in squalor. Here the present merged into the past and everywhere a sense of continuity prevailed. The city was a veritable treasure trove of Islamic architecture: Al Azhar University, one of the world's oldest, with its domes, courts and colonnades, where turbanned mullahs taught their lore to students from many lands; the famous mosques, amid scores of others rarely visited by foreigners; and the many tombs in the City of the Dead. Here was everything I had failed to find in Constantinople, and I spent my remaining days in Cairo exploring the Old City, a world far removed from the modern boulevards, from Shepheard's Hotel, the Continental, Groppi's teashop and the Gezira Sporting Club.

On my way up the Nile to the Sudan I stayed for three days at Luxor. There, as elsewhere in Egypt, I was particularly struck by the abrupt transition from the desert to the sown, marked in this rainless land by a rigid line along the edge of the irrigated fields.

On my first morning in Luxor I visited Karnak, and had the place to myself: the vociferous guides had collected their charges at the Winter Palace Hotel and conducted them across the river to the Valley of the Kings. At Karnak I was staggered by the extent and size of the ruins, fascinated by the figures carved on the walls. In their tranquil faces I could detect no sign of the brutal disregard for suffering involved in the building of the pyramids and of these massive temples. I went next day to the Valley of the Kings, but was little interested and was glad to revisit Karnak. My abiding memory of Luxor is of the sun setting in a blaze of colour behind the lifeless hills across the river. From Luxor I took the train to Aswan.

It is now over fifty years since I boarded the paddle-steamer at Aswan to take me to Wadi Halfa. Nearly forty years earlier Kitchener had used similar boats during his conquest of the Sudan. This one was spacious; my cabin was comfortable, the service excellent, the food reasonable. The great wheel churned astern, and for two days and nights we travelled upstream. It was the ideal way to see the Nile, the proper way to approach the Sudan.

We tied up at Abu Simbel. Four seated figures of Rameses II, seventy feet in height, guarded and dwarfed the entrance to the temple; carved in the cliff-face, they stared across the Nile into the desert beyond. I went inside, into the three great halls that extended for sixty yards into the rock. Here, in the dim light, were other great statues of the Pharaoh, but my thoughts lingered outside with those enormous seated figures.

As we steamed further south the scenery became increasingly desolate: occasional villages, hemmed between the river and barren, brown hills, only emphasized the solitude. We would see a cluster of flat-roofed houses, a mosque, palms, water-wheels, some cultivation, a few men and women, the odd camel or donkey, a flock of goats on a hillside – then we would be past and the desert closed in on the river once more. So vivid had been the accounts I had read of the Sudan campaign that I felt I had seen it all before. Somewhere below Wadi Halfa we must have passed in the night the battlefield of Toski where Wad al Nijumi, the gallant Dervish Amir, had been killed.

At Wadi Halfa I entered the Sudan and from there I crossed the Nubian desert by the railway Kitchener's engineers had built. Travelling first-class in a very comfortable train, I looked out, hour after hour, on the challenging starkness of this desert.

Arriving at Khartoum on 13 January 1935, I was met at the station by May Perry, wife of Walter Perry who represented the Egyptian Irrigation Service in the Sudan. I had not heard of the Perrys but May now told me she was a cousin on my mother's side. She and Walter gave me a warm welcome and a home in Khartoum whenever I was there during the next five years; I became very attached to them both. Walter had travelled extensively in the

175

Southern Sudan and done a lot of shooting, and I was interested by all he had to tell me.

Khartoum was the administrative centre of the Sudan, as it had been ever since 1830, after Muhammad Ali, who ruled Egypt, had invaded and occupied the northern part of the country. He had done so largely to acquire slaves; and slave-trading soon developed into the Sudan's major industry. Further south, Zubair Rahmah and Ahmad al Aggad, the two most powerful of innumerable slave-traders, became virtually independent rulers. Inefficiency, brutality and cupidity were the hallmarks of the Egyptian administration.

In 1877, in an attempt to improve matters, the Khedive Ismail, Muhammad Ali's grandson, appointed Charles Gordon, who had been administering Equatoria for him, to be Governor-General of the whole Sudan. Assisted by some remarkable Europeans whom he had recruited, Gordon reduced the slave-trade, suppressed rebellions, reorganized the administration and curbed corruption and oppression. But when Ismail was deposed as Khedive by the Sultan of Turkey in 1879, Gordon resigned and left. He was succeeded as Governor-General by an Egyptian, the slave-trade revived, and conditions in the Sudan became appalling once more. Such was the plight of the country, until the fifteen dramatic years which culminated in 1898 in the battle of Omdurman and the British occupation.

On Abba Island, sixty miles upstream from Khartoum, Muhammad Ahmad, a boat-builder's son, had begun preaching trust in God, the impermanence of this world and the joys of the next. Affirming that poverty was a virtue, that luxury and self-indulgence were sins, he devoted himself to prayer, meditation and fasting, saw visions and heard voices. His reputation for sanctity spread far and wide; from all over the Sudan men came to him.

Among the first was Abdullahi ibn al Sayyid Muhammad from the Taiaisha, one of the Baggara tribes, those formidable cattle-owning Arabs of southern Kordofan and Darfur. Abdullahi was a man of action and a realist, Muhammad Ahmad a visionary and an idealist; yet they felt an immediate affinity. When Muhammad proclaimed himself the Mahdi, the 'Guided One' who had come to restore Islam to its initial purity, he appointed Abdullahi his Khalifa or successor.

The Government in Khartoum, disturbed by rumours of unrest on Abba Island, sent two companies of soldiers to arrest the troublemakers; as they landed from the steamer they were attacked and wiped out. The Mahdi and his followers then moved to Gedir in the Nuba mountains of southern Kordofan, and there exterminated another inadequate force sent against them. Adherents now poured in to the Mahdi's headquarters. His followers, known as the Ansar, were distinguished by the patches sewn on their *jibbas* or shirts as a mark of avowed poverty; these *jibbas*, patched with bright colours, later became the distinctive uniform of the Mahdist armies.

The Egyptian Governor-General, now thoroughly alarmed, sent a force of six thousand men against the Mahdi, but their camp was overrun at dawn before they reached Gedir. The soldiers, mostly half-asleep, were slaughtered; their weapons and stores were appropriated by the Mahdists, who now laid siege to El Obeid, the Sudan's second largest town. Hundreds died of starvation before it surrendered to them in January 1883.

Meanwhile in Egypt, popular resentment against the British and French, who were increasingly interfering with the running of the country, had led to rebellion. The Khedive appealed to the British for help and the mutinous Egyptian army was defeated by General Wolseley at the battle of Tel el Kebir on 13 September 1882. Britain now found herself in reluctant occupation of Egypt, and consequently involved in the Sudan. The Khedive was determined to reoccupy Kordofan and destroy the Mahdist forces. Colonel Hicks Pasha was therefore given command of the Egyptian army in the Sudan, and ordered to reoccupy El Obeid. Frank Power, *The Times* correspondent in Khartoum, wrote of Hicks Pasha's army: 'We have here 9000 infantry that fifty good men would rout in ten minutes, and 1000 cavalry (Bashi Bazoukes) that have never learnt to ride, with a few Nordenfelt guns, to beat the 69,000 men whom the Mahdi had got together.'

The result was a foregone conclusion. On 5 November 1883, Wad al Nijumi, with twenty thousand men, annihilated Hicks Pasha's rabble near El Obeid. The Egyptian forces in Darfur promptly surrendered and the whole western Sudan fell into the hands of the Mahdi. In the eastern Sudan, the Hadendoa, under the skilful leadership of Osman Digna, rose in revolt, and Egyptian forces there suffered further disasters.

When the authorities in Cairo heard of the annihilation of Hicks Pasha's army, they decided, at the instigation of Gladstone's Government, to evacuate the remaining Egyptian forces from the

Sudan. Gordon was chosen in London for the task, though the selection of this gallant, devout but unpredictable man was viewed with justifiable misgiving by Sir Evelyn Baring who, as British Agent and Consul-General, virtually ruled Egypt.

Gordon, accompanied by Colonel Stewart, arrived in Khartoum on 18 February 1884. There were seven thousand poor-quality troops in the town and a large civilian population. Gordon promptly evacuated the civilian officials and any sick troops but, misled by his previous successes, assumed 'it would be comparatively easy to destroy the Mahdi'. By mid-March, however, the tribes downstream had joined the rebellion, and Dervish forces were investing the town. Khartoum was cut off; the siege had begun.

Though the British public became increasingly concerned about Gordon's personal safety, Gladstone was determined not to get involved in the Sudan. Only in August 1884, to save his ministry from falling, did he agree to send a relief force under General Wolseley. In September, Gordon, unaware of this development, sent Colonel Stewart, Frank Power and the French Consul out of Khartoum by steamer to summon help, but their boat ran ashore, and Stewart and his companions were murdered.

After their departure from Khartoum, Gordon was left with no one he could rely on, no one with whom he could share his hopes and anxieties. Beset by apathy, inefficiency, cowardice and treachery, he imposed his indomitable will upon soldiers and civilians alike, and continued to hold out, month after month. Food, however, was running short, and there could be no answer to starvation. In his *Journal* he recorded his innermost feelings. Reading it as a boy, I pictured Gordon standing day after day on the roof of the palace, staring down the river for the help that eventually came too late.

Wolseley reached Wadi Halfa on 5 October 1884, just when the Mahdi, with a large following, reached Omdurman on the bank of the Nile opposite Khartoum. Wolseley, unaware of the perilous state the Khartoum garrison had been reduced to, methodically prepared a further advance, and sent a column of thirteen hundred British troops across the desert from Kosti to Metemma. On 14 January they were attacked near the wells of Abu Klea: the Dervishes broke the British square and only after desperate hand-to-hand fighting were they repulsed.

The column reached the Nile near Metemma, where on 21 January they encountered four steamers sent by Gordon. These brought letters and his *Journal*. The last entry, dated 14 December, ended: 'Now mark this, if the expeditionary force, and I ask for no more than two hundred soldiers, does not come in ten days, the town may fall; and I have done my best for the honour of my country. Goodbye.'

Four days later, after an inexcusable delay, two of the steamers with troops on board set off for Khartoum. They came under heavy fire as they approached the town, where the Egyptian flag no longer flew over the ruined palace, and Dervishes in their patched *jibbas* thronged the waterfront. Khartoum had fallen two days earlier: Gordon had held out a month longer than he had predicted in his *Journal*. The steamers turned back.

When, on 26 January 1885, the Dervishes had overrun the defences and swarmed into Khartoum, massacring everyone they encountered, Gordon awaited them, standing on the palace steps in his white uniform, and there they killed him. They cut off his head and took it to the Mahdi.

The Mahdi himself died unexpectedly on 20 June 1885, only five months after capturing Khartoum, and was succeeded by Abdullahi, his Khalifa, who ruled the Sudan for the next thirteen years. The 'Turks' (Egyptians) and infidels had been overcome; their armies had been annihilated or driven from the land; the Sudan, for the first time, was both united and independent. The Khalifa's rule was despotic, ruthless and brutal; he would never otherwise have survived. From 1887 to 1889 he was at war with Abyssinia; hostilities began when the Abyssinians raided and looted the frontier town of Galabat. The Khalifa in turn assembled sixty thousand men at Omdurman and sent them, under the Amir Abu Anja, to invade Abyssinia. Abu Anja won a hard-fought battle near Gondar, sacked and burnt that city and returned to the Sudan with droves of slaves and cattle. He died the following year while preparing to meet an attack by a large Abyssinian army led by the Emperor John in person.

The battle at Galabat was fought two months later. Time and again, the Abyssinians hurled themselves with reckless courage against the Dervish positions and in furious hand-to-hand fighting gradually overwhelmed the defenders. Penned inside their *zariba*, the Dervishes faced annihilation. They were saved when news spread among the Abyssinian troops that the Emperor had been

179

killed; then the Abyssinian triumph turned to rout. This Dervish victory ended the war, but cost the Khalifa his finest army.

In July 1889 the Khalifa sent the Amir Wad al Nijumi, with a totally inadequate force, to invade Egypt. He penetrated as far as Toski, sixty miles north of Wadi Halfa, and there was cut off from the river by an Egyptian army under General Sir Francis Grenfell. This comprised several by now well-trained Egyptian infantry battalions with artillery and cavalry, supported by a brigade of British troops. Wad al Nijumi's fighting men had with them three thousand camp followers, all half-starved and desperately thirsty. Sir Francis appealed to Wad al Nijumi to surrender. The Amir sent back a defiant answer and, as his troops made ready for battle, exhorted them to prepare to meet their maker. They fought with their accustomed gallantry. Wad al Nijumi and more than half of them were killed; the rest were wounded or captured. The battle of Toski removed the Dervish threat to Egypt.

It was not until seven years later, in 1896, that the British Government authorized Kitchener to reconquer the Sudan, whereupon he systematically set about the task. On 8 April 1898 his army, with their bands playing, stormed the Amir Mahmud's *zariba* on the Atbara river. They suffered heavy casualties but Mahmud's army was destroyed and he was taken prisoner. Kitchener continued his advance up the Nile and on 1 September camped on the bank of the Nile below Omdurman.

Shortly after I had arrived in Khartoum I was taken to see the battlefield of Omdurman. From the Nile, a gravel plain stretched to the distant hills of Kereri and Surgham: as the Dervishes advanced on Kitchener's encampment not even a fold in the ground had given them cover.

The Anglo-Egyptian army comprised nearly 26,000 highly trained soldiers, with 44 guns and 20 machine-guns, supported by 10 gunboats mounting a further 36 guns and 24 machine-guns. The Dervish army numbered between 50,000 and 60,000 men, of whom perhaps 14,000 were armed with old-fashioned Remington rifles. Had the Dervishes attacked by night they might have overrun Kitchener's army; instead they advanced next morning in broad daylight across the plain.

Kitchener's artillery opened fire at 2800 yards, the infantry at 1200: not a Dervish got nearer than 400 yards. G. W. Steevens, who was present as a war correspondent and described the battle in his book

With Kitchener to Khartum, wrote: 'No white troops would have faced that torrent of death for five minutes. It was the last day of Mahdism and the greatest. They could never get near and they refused to hold back ... It was not a battle but an execution.'

Having shattered this attack, Kitchener had moved forward, intending to occupy Omdurman before the surviving Dervishes could enter the town. He was unaware that an undefeated force of 35,000 were still in the field. Yakub, the Khalifa's brother, with the pick of the Dervish army, was stationed behind Jabal Surgham. Under the Khalifa's great black flag they now advanced, steadily and in perfect formation, but the shellfire and massed rifle-fire tore their ranks apart. Eventually three men, surrounded by the dead and dying, still held the black flag aloft. Then two of them fell and the third, shouting defiance, hurled his spear at his distant enemies and collapsed, riddled with bullets, under the crumpled flag.

Finally, just too late, the armies of Ali Wad Hilu and Uthman Sheikh al Din poured over the Kereri hills to attack MacDonald's Sudanese brigade. Had his attack synchronized with Yakub's, the brigade might well have been overrun. Then, when all hope of victory was gone, 400 mounted men, preferring death to defeat, charged across hundreds of yards of open ground; only a few riderless horses reached the British ranks.

Going over the battlefield, I was shown where the 21st Lancers had made their famous charge. This had been a costly blunder, ending unexpectedly in a dry water-course packed with swordsmen; most of the British casualties in the battle were incurred here. Winston Churchill, who took part in the charge, wrote a vivid account of it in *The River War*.

At the end of the day the Dervish casualties amounted to some 11,000 killed and 16,000 wounded; 4000 were taken prisoner. Steevens paid them the following tribute: 'The honour of the fight must go to the men who died. Our men were perfect but the Dervishes were superb, beyond perfection. It was the largest, best and bravest army that ever fought against us for Mahdism and it died worthy of the huge empire Mahdism had won and kept so long.' I can still recall the sense of tragedy I had felt as a boy when I read Steevens's account of the battle of Omdurman. Instinctively I had sided with the Dervishes, magnificent in their savage heroism.

The Khalifa, who had taken no part in the battle, escaped to Kordofan where he recruited several thousand more fighting men.

Fourteen months later, on 24 November 1899, a flying column of nearly 4000 troops under Sir Reginald Wingate brought him and his 5000 Dervishes to battle near Abba Island, where eighteen years previously the Khalifa had first met the Mahdi. The copper war drums thundered, the horns blared and the Khalifa's army charged under banners inscribed with the name of God and his Prophet. When the slaughter was over, Wingate's troops identified the body of the Khalifa, his dead Amirs on either side of him. They had seated themselves on the sheepskins taken from their saddles to await death, in the traditional Sudanese gesture of the defeated who are too proud to flee.

It has been estimated that the Sudan's population was reduced by half during the ten years of Mahdist rule. This was due in part to wars and punitive expeditions, but principally to an appalling famine in 1889, caused by a severe drought augmented by the wholesale recruitment of cultivators into the Khalifa's armies. To administer the conquered Sudan, Kitchener established the Sudan Political Service; though originally staffed by army officers, it had been, even in the early days, essentially civilian in character. This Service soon acquired a high repute and was generally regarded as the equal of the Indian Civil Service at its best.

When I reported to the Civil Secretary's Office, the day after my arrival in Khartoum, I was delighted to learn that I had been posted to Kutum in Northern Darfur, generally regarded as one of the three most coveted districts in the Northern Sudan. I learnt later that I owed this posting to Charles Dupuis, Governor of Darfur, whom I had met at a friend's house in Wales shortly after I had been selected for the Service. Dupuis was a lean, weathered man of forty-nine, attentive, courteous and unassuming. We had had a long and, for me, enthralling talk, mostly about Darfur. I sensed at once that his heart was in that remote province. Apparently, on getting back to Khartoum from leave he had enquired and been told I was being sent to Wad Medani, a sophisticated cotton-growing area on the Blue Nile, with the intention of breaking me in to routine office work. Dupuis told Gillan he was certain I would resign if I was posted there, and persuaded him to send me to Darfur instead.

Northern Darfur was the largest district in the Sudan, covering some sixty thousand square miles. It bordered the French Sahara, extended northwards into the Libyan Desert, and was inhabited by various tribes of Berber, negroid and Arab origin.

The District Commissioner was Guy Moore; he and I would be the only two British officials in the district. Kutum, the District Headquarters, had no wireless station, and mail arrived fortnightly by runner from Fasher, the Provincial Headquarters. Well-meaning people warned me that Moore travelled incessantly about his district, covered extraordinary distances with his camels, never bothered about meal times, and ate – when he did eat – at the oddest hours, and would expect me to do the same. I welcomed the prospect of serving under such a man.

Two servants, a *sufragi* or butler and a cook, had been engaged for me before I arrived; both were from Berber, the home of professional Sudanese servants. I have forgotten their names; neither lasted very long. In Khartoum, where there were excellent shops, I bought whatever I was likely to need in Darfur, since I gathered that Fasher could supply only the most basic requirements.

I went to see Pongo Barker, the Game Warden, at his office in the attractive little zoo in Khartoum, to get a game licence. My brother Brian had given me a .350 Magnum by John Rigby and I also had with me a 12-bore shotgun and a .22 rifle. When he realized I was keen on hunting and going to Northern Darfur, Barker told me I could hope to get addax, white oryx and Barbary sheep, all highly prized trophies. I asked about lion; he said there were plenty in the district but I was not likely to get one – no one had yet managed to shoot a lion at Kutum. I had every intention of doing so.

Before leaving Khartoum I was invited to dinner by Sir Stewart Symes, the Governor-General; I had met him at Haile Selassie's coronation when he was the Resident at Aden. I enjoyed the evening. With only his wife, his charming daughter and the Perrys present, it was a friendly family party in the impressive setting of the palace, rebuilt on the site where Gordon had kept his lonely vigil.

A few days later was King's Day, with a reception in the palace grounds for Government officials and their wives, officers of the Sudan Defence Force and of the British battalion stationed in Khartoum, and important chiefs from Northern Sudan, wearing scarlet or blue robes of honour. Sayyid Abd al Rahman, the Mahdi's posthumous son, was present: it was the only occasion on which I saw him. A stately, rather portly man, he lived on Abba Island, possessing great wealth and with a considerable following, especially in western Sudan. Understandably, his activities were watched by the Intelligence Branch with some suspicion.

The journey to Fasher took four days, the first by train to El Obeid, the terminus of the railway, in Kordofan Province. Douglas Newbold was Governor here. I was looking forward to meeting him again, after lunching with him at his London club and being immediately drawn to this large, humorous and erudite man. He had told me then how he had spent one of his leaves exploring the Libyan Desert with camels, and had spoken nostalgically of 'those wonderful days', which showed me at once that his was a kindred spirit. Unfortunately, when I arrived in El Obeid he was on tour. Visiting his headquarters, I was shown bullet-marks on the walls, a reminder of the Madhist siege of the town more than fifty years previously.

I now endured three tedious days in a lorry. There was no proper road to Fasher, and over much of the route, lorries carrying supplies picked their own way across the soft sand. Our engine boiled at intervals and we had constantly to stop and let it cool. I spent the first night at Nahud with the District Commissioner. He had that day sentenced a man to death for killing his newborn twins, a killing which was obligatory under Nuba tribal custom. I can still remember how shocked I was by the sentence.

Beyond Nahud I saw baobab for the first time, odd-looking trees that gave the impression of having been put into the ground upside down. There were lots of them, and the tribesmen hollowed out their bulky trunks to store water after rain: surprisingly it did not kill the trees. We filled our radiator from one of them. Otherwise there was little to look at as I bumped along, bored, uncomfortable and out of harmony with my surroundings.

When I arrived at Fasher, Dupuis was away attending a Baggara tribal gathering in Nyala, the southernmost of his five Darfur districts. But Tony Arkell, the Deputy Governor, and his wife, made me welcome and had me to stay. Arkell, a scholar with wide interests, was later Director of Antiquities in Khartoum. He had served in Kutum in the early 1920s, and he now took me to the prison as the best place for seeing the various types I would be dealing with. Among others we found many Zaghawa, a cheerful lot, mostly in prison for stealing camels, which Arkell explained was their tribal pastime. My first impression of the tribesmen I saw was not altogether favourable: the Fur in particular looked much less refined than Abyssinians, Somalis or Danakil. When I commented on this, Arkell said, 'Don't underestimate the Fur. Men like those over there established the Fur Empire: their Sultans dominated the other tribes in Darfur. They are a very tough people.'

I thought Fasher an attractive place. The small native town was situated among trees on the slope above the *fula*, a large pond from which women fetched water and where animals were taken to drink. Opposite the town was the Sultan's palace, now occupied by Major R. S. Audas, the veterinary surgeon. It was a spacious, flat-roofed building which, despite the European furniture, retained an atmosphere of its past. The other British officials lived nearby in standard houses of conventional pattern built by the Public Works Department.

In addition to Dupuis, Arkell and Audas, there were the District Commissioner and his assistant, who ran the central district; Lieutenant-Col. G. K. Maurice the doctor; the police officer who supervised the detachments stationed in each district; and a Public Works official. Also in Fasher was the headquarters of the Western Arab Corps, one of the four formations of battalion strength comprising the Sudan Defence Force.

CHAPTER 15

Service in Darfur

Aꜰᴛᴇʀ ᴀ ꜰᴇᴡ ᴅᴀʏꜱ Arkell sent me by lorry to Kutum, sixty miles north-west. When I arrived Guy Moore was on trek, but Reggie Dingwall, whom I was replacing, showed me round and helped me install myself.

I was immediately captivated by Kutum. Below my house was a broad, sandy wadi or water-course bordered by *haraz* trees in full leaf. On the far side was a small village of thatched huts; beyond that an infinitude of bush-covered country, broken in the distance by the jagged peaks of Jabal Si. Just behind my house was a jumble of massive boulders interspersed with thorn bushes.

My neatly thatched house was built of mud, with a cement floor. There was a large sitting room, a dining room, a bedroom, two small store rooms and a bathroom, though with neither bath nor basin; for lavatory, a bucket under a seat in a shed outside. No furniture was provided with the house but I had the camp equipment I had bought in Khartoum, including a canvas bath and basin; the servants heated bath water in a kerosene tin in the kitchen. Dingwall sold me a couple of tables, four upright chairs, an armchair, a bookcase and three charpoys. I slept on one of these bedsteads on the verandah, and in time covered the other two with colourful Fezzani rugs and leather cushions, and used them as divans in the sitting room. I put other rugs on the floor and eventually some lion skins. The mud walls were riddled with white ants but I later decorated them with spears, swords, throwing-knives and the horns of animals I shot. In the bookcase I put my complete sets of Conrad and Kipling, Black-wood's *Tales from the Outposts*, Gibbon's *Decline and Fall of the Roman Empire*, Frazer's *Golden Bough*, Lawrence's *Revolt in the Desert*, Doughty's *Arabia Deserta*, Churchill's *The River War* and a number of other books, mostly historical. I soon made the house comfortable and, despite its lack of amenities, infinitely preferred it to the characterless bungalows in Fasher. Moore's similar house was nearby, with the guest house between us. The office, the prison, the dispensary, the police lines ꞓnd the houses of the half-dozen

Sudanese officials were across a small gully on our side of the wadi.

Being entitled to an allowance for a riding camel and five baggage camels, I bought Dingwall's, but his riding camel was a slow, ponderous beast which I soon got rid of. In time I replaced the other five with riding camels, preferring to travel light, fast and far rather than plod at the head of a caravan laden with tents, chairs, tables and the other customary impedimenta. My camels appealed to me far more than the two horses I also bought soon after my arrival.

The day after Moore got back, he and I went to Fata Burnu where a tribal gathering was to be held, and installed ourselves in shelters that had been built for us. I had pictured Moore as a tall, spare, weather-beaten man of few words; in fact, he was short, tubby, talkative, with a red face, very blue eyes, and an explosive temper which he generally controlled. He had been in the Flying Corps during the First World War and won an MC. After the war he had served as an Intelligence Officer among the desert tribes in Iraq, where he learnt fluent Bedu Arabic. He had now been at Kutum five years and was to remain there for another eleven. Being on contract terms, he could not be promoted higher in the service than District Commissioner, but he had no wish to be.

At Fata Burnu the tribes were camped all around us. There were the three Zaghawa clans from the desert borderlands of the north, a restive, lawless people, hardy from the circumstances of their lives, and akin to the Bedayat, Goran and Tebu who inhabited the French Sudan as far west as the mountains of Tibesti. There were the Maidob, who had ridden for a hundred and fifty miles from their volcanic fastness, Jabal Maidob, on the edge of the Libyan Desert; Berti from the Tagabo hills; nomadic Umm Jalul and Zayadia, the camel-owning Arabs from the border of Kordofan; Bani Husain from the south-west of the district, the northernmost tribe in the great Baggara confederacy; and Fur from Jabal Si and elsewhere in the district.

Several of these tribes possessed *nahas*, great copper war drums, the tribal equivalent of regimental colours. Some had lost theirs during the period of the Mahdiya, and now only the Governor-General could award them. *Nahas* beat at intervals throughout the night, an unvarying, unhurried, far-reaching sound, as one camp answered the insistent challenge of another. Only here at the

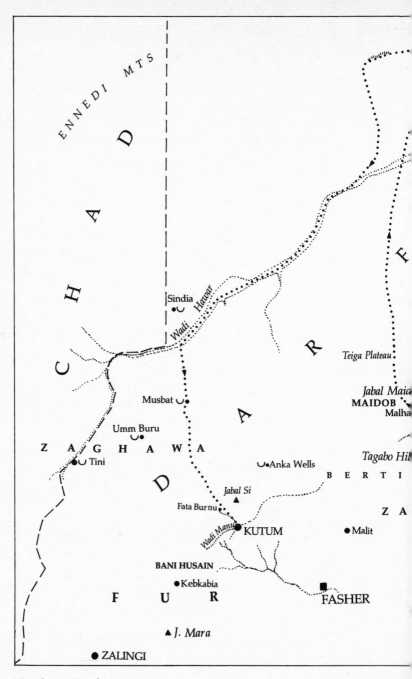

Northern Darfur, 1935–7

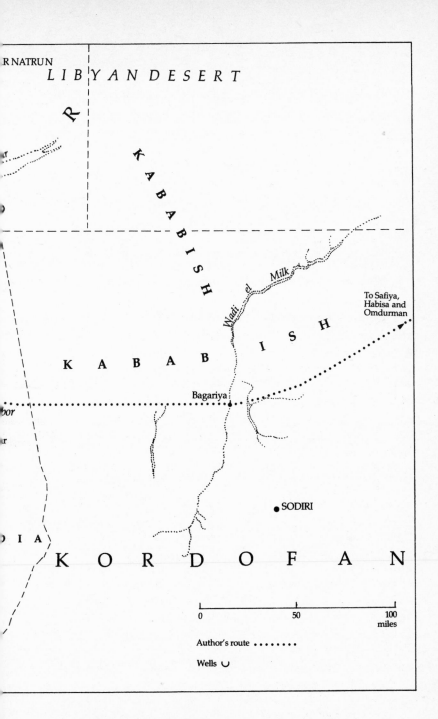

Author's route • • • • • • •

Wells ∪

gathering could *nahas* be beaten outside their tribal territory; to beat them elsewhere amounted to a declaration of war.

Dupuis the Governor arrived with his wife and his two special friends, Audas the vet and Maurice the doctor. These three had been together in Darfur for years, and had acquired the status of a triumvirate. Next day the tribes marched past the Governor, some ten thousand men in all. Mounted on horses and camels, they brandished swords and spears, and shouted their war songs to the thunder of the drums. The Zayadia were preceded by the emblem of their tribe, a decorated camel-litter, which carried the daughters of the sheikh. I had read somewhere that the great Rualla tribe in Arabia followed such a litter into battle.

The chiefs were resplendent in coloured robes, their turbans wrapped across their faces hiding all but their eyes; many of their followers, especially among the Zaghawa, wore bright-coloured *jibbas*. As they surged past I noticed a few in coats of mail, which were reputed to date from the time of the Crusades, as was the pattern of their long, straight swords. I found this parade, at which the tribes honoured their Governor, a thrilling introduction to Northern Darfur.

Dupuis stayed for two more days at Fata Burnu for discussions with the Magdum and the chiefs. In the past the Magdum had been the Sultan's representative in the north, but when the British took over the administration the office had been abolished. However, in accordance with the policy of indirect rule, it had recently been revived and Yusuf, a son of the previous Magdum, had been appointed over the tribal chiefs, with his court at Fata Burnu. Raised unexpectedly from obscurity, this elderly, rather pompous man lacked the assurance to deal effectively with such tribal barons as Malik Muhammadain Adam Sabi of the Zaghawa.

Muhammadain, a vigorous, middle-aged, hard-bodied man with an imposing, arrogant face, was the dominant personality in Northern Darfur, far too ambitious willingly to take second place. The other Zaghawa chiefs were Sultan Dosa, a kindly, white-bearded figure who ruled over only a small section of his clan, most of whom were on the French side of the border, and the young Shartai Tigani; he had been at school in Fasher and was the only chief in the district who could read and write.

A number of Muhammadain's Zaghawa, in search of easier living, had recently migrated south to Nyala District; there the Baggara chiefs found them unmanageable and had demanded their return to Kutum. This was one of the many subjects that cropped up for discussion at the gathering. More serious was the question of the Urti, a recalcitrant section of the Maidob, a large number of whom had proclaimed themselves Ansar and gone on pilgrimage to Abba Island. The Government was sensitive to such manifestations of religious unrest, particularly in the western Sudan. In 1921 a religious rising had occurred in the Nyala District in southern Darfur: the District Commissioner, the veterinary officer and a detachment of police had all been killed when the District Headquarters was overrun.

I now met Malik Sayyah of the Maidob. He looked twenty-five but was in fact about forty. He had a gentle, winning manner, a delightful smile and natural charm, but it was soon apparent that he was both resolute and responsible. The other chief I remember best from that gathering was Sheikh Hamid of the Bani Husain, the grizzled, unpretentious leader of a tribe that had fought under Yakub's black flag at Omdurman.

The previous day I had watched the Bani Husain ride past, carrying their distinctive, long-shafted, broad-bladed spears. Now they were selling horses to Audas, and I bought two. Audas had a reputation as a judge of horses, and a remarkable memory for them, claiming to remember every one of the hundreds he had bought. He was a jovial, uninhibited person and I was amused by his rather broad humour; we got on well from the start. He had travelled all over Darfur, and I enjoyed listening to stories of his experiences. He was gratified by my interest in big-game hunting, and gave me advice on how to sit up over a bait for a lion at night, and where to find Barbary sheep.

In the evenings, as we sat round a large fire over drinks, the others talked shop, ranging over the whole Province and every aspect of its administration. Listening, I realized how completely they had identified themselves with the people in their charge, and I sensed their misgivings about the changes that had inevitably to occur. Despite the difference in our ages, and my newness in the Sudan, they made me feel I was one of them. Dupuis in particular went out of his way to be understanding and encouraging. He was quietly authoritative, as well as likeable, and his wife too was friendly. In this male society she was never obtrusive, but she was obviously well informed about the country and hated the idea of leaving

191

Darfur. Dupuis, Audas and Maurice were all due for retirement, and on their departure an era ended and the Province lost much of its individuality.

Back in Kutum, Guy Moore proved to be as unconventional about office hours and meal times as I had been led to expect. He went riding each morning soon after sunrise and often did not get back for breakfast till ten or later. He would then probably stay in the office till five before returning to his house for lunch. When we were both in Kutum, which was not often, we spent our evenings together. At four thousand feet, Kutum was cold in winter and we were glad to sit by a fire. Eventually, sometimes after midnight, his servant would come and ask if we were ready for dinner.

Moore was never pompous. On duty we wore uniform, a practice inherited from the earlier military administration, and on first entering a senior's office it was customary to salute. Once, in a hurry, I forgot. Moore looked up and simply said, 'I think you've forgotten the quarterdeck.'

I found him a stimulating conversationalist, with decided and often unconventional views; these often coincided with my own, but when we disagreed he was never dogmatic. I remember we frequently discussed the diverse characters of Burton, Doughty, Lawrence and Leachman, and tried to analyse the attraction Arabia and the Arabs had for certain Englishmen. Moore's Arabian years were certainly for him the most memorable: he spoke with moving nostalgia of the desert, bringing individual tribesmen to life and firing me with a lasting desire to travel there. But usually we talked about the district and I soon realized that its inhabitants were in a very real sense his own people, that he felt for them not only responsibility but affection. Since he was unmarried, he made their welfare his prime concern; his compassion for any who were destitute or in trouble was apparent, and in such cases he was generous with his own money.

However, overshadowing those happy days was my growing anxiety about Abyssinia. In the papers, and in Reuter's telegrams which arrived with the mail, I read of the impotence of the League of Nations, the bombastic threats of Mussolini, the calm dignity of the Emperor's replies, the duplicity of France as represented by Laval, and the vacillation and pusillanimity of the Baldwin Government,

192

typified by the Hoare-Laval agreement to hand over vast areas of Abyssinia in order to appease Mussolini.

Moore was a comfort in that troubled time. Naturally he felt as I did, though without the personal involvement. But when I told him that if the Abyssinians were attacked I intended to resign and go and fight for them, he said, 'I understand your feelings, but don't jump the gun. I am convinced that we shall ultimately be at war with Italy; then you will get your chance to help Abyssinia while fighting for your own country.'

Soon after I arrived in the district, Moore sent me by camel to visit the Berti in the Tagabo hills. Although we had a boxbody car and a three-ton lorry – the only motor vehicles in the district – we seldom used them. Moore preferred camelback, which enabled him to keep in touch with the people as he rode. I had used camels in the Danakil country to carry loads, but this was the first time I rode one. Next day I was so stiff I could hardly move, but after another six hours in the saddle I loosened up and never again felt stiff from riding a camel.

On this occasion I was accompanied by the Berti chief; he rode a small but attractive thoroughbred camel but let me have it in part-exchange for the one I had bought from Dingwall. I named him 'Habib', Arabic for 'beloved', and became very attached to him; he was the first of a string of exceptionally fine male camels I gradually acquired. No one in the Sudan rode female camels, which in Arabia was standard practice; nor did they castrate their riding camels, as did the Goran and Tebu in the Sahara.

After a fortnight I got back to Kutum from the Tagabo hills, and one afternoon, on returning from the office, found several men waiting outside my house with the skin of a lioness they had speared that morning. Lying on the skin were two tiny cubs whose eyes were barely open. I reared them successfully and they made the most delightful pets. At first I kept them in a hut but as they grew I let them roam about in daytime. They liked to lie on my bedstead on the verandah.

One night months later I woke feeling something move under the bed. 'Damn!' I thought, 'The lions have got out.' I switched on my torch and looked under the bed straight into the eyes of a hyena. I made some noise like 'Shoo' and it scrambled out on the far side; it had no doubt been scrounging for scraps left by the cubs. The next night my servant, who had been carrying my bedding out to the verandah, came back in a hurry saying there was a lion there. Feeling sure it was the hyena, I went out with my rifle, put a joint of mutton, meant for my own next day's dinner, at a little distance in the moonlight, and waited on the bed. A few minutes later I shot the hyena, a striped one, and the first I had seen. This variety is smaller and much less common than the spotted hyena.

As the lions got bigger I was faced with the problem of what to do with them. Being constantly on trek I had nowhere to keep them permanently confined. I had hoped the Khartoum Zoo would take them but they had too many already. Turning them loose was obviously impractical and would be to release potential man-eaters since a lion reared as a pet loses its instinctive fear of human beings and, not having been taught by its parents to hunt, will all too readily kill people as an easy prey. I therefore decided when they were nine months old that I must shoot them, but I hated doing this, and missed them sadly.

I was trying hard to master the local Arabic dialect, which was very different from the classical form I had begun to learn in London. Soon after I arrived Moore gave me a court case to try, saying, 'See what you make of their Arabic. Remember, when I go on leave in six months' time you will be on your own in charge of the district.' This particular case, I remember, concerned the theft of a chicken, and the old woman from whom it had been stolen was as voluble and incomprehensible as her many witnesses. Moore would have dealt with the case in five minutes; it took me the morning and even then I doubt if I got it right.

Most of the cases Moore heard were appeals from chiefs' courts, and many concerned the theft of camels. Cases of homicide could be tried only by the DC presiding over a major court, assisted by two assessors. I remember one such case in particular; I was sitting on a case presided over by Moore. The accused was from Sultan Dosa's section of the Zaghawa. Two witnesses swore he had overtaken them while they were resting at midday on their way north from Kutum, and that he was accompanying a man, a woman and a small girl who had a camel with them. Next morning they had noticed vultures circling near the track. They had gone to investigate and found the bodies of the man, woman and child, all killed with an axe during the night; the child had woken and run a short distance.

They insisted that the murderer's footprints were those of the accused, whom they had seen the previous day. We accepted that they could recognize individual footprints, which are almost as distinctive as fingerprints; any of these people could have done the same. The murderer had taken the man's clothes and the camel, and when the accused had been arrested by the French across the frontier he was in possession of both. However, he insisted that he had bought the camel and the bloodstained clothes from a man he had not met before; he had suspected at the time that they were stolen, since he got them cheap. He had no witness to the transaction but denied he had been in Darfur at the time of the murder. Asked where he had been, he said in French territory looking for a stray camel, but he had not encountered anyone while doing so. In view of the emptiness of the country this would not have been surprising.

Knowing the two witnesses were of a tribe hostile to that of the accused, Moore questioned and cross-questioned them at great length but was unable to shake their evidence. The charge of murder seemed proved beyond doubt and Moore sentenced the man to death. The accused listened impassively to the sentence, then turned to his accusers, looked at them steadily for a while and said quietly: 'As for you two, I will meet you on the day of judgement': in Arabic, 'bi yaum ad din'. The death sentence was confirmed by the Chief Justice in Khartoum and the man was hanged in Fasher prison. Several of my contemporaries, at various times, had to preside over executions, but I am thankful I never had to.

I sat on a number of major court cases under Moore. I remember an especially sad one, when the accused, a young, good-looking Husaini, confessed he had killed his newly married wife because, 'She shamed me and I killed her.' She had undergone the severe Pharaonic circumcision, which leaves only a very small aperture. After a number of ineffective attempts to force an entrance, he had suggested widening her vulva with a tent-peg. She had scoffed, saying, 'Wait till I tell the girls on the well tomorrow that you were not man enough to enter me, and wanted to use a tent-peg.' He said: 'Tell them and I will kill you.' She did tell them, the women mocked him, and he killed her. Moore sentenced him to death, but put a strong recommendation to the Chief Justice that the sentence be commuted to imprisonment; and this was done.

Moore had decided to start a school at Kutum for the sons of chiefs, so that in time they could supervise the scribes who worked for their illiterate fathers and too often took advantage of it. There was no other school in the district, but few of us believed in the benefit of education for these tribal people, none of whom had yet demanded it: the British had brought them security and justice, with which, for the present, they were content. We were well aware of the disruption which must ensue from the wholesale intrusion of an alien education into their society, with the consequent breakdown of family life, drift to the towns, unemployment and discontent. That this was ultimately inevitable we recognized; we merely wished, in all good faith, to defer these consequences as long as possible. To argue, as some do today, that this reflected the policy of an alien Government to retain its hold on the Sudan is nonsense. Gordon College, founded by Kitchener soon after the reconquest of the Sudan, and the dedicated work of Christopher Cox and others in promoting education in the more sophisticated areas, effectively disprove this.

An elderly *faqih* or Muslim teacher was in charge of the school in Kutum, and responsible for the boys' religious instruction, while an agreeable young Sudanese from Fasher provided secular education. The boys came from all over the district. Between thirteen and seventeen years old, they got on well together and were a cheerful little band.

There was always plenty to do whenever either one or both of us was in Kutum. Once a week before breakfast there was the police drill to inspect, and every now and again their firing on the range to supervise. There was the school to keep an eye on and the dispensary to visit. We had a first-rate medical dresser; he always had a crowd of patients, who came from all over the district to be treated. I had acquired some medical experience in the Danakil country and by watching him I now learnt more.

I always carried some medicines with me when I went on trek and could treat wounds, infected eyes, malaria, diarrhoea, headaches, sores and such-like complaints. One of the commonest afflictions was tropical ulcers, which ate away the flesh on the shins and often affected the bone; even the hospital in Fasher had no effective cure for this. Cerebrospinal meningitis, endemic in the Nuba mountains, spread in 1935 to Darfur, and there were thousands of deaths in the province. It was dreadful to watch people dying of this disease; only worse was a death from tetanus which I witnessed.

When we were in Kutum we went to the office every morning

except Friday, which, being the Islamic sabbath, was a holiday. Since the Sudan was nominally an Anglo-Egyptian condominium, both the British and Egyptian flags flew from flagstaffs in front of the building. As soon as Moore, or I in his absence, appeared at the office, the police guard would turn out and present arms while the bugler sounded the salute. Our twenty-five police, commanded by a sergeant-major, were always smartly dressed. They were armed with service rifles, and each man had his own camel or horse; all were ready to go anywhere at a moment's notice.

In the office we had a staff of three. Khidr Efendi, who held the rank of *mamur*, was number three in the district. A distinguished-looking man, always immaculately uniformed, he had been in the service for many years and commanded general respect. Moore said he was utterly reliable, even if rather unimaginative. Abdullah Efendi was the *katib* or clerk. A youngish and very likeable man, he spoke and wrote good English, was competent at his job and well informed about the district; he helped me a lot when I first arrived and was finding my feet in the office. Yusuf Efendi, the *saraf* or accountant, was a large, fat man, with a big belly and a jolly laugh; among his other duties he was responsible for the money in the safe. The *qadi*, who dealt with religious matters, came from the Nile valley. He had his own office and we had little occasion to meet him: when we did he was invariably courteous and attentive. With his tightly-woven white turban and the long robe of his calling, this portly, dignified ecclesiastic appeared rather incongruous in our rural setting.

In the office there was the fortnightly mail to deal with, which often contained circulars that had no relevance to the district; and we had the monthly report to write; cases to try; petitions to hear; visiting chiefs and others to interview; taxes to assess or to check their payment; the money in the safe to count at irregular intervals; and a variety of other matters to cope with.

In the evening I would go for a ride on Habib or on one of my horses. Sometimes I visited the Tuareg encampment a few miles down the wadi. They were known as Kenin and except that the men dressed in white instead of the more customary blue, these Kenin wore traditional Tuareg clothes, including the veil.

Many Tuareg had migrated to Darfur and put themselves under its Muslim Sultan after desperately but unavailingly resisting the French intrusion into their land. After the British occupied Darfur, most of them had drifted back to their homeland. They were skilled leather workers and I bought from them some decorated leather cushions which I still have. These were the only Tuareg I have encountered. I thought them an aristocratic-seeming people, and I have always regretted that I never travelled among them in the Sahara.

We were due at the end of April 1935 to hold a meeting between the Maidob and the Kababish, two tribes whose mutual relationship was bad. The Kababish, the largest camel-owning tribe in the Sudan, inhabited northern Kordofan and in winter, after good rains, penetrated with their herds far into the Libyan Desert. Being Arabs, they despised the Maidob as 'blacks' and were infuriated when the Maidob, confident of safety once back in their mountain fastness, lifted Kababish camels from the neighbouring desert. Moore, who liked Malik Sayyah and his Maidob, and also felt a predictable affinity with the Kababish and respected Ali Taum, their sheikh, had instituted these annual meetings. Ali Taum and Sayyah, having met, became firm friends and relations between their tribes consequently improved.

Some weeks before this meeting, when a Kababish sheikh had visited him at Kutum, Moore, knowing I wanted a really first-class camel, suggested I should ask the sheikh to buy me one and bring it to the meeting. This I did, giving him the price he suggested.

Moore happened to be detained at Kutum so I went ahead, joining Sayyah's party at the meeting place on the Kordofan border, south of Jabal Maidob. Charles de Bunsen, who administered the Kababish, and Ali Taum and some forty Kababish arrived next day, a fine sight as they came across the desert towards us at a fast trot. The Arabs were turbanned and dressed in white, while their camels, extended at this pace, displayed an unexpected grace of movement. Leaving Sayyah and Ali Taum to foregather, de Bunsen and I camped together. He was a congenial companion, with whom indeed I found closer affinity than with any other of my Sudan contemporaries. He had been in charge of the Kababish for more than a year, and revelled in his nomadic existence.

This was my first encounter with an authentic Bedu tribe, the first time I heard the inimitable speech of the Arabian desert, very different from the Arabic used as lingua franca in Darfur. Moore had often spoken about Ali Taum, and in the evening de Bunsen took me to his camping-place. He was small, lightly-built, with the austere face of a desert aristocrat and a courtesy inherited from Arabian forebears. I noticed how attentively he listened to every word, and how, when he walked, he showed little sign of his advanced age though he had ridden far that day. The Kababish had been massacred by the Khalifa during the Mahdiya, and it had been Ali Taum who after the British occupation rebuilt his shattered tribe to its present pre-eminence.

Ali Taum now produced a superb camel, and said it was the one I had bought. Suspecting it was actually one of his own prize camels, I had qualms about accepting, but he insisted and de Bunsen supported him, saying it would give offence if I refused. It was a Bisharin from the Red Sea hills, home of the finest riding camels in the Sudan, and its name was Faraj Allah. There was certainly no other camel to equal it in Darfur, and few west of the Nile. No animal I have ever owned has meant as much to me.

Moore arrived for the last two days and was warmly greeted by the sheikhs. Sayyah and Ali Taum having by now settled all outstanding disputes between their tribes, the meeting had become a social occasion for drinking cups of sweet, black tea with Maidob and Kababish alike. In the evening Moore, de Bunsen and I sat and talked beneath the stars, while a goat Sayyah had given us roasted over the fire.

De Bunsen rode off with the Kababish in the morning, and Moore and I accompanied Sayyah back to the Jabal. This 6000-foot volcanic massif, on the edge of a desert stretching a thousand miles north to the Mediterranean, was inhabited by the Maidob, an exclusive race of mixed Berber and negro origin, with their own language. We pitched our tents near Sayyah's houses at Malha, a village where most of the buildings were huts of logs thatched with grass; Sayyah's were the same but more spacious and better constructed.

Nearby, in the almost sheer-sided crater of Malha, was a small black lake from which the Maidob collected a pitch-like substance as medicine for their camels. At midday the crater floor was alive with camels, cattle and sheep, which had gone down the 300-foot descent by barely negotiable tracks to water at some small springs and brackish wells. In the evenings sandgrouse in thousands flocked here to drink. I found them difficult to hit as they flew in and, being short of cartridges, I fired into them as they settled, killing several with each shot; these were very acceptable to the Maidob with me.

Dupuis had told me to report on the Barbary sheep in Jabal Maidob, a job he knew I would enjoy, because it gave an opportunity to shoot one. When Moore left me behind to do this, I went to Kejku, a little village a day's journey from Malha, with a white-bearded headman named Sulaiman. According to Sayyah, Sulaiman knew all there was to know about Barbary sheep on the Jabal. His village of huts, like those at Malha, was at the foot of a big mountain, Jabal Ubor. We climbed it the first morning; though it was almost vertical Sulaiman scrambled up without pausing for breath. I soon found that the old man was an exceptionally skilled stalker. He showed me several sheep, mostly ewes, and insisted that the rams all had small heads, but he eventually spotted one which he declared was very big. We had a difficult stalk to get within range, but when we did it dropped to the shot and rolled down the slope. It was a magnificent animal, rich chestnut in colour with a long fringe of hair down its chest, and far bigger than I had expected, taking three of us to lift it. With its massive back-sweeping horns measuring 28¾ inches, it had a really fine head.

I saw more of these sheep during the week I was there, but, as I had no wish to shoot another, there was no need to get close. Even so, it was hard work keeping up with Sulaiman as we scoured these precipitous mountains. I remember one cliff-face, perhaps a thousand feet high and three miles long, intersected by dramatic gorges where I expected to find water on account of their greenness. When I wrote my report I proposed that Sulaiman should be appointed guardian of the sheep, for a small salary, and this was approved.

Sayyah had suggested that from Malha I should cross the desert to Anka wells, a day's journey north of Kutum. He also offered to accompany me, saying we might well come across white oryx and even addax. I willingly agreed and decided to take only Kalol, one of my two camelmen. I therefore sent my two servants, the other camelman, the three police, with my tent and camp equipment, back to Kutum by the normal route through Melit, keeping with me just my blankets. After the others left I stayed for a couple of days in one of Sayyah's houses, furnished with a charpoy, two or three stools and some rush-matting and rugs. I wanted nothing more.

We went out of our way looking for oryx, so it took five days to reach the wells at Anka, but we were carrying enough water in goatskins. One day after a long stalk I shot a solitary bull oryx with a good head. The same evening we came on some grass that had sprung up after a recent shower, and there we found a herd of forty-two, a splendid sight as they poured over a nearby ridge, a mass of rufous and white bodies topped by long, scimitar-shaped horns. There too we saw a flock of eighteen ostrich, several herds of the large addra gazelle, and the tracks of five lion. I wondered where these found water to drink. Sayyah maintained that desert lion got the liquid they needed from the stomachs of the animals they killed, but I was still puzzled as to where their prey obtained theirs, since the scanty herbage was mostly dry. We saw no addax; they apparently lived even deeper in the desert than the oryx.

Except when I shot the oryx and we ate chunks of freshly grilled meat, we fed on *assida*, a stiff millet porridge, and *mullah*, a vegetable sauce, which one of Sayyah's four Maidob cooked for our evening meal. He would place a large lump of *assida* in a dish, scoop a hole in it and fill that with *mullah*: the seven of us fed together, using our right hands. After the meal we drank strong, sweet tea, served in small glasses. We ate otherwise only a handful of dates before starting in the morning. I found this diet wholly satisfying.

I sat or slept on a rug on the ground, with my few possessions in my saddle-bags, and enjoyed the easy, informal comradeship that this life and our surroundings engendered. It was my first experience of the infinite space of the real desert, its silence and its windswept cleanness. When I told Guy Moore of its fascination for me he said, 'When I get back from leave you can go off for a month into the Libyan Desert. I'd like you to do that. I always think of the desert as the High Altar of God.'

When I returned to Kutum I found Moore had gone on trek ten days earlier and that news had just come in of an affray among the Zaghawa, a hundred miles away near Umm Buru: two were reported killed and five wounded. I went off in the boxcar with three police and despite a badly leaking radiator arrived the same day. The fight had resulted from a blood feud involving many people; it took me three days to sort it out. I had arrested seven men and despatched them on foot to Kutum under police escort when I heard of yet another killing, at Sultan Dosa's village. I was preparing to go there when the *mamur* arrived in the lorry, so I sent him to do the investigation and returned to Kutum.

There I found twelve Urti, leaders of the religious exodus from Jabal Maidob to Abba Island, who had been arrested in White Nile Province and sent back to Kutum. They were impressive old men, with whom I felt instinctive sympathy. Moore sent them to the Magdum's court, where after swearing on the Koran not to leave the Jabal again without permission, or cause further trouble, they were released. I was glad it was settled like that.

Ever since the Sudan Service had been established, its purpose had been to administer the country as efficiently as possible, solely with the aim of safeguarding its inhabitants and improving their lot, a task i⁺ had performed supremely well. The people of Darfur had never known the like. I recognized this, yet sometimes wondered whether it had justified our invasion of the Sudan, and the slaughter at Omdurman of ten thousand men fighting to defend their religion and their independence. I also questioned whether it was right to try to impose on the Sudanese the conventions and values of our utterly alien civilization, and sometimes expressed these doubts in letters to my mother. I could not help feeling that other races were entitled to their own customs and moral standards, however much these might differ from ours. I had witnessed the incessant killing among the Danakil, but accepted it as part of their way of life, and felt no desire to see them administered and civilized.

Dupuis paid us a farewell visit; Philip Ingleson, his successor, was with him. I had felt drawn to Dupuis as soon as I met him. An individualist with a wealth of experience of an Africa that was fast disappearing, he differed markedly from Ingleson, a more conventional representative of the modern Sudan Political Service. Ingleson had never met Moore and that evening asked him many detailed questions about the administration of the district, while I talked to Dupuis about Barbary sheep on Jabal Maidob.

CHAPTER 16

Darfur:
Herdsmen and Hunters

I N EARLY AUGUST 1935 Guy Moore went on leave; before going he told me to go to the Bani Husain country to meet Paul Sanderson, a neighbouring Assistant District Commissioner, and settle a boundary dispute. Knowing lion were plentiful in that region, I hoped I should have the chance on this journey to shoot one.

I got my chance on the way, near Kebkabia. After hearing lion roaring in the night I went out to look for them at dawn with three Bani Husain; they soon found tracks of five lion, which they followed for two hours. I was amazed at the skill with which, even over stony ground, they followed the tracks with seeming ease, noting here a shifted pebble, there a crushed grass stem, before picking up yet another slight indication a few yards further on. Only occasionally did they halt and stoop to check that they were right.

Suddenly one of them pointed. I looked and saw, lying under an acacia bush about forty yards away, a nearly full-grown lion. It saw us too, and sat up, but I was hoping for a fully adult lion and did not shoot. However, the next instant a lioness sprang up and I fired and heard the bullet strike. Then the scrub erupted with lions. I counted one, two, three, as if marking birds at a pheasant drive, and killed one lioness and wounded another, firing my Rigby .350 almost as fast as I could work the bolt. Then the first lioness charged and I broke her shoulder and killed her with the next shot.

Meanwhile, the other wounded lioness had disappeared into a patch of bushes and long grass, leaving a trail of blood. Before going in to look for her we skinned the two I had killed, hoping she would die in the meantime. It was an uninviting place to have to follow a wounded lion, and when we did so we noticed she had lain down frequently and bitten everything in reach. Then she came at us from under a bush and I killed her as she charged.

At our next camp we again heard lion in the night, and soon after sunrise some Fur from a nearby village found the tracks of a very large male. About fifteen Fur, armed with spears, went with me, following the tracks at a loping pace that was hard on my wind. One would hold the spoor and the rest would fan out on either side and pick it up as soon as he lost it, attracting each other's attention with a few clicks. After about an hour and a half we came to where the lion had lain up, but he had evidently seen us and moved off again.

The country here was fairly open, with only scattered bushes and occasional gullies. Lion dislike going faster than a walk and this one only broke into a trot when we got close: by pushing him along we hoped to provoke him into facing us. We seemed to have been following him for hours before I got a brief glimpse of him among some scrub, and a little further on two dogs that were with us brought him to bay. I approached to within forty yards. He looked enormous as he stood there, flicking his tail from side to side and growling, a vibrant, hair-raising noise. I had read that when a lion flings his tail out straight behind him he invariably charges. I shot him in the chest as he did so. He staggered and the next shot killed him.

I was due to meet Paul Sanderson next day, but as we were loading the camels a man arrived from one of the Bani Husain villages, reporting that a lion had killed a horse in the night and imploring me to come and shoot it. Needing no persuasion, I sent the caravan off with a note to Sanderson to say I would join him that evening, and followed the man to his village. Nearby they showed me the horse's half-eaten carcass. I selected three men to come with me, and insisted that the others, most of them mounted, should remain behind. It did not occur to me to ride the lion down, which was what they would have done.

The country hereabouts was intersected by numerous dry water-courses bordered by thick bush and tall grass, green after recent rain. It had poured in the night and even I could follow the tracks without difficulty; they were those of a very big male. We disturbed him where he was lying up; we did not see him but heard him growl as he made off.

At first he stuck to thick cover, then took to more open country where some vultures wheeling above him indicated where he was. An hour or so later he descended into a large wadi. I shall never forget those enormous pug marks slowly filling with water where he had gone down the sandy wadi-bed before us, the drops from his coat still glistening on the pebbles where he had crossed a pool.

Every now and then he took to the bank and left a track through the reeds like a buffalo's. Once he sprang with a snarl from a nearby thicket, but I was on the opposite side. After a pause to collect ourselves we again took up his trail, which now twisted and turned. I realized he was only just ahead. Then I heard the sound of panting. It was long past noon and we had been going for hours under a blazing sun and I was exhausted. Confusedly, I thought the sound must be from a dog that had followed us unobserved. A second later, the others whispered, 'Ahu! Ahu!' ('That's him! That's him!') and I realized it was the lion. I just hoped he would not make off again.

The grass was long and he was half-concealed under some bushes: I peered for some seconds before vaguely making out his shape six or eight yards away. He had started to growl threateningly, and I was sure he was about to charge. I fired at what I thought was his head. Then he came straight at us. He kept low, only at the last moment rearing up. My rifle went off again as I was knocked over backwards; I think the lion's shoulder must have caught me. The man beside me thrust his spear like a pike into the lion's jaw; as I went down I saw him collapse with the lion on top, and his brothers close in to help him. Before I could get back on my feet one man had been pulled down and the lion had hooked the other in the shoulder. I pushed my gun into the lion's ear and pulled the trigger.

The first man had deep claw-marks in his chest; one of his brothers had been clawed across the thigh, the other across the back of the shoulder. It had all been over in seconds, too quickly for the lion to do more damage. The three of them stood there inspecting their wounds and one said: 'God be praised, that brute won't kill any more of our cattle.' None showed any sign of pain. For them it was all in the day's work; if a lion killed their stock they hunted it down and speared it, regardless of casualties.

I wondered what the hell I was going to do, with three wounded men on my hands, no transport and no idea where I was. Fortunately, the others from the village had followed us, and hearing the shots and the lion's snarls galloped to our assistance. We put the injured on horses, supported in their saddles, and sent them ahead to the rendezvous with Sanderson, while the rest of us stayed and skinned the lion. Then someone threw the wet skin over the saddle of a horse: I was astonished that it showed no alarm, but I had already noticed that these horses paid little attention when brought

205

near the dead lion, and even grazed within a few yards of it.

At Sanderson's camp I treated the injured with a weak solution of carbolic acid; they were very stoical while I did so and showed no signs of pain. In those days there were no antibiotics and even a slight wound from a lion's claw often led to death from septicaemia. This accounted for the large proportion of European hunters who died after being mauled by lion or leopard, though Africans appeared to have acquired greater immunity. In this case, however, the wounds turned very septic and I could smell them twenty yards away. The chest wound was the worst; the whole cavity was apparently filled with pus, which flooded out when I applied pressure. I treated them here for a week before taking them slowly to the dispensary at Kabkabia. All three recovered and one of them came with me again when I hunted lion.

In Northern Darfur there were few game animals except in the desert, so the many lion lived almost entirely off the tribesmen's herds. Among the Bani Husain, in particular, it was a matter of honour to hunt down a lion that killed their cattle, and they expected to lose men while doing so. In five years they had suffered more than 120 killed and mauled. The Zaghawa did the same. Unlike the much-vaunted Masai in East Africa, these tribes had no shields; as a result when they moved in on a bayed lion, whoever was charged was almost invariably killed, and others would be mauled or even killed before they could stab it to death.

In the Sudan, lion and leopard were officially accounted vermin, requiring no game licence to shoot them. During my two years at Kutum I shot thirty, which was perhaps the most beneficial thing I did there, and certainly the most exciting. I never shot lion over a bait or sat up for them at night.

Sanderson stayed with me for the week I was here; we held a number of meetings, settled the boundary dispute and mapped the area. I found Sanderson interesting, for having spent several years in the Zalingi District, comprising Jabal Marra, the Fur heartland, he was knowledgeable about the Fur. He had a great respect for this industrious race. I had visited the Fur on Jabal Si, where they were shy and elusive, keeping to themselves. I spent several days there hunting for kudu and this enabled me to establish contact with the Fur, whereupon I found them unexpectedly likeable.

On my return to Kutum, while I was inspecting the prison, I noticed a fifteen-year-old boy among the prisoners. He was called Idris Daud and came from Sultan Dosa's village of Tini but he had unusually negroid features for a Zaghawi. Idris was charged with homicide. The *mamur*, who had made a preliminary enquiry, told me that in a scuffle over the ownership of a horse Idris had inadvertently knifed a boy: it was obviously a case to be settled by payment of blood money. I disliked seeing a boy of his age locked up indefinitely with a crowd of men, so after one of his elders had guaranteed that he would not run away I released him, and told him to go and help in my house. Not long afterwards I had to sack my *sufragi* for pilfering my stores and drinking the whisky I kept for my guests, and a little later I sent the cook back to Khartoum because I wanted local tribesmen with me, not professional servants from the Nile valley. I found in the village a Furawi called Adam, who could cook, took on a boy to help him, and put Idris in charge of the house. He proved reliable and intelligent, and was always cheerful, a relief after the gloomy *sufragi*.

From now on Idris identified himself with me. I soon discovered he was a skilful tracker and utterly fearless. Once, after lion, we found some barely discernible tracks which the Zaghawa with me declared were fresh. Idris maintained they were from the previous day, and was told by his elders not to talk out of turn. However, he was right, as we discovered on following the spoor to where the lion had lain up the night before.

I now began to receive constant appeals to come and shoot lion that were killing stock. The Fur at Ain Qura, a village some forty miles from Kutum, complained bitterly that they were losing a cow every few days, so I went there in the boxcar with Idris. In the evening we walked down to a nearby spring, returning at dusk to the village. Next morning we found we had been followed by three lion which had then killed a horse in an Arab encampment close by. I sent out men to locate them; they did so and one came back in the afternoon with news.

Idris and I immediately set off with a party from the village, all of them quiet and tense like a raiding party. Some figures waved to us from the top of a steep ridge and we scrambled up to join them. Here the lions had lain up that morning, looking down on the village and the grazing cattle. There were three of them; their tracks followed the ridge and we needed only an occasional indication to keep us right. As we rounded some rocks we were greeted by rumbling growls, not unduly loud but continuous and menacing. I could see no sign of lion but standing there with every sense alert I knew they were near, and was very conscious that the last lion I had shot had knocked me down.

After what seemed hours, one of them stood up behind a rock forty yards away. He was facing me, growling and lashing his tail. I fired and he staggered out of sight. The other two growled more loudly and threateningly. I got occasional glimpses of them among the rocks and bushes, but never long enough to risk a shot, especially as there was dead ground between us. Then I saw them for a second as they topped a rise and disappeared. I went forward cautiously to where I had shot one lion, and as I did so one of the others broke back across the plateau, no doubt turned by herdsboys from below who had appeared waving sticks and spears. The lion was moving fast, a hundred yards away. I knocked him over and as he got to his feet hit him again, but it took yet another shot to kill him. Once wounded, a lion will sometimes temporarily survive a second bullet which had it been the first would have killed him dead; it is this that makes the charge of a wounded lion particularly dangerous. I found the first lion dead within twenty yards of where I had shot him.

Celebrations in the village lasted till dawn: at midnight I was fetched out of bed to watch the women dancing. I was also expected to mark the occasion with gifts of money all round, and was happy to do so. This rejoicing, however, was premature. The surviving lion, known as Abu Higl, or Father of the Bracelet, from a white mark round a front foot, continued to kill their cattle. On several occasions Idris and I followed his spoor, but he invariably lay up down wind and made off as we approached. Jim Corbett, in *Man-eaters of Kumaon* and several other interesting books, maintained that tigers have no sense of smell, but I am convinced that lions have this sense. It may not be acute, but Abu Higl's was sufficient to ensure survival.

I was in the office one morning, trying a case, when a Furawi came in, having travelled all night from a village near Jabal Si, where a lioness was constantly killing their cows. He said she had killed the evening before; would I come and shoot her? I immediately adjourned the case, sent to the house for Idris and my rifle and left for the village in the boxcar with Idris and the Furawi. We arrived in the afternoon, found the spoor of the lioness and followed it.

The tracking was difficult, mostly over stony ground, and it was late evening before I saw the lioness on the edge of thick bush; all but her hindquarters were concealed. Realizing she only had to move and I should lose her, I fired at her spine, and missed. The Fur with me said resignedly that God had not decreed her death. I got back to Kutum in the middle of the night. A few days later this lioness killed another cow. The villagers hunted her down and speared her to death, but had seven casualties, three of them fatal. Hearing the news, I felt responsible.

In November 1935 Guy Moore returned from leave and I was able to report that all was well in the district and that I had even managed to collect the outstanding taxes from some recalcitrant Zaghawa, one of the tasks he had set me to do. Ingleson, the Governor, had told Moore he was expecting both of us in Fasher for Christmas, to attend a fancy-dress party he and his wife would be giving. This appealed to neither of us.

It also meant cutting short the month Moore had promised me in the Libyan Desert, where I was planning to travel north from Jabal Maidob to Bir Natrun. Because of this exasperating invitation, there was no time to lose in setting off for Bir Natrun. I had already sent my camels ahead to Jabal Maidob on the southern edge of the desert, and I followed two days later in the car. Idris I had to leave behind, since his blood debt had not yet been paid. Moore undertook to settle this in my absence.

I had realized as soon as I arrived at Kutum how lucky I was to be serving under Moore; looking back, I know that few other DCs would have put up with me. Moore not only put up with me; he also gave me his confidence, and won mine. I found I could discuss anything with him. He never snubbed me, however extreme, unconventional or irrational the views I expressed. Some of his own views were as unexpected, and some of his actions; for instance, although a devout Christian, he invariably kept the Islamic fast of Ramadan. Predictably, Gordon was his hero; I remember he raised more than an eyebrow when I said late one night that I preferred Wad al Nijumi.

I felt from the start that Moore recognized and appreciated my craving for hardship and adventure, my preference for wild, remote places. I undoubtedly owe much of my later success as a traveller to his unobtrusive coaching. No other DC would have sent me into the Libyan Desert to learn about desert travel with camels under testing conditions.

More important, something decisive in my life, he taught me to feel affection for tribesmen. Ever since then it has been people that have mattered to me, rather than places. I have never craved magnificent scenery or opportunities for sport in the way that I have longed to be with certain tribes and, above all, certain individuals among them. Ten years later the Empty Quarter was to offer me the challenge of the unknown, but it was the comradeship of the Bedu I travelled with that drew me back to that land year after year; two among them in particular mattered to me as few other people have mattered. A similar attachment kept me eight years in the Marshes of Iraq and has now kept me longer in northern Kenya.

On 3 December I left Jabal Maidob for Bir Natrun, accompanied by Kalol, his brother Ahmad, four police, and two Maidob who knew the route. Bir Natrun, more than two hundred miles from the Jabal, was the first of the three watering places on the Darb al Arbain, the Forty Days' Road, the ancient slave route from Darfur to Egypt. Bir Natrun was visited by Maidob, Zaghawa, Kababish and even by caravans from Dongola, who went there to fetch natron and salt. In recent years, Goran from Ennedi had watered there before raiding the Kababish; this fact afforded an ostensible reason for my visit.

From Bir Natrun I intended to travel west to the Musbat wells in Zaghawa country, so I also had with me an old Zaghawa called Ghalib to guide us there. Ghalib had done this journey several times as a young man; though his sight was now failing the others were sure he would find the way. We travelled light; apart from food, and enough goatskins of water to last nine days, we only took cooking pots and blankets, though for our camels, including four baggage animals, we carried grain and large bundles of grass. I wore the local dress: a long shirt or *jibba*, loose drawers and a turban; European clothes are singularly uncomfortable on camelback.

It was now Ramadan, the fasting month. From sunrise to sunset my companions abstained from eating or drinking, and I kept them company. I found it no hardship; the weather being cool, I had no difficulty going through the day without a drink.

We started each morning before sunrise after eating some dates and drinking tea; and rode till sunset when we cooked our evening meal of *assida* and *mullah*. After this we sat round the small, dying fire, talking and drinking more tea, but I soon found it cold under the stars and was glad to snuggle under my blankets, lying on the sheepskin from my saddle; even so it was chilly before dawn. Travelling round the district I always rode at a shuffling trot, but here in the desert, to spare our camels, we never went above a walk, a pace that even on the most comfortable camel puts constant strain on the rider's back.

For the first two days we passed occasional bushes and patches of dry grass. The Maidob advised us to collect and carry with us what firewood we could, since we should find no more till the Wadi Hawar. We had seen some three hundred Kababish camels scattered over the desert and eventually spotted a mounted man, but he made off, possibly taking us for Maidob raiders. I could understand what a temptation these untended camels must be to the Maidob. The rains had failed this year, otherwise the Kababish would have been grazing their herds on the *jizu*, the desert herbage that even as far north as Bir Natrun comes up after rain. On the third day, soon after sunrise, we topped a low rise, and I caught my breath. Ahead was empty desert, an expanse of bare, red sand without a trace of vegetation; it stretched unbroken to the horizon. The next day we reached the Wadi Hawar and camped. The wadi was a half a mile across and well wooded. We turned the hungry camels loose to feed and that evening sat round a blazing fire. I was astonished to come across such a place in this stark desert.

Three days later we arrived at Bir Natrun, where the pans of salt and natron lay in a narrow depression seven miles long, enclosed by outcrops of rock partly smothered under sand dunes. In many places fresh water was within a few inches of the surface, the best at the western end of the depression near six dom palms; elsewhere it was slightly brackish. The Zaghawa caravans, when they visited Bir Natrun, always confined themselves to this area, whereas the Maidob and Kababish camped at the eastern end of the depression where there was a small grove of date palms. It was here we encountered fifteen Maidob with fifty-six camels, and four small parties of Kababish; some Zaghawa had left Bir Natrun two days before our arrival. There was practically nothing for the camels to eat: two fairly extensive areas of stiff, knife-edged grass had been grazed almost bare by recent caravans, otherwise there were only a few small patches of nearly leafless scrub.

We stayed for two days before leaving for Musbat. Our route for the first three hours wound among outcrops of rock partly covered by sand, and marked on every skyline by piles of stones. Then for four days, until once again we reached the Wadi Hawar, we rode across endless small undulating dunes, a little group of men and camels reduced to utter insignificance by the vast emptiness all around.

I was exhilarated by the sense of space, the silence, and the crisp cleanness of the sand. I felt in harmony with the past, travelling as men had travelled for untold generations across deserts, dependent for their survival on the endurance of their camels and their own inherited skills. The pattern of some camel droppings would indicate to my companions whether a caravan had been coming to Bir Natrun or leaving it; a disturbance in the sand would reveal that a herd of addax had moved south four days earlier; a trace of withered vegetation showed where a shower had fallen six months before; a score of other similar signs were subconsciously noted as we passed. Kalol, encouraged by my evident interest, was happy to instruct me in camel management as he rode beside me.

By the time we camped on the fourth day Ghalib was uneasy; he felt we should have reached the Wadi Hawar again. All that afternoon he had peered about, asking if we saw any trees. However, starting again four hours before dawn, we reached the wadi at first light. I realized we could easily have crossed it unawares in the dark, for it was marked by no noticeable depression, and the few trees were sometimes several hundred yards apart. We followed its course for the next three days before turning south for Musbat, which we reached after four more days.

South of the Wadi Hawar we came on abundant grazing and almost immediately encountered three herds of addax, respectively of fifty, forty-five and twenty-one animals. I had noticed their distinctive spoor north of Jabal Maidob, and many recent tracks north of the Wadi Hawar, but until now I had only seen three, far off near Bir Natrun. I had found no indication that any addax watered there. Indeed Pongo Barker had told me that an addax in Khartoum Zoo had never been seen to drink even in summer, even though water ran through its cage.

Addax are about the same size as white oryx, pale grey, almost white, with long spiral horns and exceptionally large shallow hooves, well adapted to moving over sand. I shot two of them. So far the only meat we had eaten on the journey had been two large tortoises, cooked in their shells; not exactly a banquet. Now we made up for it. Meat after long deprivation I have always rated high as an indulgence: this meat was juicy and delicious. It is curious, with African game animals, that the more barren the environment, the more succulent the flesh. Addax inhabit drier areas than oryx and their meat is correspondingly better.

We had seen a herd of forty-five oryx near Jabal Maidob but saw no more until we were near Musbat; there I counted two hundred and thirty in all, a hundred and seventeen in one herd. We had seen occasional Dorcas gazelle nearly every day, even as far north as Bir Natrun, but only two small parties of the large Adra gazelle. Ostrich were numerous; in one place I counted sixty-seven within a mile. We chanced on a fresh egg lying on the sand, which made an excellent omelette, enough for all of us. Just south of the Wadi Hawar we had found the remains of an addax killed two days earlier by a lion, and we saw tracks of seven other lion before we reached Musbat. Among other interesting tracks were those of giraffe and eight cheetah near Jabal Maidob, and of a pack of wild dog in the Wadi Hawar.

Since the Kababish, when they were on the *jizu*, required no water – the milk from their herds sufficing them, and the succulent green herbage satisfying the camels – they could remain throughout the winter wherever there was any *jizu*. With their old-fashioned rifles they shot oryx and addax after their dogs had brought them to bay. This provided them with meat, while the tough oryx hides made excellent ropes for loading camels. Their horns were also useful for digging out the salt and natron; I saw innumerable horns lying about on the pans at Bir Natrun.

During the summer when the oryx herds had moved south, the Zaghawa hunted oryx on horseback, but the fact that their horses needed water daily restricted the distance they could hunt from wells, even when carrying water with them. In the past, inter-tribal fighting and the fear of Goran raiders had curbed the activities of hunting parties, but by 1935 their principal handicap was competition from their fellow tribesmen and an increasing shortage of animals. However, I never anticipated that in time both oryx and addax would be virtually wiped out by parties hunting in cars.

*   *   *

I arrived at Musbat on Christmas Eve. The car was awaiting me so I reached Kutum in time for Guy Moore and myself to drive to Fasher for Christmas dinner. We wore dinner jackets since neither of us wanted to don fancy dress as required. When criticized for this, we said that we were parodying Englishmen who dressed for dinner in the jungle. I was glad Idris had not been brought to help the Governor's servants, for I felt embarrassed, wondering what they all thought of the way we Christians were celebrating the birthday of our Prophet. They saw the Governor dressed up as a prisoner, his middle-aged wife as a schoolgirl, other wives dressed as men, their husbands as sheikhs, troubadours, bull-fighters and God knows what else, and all of them drinking and dancing and getting noisier.

I was interested to meet Colonel Hugh Boustead, who had recently on retirement from the Army been appointed a contract District Commissioner at Zalingi in western Darfur; I had missed him in Cairo where he too had been staying with John Hamilton, but Hamilton had told me a lot about him. All his life Boustead had sought adventure, and revelled in hardship and danger. At the beginning of the First World War he had been a Midshipman on the South Africa station. Fearing that he might not see action, he had actually deserted the Royal Navy, joined the Transvaal Scottish, and gone with them under a false name to Egypt and to France, where he won an MC; he was later granted a King's Pardon for desertion. After the war he was attached to General Denikin's White Russian Army; later he joined the Sudan Camel Corps and rose to command it. After a noteworthy journey in the Himalayas, he had taken part in the 1933 Everest expedition.

A small, wiry man with a lined, leathery face and greying hair, he was intensely energetic, with a passion for physical fitness: he had captained Great Britain's pentathlon team at the 1920 Olympic Games in Antwerp. Although by no means an intellectual, he was widely read, and had an endearing, playful sense of humour.

At Zalingi Boustead found contentment, working to improve the lot of the Fur cultivators in his district. Being convinced that their happiness depended on a raised standard of living, he never questioned the repercussions of Western education and technology. For all his versatility he was by nature conventional, holding firmly to English ways: he would never have worn native dress. On tour he would always be seated on a chair with his tribesmen gathered round him on the ground, and he would not have shared a meal with them; yet their welfare was his main concern and years later they remembered him with affection.

Another striking personality whom I now met for the first time was Clifford Drew. A vast, red-faced, beefy man known to his friends as Pansy Drew, he had taken over as doctor from Maurice. He was a brilliant surgeon; six years later, during the Abyssinian campaign, many would owe their life to his skill, operating under primitive conditions.

While Moore and I were in Fasher, Renouf, an unpopular man who commanded the Western Arab Corps, gave a dinner party, during the course of which he mentioned that the Italians had apparently occupied Bir Natrun. The previous year an Italian force had stationed itself on the desert wells at Uwainat, just across the Libyan border inside the Sudan, and now some Arabs had reported that there were white men on Bir Natrun, presumably Italians.

From the bottom of the table I interjected: 'But I was at Bir Natrun three weeks ago and there weren't any Italians there then, only some Maidob and Kababish.' Everyone looked at me, and after a rather ominous pause either Renouf or Ingleson said: 'Then I suppose it was you. Well, you have stirred things up. Ministers in London have taken note, troops here in the Sudan have been alerted. I even think that extra aircraft are to be flown out. I'll get a telegram off at once.' I could just imagine it: 'Not Italians but Thesiger at Bir Natrun.'

Two months later I got the following note from Ingleson: 'I am directed to inform you that H. E. The Governor-General has read your "Notes on Malha-Bir Natrun-Musbat Salt Caravan Route" with interest, and to convey to you His Excellency's compliments on your report.'

Moore and I had been in a hurry to get back to Kutum as soon as the Christmas festivities were over to organize a Zaghawa tribal gathering, which Ingleson was to attend, at Umm Buru, Malik Muhammadain's village. At the last moment Ingleson sent word to cancel it, owing to the spread of meningitis. As there had been no cases among the Zaghawa, Moore motored into Fasher and persuaded him to allow the gathering to take place. Italy had invaded Abyssinia in October, so far with singularly little success, but owing to the proximity of the Italians in Libya, Northern Darfur was alive with rumours. Moore felt that to cancel the gathering at the last moment for no apparent reason would only increase anxiety, so it took place at the end of January and was a spectacular success. The march-past was particularly colourful and impressive, and Muhammadain, always a striking figure and especially on this occasion, dominated the scene in his splendid, voluminous robes.

In February, when I was to go on leave to England, Guy Moore told me he had obtained permission from Khartoum for me to follow the Maidob sheep route to Omdurman and report on it. He knew how I should appreciate making this journey by camel to Omdurman and how greatly it would increase my experience.

I had been glad to hear at Christmas that Moore, when he had visited Tini, had arranged the payment of Idris's blood money, so Idris could now go with me to Omdurman. I was pleased, for I had grown fond of him: he was always cheerful, meeting every requirement with a smile. I remembered with distress an incident of some months before. We had left Kutum on camels and Idris had packed the small tea glasses in a goatskin filled with flour. When we stopped for lunch he had to confess that the glasses were broken: since the flour was now full of splintered glass, I realized it would have to be thrown away. I lost my temper and cursed Idris for a bloody fool. When I noticed a little later that he was not with us, Kalol said, 'He is over there, under that tree.' I went over and found him sobbing. I told him to forget it and come and join us. He looked at me and said: 'I know I was a fool to have put the glasses there. At the time I thought it was such a good idea. I know it's my fault that everything has been spoilt and we have no food. I already realized that, and then you cursed me. That cut me to the heart. I would rather you had hit me.' Putting my hand on his shoulder I said, 'Forgive me.'

Whereas in Kutum I would expect my cook to produce decent European food which Idris would serve at table, on trek I invariably ate the local food, in company of whoever was with me. According to Moore, feeding with your retainers was standard practice in Arabia; but in the Sudan it was decidedly unconventional. I also stayed in the houses of important chiefs like Sayyah or Muhammadain, and in return put them up in empty quarters in my compound and entertained them when they were in Kutum.

I remember an argument with one of my contemporaries who said that my behaviour was bad for Government prestige; he maintained that British officials should keep aloof and not involve themselves socially with those they administered. Had I done this I should have missed much that was most rewarding during my time in Darfur. I refused to believe I lost face with the Zaghawa, the Maidob or indeed any of the others by feeding with them. After all, they were not savages, but as Muslims belonged to an ancient civilization. Although I was there to administer them, I could not see why this should prevent me treating them as friends.

I looked forward to riding across the Sudan on a camel from Jabal Maidob to Omdurman. Sayyah had told me that the Maidob took twenty-three or twenty-four days to get there with their sheep. Since a good sheep fetched the equivalent of one pound, a lot of money in those days, the Maidob were very dependent on this trade. However, they often met with trouble from the Kababish when they watered at their wells, and Moore wanted me to investigate this.

I left Jabal Maidob in mid-February with Idris, Kalol, a policeman and two Maidob guides. Omdurman was four hundred and fifty miles away, but more by way of Bagariya, Safiya and Habisa, where the Maidob watered. We arrived at Omdurman after eleven days, two of which I spent making enquiries at Bagariya and Safiya.

We rode long hours, sometimes seventeen or eighteen a day. This was not due to impatience on my part to reach Omdurman and start my leave: I was only too happy to see this part of the Sudan; but I could not resist the opportunity to test my endurance. On this journey there was no need to keep our camels to a walk since we could water them every two or three days and we carried grain for them; there was also abundant *haskanit*. This beastly grass, with its clinging, penetrating seeds, grew in many places along our route as tall and thick as a field of wheat, enabling the camels to grab mouthful after mouthful as they shuffled past. The going was generally sandy, though interspersed with occasional stretches of sharp stones, especially between Safiya and Habisa, where there was a succession of volcanic ridges, hard on the camels' feet.

On the whole, the country was flat and uninteresting, being devoid of trees or bushes except along the larger wadis, which were generally well wooded. Here we passed a number of encampments where we encountered old men, women and children, with goats and cattle. The able-bodied men were away in the desert with the camel herds.

Bagariya was the first watering place which the Maidob reached after leaving the Jabal. Here, since the water barely sufficed for the Kababish, the arrival of the Maidob with as many as a thousand sheep was naturally resented. Equally, after seven waterless days the Maidob would be impatient to water their sheep, and if there were large numbers of Kababish camels waiting their turn tempers could easily get short, the Kababish being arrogant, the Maidob quick-tempered. Bagariya was remote and the only people permanently there were two or three guards on the wells. When I arrived in the evening I was lucky to find two sons of an important sheikh, with whom I had a long discussion next day. At Safiya, however, there was a small permanent village and abundant water, and also at Habisa.

On our last day we rode endlessly across particularly monotonous country; I was getting tired and found it one long slog. We had started at midnight and stopped only once for a quick meal at sunrise. I had expected to reach Omdurman about midday; we finally arrived in sight of the town just before sunset and camped on the plain a mile or so outside. I could see above an expanse of low, flat roofs the shattered dome of the Mahdi's tomb.

In the morning, I reported my arrival to the District Commissioner and then, after arranging accommodation for Kalol and the others in the Maidob quarter of the town, Idris and I crossed the bridge by car to Khartoum, and to the Perrys, who said they were sorry I had not arrived on my camel. It was pleasant to relax in the civilized comfort of their house, to eat delicious food and dawdle in a hot bath that smelt of bath salts. I was in Khartoum for a week before leaving via the Nile valley for Cairo and England. This time I enjoyed the social life, dinner parties and watching polo matches; but I knew I would do anything rather than be stationed in Khartoum.

One morning Sir Angus Gillan, as Civil Secretary second only to the Governor-General in the hierarchy of the Sudan, sent for me. I had met him only once, soon after my first arrival in Khartoum, when I and two other probationers had dined with him and his wife. A large, imposing man who had been a notable Oxford rowing Blue, he had on that occasion quickly put us at ease. Now I entered his office in some trepidation, conscious of the disturbance my unauthorized visit to Bir Natrun had caused.

He asked how I was getting on at Kutum, and put some questions about the Maidob and my camel journey to Omdurman. Then he said: 'Though it was reassuring to learn that there were no Italians at Bir Natrun, you realize your presence there caused a certain amount of alarm here and elsewhere. We realized when we selected you that you were rather odd, but we felt you would be useful to us and I am sure you will be. It is up to you to fit in. Dupuis spoke well of you. But remember that you don't travel in another district without its DC's permission, and most certainly not in another province without mine. I gather you are just off to England. Enjoy your leave.'

I was indeed looking forward to my leave at The Milebrook, yet at the same time I wanted to be back at Kutum. I remembered my house there, the view over the wadi towards Jabal Si, the evenings with Guy Moore. I wanted to ride Faraj Allah again, to revisit Sayyah in the Jabal, to travel with Idris among the Zaghawa, to hunt lion with the Bani Husain. I had been happy at Kutum; nevertheless, there had been a shadow in the background, seldom out of my mind: the threat to Abyssinia.

219

CHAPTER 17

The Italian Occupation of Abyssinia

WHEN I LEFT the Sudan in March 1936 the Abyssinian armies seemed to be holding their own. I even heard officials discussing the possible repercussions on the Sudanese of an Abyssinian victory; but by the time I arrived in England the tide had turned. I can recall the intense anxiety with which each morning I waited for the papers to be delivered at The Milebrook; my feeling of sick despair as I read of the appalling casualties the Abyssinian armies were suffering, and then of the massacre in Addis Ababa.

Since early 1934, before I went to the Sudan, the Italians had been building military bases, aerodromes and roads near the Eritrean frontier with Abyssinia. That spring, Mussolini warned his troops, during manoeuvres in Italy, 'It is necessary to prepare for war . . . not tomorrow but today.' Had the clash at Walwal on 5 December 1934 not provided a pretext for invasion, he would have found another, for he was determined to incorporate Abyssinia into his new Roman Empire.

Immediately after Walwal Italy delivered a virtual ultimatum to Abyssinia, demanding apologies and monetary compensation for what was described as an unprovoked attack on Italian Somaliland. The frontier had been settled by the 1897 Treaty between Abyssinia and Italy after the Abyssinian victory at Adua. Unfortunately for the Italian claim, their colonial office map, issued in 1925, showed Walwal at least sixty miles inside Abyssinia. Mussolini ignored this inconvenient fact.

Abyssinia was a member of the League of Nations, and on 14 December 1934 when Mussolini refused to agree to arbitration Haile Selassie appealed to the League. The United States did not belong to the League and President Roosevelt, despite a personal appeal from the Emperor, consistently refused to involve his country in the dispute.

In Britain, Sir John Simon was Foreign Secretary, with Anthony

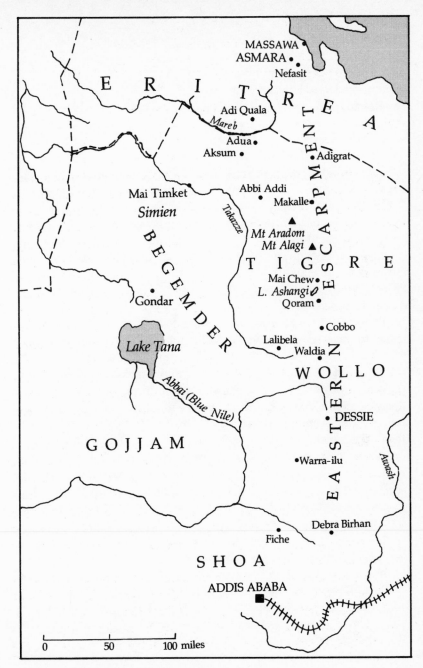

The Invasion of Abyssinia, 1936

Eden as his representative at the League of Nations Assembly in Geneva. Simon gave no help to the Emperor in his dispute with Italy: after doing his best to stop him appealing to the League, he next tried to persuade him to make concessions. On 7 June 1935 he was succeeded as Foreign Secretary by Sir Samuel Hoare, with Eden as Minister for League of Nations Affairs, but subordinate to him. If the Emperor hoped Hoare would be more helpful than Simon he was to be disillusioned. Hoare announced he was a friend of Italy and while he held office behaved as such.

Baldwin, who became Prime Minister on 7 June, took singularly little interest in foreign affairs, being content to leave them to his Foreign Secretary; and Hoare, with the approval of Sir Robert Vansittart, Permanent Under Secretary at the Foreign Office, vacillated and prevaricated in order not to offend Mussolini. Vansittart was prepared to concede anything rather than drive Italy into the arms of Hitler, who in March had reoccupied the Rhineland. In Laval, the French Premier, the Foreign Office found a sinister and unscrupulous accomplice.

On 25 July 1935 Hoare stated in the House of Commons that in order to encourage a peaceful settlement the Government would issue no licences to export arms to Italy or to Abyssinia; this despite the Treaty of 3 August 1930, whereby Britain had undertaken to help the Emperor obtain 'all the arms and munitions necessary for the defence of his territories from external aggression'. Britain and France now banned the passage of arms to Abyssinia through their territories, and Belgium, Czechoslovakia and Denmark cancelled orders for arms from the Abyssinian Government. The British controlled the Suez Canal, through which Italian troops and weapons were constantly passing on their way to Massawa and Mogadishu. In justice to Abyssinia, the British should have closed the canal to Italian military use: they did not do so.

However, Haile Selassie, despite his earlier disappointments, was greatly encouraged on 11 September 1935 when Hoare affirmed to the League Assembly that 'His Majesty's Government ... in spite of all difficulties ... will be second to none in its intention to fulfil, within the means of its capacity, the obligations which the Covenant lays upon it ... We believe that small nations are entitled to a life of their own and such protection as can collectively be afforded them.' The Emperor did not realize at first how insincere this protestation was.

During the morning of 3 October 1935 the Italian forces in Eritrea, under General de Bono, invaded Abyssinia by crossing the Marib river unopposed in three columns, each comprising an army corps. The Emperor, to avoid any incident during the negotiations, had withdrawn all his troops from the border areas. The only Abyssinian armies in the north, on the outbreak of war, were those of Ras Seyum, King John's grandson, at Adua, and of Dedjazmatch Haile Selassie Gugsa, the Emperor's son-in-law, at Makalle. The Italians had made every effort to induce these two chiefs to defect. They succeeded with Haile Selassie Gugsa; Seyum, while accepting their bribes, remained loyal to the Emperor.

After Seyum had withdrawn his troops from Adua south-west into the mountains, the Italians entered the town, which was only twenty miles from the frontier, on the second day of their advance. The small primitive township had been bombed and some civilians killed. Before the Italian soldiers, with their bands playing, marched into the virtually empty town, it was reconnoitred by Eritrean native troops. De Bono then erected a monument inscribed 'To the dead of Adua, at last avenged'. On the same day Adigrat, fifteen miles from the frontier, was occupied without resistance. De Bono then halted for a month.

As soon as the Emperor heard of the invasion he ordered the war drums in the palace to be beaten and issued orders for mobilization, nine months after Mussolini had mobilized. On 19 October he reviewed Ras Mulugeta's sixty thousand troops before they went north to Dessie. The Imperial Guard were now dressed in khaki uniforms and had been trained by Swedish officers; the rest of the army differed little from the one that had fought at Adua thirty-nine years earlier.

It was now apparent how crippling had been the British and French ban on the import of arms. The Abyssinian troops were armed with every sort of rifle, many dating from the last century; too often their cartridge-belts were almost empty. Not a few had only swords and spears. To meet a modern army, the Abyssinians lacked everything but courage. The Emperor consistently stressed the need for guerilla tactics, for concealment, ambushes, sniping and attacks on communications; but Mulugeta, that stubborn old warrior who had fought under Menelik at Adua, still believed in traditional hand-to-hand fighting which ended at sunset.

De Bono was only induced to advance a further forty-five miles to

Makalle after receiving increasingly peremptory telegrams from Mussolini. The treacherous Haile Selassie Gugsa had hurried north from Makalle on the first day of the war to join the Italians. He had undertaken to bring in twenty thousand troops, but arrived at de Bono's headquarters with only twelve hundred: when the rest had realized what he was doing, they deserted him.

The first serious fighting did not take place till 12 November 1935, when an Italian force of twelve thousand under General Mariotti, guarding de Bono's left flank, was ambushed in a gorge of the great escarpment that overlooks the coastal plain. It suffered heavy casualties and had the Abyssinians only renewed their attack next day would probably have been wiped out. On 14 November, de Bono was replaced by General Badoglio who, however, showed no more initiative than his predecessor.

Italian dilatoriness gave time for the Abyssinian armies to arrive, and by mid-November Ras Mulugeta's army was in position round Amba Aradom, a mountain twelve miles south of Makalle. Ras Kassa had now joined Ras Seyum in the mountainous area of Tembien, where their combined forces totalled forty thousand. Meanwhile, Ras Imru was further north with twenty thousand men, on the south side of the Takazze river; there Dedjazmatch Ayalew Birru had joined him with ten thousand more, but the Dedjazmatch's loyalty was suspect. Imru was to prove by far the ablest of the Abyssinian commanders. The Emperor, however, subordinated him, as well as Seyum – and even Mulugeta, Minister of the Spear, or of War – to Ras Kassa, whose status as a Ras was senior to theirs.

At dawn on 15 December Ras Imru crossed the Takazze river with five thousand men, routed an Italian garrison at the Mai Timket ford, driving the remnant back to the Dembeguina Pass; he had sent another five thousand across seemingly impassable mountains to cut the only road between Dembeguina and Adua. The Italians had nine light tanks at Dembeguina, but the Abyssinians swarmed round them, thrusting spears through the slits and damaging their tracks. The Italian native troops fought well and eventually broke through to another position further back, but next day Imru captured that. He had inflicted four hundred casualties and taken twenty-eight machine-guns, hundreds of rifles and large stocks of ammunition. He was now within ten miles of Aksum and in a position to attack the communications of the Army Corps at Adua or even to invade Eritrea.

Two months earlier, on 10 October, a week after Italy had invaded Abyssinia, the League of Nations condemned her as the aggressor by fifty votes to four. The Committee of Eighteen met on the same day to discuss the imposition of certain sanctions, which came into effect on 19 October. When Eden had called on Laval in Paris on his way to Geneva for this meeting, Laval had showed him a plan he had drawn up to stop the war: Mussolini was to be bought off by being awarded a Mandate over all parts of Abyssinia not originally inhabited by the Amhara, which meant three-quarters of the country. The Foreign Office in London had worked out a similar proposal, but for the moment these plans remained secret and the British Government continued to profess adherence to the principles of the League of Nations.

The outstanding question now was whether to impose sanctions on oil. A majority of the League favoured this since such sanctions as had so far been imposed had merely united the Italians behind Mussolini. Later Mussolini would confess to Hitler that if the League had banned the import of oil the war would have ended in a week. Meanwhile, by blustering and threatening war against England, he thoroughly alarmed Baldwin and his Cabinet. An election was pending in England and Baldwin assured his electorate that there was no question of military sanctions. On 14 November he won the election with a greatly increased majority largely because of his apparent support for the League.

On 8 December Hoare and Laval formally initialled a plan to give Mussolini the greater part of Tigre, where the Italian armies at that moment were making no progress, and the Danakil country as far south as Aussa, and the Ogaden, together with an economic monopoly over the country south of Addis Ababa. In return the Abyssinians would be given the undeveloped port of Assab, but on the understanding that they did not build a railway there, which would compete with the French railway from Jibuti. Laval urged that this plan should be approved by Mussolini before being shown to the Emperor. He hoped Mussolini would accept it and then, if the Emperor rejected it, France would feel excused from further action.

The British Cabinet saw nothing wrong with the proposals, but insisted that Haile Selassie be informed of them at the same time as Mussolini. Laval would only agree to this on condition that the British withdrew their support in the League for a sanction on oil. However someone leaked the Hoare-Laval Plan to the French press;

an accurate version appeared next day in two French papers and in the *New York Times*.

There was immediate uproar in England. Members of Parliament were inundated with angry letters, and the Government, despite its large majority in the Commons, was threatened. Hoare, who, with the approval of Vansittart, had drawn up the plan, was eventually forced to resign, though still supported by the Cabinet. With his resignation Mussolini was deprived of a powerfully placed collaborator. Many expected Eden also to resign, but Baldwin appointed him Foreign Secretary in place of Hoare.

Eden faced embarrassment on 12 December at the League meeting, where most of the other delegates were indignant at the Hoare-Laval Plan. Ten of the Committee of Eighteen had already agreed to support oil sanctions and expected Eden to vote with them. He now explained that his Government was unwilling to impose further sanctions while peace proposals were being discussed. Abandoned by Britain, the others withdrew their support for oil sanctions.

Haile Selassie had gone to Dessie to be nearer the front. Shortly after his arrival, eighteen Italian aircraft had bombed the little town, inflicting casualties. Though his staff urged him to take cover, he manned an Oerlikon machine-gun throughout the attack. Here at Dessie, the day after Imru's victory at Dembeguina, Haile Selassie, still unaware of that victory, learnt of the Hoare-Laval Plan.

Though he reiterated to the assembled reporters his willingness to help find a peaceful solution of the war, he absolutely rejected the proposal to dismember his Empire and deprive his people of their age-old independence. He insisted that it was a negation of all the principles for which the League had been formed. To accept it would amount to betrayal both of his people and of the League, and also of all those states that had shown confidence in the system of collective security. For him Abyssinian interests took precedence over all others, but he was also aware that the security of other weak states would be endangered if the proposed concessions were awarded to a state that had already been declared the aggressor, at the expense of its victim.

For the six weeks following his victory, Imru's troops raided as far as the Mareb river, attacking road convoys, and on one occasion capturing trucks carrying 100,000 cartridges. The Abyssinian forces, having cross-country mobility, neither needed roads nor had to worry about physical communications. They were handicapped however by lack of wireless links between their armies.

On hearing of Imru's victory, Seyum, with four thousand men, had advanced on Abbi Addi. This important town in the Tembien, thirty miles west of Makalle, was held by eight battalions, mostly of Eritrean native troops. Seyum's force was bombed and strafed from the air throughout the day as it approached Abbi Addi, but attacked at dawn on 18 December and, in face of artillery firing over open sights, closed with the defenders. Bitter fighting, largely swords, spears and shields against rifles, bayonets and hand grenades, lasted until nightfall, when the Abyssinians withdrew. Four days later they renewed the attack, captured the town and drove the remnant of their enemies back some miles to another fortified position; this also they captured. The Abyssinians were now more than holding their own; it seemed possible that they might win the war.

Earlier, only five days after the outbreak of war in October 1935, Dedjazmatch Nasibu, the Abyssinian commander in the Ogaden, had accused General Graziani, commanding in Italian Somaliland, of using poison gas. The Emperor had refused to believe it. He had said: 'Let us try to mitigate the inherent horrors of war by being frank and honest and giving our enemies credit where credit is due. Is not war horrible enough without investing it with such horrors?' However, in that month Mussolini did send Graziani a secret telegram: 'Authorized to use gas as a last resort in order to defeat enemy resistance and in case of counter-attack.'

Now, on 23 December, Badoglio ordered planes to drop containers of mustard gas on Abyssinian troops crossing the Takazze river to reinforce Ras Imru's forces holding Dembeguina. The effect was appalling; anyone who was splashed with the fluid or who breathed its fumes writhed and screamed in agony. There was utter bewilderment, too, for no one understood what was happening to them. The pilots found with practice that it was more effective to spray the gas than to drop it in containers. On 28 December Mussolini sent Badoglio a telegram: 'Given the enemy system of warfare, in answer to your despatch No. 630, I authorize your Excellency to use, even on a vast scale, any kind of gas and flame thrower.' He even suggested the use of 'bacteriological war' but Badoglio advised against this.

On the southern front Graziani, who, though operating in open desert country, had shown even less initiative than de Bono and Badoglio, was at last preparing to attack the army of Ras Desta, another son-in-law of the Emperor, at Dolo on the Ganale river near the Kenya border. Not wanting international observers of his methods of warfare, on 30 December 1935 he deliberately bombed the Swedish Red Cross camp fifty miles behind Desta's position, though all its tents were clearly marked with the Red Cross. About a hundred bombs were dropped and forty people, including a Swedish orderly, were killed. Dr Hylander, who was in charge of the unit, and fifty others, were wounded and all the transport and tents were destroyed. Graziani justified the attack by claiming that the camp sheltered Abyssinian troops.

Ras Desta was an educated, progressive and likeable man, who spoke good English and had been for some years Governor of Sidamo. On the outbreak of war the Emperor had given him command of the southern army. Now, though operating in an area with which he was familiar, he proved highly incompetent. When Graziani attacked his army at Dolo on 12 January 1936, it had dwindled to barely five thousand men, and these were starving: they were routed and massacred. Desta escaped but was later captured and, on Graziani's orders, shot.

Mussolini could now proclaim a local victory, but he was dissatisfied with Badoglio's progress in the north, and kept ordering him to destroy Mulugeta's army and advance on Addis Ababa. Badoglio, however, determined not to move till he had secured his right flank at Makalle. On 20 January he sent a strong force of Eritrean troops against Kassa's right near Abbi Addi.

Badoglio's Eritreans were trained soldiers and as brave as the Abyssinians; where possible he used them in preference to his white troops. They now captured some of the positions held by Kassa. To support them, Badoglio ordered the Italian Black Shirt Division, holding the Warieu Pass, to feint against Kassa's left. This they did next day, but were routed and driven back on their fortifications in the pass, and by nightfall were almost surrounded.

To hold the Warieu Pass was vital for the Italians. To lose it would isolate their army corps at Adua and expose all their communications with Eritrea. Defeat here could precipitate disaster, perhaps even end the war. In this crisis Badoglio called on his air force. Mussolini had authorized him to use 'all means of war – I say all, both from the air and from the land'. Badoglio concentrated a hundred aircraft and, for the four days of the first battle of the Tambien, these bombed the Abyssinian troops pouring forward to the attack, and drenched their rear positions with mustard gas; there, villagers, camp followers and baggage animals died in agony.

Despite the air assault, to which they could not reply, Kassa's troops raced forward and hurled themselves in wave after wave on the Italian defences. The enemy's machine-guns took a fearful toll but still they came, scrambling over the piles of dead to drive the Italian troops to alternative positions. In this hand-to-hand combat, which the Abyssinians understood and excelled at, they inflicted over a thousand casualties on Badoglio's troops.

By nightfall on 23 January a large Italian relief column had still not succeeded in fighting through to the beleaguered garrison, but next day it did so. To renew his attack, Kassa needed reinforcements: he had lost eight thousand killed and wounded, nearly a third of his force. Imru was out of reach and Mulugeta, with whom Kassa was in touch, made excuses and sent no help, resentful of subordination to Kassa. Accordingly, short of ammunition and deprived of reinforcements, Kassa's force no longer threatened Badoglio's rear at Makalle. Badoglio therefore decided to attack Mulugeta's army at Amba Aradom.

The battle began on 12 February when Dedjazmatch Wodaje, with twenty thousand men, tried to halt the advance on Amba Aradom of the First Corps, with two other corps in support, a total of nine divisions. Since Mulugeta's occupation of the mountain in December the Italians had been bombing it, and now 170 of their aircraft dropped 380 tons of bombs on the Abyssinian positions, in four days, while their artillery fired some 23,000 shells. Under this onslaught Mulugeta's few field pieces, captured forty years before at Adua, were never even fired.

Mulugeta had believed the mountain to be impregnable. Now, shaken by the continuous bombardment, the old man stayed in his command cave, completely out of touch with the battle. His entire army would have been surrounded and annihilated had not Bit-woded Makonnen, a chief from Walega, with his four thousand men, held up two Italian divisions long enough for it to escape. In this battle the Abyssinians lost six thousand men, and in the next three days at least ten thousand more as they were bombed, machine-gunned and sprayed with poison gas from the air. The Abyssinians were barefoot, which normally contributed to their mobility but now, on mountain tracks contaminated with mustard gas, was disastrous. The Emperor's largest army thus disintegrated. Its remnants were attacked, further south, by the Raya Galla, a fierce tribe, who had been suborned by the Italians; in one of their ambushes Mulugeta was killed.

The Emperor heard of the catastrophe on 19 February at his new headquarters, a hundred and fifty miles south of Amba Aradom. He immediately sent messengers to Kassa and Imru to withdraw and occupy Amba Alagi, but Badoglio forestalled them and occupied it on 25 February, unopposed.

After his victory at Amba Aradom, Badoglio next concentrated his army of two hundred thousand against the forces of Kassa and Seyum, who together could now muster only some thirty thousand. Seyum held a strong position overlooking the Warieu Pass, but Badoglio, in the knowledge that Abyssinians traditionally fought only by day, assaulted it during the night with elite Alpine troops. The sleeping Abyssinians were taken by surprise and driven off the mountain-top. Elsewhere, though Italian aircraft bombed them heavily during the following day, Seyum's troops more than held their own. By that evening, however, they had suffered heavy losses and practically exhausted their ammunition, so Seyum decided to avoid encirclement by withdrawing across the Takazze. Next day his remaining men, crowded together in the gorge, offered the Italian airmen an unbelievable target. Soon, shattered by bombing and drenched with mustard gas, Seyum's army, like Mulugeta's, ceased to exist.

Kassa, near Abbi Addi, learnt on 27 February of Seyum's retreat and saw that he himself was now in danger of being trapped between the Italian First and Third Corps. He therefore ordered a withdrawal, during which his troops were subjected to incessant air attacks. When, a fortnight later, Kassa and Seyum joined the Emperor at Qoram they had with them only a few hundred men; any others who had survived the bombing had made for their homes.

Imru's army was now isolated up on the Eritrean frontier. The Emperor had already sent messengers instructing him to withdraw; these arrived at the end of February. Imru had been unaware of Mulugeta's catastrophic defeat or of the fighting in the Tembien. He now detached a force towards Aksum, so as to cover his withdrawal.

On 29 February Badoglio had ordered his Second Corps under General Maravigna to advance against Imru at Dembeguina, while the Fourth Corps made a forced march through the mountains to threaten his rear. The Second Corps, deployed in wooded country without adequate precautions, was ambushed. The Abyssinians had several machine-guns and ample ammunition obtained in raids on the Italian supply lines; they now brought a devastating fire to bear. While the leading Italian division tried desperately to sort itself out and bring its artillery into action, Maravigna, fearing that he had run into Imru's entire army, halted and ordered his corps to adopt defensive positions. The Abyssinians attacked repeatedly and fighting went on all day. In the words of an Italian officer, 'They threw themselves on the guns as though to silence them. Their courage was unbelievable. They were utterly oblivious of danger.'

After staying in position for another day, Maravigna resumed his march, whereupon he was ambushed again and his entire corps was brought to a standstill once more. Imru's rearguard of a few thousand men had succeeded in delaying three divisions for nearly three days. Meanwhile the Fourth Corps, engaged in a fifty-mile march through difficult and unreconnoitred country towards Imru's rear, suffered even worse delays.

However, for all that he had successfully disengaged his army on the ground, Imru now saw it destroyed by the Italian air force. For a second time the fords over the Takazze proved a death trap, and having crossed the river Imru was left with only ten thousand men. He himself was undaunted, and planned to fight on in the Simien mountains; but by now his troops had had enough and it was not long before all that remained to him were three hundred of his personal bodyguard. Only the army at Koram, commanded by the Emperor himself, now stood between Badoglio and Addis Ababa.

On 4 March 1936 a British Red Cross camp near Koram, under Dr John Melly, was bombed by an Italian aircraft, which dropped explosive and incendiary bombs, killing five people, wounding others, and destroying tents and equipment. The site was by itself on an open plain, unmistakably marked with large ground flags; the Italians acknowledged the incident but claimed that the plane had come under fire from the camp.

Ten days later Dr Marcel Junod, the Swiss delegate of the Red Cross, visited Koram. Approaching the Emperor's cave he was appalled to find men lying about everywhere, covered with mustard gas burns and crying in their agony, 'Abeit! Abeit!' This was the traditional appeal for help, 'a heart-breaking chant that came and went in a slow but persistent rhythm'. The Dutch and the damaged British Red Cross unit did all they could, but it was pitifully little. Dr Junod estimated that the sufferers numbered thousands.

Dr John Macfie, of the British Red Cross wrote: 'The patients were a shocking sight. The first I examined, an old man, sat moaning on the ground, rocking himself to and fro, completely wrapped in cloth. When I approached he slowly rose and drew aside his cloak. He looked as if someone had tried to skin him, clumsily; he had been heavily burned by mustard gas all over the face, the back and the arms. There were many others like him; some more, some less severely afflicted; some newly burned, others older, their sores already caked with thick, brown scabs. Men and women alike, all heavily disfigured, and little children, too. And many blinded by the stuff, with blurred, crimson apologies for eyes. I could cover pages recounting horrors, but what would be the use?'

On 19, 22 and 24 March, *The Times* published reports describing the sufferings of the Abyssinians from the use of mustard gas. The British Minister, Sir Sidney Barton, had sent an official report to the Foreign Office with affidavits from several doctors, including Dr Macfie, testifying that they had treated burns caused by mustard gas. Yet on 30 March, in answer to a question from Lord Hugh Cecil in the House of Lords, Lord Halifax for the Government stated that he had no information that the Italians were using gas in Abyssinia, and added: 'It would be quite wrong and quite unjust to prejudge a matter so grave and so vitally affecting the honour of a great country ... The first step must be to obtain the observations and comments of the Italian Government.'

The Emperor had repeatedly appealed to the League of Nations to condemn the Italians' use of gas. The Italians invariably countered with charges that the Abyssinians used dum-dum bullets and killed prisoners, though they could cite only one instance, of a captured airman who had his head cut off. On 18 April, when the question of gas was raised in the League for the last time, Flandin, the French Foreign Minister, persuaded the Committee of Thirteen to drop the subject. In a private conversation he remarked to Eden that the Italians had been stupid to use gas.

The Emperor realized that he must now risk everything on a final battle, in personal command of his army. Had he been able to withdraw his forces to Dessie or beyond, he would have lengthened the Italian lines of communication; then, using the guerrilla tactics he had always advocated, he might have delayed their advance until the rainy season. But he knew that if he attempted to do so his army would disintegrate under incessant bombing. He must fight where he stood at Koram; honour demanded it. Indeed he must fight as soon as possible, since his chiefs and their troops were becoming demoralized by daily air attacks, and the general widespread depression was increased by the arrival of Ras Kassa and Ras Seyum on 20 March with the pitiful remnants of their shattered armies. Until they came, the only Ras with the Emperor had been Gatachew from Kaffa, who had no experience of war.

Now the Emperor daily urged on his followers the necessity for an attack. Meanwhile the treacherous Raya chiefs, already bought by the Italians, visited his camp, pretended support, were given presents, and went back to report to the enemy. Finally the Emperor won over the waverers, and on 30 March gave orders for the next day's battle. He detailed a few hundred men to attack the Italian centre at first light, which would serve as a diversion while Kassa, Seyum and Gatachew, with some nine thousand men, stormed the Mehan Pass on the Italian right and attacked their rear. A large force, including the regular soldiers of the Imperial Guard, would then smash through the Italian centre.

In the dark the troops detailed to make the diversionary attack on the centre crept close to the Italian outposts undetected. Then as it grew light, they charged, supported by accurate machine-gun fire. Though the Italians had been warned by the Raya to expect an attack, the Abyssinians swarmed over their forward positions; however, they were too few to storm the main defences.

Meanwhile, the attack on the Mehan Pass had started. It was supported by the few guns the Abyssinians had, and it met with initial success, but was halted up against the trenches and stone breastworks manned by two Eritrean divisions. The Emperor thereupon reinforced that attack with his Imperial Guard. These fought magnificently, virtually wiping out the 10th Eritrean Battalion, but suffered very heavily while attacking across open ground. Badoglio later described how they charged repeatedly into what he described as 'a veritable avalanche of fire'.

Realizing that this was the crisis of the battle, the Emperor now threw in his last reserves. In their final assault the Abyssinians drove a wedge between the 1st and 2nd Eritrean Divisions, but by now were simply too few to exploit their success. All the Emperor's surviving troops were in action; he had nothing left to reinforce them. The last chance of victory was gone, but they fought on.

During the day the Abyssinians' few Oerlikon anti-aircraft guns had brought down seventeen planes. The Emperor himself had manned one of the guns, first in support of his attacking troops and then against the waves of Italian aircraft. At last, late in the evening, he ordered a withdrawal. As his troops pulled back from the assault, the Raya, who had been awaiting the outcome, turned on them and inflicted further casualties.

The Red Cross units having been withdrawn before the battle, there was no one in the Abyssinian camp to tend the innumerable wounded. Worse was to come during the nightmare days ahead. The Abyssinians began their retreat in the afternoon of 1 April, and Badoglio loosed every plane he had against the dense columns of fugitives winding across a treeless countryside, devoid of cover. Day after day the slaughter continued. The Emperor later described the scene: 'Of all the massacres of this terrible and pitiless war this was the worst. Men, women and pack animals were blown to bits or were fatally burned by the mustard gas. The dying, the wounded, screamed in agony. Those who escaped fell victim to the deadly rain. The gas finished off the carnage that the bombs began. We could do nothing to protect ourselves against it.'

With his army shattered and dispersed, Haile Selassie went to Lalibela, though it was not on his way to Addis Ababa. There, in one of its famous rock-hewn churches, he sought help and comfort from God; for forty-eight hours he prayed and fasted before continuing his journey. Near Magdala he learnt that the Italians had reached Dessie, so he followed a little-used upland route to Addis Ababa and arrived there on 30 April. Though he was mentally and physically worn out, there was no rest, and everyone turned to him, clamouring for help and advice. The town was in chaos, authority had broken down, looting had started. Here, clearly, was no hope of further resistance; his appeals met with no response. He was still determined to continue fighting, and to go south and raise another army. However, his chiefs argued that it was useless to do so, since there was no answer to bombs and gas: instead he must go to Europe and appeal in person to the League. Against his every inclination, he was persuaded at last that they were right.

On 2 May 1936 the Emperor left Addis Ababa by train for Jibuti and two days later boarded a British cruiser, HMS *Enterprise*, on his way to Jerusalem. Later he sailed in HMS *Capetown* from Palestine to Gibraltar and then by liner to Southampton, where he landed on 3 June; he went by train to London on the same day. I was present at Waterloo Station when he arrived there. No official reception awaited him; he was met by a few friends and a representative from the Foreign Office. To avoid the crowds assembled to welcome him, he was driven by back streets to his Legation at Queen's Gate.

On his earlier visit to England, in 1924, he had been met by the Duke of York and had been received at Buckingham Palace. Now he found himself treated as an unwelcome refugee by the country he had always most admired and trusted. He would soon be destitute, when the funds he had officially invested in Britain were held for the King of Italy, to whom Mussolini had awarded the title 'Emperor of Ethiopia'.

However, when two days later, Haile Selassie received my mother and me at his Legation he greeted us with all his customary courtesy. He looked worn and tired but otherwise unchanged since I had last seen him in Addis Ababa in 1934. His world was in ruins; his armies had been annihilated; his country was overrun; his relatives and friends were even then being hunted down and butchered. He had put his trust in the League of Nations. The League had almost unanimously condemned Italy as the aggressor, but then done nothing to help Abyssinia. Yet, as we sat there looking on Hyde Park, he evinced no bitterness, gave no sign of the despair he must have felt. Only when he spoke briefly of the horrors he had seen was I conscious of his inutterable sadness.

I should of course have liked to have joined one of the Abyssinian armies in that war. I had known Ras Kassa ever since my childhood, and he had given me a silver-gilt goblet when I was christened: Imru, Seyum, Mulugeta and Desta I had met at the Emperor's coronation. I was well aware that if I had taken part in the fighting I should have achieved nothing, beyond retaining my self-respect. Now I could only trust that sooner or later Britain would be at war with Italy. Thinking of Mussolini posturing and ranting on the balcony of the Palazzo Venezia, I felt a bitter, personal hatred. I remember my savage satisfaction nine years later on learning that he had been executed by his own people and his carcass had been hung, appropriately, on a meat hook.

On 5 May 1936, three days after Haile Selassie had left Addis Ababa, the Italians marched in. Mussolini had given orders that as soon as the town was occupied anyone found carrying arms was to be summarily shot, together with all who failed to surrender their weapons in twenty-four hours. He also ordered Badoglio to shoot all the 'young Ethiopians', meaning the young men who had been educated abroad at the Emperor's expense. Many of these, including Dr Martin's two sons, were duly rounded up and executed. On 22 May Badoglio returned to Italy, and Graziani succeeded him as Governor-General and Viceroy of Ethiopia.

Graziani, who had already earned a butcher's reputation while suppressing the Senussi in Cyrenaica, now adopted the same methods in Abyssinia. He is alleged to have said, 'The Duce shall have Ethiopia with or without the Ethiopians, as he pleases.' On 19 February 1937, at an outdoor celebration in Addis Ababa, some young Abyssinian Patriots threw nine small plastic hand-grenades into the crowd around Graziani; no one was killed but several Italians were wounded, including Graziani. In retaliation he loosed his Black Shirts on the town. The Italian mayor told them: 'For three days I give you permission to destroy, kill and do all you want to the Ethiopians.' The massacre duly went on for three days. Between five and ten thousand people were killed in the capital, and thousands more in the provinces. On the third day a notice was put up in Addis Ababa: 'Reprisals must stop at noon. Guido Cortese, Mayor.' When I was in Gojjam during the Second World War survivors described how the Black Shirts in their dress uniform had lit the thatch on *tukuls* and stabbed men, women and children to death with their ceremonial daggers as they tried to escape from their burning houses. The bodies were later collected in lorries and buried in pits.

Sporadic resistance had continued after the occupation of Addis Ababa in May 1936, and on 5 June Mussolini ordered all captured 'rebels' to be shot. Among those shot were Ras Kassa's three eldest sons. On 8 June Mussolini authorized Graziani to use gas 'to get finished with the rebels'. This policy of terror, far from cowing the Abyssinians, intensified their hostility; active resistance spread over large areas of the country.

On 8 July Mussolini authorized Graziani 'once again to begin conducting systematically the policy of terror and extermination against the rebels and the accomplice populations. Without the law of tenfold retaliation the wound will not heal quickly enough.' One result of this was that 425 deacons and monks in Debra Libanos, the foremost southern monastery in the country, were shot. Such was the 'civilizing mission' of which Italy boasted, and of which Evelyn Waugh saw fit to write: 'It is being attended by the spread of order and decency, education and medicine, in a disgraceful place.'

On 30 June 1936 Haile Selassie had appealed on behalf of his people to the League of Nations in Geneva; he was cheered outside the Assembly Hall by enormous crowds assembled to greet him. Inside the Hall, most of the representatives were embarrassed and shamed by the presence there of this small yet immensely impressive figure, whose cause they had betrayed; some had even questioned his right to address them now that he no longer represented an independent state. As he ascended the rostrum, Italian journalists booed, whistled and shouted abuse. He waited impassively until police had removed them and then he spoke.

'I, Haile Selassie the First, Emperor of Ethiopia, am here today to claim the impartial justice that is due to my people, and the assistance promised to it eight months ago by fifty-two nations who affirmed that an act of aggression had been committed in violation of international treaties ... It is my duty to inform the Governments assembled in Geneva, responsible as they are for the lives of millions of men, women and children, of the deadly peril which threatens them, by describing to them the fate which has been suffered by Ethiopia.' He then described the appalling effect of poison gas sprayed not only on his warriors but on the civil population far from the battle areas with a view to terrorizing and exterminating them.

'Despite the inferiority of my weapons, the complete lack of aircraft, artillery, munitions and hospital services, my trust in the League was absolute. I thought it impossible that fifty-two nations, including the most powerful in the world, could be successfully held in check by a single aggressor.' He told them how when the danger to his country became more urgent he had tried to acquire armaments. 'Many Governments proclaimed an embargo to prevent my doing so, whereas the Italian Government, through the Suez Canal, was given all facilities for transporting, without cessation and without protest, troops, arms and munitions ... On many occasions I asked for financial assistance for the purchase of arms. That assistance was constantly denied me. What then, in practice, is the meaning of Article 16 of the Covenant and of collective security?'

He insisted that 'The issue before the Assembly today is not merely a question of the settlement in the matter of Italian aggression. It is a question of collective security; of the very existence of the League; of the trust placed by States in international treaties; of the value of promises made to small States that their integrity and their independence shall be respected and assured ... if a strong Government finds that it can with impunity destroy a weak people, then the hour has struck for that weak people to appeal to the League of Nations to give it judgement in all freedom. God and history will remember your judgements ...'

He deplored the initiative that had been taken that day to raise sanctions and asked: 'What does this initiative mean but the abandonment of Ethiopia to the aggressor?' He demanded that the League should use all means to secure respect for the Covenant, and assured the Assembly 'that the Emperor, the Government and the people of Ethiopia will not bow before force, that they will uphold their claims, that they will use all means in their power to ensure the triumph of right and respect for the Covenant.

'I ask the fifty-two nations who have given the Ethiopian people a promise that they would come to their aid at the time of aggression against them, to prevent the aggressor defeating them: what are they willing to do for Ethiopia? I ask these fifty-two nations, who have promised the guarantee of collective security to small States over whom hangs the threat that they must one day suffer the fate of Ethiopia: what measures do they intend to take? Representatives of the World assembled here! I have come to you in Geneva to discharge in your midst the saddest duty that has befallen an Emperor. What answer am I to take back to my people?'

A week later the League suspended all sanctions against Italy.

CHAPTER 18

Last Year in Darfur

I DECIDED TO SPEND the last month of my 1936 leave travelling through Syria and Palestine, and then to Cairo, for I was anxious to see something of the Arab world about which I had read so much. I therefore took the Orient Express to Aleppo, where I changed trains for Beirut. I have always enjoyed long train journeys through undeveloped countries, finding it absorbing to see the varying types at the stations, and the changing village scenes. Also, confined as they are to a railroad, trains do little to disturb the pattern of life in the surrounding countryside, in contrast to motor transport, which is forever increasing in numbers and expanding in range.

I was convinced I was going to dislike Beirut – as indeed I did. Its fashionable hotels, smart restaurants, crowded bathing beaches and hybrid culture roused my instant resentment. I would not have gone, but that Robin Buxton, who had served with Lawrence in the Arab Revolt, had given me a letter of introduction to Amir Arslan, one of the Druze chiefs, to enable me to visit Jabal Druze.

The Druze had won my sympathy during their revolt against the French in 1925–6; reading the daily accounts of this war in the papers at the time, I had been filled with admiration for their bravery and skill. I knew that the Jabal was now a restricted area, virtually closed to visitors, but the Amir obtained permission from the French authorities for me to visit it, on condition that I should report to the Commandant as soon as I arrived.

I spent two days in Damascus on my way there. The older parts of the city made an immediate appeal to me, but my recollections of Damascus and Jabal Druze from this fleeting visit are now confused by others of a later date. On this occasion I saw little of the Druze, though the fact that I had been in the Jabal was to prove helpful to me later, during the war. On this first visit the Commandant sent me with a Druze camel patrol from Suaidah to the Arab Legion post at Azraq in Trans-Jordan. On our way we rode across a volcanic wilderness devoid of trees and bushes, without, if I rightly remember, passing a single village; the impact on me of Azraq was consequently all the greater. I had always wanted to see it after reading Lawrence's account of how he emerged from the desert and first saw its ruined castle, palms, marshes and lagoons. At Azraq, Glubb's Arab Legionnaires, in their spectacular tribal uniform, killed a goat and feasted us before taking me in their truck to Amman.

In Amman Peake Pasha and Glubb, who were sharing a house in this small and still unspoilt Arab town, had me to stay. Next day I accompanied Glubb to an encampment of Bani Sakhr, where we feasted in the sheikh's large black goat-hair tent. As my first encounter with one of the nomadic tribes of Arabia, and in the company of Glubb, I could have had no better introduction to Bedu life. I was singularly lucky to be staying with these two remarkable men, and during my three days with them I learnt much about Arabia.

Peake had been seconded to the Egyptian Army in 1913 and three years later had served in the Darfur campaign and in the Flying Corps in Salonika, before taking part in the Arab Revolt. In 1922, in the newly established country of Trans-Jordan, he had raised and commanded the Arab Legion. Recruiting from villagers, he had brought security to the settled areas; however, the nomads remained vulnerable to fanatical Ikhwan raiders from Saudi Arabia. Similar conditions had prevailed in Iraq until Glubb recruited a force from the Bedu tribes there, held off the Ikhwan and established peace in the Iraqi desert.

When Iraq became independent in 1930, Glubb was transferred to Trans-Jordan, where he achieved the same results by incorporating into the Arab Legion a Desert Patrol recruited solely from the Bedu. When I visited Trans-Jordan he was Peake's second-in-command, responsible for the desert areas. Even by 1936 his prestige among the Bedu was remarkable, not only in Iraq and Trans-Jordan but over much of Arabia. No other European has ever acquired comparable knowledge of Bedu custom and understanding of their character, nor won from these proud tribesmen a like respect.

By 1936, when I arrived in Palestine, the Arabs there had been provoked into revolt by the Government's authorization of Jewish immigration. My sympathies were entirely with the Arabs, and I could see no justification for this influx of Jews into an Arab land two thousand years after they had been expelled by the Romans. Country roads were now being ambushed, and in the hills there was sporadic fighting between British troops and Arab guerrillas, while in Jerusalem all the shops in the Old City were shut and troops patrolled deserted streets. It was impossible to visit the Dome of the Rock but I have never forgotten Jerusalem as I saw it for the first time from the Mount of Olives; only the ancient walled city was visible, the tragic scene of so much strife and hatred down the ages; the golden Dome of the Rock rose in splendid simplicity above its spacious court; in the far distance were the blue mountains of Moab.

Dan Sandford and his wife Chris were in Cairo when I arrived there, so I spent the three days with them. I had not seen them since I left Addis Ababa for the Danakil country. Since then so much had happened.

In 1935 Haile Selassie had appointed Sandford Advisor to his newly formed administration in the southern province of Jimma. When the Italians reached Jimma in 1936, he had withdrawn at the last minute into the Sudan, and had but recently arrived in Cairo. His wife and family had left for Jibuti before the Italians entered Addis Ababa.

Abyssinia had been the Sandfords' home since 1921; now, the loss of their farm at Mullu deprived them of all they possessed. Yet they were undaunted, confident that they could somehow get by while waiting to see what would happen in Abyssinia. Sandford was convinced that the Italians now faced widespread and formidable irregular resistance, far harder to contend with than armies in the field, and that their calculated but senseless brutality would only inflame this resistance. He was also confident that if Britain found herself at war with Italy, he and I should both be employed in Abyssinia.

From Cairo I went straight to Kutum without stopping in either Khartoum or Fasher. Guy Moore was there when I arrived; he told me the rains had been exceptionally heavy and that all was well. That first night we sat up even later than usual. Moore had served with Glubb in Iraq, and was pleased that I had met him, and that he had taken me to visit the Bani Sakhr. 'I'm glad you came back that way,' he said. 'Now you've got an idea what the Bedu are like in Arabia.'

241

Idris was delighted to see me. He had looked after my house and had taken special care of my guns, cleaning and oiling them. He had once told me that the three things he wanted most were to own a sword and a carpet and to make the pilgrimage to Mecca. I had already given him a sword; now I brought him a carpet from Cairo. Faraj Allah, Habib and the other camels were in excellent condition, as were the two horses. I was happy to be back.

Moore sent me off a few days later to the Zaghawa country, telling me to go north from Tini to the wells at Sindia, somewhere in the desert to the north of the Wadi Hawar. He said, 'These wells are a hang-out for scoundrels from both sides of the frontier,' and added, 'just the sort of people who would appeal to you.'

I was away altogether for six weeks. The rains had been phenomenal; even old men could not remember the like. Some people complained that they had been so heavy they had ruined the crops. Ordinarily most of the millet in the district died from lack of rain, and the Zaghawa then lived largely off berries and a flour made from the seeds of a small grass. At Tini the normally dry Wadi Hawar had been in flood for weeks. The day after we arrived there Idris and I followed the exceptionally large pug marks of two lion that had killed a horse during the night, until we found they had swum sixty yards across the wadi into French territory.

As usual I was travelling light, accompanied only by Idris, Kalol, Ahmad and a policeman. We got soaked several times during the nights, once, about eleven o'clock, by a real downpour. Water was lying everywhere and the deep wells at Sindia were not in use. However, north of the wells we dropped out of the blue on several Badayat *fariqs* or encampments. The Badayat lived indiscriminately on either side of the frontier, keeping as far out of reach of the administration as possible. These particular ones had never seen a District Commissioner. As Moore had predicted, I liked them at once.

One night they were boasting of their skill as camel thieves, so I challenged one of them to move Habib, who was couched a few yards from me, and take him a hundred yards without me hearing him do so. Couched camels grunt and roar when anyone tries to shift them and Habib was always especially noisy. However, the man approached Habib very slowly, undid the fetter round his doubled foreleg, and prodded him, always stopping when Habib turned his head or opened his mouth. Having got him to his feet, he took off his hobble and disappeared with him into the night. I had not heard a sound. Returning, he said triumphantly, 'I could have stolen the lot and you would have known nothing till you woke in the morning.'

I was now known in the district as *samm al usud* or 'Lion's Bane', and as such these Badayat had heard of me. At one *fariq* they asked me to shoot three lion that had been killing their camels. It had rained heavily in the night and it was easy to follow the lions' spoor at a trot on our camels. The three lion kept separating and joining up again but we followed the tracks of the largest. Suddenly I saw him about forty yards off, asleep on his back under a bush.

My mother had given me a double-barrelled Rigby .450 rifle, a more effective weapon than a magazine rifle for stopping a charging lion at close quarters, and considerably more powerful than my .350. I now handed it to Idris who was on Habib, jumped off Faraj Allah, and all in a second collected it again. Faraj Allah had grunted as I left the saddle. The lion woke, rolled over and sat up, and I killed him stone dead. Idris, still mounted, called to me to shoot another, but this I could not see from the ground until it rose to its feet, and then I shot it. The same day we came on some four hundred oryx, one of which I shot, which gave us all a feast.

I now returned to Tini and joined Guy Moore, and from there for the next fifteen days we travelled together, something we did all too seldom. When we arrived at Sheikh Hamid's village we found that the Bani Husain were having trouble as usual with lion: two men had been killed and several mauled in the past week.

Next day at dawn Idris and I set out with ten Bani Husain, all of us on horseback. We rode a long way to a village where a lion had killed a cow; there we were joined by the headman and two other horsemen, and we all spread out and beat across country. An hour or two later we picked up the spoor of a lion and lioness. Idris and I dismounted and followed the tracks through the bush, with the horsemen on either side.

Suddenly we heard the thunder of hooves and the wild, exultant *kororak* as the others tore in pursuit. They bayed the lion three or four hundred yards away, but he broke through them before Idris and I could catch up, They brought him to bay again almost immediately. As we ran up, the Bani Husain were circling a small isolated patch of bush, waving their spears, yelling their war cries and shouting insults at the lion, which was growling furiously. As we approached, he faced us, his tail lashing. I fired one barrel into his open mouth and then killed him with the other. He was a large lion with an unusually good mane.

We rode back to the village where the cow had been killed, the Bani Husain exultantly singing their triumph song. As we approached the village they broke into a wild gallop and poured through a gap in the fence, a cataract of horses and men. Idris missed the gap and came down with his horse on top of him. He was shaken but otherwise unhurt, and the .350 was undamaged. The headman slaughtered a sheep and fed us, and then we started back under a full moon for Shaikh Hamid's village. My companions sang most of the way, and whenever we passed a village broke into a gallop. It was midnight when we returned to camp.

After that, with sometimes as many as thirty horsemen, I rode down more lion with both the Bani Husain and the Zaghawa. Now, when we found tracks, Idris and I would stay mounted, leaving someone else to follow the spoor on foot. This gave us the excitement of the headlong pursuit, with the risk, in bush-covered country, of riding right on top of the lion. In the open a lion would not face us; instead after its first burst of speed it would slow to a lope, and search for somewhere to make a stand. Meanwhile we would close up behind it, a mass of jostling, excited horsemen, all shouting and singing as the hunt approached its climax. When the lion finally stood at bay, often in a patch of thick scrub, we would ride round and round its cover at some thirty yards distance. The others would shout to me, 'There it is! There! Can't you see it?' and very often I could not.

I soon learnt from experience that if I dismounted while the lion was facing me it almost invariably charged, and would then be almost on me before I could fire. Had I not been with them, armed with a rifle, my companions would have dismounted, advanced together on the lion and speared it to death. I did sometimes feel that I ought to have joined them armed only with a spear.

At the end of September 1936 there was another meeting on the Kordofan border between the Maidob and Kababish, attended this time by some sheikhs from our Zayadia Arabs. Moore could not get there but sent me as his representative.

For me the most memorable occurrence was the presence of Douglas Newbold; I had met him briefly in London and had longed to meet him again. Now I had the rewarding experience of three days in his company. He was Governor of Kordofan, and soon to be Civil Secretary of the Sudan, whereas I was still a probationer, but I found I could talk to him without constraint. In this setting, among the tribesmen he loved, he was at his most relaxed and happy.

He spoke of his journeys into the Libyan Desert, one with camels, another with Ralph Bagnold in cars. While agreeing with me that cars were an abomination, he said we had to accept them now as an essential part of modern desert exploration. 'All the same, I would have liked to have made a camel journey from the Sudan to Tibesti. Now I don't have time, and am too old and fat.'

Soon after my return to Kutum we were expecting a visit from our own Governor, Ingleson, but three days before he was due we had news of another affray among the Zaghawa, with several killed. Moore said, 'I must get up there and sort things out. I'm getting fed up with these Zaghawa. You'll have to hold the fort when Ingleson arrives,' and he explained in detail what he wanted me to discuss.

Ingleson duly arrived with his wife and a niece who was staying with them. He was a different type from Newbold, and I always felt he was principally concerned with the efficiency of the administration, and had little personal relationship with the Sudanese, whereas for Newbold, friendship with many Sudanese was all-important. The Inglesons had brought a lorry with servants and camp equipment and installed themselves in the guest house. Except for breakfast, I fed them in my house, hoping my cook would provide reasonable meals and that Idris would serve them properly. In fact, all went well. They stayed for two days, and on the second the Sudanese staff invited them to a tea party, presided over by the qadi, at which we ate tinned fruit and sweet biscuits.

Ingleson inspected the prison, dispensary and police lines, and checked the office work. We discussed at length the subjects Moore had told me to raise and I took a lot of notes. Ingleson was friendly and interested in what I had been doing, and as he left he said, 'Just take care you don't get yourself killed by a lion.'

During the next two months Moore was almost continuously on trek so I was in Kutum running the office. One night Yusuf Efendi, our accountant, died in his sleep. I sent prisoners to the cemetery to dig his grave, and when it was reported ready I joined the funeral

245

procession, headed by the *qadi*. On arrival at the grave we found it was too narrow to take his body; as the ground was rocky it took another hour's work before it was wide enough. I missed Yusuf, a cheerful, friendly soul who used to waddle into the office, smiling broadly and carrying a sheaf of accounts which I knew would be meticulously correct.

Moore, too, was upset by Yusuf's death. He took a lot of trouble over his staff, and in return they would do anything for him. When both Moore and I were on trek Abdullah Efendi, the clerk, would have everything ready in the office for our return. On one occasion I came in to Kutum at the end of a month and Abdullah had made out the monthly report; I read it, signed it and sent it off to Fasher. There had been twenty-nine cases of chickenpox in the prison. However, Abdullah had written 'smallpox' and I had missed this disastrous slip, which caused consternation when the report reached Fasher. Luckily Pansy Drew, the doctor, asked for confirmation before taking action. When the flap was over, Moore said, 'That should teach you not to be slipshod in future. Imagine what would have happened if this report had reached Khartoum. We'd have had the whole medical department here!'

Soon after Christmas 1936, an occasion for which we again had to go into Fasher, Moore sent me back to the desert.

In recent years the Goran had made occasional raids, none on a large scale, from the Ennedi mountains in French territory, and had captured Kababish camels. To counter these raids, Moore had raised and armed ten Zaghawa Scouts to patrol the frontier. He told me: 'You'd better go up again as far as Sindia, take a look round and see what news you can get. This year there must be camels scattered all over the desert, just what the Goran would be hoping for.'

There was no one at Sindia, but in the Wadi Hawar we found several Badayat encampments, including those of our friends. With them was an elderly Badayi called Kathir, whom Moore had recruited among his Scouts; I found him absorbing to talk to. He was well acquainted with Ennedi and spoke of other great mountains which he called Tu, inhabited by a people called the Tedda, many days' journey towards the setting sun. He claimed to have been there as a young man about 1910, when Ali Dinar was still Sultan of Darfur.

I felt certain that Tu was another name for Tibesti, the place that Newbold had always wanted to visit. Talking to Kathir, I made up my mind to travel there, and asked him endless questions about wells and distances, about the mountains themselves and above all about the Tedda. Idris was curious why I wanted to know so much about Tu, and I told him that one day we would go there together. Kathir said at once: 'When you go there, take me.'

The Badayat told me that Kababish and Zayadia were far away to the north, with thousands of camels. No living person, they said, had seen such a *jizu*. They had no news of Goran raids but said their own herds were being raided by two lion. God had brought them *samm al usud*. Tomorrow we would go together and kill them.

We went at dawn, the Badayat on eight camels, two on each, Idris with me. The others I left in camp. We soon found the spoor, easily visible on the sand. Two young Badayat followed it at a run; after a mile or so others took over and the first pair scrambled up on to a camel. We found the lion in some scrub. I saw one, fired, and wounded it; when it roared, the other, which I had not seen, immediately attacked it. They were about forty yards away, an extraordinary spectacle as, snarling and growling, they hit and bit at each other. I watched fascinated for a minute or so, then shot them both. The Badayat were triumphant.

On my return to Tini I stayed as usual in one of Sultan Dosa's large, neatly thatched huts. This venerable, white-bearded old man ruled his small section of the Kobe Zaghawa, the majority of whom lived across the frontier, with fairness and authority, and there were seldom disputes for us to settle among his people. Daud, Idris's father, a quiet-spoken, middle-aged man, was usually in attendance on the Sultan. Both were grateful for what I had done for Idris, who was Daud's only son.

At Tini I rode down four lion with the young squires from Sultan Dosa's house; two months earlier one of them had had both his brothers killed spearing a lion. Idris was especially elated to be hunting lion here among his own people. One afternoon he and I had a long chase after a striped hyena. Only one other person was up with us, the others being caught on the wrong foot by this unexpected quarry. The hyena kept twenty yards or so ahead, increasing its pace each time we drew nearer. We must have been chasing it for two miles when Idris fired from the saddle at full gallop and hit it in the head.

In early March 1937 I went to Khartoum to take my official Arabic and Law examinations, and stayed with the Perrys. I was now reasonably fluent in Arabic and had done some work on the written language, and I hoped to pass; however the dictation ploughed me. In Law I easily passed the paper on Criminal Code but failed the one on Sudan Government ordinances.

I had been thinking a great deal about my future. I realized that inevitably, probably quite soon, I should be transferred to one of the northern provinces along the Nile, possibly posted to Wad Medani, Atbara or even Khartoum to learn about modern administration. I had had a foretaste of what this would involve, for as soon as we had finished the examinations the other probationers and I had been lectured on rural development, cooperative farming, town planning, education, and urban and district councils. I therefore asked for an interview with Gillan, the Civil Secretary.

When I saw him I proposed that I should resign from the permanent Political Service and rejoin on a contract basis, with the understanding that I should only serve in the wildest and remotest districts. At first he refused to contemplate this, insisting that I would later regret throwing away my pension rights and any prospect of becoming a Governor or even a Deputy-Governor. However, he listened with great patience, sympathy and understanding to all I had to say. Eventually he replied, 'Well, I have said everything I can to dissuade you, but if you insist I will agree to the change.'

I was given a contract on a higher rate of pay for seven years, with the option of renewing it for another seven, and was told that my standard of Arabic and Law would now be accepted as adequate. For this I was thankful, for I always dreaded exams. When I saw Ingleson on my return to Fasher, he said he too was worried because I had renounced my rights to a pension, which I might well need, especially when I got married.

Though grateful for his concern, I had no intention of marrying: I valued personal freedom far too highly for that. As for money, I had no expensive tastes, and wanted only to serve in places remote from civilization, where the cost of living would be minimal. At Kutum, for instance, my cook provided me with meat, eggs, and milk for a shilling a day. I had £400 a year of my own and was now to get a salary of £500, most of which I knew I could save. In any case, I was concerned with the present, not with my problematical old age. When I told Guy Moore what I had done he said: 'I think you were probably wise; now I hope you will get at least a couple more years with me here at Kutum.'

Moore went on leave at the beginning of April and I spent most of the next four months touring the district. I dealt with the office work on occasional visits to Kutum, but most cases could be handled on the spot with far less inconvenience to those concerned. It was a long way to Kutum for a plaintiff from Tini or Jabal Maidob, as far as from London to Bristol, or further; then he would have a long wait while the defendant and witnesses were summoned. At that time there were no merchants' lorries to give people lifts; our cars were the only two in the district.

I went to Umm Buru and stayed for several days with Muhammadain, something I always enjoyed. Both Moore and I were fond of the old villain; he belonged to a past age, more colourful and violent than our own. I knew he was ruthless and unscrupulous, and, unlike Dosa, extremely autocratic in dealing with his fellow tribesmen, who feared and admired him but did not like him.

Moore maintained that it was our job to ensure Muhammadain's people got a fair deal, without diminishing his authority. Warning me that one of Muhammadain's sections was making trouble, he had said: 'I settled it when I was up there the other day. Muhammadain is partly to blame, but the headman is a real bastard, and I suspect may make more trouble as soon as I've gone on leave.'

One morning as Muhammadain and I came out of his house, we were met by a noisy, truculent crowd. Muhammadain spoke to them in Zaghawa but was constantly interrupted. The headman, a scraggy individual who was shouting angrily, whipped out his arm-knife and lunged at Muhammadain. I stepped forward and hit him on the jaw, knocking him unconscious, the only time I had hit anyone since boxing at Oxford. I later sent the man to the Magdum's court at Fata Burnu and the Magdum sentenced him to a year's imprisonment.

On 3 June 1937 I celebrated my twenty-seventh birthday by riding from Umm Buru back to Kutum, a hundred and fifteen miles, in just under twenty-four hours. I was riding Faraj Allah, accompanied by Idris on Habab. We started at sunset from Muhammadain's house and followed the motor track; the moon did not rise till three in the morning but the sky was clear and the stars gave some light. I found it difficult to stay awake as the camels shuffled through the dark at their most comfortable pace of five miles an hour. Late in the morning we halted for an hour at a spring near Jabal Si, watered the camels, made tea, ate dates, and rested briefly. We reached Kutum just before sunset. Neither camel showed signs of exhaustion.

At Kutum I found a copy of a petition addressed to the Governor. In it a Zaghawa stated that his brother, the headman, had appealed to the Assistant District Commissioner against oppression by Malik Muhammadain. The Assistant District Commissioner had immediately hit his brother in the mouth, knocking out his teeth, and had then imprisoned him. Ingleson had sent it to me with a request at the foot of it: 'For your comments, please.' I wrote explaining what had happened, and heard no more.

In late June 1937, with massed banks of black clouds, the rains broke. They were heavy again this year, in a district which usually had only about nine inches of rainfall annually. Everywhere the villagers turned out to plant their crops, poking holes in the earth with sticks and dropping in the millet seed. God willing, they said, we shall have another good harvest. All too often they knew scarcity. My fear was that the desert locusts might come. I had seen them as a child in Abyssinia, swarms that darkened the sky as they passed over, and I knew what devastation they caused when they settled.

At Kutum the wadi came down in short-lived spates, and the boys in the village stripped and romped in the racing brown water. It was an exhilarating time of year; the damp earth smelt good; bushes and trees turned green overnight; only the perverse *haraz* trees now shed their leaves, to renew them when the rains were over.

At night while rainstorms beat on the roof, I was glad to be in my house and not on trek. There were books my family had sent me, to read by the light of my Petromax lamp, and luxuries to eat from a Fortnum and Mason hamper sent by my mother.

I planned to tour Jabal Maidob before I went on leave. Mark Leather, a young Bimbashi in the Western Arab Corps who was due some local leave, had asked if he could come with me, so I went to Fasher in the car to fetch him. While I was there Ingleson gave me disastrous news: on return from leave I was to be transferred to the Western Nuer District in the Upper Nile Province. He said he would be sorry to lose me.

I had counted on several more years at Kutum and was very upset. I realized that Western Nuer was one of the wildest and most primitive districts in the Sudan, which after all was just what I had asked for when I had taken a contract. Yet the thought of leaving Kutum was a wretched one. I liked serving under Moore; I loved the country and the life; I had made many friends among the Maidob, Zaghawa and Bani Husain. I realized that during my first year while I was learning the ropes I had been almost useless to Moore, but I was now fluent in Arabic, and after travelling all over the district, I knew the different tribes and their chiefs, and had some of that understanding of their ways which among people whose lives were largely governed by tribal custom is essential. While Moore was on leave I had felt competent to deal with any problem. Now I would have to start all over again, in a totally different environment, among pagans whose language I could not speak.

Anyway, Leather and I drove to Kutum on 2 August and picked up the lorry for our drive to Jabal Maidob. We had an unpleasant journey. Near Melit it poured with rain; we only just got across a flooded wadi and were frequently bogged down; we became separated from the lorry; and then, after ten hours' driving, when we were only a dozen miles from Malha, our lights fused.

When we eventually reached Aidrur, Sayyah provided us with camels and came with us to Sulaiman's village at Kejku. The narrow, rocky track was often steep, sometimes with a sheer drop below. These mountain-bred camels were sure-footed, but for Leather, perched high on an animal he did not know how to control, it was an alarming introduction to camel-riding. I had been chary about travelling with an Englishman I did not know, on my last visit to the Maidob, but I need not have worried. Leather was an admirable companion. He liked the Maidob at once, made friends with Sayyah, was enthusiastic about everything, and desperately keen on his hunting.

I had brought the tent. In the night it poured again, and in the early morning the mountains were wrapped in mist, which gave them an almost Highland appearance. We spent a week at Kejku, at the end of which Leather shot a magnificent ram with a record head of thirty-one inches. When we got back to Malha, Leather still had a week of his leave left, and as he was anxious to get an oryx, we rode out next morning with Sayyah into the desert. We pitched the tent as a base camp and Leather and I hunted separately, Idris and two young Maidob going with me. I shot an oryx with forty-two-inch horns, and Leather shot an oryx and an Adra gazelle, so we had plenty of meat for the Maidob who came to see Sayyah and spent the nights at our camp.

On the last day I shot another oryx. Towards evening, when we had ridden far and were still a long way from camp, we came on five young boys rounding up their sheep and goats. They gathered round, urging us with shrill voices to stop with them for the night; when we agreed they led us to their camping place beside a small tree. Here on the sand were some pieces of wood, the ashes of a small fire and two tin bowls; they had nothing else but their spears and the shirts they wore. As we unsaddled, two of them took the bowls and went over to milk their goats for us. We had meat from the oryx, some dates, sugar and tea, and a goatskin of water. We grilled quantities of the meat, a veritable feast for these half-starved children, who for weeks, even months, had been living on milk and nothing else; yet as they fed they showed no sign of greed, but waited courteously to help themselves in turn. Indeed we had to insist before they would eat enough.

We had turned our camels loose to graze and at sunset the two Maidob who accompanied us brought them in and couched them nearby; contentedly they chewed the cud, every now and then shifting and fidgeting a little. The dusk deepened and one by one the familiar stars appeared, growing in number and brilliance as it grew darker. Round us were the huddled sheep and goats, several hundred in all, their bleating a homely not unpleasant noise. At last I stretched out on my sheepskin. A boy played snatches on a flute, and very sweet it sounded. The late moon rose and still they talked beside the dying fire. Here in Northern Darfur among these people I had been utterly content. As I drifted off to sleep I felt great sadness at leaving them.

Guy Moore arrived back at Kutum from leave a few days before I left for England; he said he had done all he could in Khartoum to keep me, and that Ingleson in Fasher was still trying to get my posting deferred. I therefore went on leave hoping against hope that I should be left at Kutum. However, on reaching Khartoum on 15 December I learnt that my posting to the Western Nuer District had been confirmed.

Moore had called at The Milebrook and stayed with my mother and my brother Dermot. I was glad of this; it brought him more closely into my life. Years later, after my mother's death in 1973, I found this letter to her from Moore among her papers.

Tini
On the French Frontier
20.12.37

Dear Mrs Astley,

Will you please forgive this unpleasant demi-official notepaper; I had hoped to send you a letter for Christmas from the more or less orthodox surroundings of my house in Kutum where I might have found the proper materials and an atmosphere more in keeping with the quieter tones of Christmas greetings. But now that the battle is lost and they have deprived me of Wilfred I have to jog about even more than formerly and, apart from the personal side – which needs no comment – his absence has caused me a whole mass of extra work. This was one of his beats – which he had come to know very well and, largely because it borders on the desert side with all its funny will-o'-the-wisp nature permeating man and beast, he was very happy always when he had to come into this part of the world. But, as for our neighbours the French – to say the least of it – they are not easy and our little frictions with them along this rather open and lengthy line of frontier don't allow one to get all the enjoyment one might out of it all. I will say this for Wilfred – his head was, on the whole, far above such trivialities and he seldom allowed them to interfere with the course of his existence ...

Apart from all the work, it is very hard losing Wilfred – I have said it needs no comment; nor does it, but I must say this – I am not likely to find anyone again who fitted in so well to this kind of life – who very quickly found his contact with the people and, having done so, only wanted to be with them and help them. And, above all, relished what other people would call 'hardships'. I fear I am a little unorthodox myself probably because I served my apprenticeship with the Beduin (I don't think anyone has ever liked those conditions and remained completely sane); and so, I suppose, I may have done Wilfred some harm in his administrative outlook; but, by Jove! What a joy it was to find someone who liked sitting and sleeping on the ground, who felt completely at his ease and really *happy* 200 miles out in the blue with nothing much to eat – in that ocean of sudden surprises and disasters, who was more concerned with tribal affairs and their acute and absurd problems than with the question of marriage allowances or, even, his next leave! As for his next meal – it was always in the hands of God and never a matter to be determined by the chiming of a clock.

For me, and for the people here, it was a very happy and prosperous companionship; I remember so well at the last tribal gathering when we had been keyed up for a day or two – our hearts rather full of the happiness and élan of that large and varied parade of tribes – we both of us thought 'This is the climax' – it was too good to go on; I suppose those sort of things generally are. Well – this year we are to have another tribal gathering to greet the Governor-General – I am planning a big one – I shall not be able to do it as I want to without Wilfred's help – the new lad is bound to be a passenger (I *hope* – a willing one!) and so the thing is certain to be an anticlimax. Allah Karim!

I know he has felt a sting at leaving here – I can only hope he will soon find his feet and a vital interest in his new surroundings; I am old enough now to criticise my superiors: and I think they have done wrong in moving him – but I feel pretty sure that if there is anything to grip on to in those parts he has gone to (and I think there is bound to be) he will soon get hold of it and, with his eye for fundamentals, won't let it go.

Anyway our wishes go with him from here; and now may I do what I set out to do in this letter, – wish you a happy new year. I fear this will not arrive in time for Christmas.

> Yours very sincerely,
>
> Guy Moore

PART IV

The Southern Sudan

1938–40

CHAPTER 19

The Western Nuer

I SPENT THE LAST month of my 1937 leave travelling with my mother in Morocco. I had long wished to visit this country and I was not disappointed: the cities still retained much of the romance associated with their past. This was largely due to Marshal Lyautey, who, during the years 1912–16 and 1917–25 when he governed Morocco, preserved its customs and traditions, insisting for instance that the modern French towns should be kept geographically separate from the ancient native cities, and that only Muslims should enter mosques.

We had gone to Morocco by train across France and then by boat from Marseilles to Tangier. In those days there were no passenger flights from London to Morocco; Marrakesh still seemed a long way off. The first view of that walled city excited me, surrounded as it was by palm groves, and behind it the snow-covered Atlas, stretching east to west out of sight. I still vividly remember the Djamma al Fna, that great open space where boy-dancers, acrobats, conjurors, musicians, snake-charmers and story-tellers regaled an ever-shifting throng of people clad in burnous and turban. I remember, too, horsemen firing their muskets as they cavorted and charged beneath the city walls in celebration of a festival; the booths, each selling the merchandise of its own quarter, opening on to colourful, crowded streets; Islamic schools which we might enter and admire; mosques from which we were debarred. My brother Roddy had arranged for us a letter of introduction from his friends, the de la Mottes, to Hajj Thami al Glawi, Pasha of Marrakesh, and that formidable Berber potentate gave us a banquet at Telouet, his spectacular castle in the Atlas mountains.

Another day we drove over the mountains to Taroudant. The French had only recently completed the conquest of the Anti-Atlas tribes, and the narrow, steep-sided earth road was crowded with military convoys. Back in Marrakesh I was shown over the Foreign Legion barracks by an Englishman serving in the Legion. As a boy, I had read *Beau Geste*, Wren's romantic novel about the Foreign

257

Legion: joining the Legion had then seemed the acme of adventure, like sailing round the Horn in a windjammer. Now I only felt regret for the tribesmen they had defeated.

From Marrakesh we went to Meknes and then to Fez. Of all the cities I have seen, only Constantinople, viewed across the Golden Horn from Pera, and Jerusalem from the Mount of Olives, compared with Fez from its encircling hills.

This journey in Morocco was the first of many such travels I was to make with my mother. After the war we travelled in Palestine and Syria, in Turkey, Greece, Italy, Spain and Portugal, and several more times in Morocco. On our last journey there my mother was eighty-nine, with a hip that gave her incessant pain; yet, undefeated, she visited Goulimime to see the 'Blue People' and then motored along the edge of the Sahara, where we put up each night in primitive native hostels. Travelling with her was always fun: she was good company, indefatigable, uncomplaining, interested in all she saw. After that first journey we sailed back from Algiers, which seemed a sorry contrast with the cities we had seen in Morocco; from Marseilles my mother returned to England and I to the Sudan.

On the way, in Cairo, I stayed for a few days with John Hamilton. He had been in Fez in 1926 when the city was under threat from Abd al Karim's forces stationed on the nearby hills. I envied him what must have been an exciting and intensely interesting experience. Like me, he had been enthralled by Fez but, in that fervently Islamic city, conscious of the same sense of exclusion.

Geoffrey Dawson, then editor of *The Times*, had invited me to write an article on Morocco. When this was published as 'The Mind of the Moor' I thought its title pretentious and was glad I had insisted it should be anonymous. In it I had described the resentment felt by the Moors for the French, who were competing with them on all levels, even as drivers of horse-drawn cabs in towns; the desperation of unemployed tribesmen starving in the shanty slums of Casablanca; and the inevitable growth of nationalism fostered by a frustrated intelligentsia.

When I reached Khartoum on 15 December 1937 Idris was waiting at the Perrys to go south with me to Malakal; he had brought all my things with him from Kutum. A few days later we went by train to Kosti, where we boarded the *Kereri*, the paddle-steamer that served as the mobile Headquarters of the Western Nuer District. Wedderburn-Maxwell, the District Commissioner, was at Malakal awaiting my arrival. We should be the only two Englishmen in a district of twenty thousand square miles: my predecessor, I gathered, had died of blackwater fever, which was the reason for my transfer.

My accommodation on the *Kereri* consisted of two adjoining cabins, each eight feet square, at the stern; I slept in one and stored my possessions in the other. Another more spacious cabin was for Wedderburn-Maxwell, with a bathroom, which we would share. The saloon was forward of a companionway that led to the lower deck, engine room, and accommodation for our six Northern Sudanese crew and our servants. Beyond that, the deck up to the bows was meshed with mosquito netting, providing us with an agreeable place to sit; on the upper deck aft of the wheelhouse was another netted enclosure.

Lashed alongside the *Kereri* was a large, roofed, double-decked barge, at present empty. Once back in the district it was soon packed with porters, tribal police, prisoners and a variety of women, as well as with our four horses, some sheep, goats and chickens, and any cattle we were transporting: conditions aboard it were crowded and chaotic, but no one seemed to mind. A smaller medical barge was pushed along ahead of the *Kereri*: on it the Sudanese dresser and our clerk had their quarters.

The *Kereri* took four days to reach Provincial Headquarters up-river at Malakal. The country south of Kosti was completely flat, with a mile or so of marsh and reedbeds bounding the river on either side: beyond these stretched a scrub-covered plain. We tied up several times at landing stages, to refuel. Most of the tribesmen who loaded the wood on to the steamer were completely naked; only the Shilluk, in accordance with their tribal custom, wore a length of cloth knotted across one shoulder, but this was in no way intended to conceal their nakedness, of which, like the others, they were totally unconscious.

The town of Malakal extended along the east bank of the White Nile. Downstream were government offices and the bungalows of officials. Upstream were the prison and police lines, the market and the tin-roofed shops of some Syrian merchants, and the native quarter inhabited largely by de-tribalized southerners, who had mostly adopted Islam and northern dress, though among them

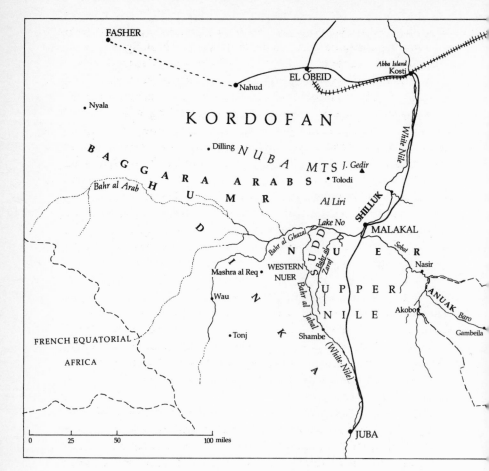

Upper Nile Province, 1937–40

were many naked Dinka and Nuer. The town struck me as meticulously clean but devoid of interest, just an administrative imposition
on the emptiness of a primitive land, around which had accumulated the flotsam of disrupted tribal lives. As we tied up,
Wedderburn-Maxwell, a stocky, fair-haired man, in conventional
bush shirt and shorts and Wolseley pith helmet, came aboard.
Wedderburn, as he was always called, had a frank, open face with
wide-set eyes, and impressed me at once as friendly and utterly

260

reliable. While we talked, he puffed at his pipe; during my two years with him he always seemed to be lighting it or smoking it.

He had now achieved his ambition by being posted to the Western Nuer, and hoped to spend the rest of his service among them. I soon found I was lucky to have him as my DC, for in the cramped quarters of the *Kereri* he was easy to live with, accommodating, good-natured and imperturbable; I never saw him lose his temper. Though no great conversationalist, he was enthusiastic on the subject of fishing, and always interesting about the Nuer. He had only arrived in this Western Nuer District a fortnight before me, but he had served in other Nuer districts and spoke Nuer. He said the first thing we must both do was to get to know our district, and this would entail spending nearly all our time on trek. I asked for nothing better. Wedderburn was anxious to be off as soon as possible, so told me to buy rations for at least four months; he helped me find a cook, a cheerful-looking Zande who could speak some Arabic, though whether he could cook remained to be seen.

That first night we dined with George Coryton, the Provincial Governor, a tall man in obviously hard condition, with a quiet, friendly manner, who quickly made me feel at home. He had a long discussion with Wedderburn about the Western Nuer. Both were concerned because it appeared that some Nuer in the district were eating dogs: as this was unheard of, Wedderburn and Coryton thought the Nuer may have deemed it to have some magical attribute, which could possibly portend trouble. Listening to them gave me an inkling of the strange life I was about to lead. As we left Coryton said to Wedderburn: 'Be sure and send me a letter whenever you get the chance, just to let me know you are both all right.' This did not sound as if we were going to be burdened with paperwork, and I went to bed content.

The Western Nuer had only been administered since 1921: their country had long been regarded as virtually inaccessible, and their warlike reputation was comparable with that of the Masai in East Africa at the end of the last century. However, their repeated raids on administered Dinka tribes made eventual government intervention inevitable.

When this happened, Captain Vere Fergusson, serving as a DC with the Dinka, volunteered to enter Nuer country and try to bring them under control. His offer was accepted and he was given a free hand. I had read about this in *Fergie Bey*, an account of his life published in 1930. This eulogistic book, written by his friends shortly after his death, contained many extracts from letters he had written to his mother. He travelled over much of the country, imposed his authority on the Nuer chiefs, largely stopped the raiding and, single-handedly, did a great deal of medical work.

Several times he had to call for troops to support him. Once, after two hundred of the Equatorial Battalion had beaten off a fierce Nuer attack, he wrote: 'It was a fine sight to see them coming on, and I give them full marks for bravery in face of a pretty hot fire helped by a couple of machine guns. It *has* taught them a lesson ... I must say I am awfully glad they attacked as they did, for never again will any of them try to be truculent with me, and I ought to have them feeding out of my hand.' In fact he was obliged to use troops on two further occasions and in 1927, when going ashore from the *Kereri*, was murdered by the Nuer. He had roused great resentment by depriving their chiefs of cattle taken from the Dinka in past raids.

After Fergusson's death, the Sudan Government instituted the Nuer Settlement. At first this involved the use of troops, who met with courageous resistance from the Nuer. I remembered that while we were sailing on the *Rampura* to Haile Selassie's coronation in 1930, Sir John Maffey, then Governor-General of the Sudan, had spoken of these events, which had taken place only two years earlier. He said he had insisted that the civil administration should take over from the military as soon as possible, and this had been achieved within a year of Fergusson's death.

Neither slave traders nor Mahdists had penetrated Nuer country; all that its inhabitants had asked of the outside world was to be left alone. In Nuer eyes the British occupation of their land had no justification, but against disciplined troops, machine-guns and aeroplanes their bravery was unavailing. British officials had then forbidden raiding, restored looted stock to the Dinka, and insisted the Nuer should lead peaceful lives. The Nuer, however, were an intensely proud people who held all other races in contempt, and had always taken fierce delight in fighting, their ultimate answer to every dispute; they encouraged even children to fight among themselves. They had naturally resented this seemingly unwarranted British intervention, as Professor Evans-Pritchard, the ethnologist employed by the Sudan Government, found when he first went among them in 1930.

Wedderburn's predecessor, Romilly, had both admired and genuinely liked these remarkable people, and in the end had won their respect and trust. For their part, in accepting Romilly's authority they were accepting him as an individual: but he had now been transferred to the Eastern Nuer District and been replaced by Wedderburn and myself, two strangers, one of whom could not even speak their language.

We left Malakal at the end of December 1937 and sailed upstream past the confluence with the Sobat, which, rising in Abyssinia, joined the White Nile near the town. When we came to Lake No, an insignificant stretch of water ringed by papyrus swamp, we had arrived on the edge of the Western Nuer District. Upstream of Lake No the White Nile, known there as the Bahr al Jabal, formed our eastern boundary almost as far south as Shambe, a hundred and fifty miles away. At the lake it was joined from the west by the Bahr al Ghazal, which lay within our district as far upstream as Mashra al Req; the Bahr al Ghazal in turn was joined from the west by the Bahr al Arab. North of the Bahr al Ghazal, beyond the ill-defined boundary with Kordofan, were the Nuba mountains.

A part of the district consisted of Sudd, a vast accumulation of floating papyrus and other aquatic vegetation; but the greater part consisted of black cotton-soil plains interspersed with occasional low sandy ridges that supported some thorn scrub and a few large trees. Except for this higher ground, the plains were under water six months of the year, owing to the heavy rain and flooding by the rivers. Afterwards they were covered with coarse grass, four or five feet high, much of which the Nuer burnt off in the dry season to ensure fresh grazing for their cattle. After the cotton-soil had dried, the ground was seamed with deep cracks, and away from the rivers the only water lay in occasional creeks, sometimes ten or fifteen miles apart.

The Nuer sited their villages on the high ground, building large conical byres, known as *luaks*, for their cattle, and small huts for themselves; in the dry season they moved into cattle camps near rivers, lagoons or creeks. I had assumed that they possessed vast herds of cattle, but was to discover that few families had more than a score of cows and many had less. Each family would be anxious to own at least one cow: without it they felt deficient, for cattle were the be-all and end-all of Nuer existence. However, rinderpest, probably introduced into their country in the period of the Mahdiya, had devastated their herds and continued to do so. The consequent paucity of cattle obliged the Nuer to supplement their traditional diet of milk, blood and meat with millet and maize cultivated round their villages, and with the fish they caught when they were in their dry-weather camps near the rivers and lagoons.

The Bahr al Jabal, the Bahr al Ghazal and the lower reaches of the Bahr al Arab were navigable by the *Kereri*; we could therefore go ashore with our porters at a convenient landing place, set off into the interior of the district and rejoin the *Kereri* somewhere else, perhaps on one of the other rivers.

Now, leaving Lake No, we churned our way up the Bahr al Ghazal and eventually tied up at a landing stage in the Jikany territory; here was a small tin-roofed shop, kept by a Northern Sudanese, but nothing else. From our top deck we looked over a plain covered with tall grass to some *luaks* two or three miles away. Wedderburn told me that this village belonged to an important chief. He proposed that I should set off from here and rejoin him a month later on the Bahr al Jabal, where he was meeting Romilly.

'The chief here', he said, 'will provide you with porters. Take it easy and get some shooting. In that way you should get an idea of what the district and the Nuer are like.'

After we had been tied up to the landing steps for an hour or so, the chief, in a pair of shorts and with a leopard skin over his shoulders, turned up with some naked followers, and had a long discussion with Wedderburn. He came back early next morning with a crowd of both sexes and all ages; among them were thirty men who were to be my porters.

This was my first contact with the Nuer. I am six foot two; many of them were taller and were especially long in the leg, with the graceful figures of track athletes. In general they had fine features, and I thought what superb models they would make for a sculptor. Some wore their hair long, dyed a golden colour with cows' urine, and this enhanced their good looks. Unlike the Dinka, the Nuer wore few beads, seldom more than a single string of red beads round their waist, two or three bead necklaces, and some flat, light blue beads round their foreheads, which were marked with six parallel rows of scars, the result of their initiation as warriors. Some wore highly prized necklaces of giraffe hair, while a few had amulets of brass wire bound tightly from wrist to elbow; when first put on this wire caused much pain, which lasted for days. Married women had tasselled leather skirts that just covered their bottoms; girls wore nothing but bead necklaces.

I soon accepted the nakedness of these people as perfectly natural, and never gave it a thought except to regret that Christianity, with its roots in Judaism, should so generally equate nakedness with shame, and even regard it as sinful. Fergusson had encouraged the Nuer to wear clothes but they disliked them, and when he was killed discarded them. However, some chiefs, like this Jikany chief, would put on shorts when they were with us. I once met a chief whose shorts were evidently uncomfortably tight, so he had left his fly buttons undone and hung everything outside. This was convincing proof of his sartorial innocence but it did look startlingly indecent. It seems to me that concealment is a greater stimulant to eroticism than nakedness. During my two years with the Nuer I never saw one with an erection, even at a dance with both sexes joining in.

Being new to the district, Wedderburn's and my immediate aim was to tour extensively so as to make contact with as many Nuer as possible. We could have managed with eight or ten porters each; instead, we each employed at least thirty, even though most of them would be carrying food for the other porters; what we hoped was to make friends with them and through them to get to know their fellow tribesmen. We paid each of our porters the equivalent of a shilling a day: they had few requirements and little use for money, though they might buy some beads or tobacco at a merchant's shop on one of the landing stages. What they wanted were cows, and no Nuer would sell a cow. A few years earlier they could have looted them from the Dinka, but raiding was now more or less suppressed. The chiefs, however, were entitled to try cases and to impose fines in cattle. We would collect these cattle, transport them in the *Kereri* to another area and sell them there, letting our porters buy some at a nominal price and keeping a fund into which we put the money from these cattle sales. This money should strictly have been forwarded to Headquarters, but Wedderburn knew from experience what endless correspondence ensued if we needed money, for instance to build another landing stage. It was far easier to keep the money, pay it to the Nuer we employed for building it, and get on with the job.

265

Wedderburn and I each had two horses which we took with us on trek and the Jikany chief found me a young Nuer as my *syce*, who stayed with me until I left the district. Unlike most Nuer, he was not apprehensive of horses and took good care of mine.

All British officials who served among the Nuer were known by their 'bull names'. Wedderburn was called 'Dhouryan' and Romilly 'Yangwan'. This same Jikany chief formally presented me with a black ox marked with white, which was known from its colouring as 'Kwechuor'. This now became my name among the Nuer and I was known by no other. For an adult Nuer, the ox bearing his name had an almost sacred significance; he decorated its horns with tassels and frequently made a boy lead it round his encampment while he sang its praises. On Wedderburn's advice, I asked the chief to keep Kwechuor for me with his herd.

Idris and I had sorted out my baggage, to be ready to start when the porters arrived in the morning. Here in the Southern Sudan I travelled in a conventional manner, with a tent, camp bed, table, chair, canvas bath and a couple of tin boxes for clothes, books, medicine, ammunition and odds and ends. I also took my Zande cook, with his pots and pans and a selection of tinned food, and expected him to produce reasonable European meals, which he did.

I had an interpreter, Malo. I had been afraid that Idris might be lonely, but Malo and he soon became close friends. Idris got on well with the Nuer and picked up enough of their language to make himself understood, showing in this a greater aptitude than I did. They in turn liked him, and gave him the bull name of Bor Jagey, a singular honour for an African stranger.

We left the *Kereri* at noon and made a short march. At this time of year it was never really hot and at night was cold enough to sleep under three blankets. Travelling with porters, nothing got upset or broken and no time was wasted loading or unloading: each man just picked up his forty-pound load and set off with it on his head. They all carried two or three barbed spears and a hollowed-out section of *ambach*, a soft light wood, in which they kept tobacco and other oddments. The Nuer had no shields and, when fighting, tradition-ally used this length of *ambach* to deflect spears thrown at them. We usually marched for four or five hours with occasional halts before pitching my tent and camping for the day; the porters then settled down in groups close by. Later in the season, as the country dried up, we often had to make longer marches to camp near water.

I went out each afternoon with Idris, Malo and some of the porters to look for lion or buffalo, or to shoot meat for the men. I discovered almost at once that Malo was a skilled and enthusiastic hunter; accompanied by him and Idris, I could not have been in better hands. I had bought a Rigby .275 express in London, so, with my .350 magnum and double-barrelled .450, we each carried a rifle. Although on this first journey the grass was high and still unburnt, topi and white-eared kob were so numerous that I had little difficulty in shooting one whenever I required it. The Nuer seldom killed these antelope. They did, however, spear elephants to make bracelets from their tusks, and in time of famine hunted buffalo for meat. I felt it would take a brave man to stand up, armed only with a throwing-spear, to a charging buffalo. The Nuer were particularly fond of hippo meat, relishing its fat. None of them would eat any kind of bird or eggs, though they ate crocodiles and turtles. On getting back to camp, I would find the porters squatting round their fires, boiling their maize, then Malo would divide any meat we had brought back and they would roast it, well satisfied with this addition to their rations.

Next time I was back in Malakal I bought my porters mosquito nets, which were much appreciated. Whenever we had camped near a village, strange, grey, ghostly figures would appear in the morning, bringing us milk: like all Nuer, they had been sleeping on a soft carpet of ashes, but they looked particularly odd when they had waded across a stream and become half grey and half black. Since there was no salt in their country the Nuer compensated for the deficiency by mixing cows' urine in the milk. I always gave someone else my share of this blend.

A contract DC could expect to remain for six or seven years in the same district, or even longer. At Kutum I would have been happy to do this but not here. Had I been posted to the Nuer on first arrival in the Sudan, I should have been utterly content and ready to remain among them indefinitely; but instead I had been sent to Darfur, and there, under Guy Moore, I had learnt to want for more than the Nuer could give me. I knew these naked savages could never provide me with the comradeship I most enjoyed, that I could never find among them a Sayyah, a Muhammadain or an Idris.

The cultural gap between the Maidob or Zaghawa and the Nuer was brought home to me when I watched one of my Nuer porters grab a handful of maize from a pot, step a yard aside and stand there urinating while he fed. All the same, it was rewarding to travel with these exciting tribesmen through a land teeming with game, which few strangers had ever seen. I liked being with the Nuer and having them grouped round my tent; I enjoyed listening to the sound of their voices, or watching their perfect physical coordination as they strode in front of me along a path, seeing them slip through the bush when we hunted buffalo, or beat across-country when we looked for lion. I was soon on good terms with my porters, most of whom remained continuously with me while I was in the district.

After a month's easy trekking I approached the Bahr al Jabal and there found Wedderburn camped with Romilly at a village in the Nuong country: the *Kereri* was moored a short march away. Romilly, who had arrived two days before me, stayed with us for ten days; I wished it had been longer.

Before joining the Sudan Service as a contract DC, Romilly had been a regular Army officer and had seen active service in a line regiment on the North West Frontier of India. Like his close friend Wedderburn, he was a bachelor; this was certainly no life for a married man. Romilly had a strong face, with steady, friendly grey eyes above a lean and leathern body; he also had the curious habit, on the march, of chewing the end of his handkerchief and I always think of the pair of them, Wedderburn with his pipe, Romilly with his handkerchief. As a self-sufficient man, combining authority with lack of pretentiousness, Romilly put me in mind of Arnold Hodson and those others who used to trek up from their lonely consular outposts in Abyssinia to report to my father in Addis Ababa. I felt far closer to such men than to my young contemporaries in the Sudan, many of whom, before they joined the Service, had hardly been out of England.

Romilly had identified himself with the Nuer and was content to spend his life among them; the crowds that gathered round the camp to greet him were a testimony to the impact he had made on them. Here the Nuer belonged to the very section who had murdered Fergusson and who in the subsequent fighting had suffered most. As Romilly described the courage they displayed and the losses they suffered while they charged, driving their sacred ox before them, I sensed the compassion he had felt at the time. He could never have written, as Fergusson had done, 'These fellows of mine are brutes of the first order but I'll get them to heel yet.'

Romilly never employed any Sudan Government police in the district but relied on his tribal police, who were only distinguished from their fellow-tribesmen by a metal badge worn on the left arm, bearing the Provincial arms of a shield and crossed spears. We followed his example and usually kept a few tribal police on the *Kereri*; but since most chiefs had one or two in their village, we did not take any with us when we were on trek, unless there was a specific job for them.

One day, after going down with a bad attack of malaria, Romilly got into bed and told his cook to pour buckets of cold water over him; this drastic treatment brought down his temperature and next day he was up and about. Much of the time he and Wedderburn held discussions with the chiefs; the most influential was Garluak, a large, overweight man who had been tried for instigating Fergusson's murder but exonerated. They heard a number of appeals against the chiefs' judgements: for these the plaintiff had to produce a calf, and if he lost his appeal he forfeited it. Though I understood nothing of what was being said, I was content just to watch the gestures and facial expressions of the Nuer, knowing that in the evening, over drinks, Wedderburn and Romilly would talk over the day's work and bring me into the picture.

One morning a Nuer complained that lion were killing his cattle, and Wedderburn sent me off to shoot them. I was away four days and shot four, but through stupidity had a narrow escape. The porters had flushed a lioness out of a patch of grass, and after a fast gallop across open ground Idris and I rode her down, pulling up when she came to bay about sixty yards away. I jumped off my horse and gave the reins to Idris. The lioness was facing me and looking very vicious: I expected her to charge at any moment. Still shaky from the gallop, I fired at her chest and missed, and without reloading fired the other barrel and missed again. Then she did charge. As I fumbled in my belt for two other cartridges and reloaded I felt sure she would be on me, but when I looked up she had disappeared. Idris, sitting seemingly unperturbed on his horse and holding mine, said: 'She came as far as there,' – pointing to twenty yards away – 'then she stopped and went into the grass.' When the others caught up with us we searched for her but failed to find her. I was not sorry.

Romilly spent his last night with us on the *Kereri* before starting back to Nasir in Eastern Nuer. The next day the fortnightly mail boat passed on its way from Malakal to Shambe and gave us our post. In a letter from my mother I learnt that Haile Selassie had visited her at The Milebrook, and I was sorry I had not been there to help receive him.

There was also a letter from the Civil Secretary's office. While I was in Khartoum I had asked for permission to spend my next leave travelling to Tibesti in the French Sahara. I was now told this was granted; they were applying to the French authorities for permission for the journey. This was a positive concession on the Sudan Government's part; for health reasons its British officials were expected to spend their leave in Europe, certainly not riding camels in the Sahara in summer. When I told Idris that we should be going to Tu during my leave, he remembered my discussion with Kathir on the Wadi Hawar and said, 'Kathir told us Tu was very far away and it was a difficult journey. He knows the way. We must be sure to take him with us.'

With our private mail was the official mail. We looked through it, and threw most of it overboard. We maintained a couple of files for our own convenience but circulars from Khartoum about collecting gum arabic, or enquiries whether the district was suitable for growing groundnuts, bore no relevance to our existence here.

I always enjoyed a few days on the *Kereri* between treks, reading in an easy chair, eating at a proper table, having a hot bath, and for a change sleeping in a comfortable bed. In the evenings, Wedderburn and I generally sat on the top deck: the *Kereri* might be nosing her way through the Sudd, along the narrow waterway of the Bahr al Jabal with papyrus on either side as high as the middle deck or, in more open reaches, thrashing past mudbanks and rows of basking crocodiles.

I disliked crocodiles and when I got a chance shot them. Like all river crocodiles, these ones were dangerous. Most were eight or ten feet long, but I shot one of sixteen and a half feet. It looked enormous, with a vast girth, and even the Nuer were visibly impressed, declaring they had never seen one so big. Since then I have always been sceptical of alleged twenty-foot Nile crocodiles, though I know Myles Turner, a game warden in Tanzania, has more recently shot one of eighteen feet there.

The Dongalawis, who formed the crew of the *Kereri*, valued

crocodiles' penises as an aphrodisiac. The penis was retracted inside the body and sometimes a seemingly dead crocodile that had been hoisted on board caused panic by coming back to life as they groped and operated.

We often fished when the *Kereri* was tied up to the bank; Wedderburn had two rods and lent one to me. One of the crew would row us upstream in our boat while we trolled a spoon or artificial bait. I once caught a 150-pound Nile perch after losing another that had straightened the hook; but these fish, unlike the much smaller tiger-fish, were poor fighters and never jumped. However they were excellent eating, whereas tiger-fish were a mass of bones. On one occasion, while I was unhooking a fish Wedderburn had caught, the hook was jerked into the joint of my finger, beyond its barb. Luckily Wedderburn refused to cut it out, and suggested that we should go five or six hours away down the Bahr al Gharaf to a Protestant medical mission, run by the MacDonalds. There Mrs MacDonald cut it out without damaging the joint.

The MacDonalds were concerned with the physical welfare of the Nuer rather than with trying to convert them, and they discouraged them from wearing clothes or abandoning their traditional way of life. They told us how a boy had once turned up for prayers wearing shorts and how the others had said to him in shocked voices: 'You can't pray in shorts!' Unfortunately the MacDonalds were not in our district. We had a Catholic mission, and neither of us approved of what they were doing. The fathers insisted that their converts, most of whom were orphans or destitute, should cover their nakedness by wearing clothes. This divorced them from their fellow tribesmen, and as a result they hung about the mission or drifted into Malakal where they had themselves circumcised, became nominal Muslims and were then accepted into the large de-tribalized community of the town.

I was now almost continuously on trek, sometimes for six weeks at a time before returning for a few days to the *Kereri*. In early March I found a delightful camp site on a shady ridge under some large tamarisk trees; their heavy shade was very restful in this shadeless land. Here was good water, few mosquitoes, plenty of game, with several large cattle camps nearby. In these camps the shelters, made of reeds plastered with mud, were little more than windbreaks surrounded by stakes to which the cattle were tethered at night. I remained here for a while, getting acquainted with these Kilwal Nuer. Rai Wur, their chief, had been speared in the arm while hunting hippo, and I treated the wound, which was going septic.

On my way to join Wedderburn and Romilly I had shot a buffalo. Though I had hunted them in Danakil country, these were the first I had seen and I was astonished at the size of this dead bull. I now shot two more, out of a herd of a hundred and fifty, one with a fine head, and the meat gave the Nuer a splendid feast; they much preferred buffalo to antelope.

Hunting buffalo was always exciting; some experienced hunters rate them more dangerous than lion. When I was in the district I shot a dozen, and also let Idris shoot one, which gave him great satisfaction. One of them gave me an anxious moment. I had followed a small herd into tall reeds, where I shot the bull at close range, through the heart. It still charged and was within a few yards when my second shot, hitting it on the boss of the horn but without penetrating, knocked the already dying animal off its feet. Perhaps mistakenly, I used soft-nosed bullets on buffalo.

I hunted lion whenever I got an opportunity, and while I was in the Southern Sudan I shot forty. On several occasions I was charged, often at close quarters, but though I half-expected to be killed by a lion, the compulsion to go on hunting them was irresistible. I fancy some jockeys who ride year after year in the Grand National may have something like the same feeling.

My porters were always eager to join these lion hunts: perhaps the excitement to some extent compensated them for the prohibition we had imposed on raiding. I remember in particular an occasion when I had wounded a lion on the edge of a dense, tangled reedbed. I had never yet lost a wounded lion but, even armed with a heavy rifle and with Malo and Idris behind me, it seemed almost suicidal to look for this one in such a place. However, there was no restraining the Nuer: they ignored my orders and plunged into the reeds on either side of me. Armed only with light throwing-spears, not one of them would have stood a chance had he stumbled on the wounded lion. Among the foremost I saw my young *syce*, his spear raised, his face wild with excitement, thrusting his way through the reeds. We beat right through that reedbed but the lion was gone, and we never found him.

Many DCs, even in the Southern Sudan, had no interest in

hunting. I am sure in consequence they neglected a means of getting on closer personal terms with the tribesmen they administered. This would have been especially so if the quarry were dangerous and the hunt a joint venture. After the war Philip Bowcock served as an Assistant DC among the Western Nuer. Recently he told me that when he had asked them about me they had said, 'Oh, Kwechuor! He was like one of us.' Since I was only with them for two years and never acquired more than a smattering of their language, this appreciation must have been due to the hunting we did together.

I know that today it sounds unforgivable to have shot seventy lion in five years, but that was fifty years year ago and circumstances of that time cannot be judged by those of today. Lion were then rated as vermin in the Sudan, and were especially abundant in the Western Nuer District. Now wildlife is everywhere endangered; but in those days, with few exceptions, it was under no apparent threat.

One day I joined a party of Nuer who were setting off to harpoon hippo; we went to a lagoon a few miles away, where there was a school of some thirty-five. When we arrived there, the Nuer cut off sections of the floating vegetation to form five primitive rafts, eight to ten feet across. Armed with two heavy-bladed Shilluk stabbing-spears, and accompanied by Idris, who refused to be left behind, I stepped on to the largest of the rafts with three harpooners. Their harpoons had thirty-foot ropes attached, and these were tied to part of a tree trunk driven into the tangled mat of papyrus we were standing on. When five of us were on this improvised raft, the water came up to our knees, and the ropes somewhere about our feet.

We poled across the lagoon; the water was six to eight feet deep and on the far side of the lagoon, about three hundred yards away, more Nuer were massed in the shallows. As we drove the hippo in that direction, they tried to break into deeper water by swimming back under our advancing line of rafts. Though they were completely submerged, we could follow the course of individual hippo by their wakes and the bubbles they emitted, and the men flung their harpoons at any hippo within reach. When a harpoon struck, the shaft would detach itself, but the single-barbed head came out each time after a short but violent struggle. One man was dragged off his raft and under water, with a rope round his leg, but his brother cut the rope and hauled him back on to the raft. As they turned for the shore I noticed that his leg was badly lacerated.

At last we got one of our harpoons firmly home. The hippo was now held on thirty feet of rope. The men on the other rafts closed in and tried to sink their harpoons into the infuriated animal, or to spear it when it came half out of the water, grunting and shaking its head before submerging again. It looked enormous. Then it surfaced at my feet, with cavernous mouth, enormous teeth and angry, pig-like eyes. I hurled my spear between its jaws. This turned it, and with all my strength I drove my other spear into its body behind the shoulder. After that, each time the hippo rose I saw blood flooding down its side. In its death flurry the harpoon came out and the body sank, but we recovered it next day: the carcass was towed ashore and cut up, and the meat carried off to the various camps.

Before my next leave I travelled over most of the district, including some forest country along the Bahr al Arab which afforded a welcome relief from the swamps and the treeless cotton-soil plains. Here I shot a roan antelope, and a leopard which I treed from horseback. In the swamps of the Bahr al Jabal I had already shot a situtunga and Nile Lechwe, both much-prized by hunters. I had also been lucky enough to see a white rhino; this northern race of white rhino was rare and strictly preserved.

Elephant frequented the swamps bordering the Bahr al Jabal, only moving into the open country when it rained; it was there, on the edge of the swamps, that I hunted them. My game licence permitted me two elephant a year, and while I was with the Nuer I shot the four to which I was entitled.

The really exciting encounters came when, with Malo and Idris, I followed elephant into the swamps where the papyrus grew close together to a height of twelve feet or more. In so doing we faced the possibility of having to shoot an unwanted small-tusked elephant in self-defence.

One morning a Nuer came to my camp with news that two elephant, one of them very big, were in the open not far from his village. With Malo and Idris, I hurried there, arriving just in time to see them disappear into the papyrus. The wind was tricky, but when it had steadied we followed. This was not easy, as the water was at least two feet deep, more so in the holes made by elephants' feet, while the broken papyrus stalks were as thick as a man's wrist. We eventually got close to the elephant but could still see nothing, though they were rumbling less than twenty yards away. They moved on and we followed them until they stopped again on the far side of a small clearing of water, where we could hear them breaking papyrus as they fed. We waded across the clearing, the water deeper here, and into the papyrus on the far side.

We were watching a place where we could hear one feeding, when within a few yards of us a trunk and tusks parted the papyrus; even through thick reeds and water, an elephant can move silently. As he loomed above us, we withdrew as quickly and quietly as we could, though confined by the walls of papyrus to the elephant's track we had been following. Now he heard us and moved forward, with his enormous ears fanned out. I stopped and aimed at his brain but held back from firing, since he only had small tusks. The elephant, no longer hearing us, stopped likewise and then disappeared into the reeds.

In order to look at the tusks of the other much bigger elephant, we followed them both again and some hours later reached a small island with two or three large ant-hills on it; but even climbing on to one of these all I got was an occasional glimpse of black backs among the rushes. It was now nearly sunset, and we had been following them for eight hours, so we went back to camp.

Although I never succeeded in shooting an elephant in the swamps, I was more successful when they moved into the open country during the rains. I had hoped to get one with hundred-pound tusks, but my best had tusks of eighty-three and eighty-one pounds; the others were in the seventies.

Each time I shot an elephant the Nuer – men, women and children – appeared in large numbers and in a few hours the enormous mass of meat was cut up and carried away, only the largest bones and the skull, from which we would have extracted the tusks, remaining on the ground. It was extraordinary to see these naked men swarming all over the carcass and even inside it, most of them covered with blood, partly from the elephant and partly from cuts on their own bodies, as they hacked and slashed with their spearheads.

In 1936 there had been a mass migration of elephant through the district and the Laik, Bul, Jakaing and Jagey had killed between two and three hundred with their throwing-spears. They hunted them on dry ground, and maintained that a man should be able to escape from a charging elephant. Even with the help of other men to distract it, this seemed almost unbelievable to me: I knew I should never have stood a chance.

Coached by Wedderburn, I was gradually learning something of Nuer customs, and was beginning to get an understanding of their mentality. In this I benefited from the company of my porters: hunting, travelling and camping with them had established a personal relationship and Malo told me they called themselves 'Kwechuor's men'. With his help, I was now reasonably competent to try cases brought before me. The Nuer were not litigious, and though quick-tempered and naturally aggressive they were too proud to steal or lie. Many cases involved accusations of witchcraft, that a man had bewitched someone or his family or his cattle. My task was to judge intent, but seeing the evidence I sometimes found myself half-believing in the efficacy of spells. This judicial work brought me closer to the people and added considerably to the interest of living among them.

Back in Malakal at the end of April 1938, I felt unwell and saw the doctor, who diagnosed malaria and wanted to put me in hospital; but at first it seemed a mild attack so I insisted on going back in the *Kereri* to the district. Next day I was really ill, with a high fever and constant vomiting. Wedderburn was out on trek but Idris looked after me. The doctor had given me Atabrin tablets and after five days these cured me. He had also given me other tablets to be taken when I recovered, to prevent recurrence, and in fact I have never had malaria again. A few days later Idris went down with it, and it was my turn to nurse him; in a few days he too was well again. However, the fever had left me very weak, and when I left the boat to go on trek shortly afterwards I could hardly muster the effort to shoot meat for the porters. In Malakal I had been informed that the French had now approved my visit to Tibesti, but I wondered despondently whether I would be strong enough to undertake such a journey. However, by July I was as fit as ever.

I had thoroughly enjoyed the last seven months. I was lucky to be serving under Wedderburn, who not only approved of the life I led but encouraged it. All this time I had been almost continuously on trek in a remote, hardly accessible area of Southern Sudan, among a war-like, barely administered people whom I had grown to like and admire. I had become attached to the ones who had chosen to remain with me as my porters, while Idris gave me the comradeship I required. Above all, I had amply fulfilled my boyhood dreams of big game hunting. As an experience, I could not have asked for more. Then, at the end of July 1938, Idris and I left Malakal for Kutum and the mountains of Tibesti.

CHAPTER 20

A Journey to Tibesti

I KEENLY LOOKED FORWARD to seeing Tibesti. This unbroken mass of mountains, situated near Chad's frontier with Libya, extends some two hundred miles north to south and two hundred and fifty east to west, and includes what are by far the highest summits in the Sahara.

The first European to reach Tibesti was Gustav Nachtigal in 1863, during his extensive travels in the Western Sahara. However, he had only penetrated as far as Bardai, and he had barely escaped with his life. The French, during their expansion eastwards across the Sahara, had established a military post at Bardai and another at Zouar. In 1916 during the Tuareg revolt in Aïr they had evacuated both, and not till 1930 did they again occupy Tibesti, though various military expeditions, of which Colonel Tilho's in 1925 was the most important, explored and mapped the Tibesti mountains. When I went there in 1938, Nachtigal was still the only European to have been to Tibesti, other than the French officers who now served there.

From the Tedda, who inhabited Tibesti, the French had never met with serious opposition such as they encountered from the Tuareg and Senussi: being essentially individualists whom no chief had effectively controlled, the Tedda had always been divided by blood feuds. However, with incredible powers of endurance and unrivalled knowledge of the desert, they had been famous raiders. They had raided the Tuareg, their age-old enemies, as far away as Aïr in the west; they had also raided northwards deep into the Fezzan and east as far as the Nile valley; and they had harried the rich lands beyond the desert to the south.

The Tedda can perhaps be identified with the ancient Garamantes referred to by Herodotus and Ptolemy. The Garamantes hunted the troglodyte 'Ethiopians', rode in four-horsed chariots and lived somewhere between Tripolitania and the Fezzan; eventually they may well have withdrawn into the inaccessible mountains of Tibesti, which may be looked on as the cradle of the modern Tedda

277

race. These are certainly related to the Badayat and Zaghawa, though their language is different: all three tribes are generally held to be of Libyan origin, with a mixture of negro blood that is especially pronounced among the Zaghawa.

When the French assumed control they confiscated the rifles of the Tedda; their camel-mounted desert patrols of Groupes Nomades effectively prevented further raiding. Armed now only with their barbed throwing-spears, crudely forged swords, long knives carried above the elbow, and throwing-knives, the Tedda could still carry on their blood feuds but posed no threat to the French.

On our way north from the Western Nuer Idris and I arrived at Kutum on 30 July 1938. Guy Moore had gone on leave, but his assistant, Miles Stubbs, sent us by car to Tini where Moore had arranged for Kathir and five Zaghawa to meet us with camels. Kathir gave us a warm welcome and greetings from his Badayat kinsmen in the Wadi Hawar. The five Zaghawa were from Muhammadain's people; the only one I knew was a tough, thickset, middle-aged man called Ali Bakhit whom I had seen several times at Muhammadain's house. Muhammadain had now given him orders to remain with me all the time and ensure my safety. At Tini I stayed with Sultan Dosa, very content to be back here, if only for a night. The old man urged me to stay longer but I explained that we had a long journey ahead of us and only three months in which to make it. That evening Idris had many stories to tell of his adventures among the Nuer, and he presented his father with the tusks of a hippo he had shot.

Next morning we crossed the Wadi Hawar into French territory. I had my .275 rifle and field glasses, and in my saddle bags my camera, films, two or three books, some medicine and spare clothes. For rations we carried flour for *assida*, dried meat, onions, ladies' fingers, and ghee for the *mullah*. We took our blankets and a small tent. There had been heavy rain this year and it poured during that night, but by crowding into the tent we all kept dry.

From Tini our route was northwards to Fada, the headquarters of the Ennedi *circonscription*, and then westwards across the desert to Faya in Borkou, where the French had their main headquarters. Tibesti was a hundred miles north of Faya. For the first day or two we travelled among the Kobe Zaghawa, Idris's kinsmen, but beyond the Wadi Hauash we found ourselves among the Badayat. They owned fair-sized herds of cattle as well as camels but, though nomadic, did not range far afield. Their encampments consisted of mat huts or crude shelters of grass and branches woven through a framework of sticks. They spoke a dialect similar to the Zaghawa, whom they resembled in appearance and in many of their customs, but they were a wilder, hardier race who retained many pre-Islamic practices. North of the Badayat, the Goran inhabited the desert as far as Erdi; they had camels and goats but no cattle, and were entirely nomadic.

Beyond the Wadi Hauash we followed the western edge of the Ennedi massif, where a series of plateaux, weathered peaks and pinnacles rising to five thousand feet were intersected by sheer-sided gorges. In their rock faces were many caves, in some of which I found paintings in different colours, depicting hunting scenes, horsemen, camels, long-horned cattle, and human figures clothed and naked. I copied some, and they later proved similar to paintings from Uwainat and the Hoggar mountains. The Badayat said there were many such drawings in the Basso, the heart of the Ennedi mountains, which I hoped to visit on my way back from Tibesti.

On 10 August we arrived at Fada where I was welcomed by the French officers stationed in the large, well-designed fort. The garrison was a company of Tirailleurs Sénégalais, recruited from Senegal and from negroes round Lake Chad, with several French sergeants. Owing to the mounting tension in Europe, the French had recently reinforced their troops on the Libyan border. Two Groupes Nomades, returning on camelback from frontier patrols, passed through Fada while I was there. They, too, were Tirailleurs, with locally recruited *goumiers* and guides attached to them.

From Fada we crossed the desert to Borkou with a Gorani, Isa Adam, as our guide; we were following the main caravan route from Borkou to Wadai and Darfur, and we watered at the three small oases of Oueita, Oudai and Moussou. For the first day we wound among great bergs of rock that rose abruptly four to five hundred feet from the sand, and here I noticed several Barbary sheep high on these bare faces of rock. We passed by moonlight along a narrow valley under Jabal Bishagarah, an eerie place of glistening rock faces weathered into curious shapes, and steep-sided sand dunes. A Goran raiding party had made a last stand on this jabal and had been wiped out by a Groupe Nomade. The next day Isa Adam showed me

279

Tibesti, 1938

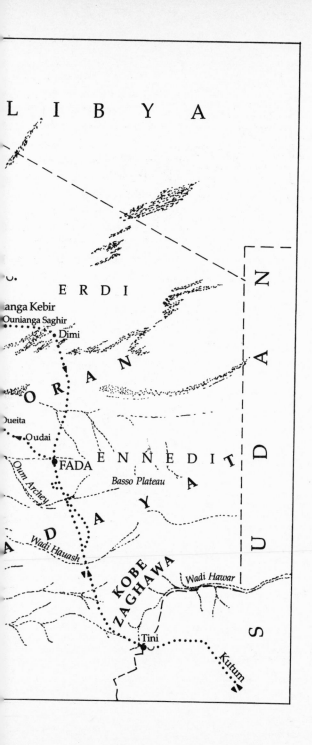

where a French patrol had fought with Senussi from the Fezzan before the French occupation.

We watered at Oueita and Oudai, shallow depressions where the water, much of it brackish, was close to the surface. However, every bush had been grazed bare so from now on, to spare our hungry camels, we travelled mainly by night, for it was midsummer and the sun was burning hot. On the last stage to Moussou we halted at sunset for a meal among the dunes, intending to go on as soon as the moon rose. Then, without warning, a sandstorm swept down, and lasted for three hours. Swathed in my *tobe* and sheltering against the side of my camel from the driving sand, I felt utterly isolated. When the storm had finally blown over, all our things were more or less buried. Digging them out, we found that the weight of sand had squeezed our water out of the goatskins. Isa Adam assured me we could reach Moussou in the morning if we started at once, and I was relieved to hear it; I did not fancy travelling all day in this heat without water.

The sky being overcast, no stars were visible, and though the moon had risen it gave only a dim light. After we had been going an hour or so, Isa Adam confessed he had lost all sense of direction and insisted we must wait till dawn. However, since Moussou was marked on my map, I knew the general direction, so I took over as guide, using my compass. We passed some scattered rocks, which became more numerous as we went, but I began to have a horrid feeling that since they were volcanic they were interfering with my compass. Still, we could but hope for the best and carry on. At daybreak, to my relief, Isa Adam saw some hills he recognized, and said Moussou lay just beyond.

Early on 19 August we reached Faya, an attractive little Saharan town surrounded by palm groves that on the west stretched fifty miles to Ain Galakka. As the headquarters of the Borkou, Tibesti and Ennedi administrations, Faya corresponded to Fasher in Darfur. Colonel Colonna D'Ornano was on trek when I arrived, but the captain and lieutenant were very kind and gave me every assistance.

I had thought that some British officials in the Sudan led fairly arduous lives, but they bore no comparison with those of the French here. Getting to Faya from Brazzaville took them three months, which included a long camel journey from Fort Lamy. When they arrived there were no luxuries, and no wives were allowed. The officers and sergeants in the Groupes Nomades lived under continuous active service conditions, incessantly on the move on their camels and covering great distances in order to patrol the desert. They led as a matter of course a hard life, which in the Sudan would have been quite exceptional and regarded as positively eccentric. This I envied them, and their vast area of unbroken desert; twelve hundred miles of Sahara from Ennedi to Mauretania.

On 21 August I left Faya on my way to Tibesti, with Idris, Kathir and Ali Bakhit, leaving the other four Zaghawa to look after our camels until we returned. The captain at Faya had engaged two Tedda with eight camels to take us as far as Gouro. At first we passed through a waste of volcanic rocks half-buried in sand, and did long marches to put it behind us, though this did not meet with the approval of the two Tedda. One of them, a young man called Ibrahim, soon earned the nickname of 'Abu Shakwa', or 'Father of Complaints'; yet his grumbles hid a ready laugh and his endurance was our envy. On the third day, starting in early afternoon, we made a forced march of twenty hours across the worst of this shadeless, scorching desert to the Kada wells near Gouro. When dawn broke, I saw, like a cloud on the desert's edge, the faint outline of Emi Koussi, at 11,200 feet the highest mountain in Tibesti.

At Gouro was a grove of palms and small fresh-water marshes, ringed by a black wall of rock against which the sand had drifted deep. This was the territory of the Arnah, a Tedda tribe whose chief, Adam Nater-Mi, before finally surrendering to the French, had acquired great fame as a raider and outlaw. Muhammad Abai-Mi, his even more famous brother, had died recently in Kordofan, preferring exile in the Sudan to submission. The small French fort was built on the site of the stronghold of Sayyid Muhammad al-Senussi, generally known as al-Mahdi, of which, however, scarcely a trace remained. Nearby was his tomb, a small, square, white-washed building containing his bed, draped in white cloth, and a few ostrich eggs hanging from the ceiling. It had been built to replace the original tomb which the French had destroyed.

Many Arnah had come to the oasis to pick dates and were camped on the sands near the palms. Since neither of the Tedda with us knew the tracks on Emi Koussi, I engaged an elderly Arnah named Kuri as our guide; thirteen years before he had been to the crater on

Emi Koussi. With him we travelled north to the wells of Modiunga, dominated even at a distance by the great hump-backed mass of Emi Koussi. On our way there I shot two gazelle; Kuri said it was the first meat he had eaten since the feast at his fifteen-year-old son's circumcision more than a year before.

We now climbed with difficulty on to a sun-scorched tableland of volcanic rocks riven by great gorges descending from the mountain range to which this tableland formed a base. All life was absent here; even the camel flies seemed to have left us. At the foot of the mountains we separated. Idris, Kathir, Kuri and I, with the two best camels, turned south to work back along the mountains and then up to the summit of Emi Koussi, while Ali Bakhit, the two Tedda and the rest of the camels crossed directly by an easier pass into the Miski valley, where we arranged to meet them.

We struggled along, climbing and descending but slowly working upwards, until we came to the great gorge of the Mashakazy, a thousand feet deep or more, and so sheer that a stone tossed from the top fell clear. A faint track marked with donkey droppings disappeared over the edge. Somehow the camels went, protesting, down that winding track, while we hung back on their tails and saddle-ropes, and loosened boulders crashed down ahead of us. We reached the bottom at last, but I could not imagine how even these small, agile camels would get up the far side: it looked too steep and difficult even for a loaded donkey. Yet somehow they did it, slowly and with many pauses, often dropping on to their knees to heave themselves up the worst places.

At sunset we reached the farther side of the gorge, the two camels trembling and exhausted, and camped among some prehistoric stone circles. We had been going for eleven hours. A light shower had recently fallen and pools were still lying among the rocks. I was astonished to find in one such pool, perhaps two feet across and six inches deep, a few tiny fish, half an inch long, silvery in colour, with crimson tails and dorsal fins. During the night we were troubled by mosquitoes.

Next morning Kuri found fresh camel-tracks which led to a Tedda encampment nearby, where a woman and a little boy herded two camels and a small flock of goats. She lent us her two camels to take us to Emi Koussi, and brought us a bowl of milk, which must have been about all she had; we left our camels with her and gave her some dried meat and flour. These mountain Tedda lived in caves or in unroofed stone circles, eking out a livelihood with small herds of goats and an occasional camel, and enduring extreme hardship of hunger and cold. No proper rain had fallen here for two years, and this was not exceptional. During the worst times they kept their goats alive on crushed date stones, and the camels on a handful of dates, fetched in season from the oases in the Miski, the Modra and other large valleys. Beyond the woman's encampment we passed other stone circles, some of them extensive, with great boulders aligned upon a level space. They had been built by giants of old, my companions declared; for who could shift such stones today?

We reached the mountain-top and camped. To the north was an awe-inspiring view across range after range of mountains, rising to jagged peaks above shadow-filled gorges. To the north-west, beyond the yellow streak of the Miski far below us, were more mountains, while to the east was a limitless expanse of sand. Southwards, the shoulder of Emi Koussi shut out the view. Towards evening the air turned bitterly cold, and the mountains stood out in the sunset, dark purple and sharp-cut under massed banks of molten cloud.

Next day, after several failures, for Kuri's knowledge of the route proved understandably vague, we found a track down into the great crater of Emi Koussi. This crater, eight miles long and five across, looked to us like an extensive plain ringed by mountains, for the crater wall rose as much as thirteen hundred feet. On the north side it fell in two steps to the floor, which was stony and sparsely covered with a heath-like plant, useless as camel fodder but welcome as fuel. When we camped for the night under a small hill, close to the great vent of Kohor near the crater's southern edge, once again it was bitterly cold.

Next morning we climbed down into Kohor, a huge hole perhaps a mile across at its widest and a thousand feet deep, with almost sheer sides except to the north, where steep screes lay below a small cliff; the bottom was covered with a deposit of sodium salt and ash. Idris and I then climbed the crater's southern wall, thereby attaining the highest point in Tibesti. It was hard work, and as I scrambled up behind him a ridiculous jingle kept running through my head. Even at noon it was very cold, and unfortunately hazy even with a strong wind, but despite the haze the view was tremendous. Near the summit we saw a Barbary sheep and under rock ledges we found the tracks and droppings of others. The Tedda snare them with noose and drag-log; for them the trapping of game is not confined, as it is among the Zaghawa, to the outcast community of blacksmiths.

Returning to our camp, we loaded the camels and climbed out of the crater by an easy track for which Kuri had searched in vain the previous day. Next morning we went back to the Tedda camp and exchanged the woman's camels for our own. Kuri, more than ever uncertain of the way, persuaded her to accompany us to the Miski. She strode ahead in her blue robe, an impressive figure with a naked knife in one hand and an oryx horn in the other. After crossing another gorge we descended at last into the valley and rejoined the others.

While we had been away, Ali Bakhit had been treating a sore eye with a strong solution of Boric acid which someone had given him in Faya. Now he was almost blind in that eye, and in great pain, so I sent him back to Faya with Ibrahim. We held a farewell feast. Meat being luxury to these people and Dorcas gazelle being plentiful, I shot several. One unfortunate boy who had helped us prepare the food was prevented from eating it by the untimely arrival of his stepfather; that a stepson and stepfather should feed together was contrary to tribal custom.

Ibrahim had found two more Tedda, who, with six camels, were prepared to take us to the French fort at Bardai. They belonged to the Tikah section and one of them, a lad called Dadi, distinguished by his great mop of hair, was a nephew of the Tikah chief; he had been born in Kufrah and brought up by the Senussi, so he spoke good Fezzani Arabic. The six camels were fine beasts in splendid condition, for the Miski was renowned for its grazing, mainly a variety of salt bush called *siwak*. To eat their fill of it, camels need to be watered daily.

Three days later, with Idris, Kathir and the two Tedda, I arrived at the Modra valley and camped in a village on the mountainside. Tieroko, the most magnificent of the Tibesti mountains, loomed above the precipices that confined the valley at our feet, where a small, swift stream, bordered by bullrushes, ran past palms and gardens. The village headman was away but his two sons, small, handsome boys, brought us food: sweet, stoneless dates and *assida* seasoned with curdled milk. That night the moon was full; it lit Tieroko and filled the misty valley with shifting lights and shades, while the music of running water rose to us in the stillness. In the morning we climbed the pass and crossed a desolate, stony table-land where the wind blew in tearing gusts. Then, after skirting Tarso Toon, we descended into the Zoumorie at the small oasis of Edimpi.

In the valleys of Zoumorie and Bardage and at Aouzou, the Tedda grew the bulk of the dates on which they depended for their liveli-hood, but since these were not sufficient they imported more from Borkou, Taisser and al-Gatrun. In their gardens these Tedda grew a little wheat, barley, maize, rye and millet, as well as some tomatoes, melons and peppers, but the gardens were small and fewer than of old. In the past they had been tended by slaves, many of whom had since been freed, and most Tedda would not degrade themselves by working on the soil: to own a garden was a sign of wealth but to work in it was accounted proof of servile origin. The Tedda claimed they were too few to tend both their herds and their gardens, and they preferred the harder but more traditional life of herdsmen. All owned a few goats, and the rich owned several hundred. To possess a camel was a distinction; to own fifty was to be extremely wealthy.

Next day we arrived at Bardai. The square mud-built Turkish fort had been reconstructed by the French and was garrisoned by forty Tirailleurs commanded by a lieutenant and two sergeants. Like all the French I met during this journey, they were hospitable and helpful. The lieutenant was convinced that the desiccation of the whole region was increasing yearly. Apparently the failure of the rains had been especially pronounced since 1914, and valleys on the northern slopes that had once had good pasturage and been popu-lated were now barren and deserted. In the past the Tedda had been nomads, herdsmen and raiders by inclination; it remained to be seen if they would become settled, under force of circumstances.

I noticed that the Tedda varied considerably in colour; many were little darker than Fezzan Arabs, while others were darker but never black. Generally small and lightly built, they were capable of aston-ishing endurance. During our journey to Bardai, being pressed for time, we marched long hours, but the Tedda with us seldom rode, striding along beside their camels on foot. One of them had already walked to Kufrah and back, and the soles of his feet were worn through; yet when we urged him to ride he insisted on walking, to spare his camel.

While I was at Bardai, accompanied by Kathir and Idris I visited

Dirda Shihai Bogar-Mi. He was of the Tuaqarah, the royal section of the Tedda, and had been the nominal ruler of Tibesti since Turkish and Senussi times. Though almost blind and now nearly deaf, he was still clear-headed and his judgements were much respected. He could only walk with difficulty but he rode his camel across the mountains to Aouzou and elsewhere. He was wearing a fine, gold-embroidered black robe lined with crimson, and a white turban, its end wrapped, as was customary, across his nose and mouth. Salah, his second son, was present and served us with tea and dates. Dirda Shihai spoke little but his son was interesting and easy to talk to. The chieftainship was customarily held by three families in turn but I had little doubt that Salah intended to succeed his father.

Kathir seemed worn out, so I left him in Bardai to recuperate while I went next day to Aouzou with Idris and Dadi. We crossed the high pass of Tirenno and the following day entered the Nanamsena gorge: for three miles the water-course wound between sheer cliffs that were from four to seven hundred feet high, though sometimes only twenty-five feet apart, and never more than ninety.

Aouzou, which we reached in the evening of the second day after an unexpected descent off a bare, black plateau, came as a complete surprise, its tranquil loveliness in striking contrast to the wild beauty of Bardai. In the morning we visited a small village called Erbi. The miniature valley, with crystal-clear water gushing from a cleft in the rocks, the green grass, the palms, the small gardens and clusters of houses shaded by tall acacias, symbolized for me the paradise for which desert-dwellers have always yearned. Three boys, bringing us a tray of dates, climbed the small cliff to join us where we sat; their grace and simple courtesy were touching.

The sergeant who commanded the small fort in Aouzou had served in French Somaliland from 1932 to 1935, and remembered hearing of my journeys among the Danakil. Wine, which I never wanted, was seldom in short supply in these forts, and the sergeant was embarrassingly hospitable. The day before I arrived he had been out shooting, and he told me that with a light automatic he had killed four gazelle and wounded five more. Like all the French in Tibesti, he had made no effort to learn even the basic Arabic which some of the Tedda spoke, but relied on an interpreter. The attachment of the French was to their Tirailleurs Sénégelais, who could speak French, rather than to the people they administered, with whom indeed they appeared to have little contact except through the chiefs. I was disconcerted to hear them repeatedly refer to 'les blancs et les noirs', a colour discrimination unheard-of in the Sudan. The loquacious sergeant at Aouzou, the only Frenchman I met in Tibesti whom I disliked, assured me that when a white spoke it was to the blacks as if God spoke. I wondered what Dadi thought of him.

On my way back to Bardai I copied a number of petroglyphs. Some were hammered, others chiselled, as much as half an inch deep in the hard rock. The largest, of a cow, was eleven feet long; human figures were also represented, several with three-feathered head-dresses; also a few camels, two large addax and an elephant. In Tibesti, unlike Ennedi, I found only one set of coloured drawings; they were of tailed figures, one of whom carried a double-bended bow. All of these had been skilfully executed but were much damaged by exposure.

At Bardai we ate a midday meal before setting off again for Doon, which the French called 'Le Trou au Natron', a crater dominated by the twin cones of Tousside and Ehi Ti, respectively 10,600 and 9940 feet high. We reached Tarso Tousside the following afternoon after a steep climb, eventually finding ourselves standing unexpectedly on the edge of the enormous cavity of Doon. It was eighteen miles round and more than 1500 feet deep. Much of its floor was covered with a white carpet of natron in the midst of which were three small black cones of volcanic debris. The crater walls were precipitous; Dadi said it took a day to get down into it and another to climb back.

We camped that night in a gorge, so as to be out of the wind. Idris was cooking our *assida*; suddenly he pointed to the cliff immediately above; looking up I saw a Barbary sheep silhouetted against the sky. I reached for my rifle and fired, and it dropped within a few yards of us. It was an old ram. As I helped Dadi to skin and cut it up he grinned; this unforeseen addition to our meal was a gift from God, he said; but the meat, as I expected, was rank-smelling and very tough.

When we returned to Bardai, we found Kathir had benefited from his rest. On 22 September we regretfully bade the lieutenant and his two sergeants farewell and left for the hot springs of Sobouroun, passing through spectacular mountain scenery on the way. The springs lay in a small valley among jumbled rocks fantastically streaked with varying shades of purple, red, orange, green, yellow and white. The many jets of boiling water were surrounded by basins of bubbling mud; clouds of steam escaped noisily among the rocks and the air stank of sulphur. It was an astonishing but pestilential place which we were glad to leave.

Beyond Sobouroun we travelled through the wildest country I had seen in Tibesti, to the gorge of Forchi. This gorge was twenty-two miles long and its walls, thirty to ninety feet apart, were never less than two hundred and more often five or seven hundred feet high, falling not in tiers but in clean, unclimbable faces of hard rock. A clear stream fringed with rushes, among a tangle of tamarisk and acacia, ran through much of the gorge. Then, passing through groves of dom palms in the wadis Tehegam and Moussou we reached Zouar, headquarters of the Tibesti *circonscription*. There were no palms or villages here, just the fort dominating the wells on a plain surrounded by rocky foothills. It was a desolate place made worse by the news I heard: I had arrived on 27 September 1938, in the middle of the Munich crisis. War with Germany, the captain told me as soon as I arrived, now seemed inevitable. That evening, I drank to the Anglo-French *entente* with him and his lieutenant.

Next day we trekked south as fast as possible towards Faya on my way back to the Sudan. At first our route lay along the edge of the Tibesti foothills, all of which were utterly barren. Then we left Tibesti behind and were once again in Borkou. In this country even the best camels were never trotted, and to spare ours, which were showing signs of exhaustion, we walked on foot for long hours: indeed I found, especially at night, it was the only way to stay awake.

We filled our waterskins at the deep pool of Oudigue, where the water was yellow by now after years of staling by countless camels, and almost as bitter as quinine. We watered again at Tigui and then at Bedo, two small oases in the wastes of sand-covered rock north of Faya. Much of the salt for which Borkou was celebrated came from Bedo, where the water was run off to evaporate in shallow pans; the residual salt was then moulded into broad cones nine inches high. We stopped only briefly at Tigui, a pleasant spot with sheets of blue water surrounded by green grass and palms, but it gave us an agreeable break. From Zouar it took us seven days to reach Faya, averaging thirteen and a half hours a day.

At Faya Colonel D'Ornano was back from patrol, and from him I heard that the crisis in Europe was over again. D'Ornano was renowned in the French Camel Corps and had an extensive knowledge of the Sahara. He had served in Mauretania, among other places, and there he had led a hard, exciting life, frequently engaging formidable raiding parties based on the Rio D'Oro. Now near the end of his service, he had been posted to Faya at his own request; he told me he had always wanted to see Tibesti. Four years later he was killed, I believe in a bombing raid, while advancing from Tibesti with Leclerc's force to link up with the Eighth Army. He must have been among the finest of those remarkable French officers who, over the years, had served as *méharistes* in the Sahara, and I shall always regret I saw so little of him.

I stayed two days in Faya, and while I was there I visited Fezzan merchants in the bazaar; most of them were refugees from Kufra. One of them asked me, 'Why do the British allow the Jews to immigrate into Palestine, and give them the land which belongs to the Muslims? Do you not realize how this tears our hearts?' I certainly had not then realized that the resentment was so widespread, but I could sympathize without reserve.

I was now on my way back to Fada and the Sudan, but the colonel insisted that on my way I should visit the strange lakes at Ounianga Kebir. My leave was running out, but by sending the Zaghawa direct to Fada and taking only Idris, Kathir and a guide, I reckoned I could do it in the time. Ali Bakhit's eye no longer pained him, though he had almost lost the sight in it, and he was anxious to accompany me to Ounianga; but I persuaded him to take the other Zaghawa to Fada and await me there.

I was sorry to part with Dadi. He had been always light-hearted and indefatigable, swinging along beside his camel and singing interminable, lilting camel songs. I had never known him grumble, however long the march, and the hours passed quickly in his company. His hair was even longer now than when he had joined me in the Miski, but he told me he would never cut it until he had settled a blood feud. At present his enemy was a military guide at Zouar, but Dadi assured me that one day he would kill him. The four new camels, hired from the sedentary Doza, turned out to be clumsy, slow-plodding brutes, and soft-footed, so they limped among the rocks. There was water on this route but little grazing among the volcanic rocks and sand. However, by doing as much as fourteen hours on the longest day, we reached the fort at Ounianga in four days, arriving at dawn on 10 October.

The lakes lie in a deep depression and our first view of Yoa, the largest of them, was lovely. The sands were golden in the early light and the dense palm groves along the water's edge cast heavy shadows; the water was a deep Mediterranean blue and the cliffs were of rose-coloured rock. This lake was two miles long and three-quarters of a mile wide; nearby were the smaller lakes of Ouma, Midji and Forodone. The water of Ouma and Midji was deep red, of Forodone vivid green. All four lakes were impregnated with salt, though warm springs of fresh water flowed into Yoa and Ouma; in Midji the salt formed crusts which were thrust up throughout the lake, and collected by the Ounia. The Fezzan have legends of great lakes covering most of the Ounianga, Gouro and Tekro areas, and it was evident that these present ones were but remnants from the past: on the plateau two hundred feet above Yao, and five miles from its present shores, I found some fossilized bones of a hippo.

The Ounia, who lived round the lakes, were a small tribe. In the past they had been entirely settled, owning palms and small gardens; when raided by the Tedda they escaped by swimming out into the lakes. Recently they had acquired camels, and now they neglected their palms and had abandoned their gardens, and were making money by transporting salt. Only the old men still spoke their own language, which was being superseded by Goran.

I stayed for two interesting days with the French officer who commanded the fort here, and then, with camels hired from the Ounia, left for Fada. Thirty miles from Ounianga Kebir we passed the dozen small lakes of Ounianga Saghir, only one of which was salt; the others were half-hidden in thick reedbeds. Colonel D'Ornano had told me that as many as ten thousand camels visited the saltworks at Dimi every year; being anxious to see these, we left the direct route from Ounianga to Fada and continued eastwards towards Erdi, joining up with a large caravan of Mourdia Goran. Their long line of camels was an impressive sight, silently wending its way by moonlight among the soft, steep-sided dunes.

We arrived at the saltpans of Dimi in the red light of dawn. Low black hills, landmarks from afar, dominated this sterile depression where a few shadeless acacias struggled to keep alive round the wells. When we arrived, only scattered groups of men were there, digging up the crusts of salt, but during the next four days on our way to Fada we met caravans of Badayat, Kobe Zaghawa and Mahamid Arabs, all bound for Dimi. With each caravan in turn we exchanged our news. One of our camels now sickened, and even if lightly loaded lay down, so although we marched long hours we made poor progress. The wind blew with great violence throughout the day, and the driven sand made the midday halt a continuous discomfort. In the Wadi Nkaula we passed the grave of Nkaula, reputed ancestor of the Gaida Goran, a rough stone wall around a tattered mat shelter before which offerings were left. Then, crossing the north-west edge of Ennedi, where the wadis seemed very green after the harsh mountains of Tibesti and the deserts to the north, we entered Fada on 19 October.

My leave was almost over, so I regretfully had to abandon my original plan of returning through the Basso, and instead took the direct road to Tini with the Zaghawa, who were waiting for me at Fada with our camels. We left next day and passed a string of deep freshwater pools in a narrow, sheer-sided gorge called Archey; here I saw five crocodiles, the largest five feet long, the others between two and three. Near the pool was a deep cave with many drawings of men and animals, but I had no time to copy them.

We were now back in the territory of the Warrah, a section of the Kobe Zaghawa. Hamid, Idris's grandfather, had been their *malik* until the French, during the reign of Ali Dinar, had destroyed the Kobe forces at Tini and killed their aged Sultan. Hamid, with a shattered thigh, had been carried from the field by Daud, Idris's father. Idris's uncle was sheikh of the village where we camped on 24 October, and here we saw at sunset the new moon that marked the beginning of Ramadan. That night we feasted well; then, sitting among our camels, I listened to stories of bygone fights, of successful raids and also of crippling losses, until far into the night.

Like many young Zaghawa, Idris fretted at security and craved at heart for those wild, lawless days, when the *nahas* beat for war and young men could prove their manhood and win the approval of the girls. He had once said to me, 'The only excitement I have had in my life has been riding down lions with you.' Listening to him, old men shook their heads, saying that the young these days were suffering from *sakar al laban*, were drunk on too much milk.

293

Idris had found satisfaction, I think, in the very hardship of this journey, which had given him the chance to match his endurance against the redoubtable Tedda; predictably, he got on well with them and was much liked. Never once on this journey did I see him sulky or ill-tempered. However arduous the march, he remained cheerful and tireless, meeting every demand made upon him with a smile. I remember one occasion in particular, when, after travelling throughout the night and late into the morning, I had unsaddled my camel and dropped on the sand, caring only to sleep for the few hours before we would have to move on. Three hours later Idris woke me. The others were still asleep, but he had collected wood and cooked a meal for us to eat before we left. He was invariably interested in what he saw or heard, and he made a point of sharing his interest with me; this added greatly to my enjoyment and to a sense of comradeship with him.

At Tini, where we arrived on the morning of 26 October, I found that Guy Moore had been there but left two days earlier, leaving a letter for me, in which he explained that he had come up in the car on chance, not knowing when I would arrive. Stubbs had seemingly not given him my letter of 30 July in which I had said I would reach Tini on 26 October – the very day I did indeed arrive.

Our camels were worn out, our flour, sugar and tea were finished, and only four days of my leave remained till I was due in Fasher. But Idris produced fresh camels and, after parting with regret from Kathir and the five Zaghawa, he and I rode south through my old district. When we reached Fasher on 1 November we had been seventy hours in the saddle out of the ninety-six.

When I arrived Ingleson sat me down to write a report on my journey. I recently came across a copy of it among my papers, with the following letter to him attached:

Governor,   Civil Secretary's Office
Upper Nile Province   Khartoum
                                  27 December 1938

I am to request you to inform Mr W. P. Thesiger, whose report on his trek in French Equatorial Africa has recently been prepared here, that His Excellency has studied the report and wishes to compliment Mr Thesiger on this very interesting and profitable account of his journey.

Copies are being forwarded to the Embassy and to the military authorities as well as to other persons interested.

T. R. H. Owen
for Civil Secretary

My report had dealt with the distances between wells, the different types of terrain, the productivity of the various oases, the distribution of the tribes, their relations with each other and with the French, the French methods of administration, and the location and composition of their forces, with diagrams of all the forts I visited. Since we were faced with the probability of a conflict with Italy, these details about a potential theatre of war on the Libyan frontier, an area of which the British knew nothing, was officially opportune.

For me, this journey in the heat of summer served as an apprenticeship to the five years I would later spend in Arabia. It so conditioned me that even under the worst conditions there, with thirst and hunger my daily lot, I would never wish I were elsewhere. On this Tibesti journey, I had in fact suffered neither thirst nor hunger, but I was never again to ride for such long hours, day after day, for weeks on end. In Arabia we would spare our camels as much as possible, for our lives depended on their survival, whereas in Tibesti, where I was always pressed for time, when they were exhausted we could change them for others.

Looking back on my attitude to the commonly accepted pleasures of life, I can say that I have never set much store by them. I hardly care what I eat, provided it suffices, and I care not at all for wine or spirits. When I was fourteen someone gave me a glass of beer, and I thought it so unpleasant I have never touched beer again. As for cigarettes, I dislike even being in a room where people are smoking. Sex has been of no great consequence to me, and the celibacy of desert life left me untroubled. Marriage would certainly have been a crippling handicap. I have therefore been able to lead the life of my choice with no sense of deprivation. Existence in the desert had a simplicity that I found wholly satisfying; there, everything not a necessity was an encumbrance. It was those three months in the Sahara in 1938 that taught me to appreciate things that most Europeans are able to take for granted: clean water to drink; meat to eat; a warm fire on a cold night; shelter from rain; above all, tired surrender to sleep.

The Danakil country in 1934 had afforded me the challenge of the unknown, the excitement of travelling among dangerous tribes, but throughout that journey I had remained apart from my followers. Tibesti, on the other hand, had been explored and was effectively administered, but during those three months there I had lived on equal terms with my companions, and the hardship of our journeying had drawn us close together. That closeness had been my reward. Now, however, I was going back among the Nuer, and I knew that with them I would never attain a like relationship, would always feel apart.

Ingleson had told me to go and report in Khartoum before returning to Malakal. Idris came with me: I had promised to help him go from there on his forthcoming pilgrimage to Mecca. On his return I wanted him to leave my employment and go back to his family. I felt desolate at the thought of parting from him, since he had been my inseparable companion for three years; we had shared many experiences, and our recent journey had confirmed the confidence I had always felt when we faced lion or elephant together. But I knew that if he stayed permanently with me, separated from his kinsmen, he would inevitably acquire by associating with servants the status of a servant, and I was determined this should not happen. Idris was a tribesman with a tribesman's values: I was only anxious that he should keep them.

CHAPTER 21

Return to the Swamps

I N KHARTOUM I had another interview with Sir Angus Gillan and explained to him my feelings about serving in the south. I told him I had hoped that working among the Nuer would bring me contentment, but now, especially after the months in Tibesti, I knew this would never be so. I therefore felt that for my own sake and the Government's it would be better to resign rather than stay on without my heart in it.

I had previously offered to serve in Kutum without pay but with my expenses paid, in order to patrol the frontier with the Zaghawa but this was turned down as taking advantage of me. Now I asked what my chances were of getting back to the north. Gillan said: 'I have read your report on Tibesti with great interest and I don't want you to leave the service. The trouble is that only three districts in the whole Sudan would suit you: Kutum, the Kababish and the Hadendoa in the Red Sea Hills. At present all three are filled. If war comes there will be just the job for you; in peacetime it's more difficult to fit you in. Go back to the Western Nuer and I will see what I can do.'

Looking back on this interview, I am astonished that he did not immediately accept my resignation. I had failed my Arabic and Law exams; at the previous meeting, to avoid posting to Wad Medani I had resigned from the permanent service, and had asked him to re-employ me on contract in a wild and remote district. He had sent me to the Western Nuer, which he must have thought would satisfy even me. Now I was pestering him again and asking for another transfer. He was head of the Sudan Political Service and an extremely busy man; I was a tiresome young man with only three years' service. Yet he had listened with patience and sympathy. I am sure this could only have happened in the Sudan Political Service which, unlike the Colonial Service or the Indian Civil Service, was a small, intimate body, numbering a hundred and thirty in all.

On 23 November 1938 I got back to Malakal. Wedderburn was still

297

on leave. I had brought with me a Fur, called Salih; he had been my *syce*'s assistant in Kutum and I had met him again in Fasher, looking for a job. I felt I could make do with him and my Zande cook.

Before I returned to the Western Nuer District on the *Kereri*, I had a long talk with the Governor, Coryton, confessing that I had asked the Civil Secretary for a transfer. I liked Coryton too much not to feel upset at disappointing him. I knew he had been confident that I should enjoy serving under Wedderburn in this remote district, and that he had expected me to learn the Nuer language and remain contentedly among them for years. I told him how much I had enjoyed the last year, which had been a unique experience; but unless he realized it was on a temporary basis I should not feel justified in remaining, knowing I would be keeping out someone else whom Wedderburn could have been training. If Coryton would rather I resigned at once, I should therefore understand. He thanked me for my frankness, urged me not to resign in a hurry and said he would write to Gillan on my behalf.

When I left Malakal, Coryton sent a young, newly appointed veterinary officer with me to see something of the province, but all he saw during the month he was on the *Kereri* was endless swamp and flooded land. This year the rains had been exceptionally heavy and the rivers continued to rise for two months after they should have been subsiding. I wrote to my mother:

> The boat is tied up in the middle of a vast swamp. The only dry land is on some islands in the distance where there are some Nuer villages: between them and the boat there is nothing but high grass with water up to one's arm-pits, a typical scene. They have been fighting a good bit here; after all, why shouldn't they, and they were having a fight this morning when they heard our siren and stopped. However, I shall have to stop it now I have arrived. It's the end of the holidays as far as they are concerned. I must now try and get hold of the chiefs, no easy matter when you can only get about in a dug-out, and I must also get the wounded down to the boat.

I went back into Malakal at the end of December; Wedderburn had just returned from leave. I was glad to get rid of the vet. I had found him uncongenial, and his presence on board had made me more conscious than ever how lucky I was to be sharing the boat with Wedderburn.

Now, day after day, we were confined to the *Kereri*. There was little to do but read, sleep and eat: nothing to look at wherever we went except swamp and floods. With this high water, it was not even worth while trying to fish, and the only interest was the sight of an occasional shoe-billed stork. I found it most depressing.

We picked up my porters at various landing-stages to which they had waded across-country when they saw the boat, and they settled down contentedly once more on the barge. The exceptionally high floods had swamped the millet and maize crops around many of the villages, and swarms of hairy-chested locusts had eaten most of what remained. In addition to these disasters, there had been outbreaks of rinderpest, and the high water still prevented the Nuer from spearing fish. They were going to be very short of food this year, and there was little we could do to help, though I should certainly shoot what I could to feed them.

One day we found a dead hippo floating down the river. It had been speared, and though already very inflated, had only been dead a day or two. In the surrounding swamp there was nowhere we could land to cut it up, so the hungry Nuer implored us to get it on board. Eventually, with ropes and tackle and their enthusiastic help, we succeeded. They carved it up on deck in a welter of blood and guts, and roasted great chunks on the barge; it afforded them meat for several days.

As soon as conditions allowed, Wedderburn and I went our various ways. With the country still largely under water, I sometimes had to cross as many as forty or fifty *khors* during a day's march. Most of them I could wade but some I had to swim. The porters carried segments of *ambach* which grew locally, and with these they fashioned small rafts to ferry the loads across the deeper *khors*. Later in the season I should be adjusting my marches so as to camp near water; the problem now was to find dry land. Though the grass was tall and hunting difficult, on most days I managed to get meat for my Nuer; occasionally I shot a hippo for them as a treat.

One morning at a village where we had camped, I watched a seventeen-year-old Nuer boy's ceremony of initiation into manhood. It took place soon after dawn, when it was cold and singularly cheerless. A large crowd, including women and children, gathered round to watch. The boy, not even wearing a string of beads, was lying on his back, his arms folded across his chest, and his head on a grass pad above a small hole dug to catch the blood.

An elderly man squatted beside him, and, using a small knife

shaped like a miniature spear, cut him from the centre of his forehead round to behind his ear, six parallel cuts, first on one side of his
head, then on the other. As he cut I could hear the knife grating on
the bone. He then drew the knife through each cut in turn to make
sure they were deep enough. The wounds bled profusely. The boy
never twitched or made a sound, though towards the end he
screwed up his mouth a little: to have shown any sign of pain would
have been an indelible disgrace. Later his family would rub cow
dung and ashes into the cuts to cause inflammation which would
ensure that the scars, which distinguished him as a warrior, were
prominently ridged. Far from seeking to postpone this agonizing
ordeal, all boys who considered themselves old enough to be initi-
ated pestered their fathers for permission to undergo the ceremony.
I later noticed, on a male Nuer skull I came across, how every cut
was scored into the bone.

One morning the *Kereri* was tied up to a landing stage on the Bahr al
Jabal, and I was preparing to go ashore and hunt, when a paddle-
steamer came alongside. It was taking the Anglican Assistant
Bishop in the Sudan from Khartoum to Juba on a tour of the diocese.
Wedderburn was away on trek so I invited the Bishop, whom I had
not met before, to come aboard, and we sat in the saloon drinking
coffee. He expressed admiration for the dedication of young men,
like myself, who lived such lonely lives in remote plates, and he
offered me Communion to strengthen me, as he said, against the
temptations to which I was exposed.

This embarrassed me. While still at Eton I had refrained from
repeating the Creed, being unwilling to affirm something which I
was unable to believe. Since then, under the stars in the desert, I had
found it impossible to reconcile belief in a personal God, to whom I
could appeal, with whatever abstract force governed the universe
and regulated all things from the movement of stars in the outer-
most galaxy to the pollination of plants on this planet. However, I
had grown up in the Christian tradition and, though I did not
believe in Christ's divinity, I accepted Christian ethics and to that
extent regarded myself as Christian. It was years since I had taken
Communion, which had never had any significance for me. Now I
accepted the Bishop's offer rather than disappoint this devout and
well-meaning man. He gave it in an abandoned Nuer hut, the only

building there on the river bank. He then went on to Juba, and I hunted, and shot a lion.

In February 1939 I visited Tolodi in the Nuba mountains in southern Kordofan, in order to liaise for a few days with Reggie Dingwall who was stationed there. Each group of these hills rose abruptly from the surrounding plain; among their massive boulders and many caves, the warlike Nuba, armed with Remington rifles they had captured during the Mahdiya, had successfully resisted the surrounding Arab tribes and had involved the British in a number of military patrols. Most of the Nuba remained naked and pagan, but each separate group retained its individuality.

On my way to Tolodi I stopped in the al-Liri jabals; the Nuba here were Muslim and wore Arab dress. When I arrived they were celebrating Id al-Adha with feasting and dancing. In the evening their chief took me to watch the dancing, vigorous and unrestrained, to the incessant throb of drums. There was also a constant firing of rifles; men were letting them off just above the heads of the girls with whom they were dancing. The young men's hair was twisted back in plaits which curled up behind, decorated with silver plaques. This striking hair-do, topped by a nodding ostrich feather, set off their youthful good looks.

I stayed two days with Dingwall, and went with him to a remote Nuba village in attractive country. It was pleasantly green after recent rain, with the trees and bushes in flower on the boulder-strewn hillsides. We camped beside the village, with the plain spread out below us; a crowd of villagers soon assembled to confer with Dingwall. They struck me as a cheerful and good-looking people, more massively built than the Nuer, as became a race whose sport was wrestling: when they moved their naked bodies rippled with muscle. As I wandered about their village, I sensed that the Nuba were people who required nothing from the outside world, except perhaps sugar and tea, and in the seclusion of their jabal were content to live as their fathers had lived. I was sad that in pursuance of a policy of economic and agricultural development they were now being made to grow cotton as a cash crop. I had been assured in Tolodi that it was to their ultimate advantage. Perhaps this was so, but I found the sight of cotton-ginning factories and queues of lorries loaded with cotton bales depressing. The Governor of Kordofan, Douglas Newbold, must have approved the policy. I remembered him, at the meeting with the Kababish two years before, insisting that the Sudan Government could not retain human 'game reserves' for ever.

When I returned to Malakal I heard that after my next leave I was to be posted back to Kutum. Years later I came across a letter that Douglas Newbold, who by then had taken over from Gillan as Civil Secretary, had written to Guy Moore. It was included in *The Making of the Modern Sudan*, a selection of Newbold's letters published in 1953, and contained the following passage:

> You will have heard we are sending Wilfred Thesiger back to you. He has sent his articles on Tibesti to *The Times* but I doubt if they'll publish them as they are a bit long, and not 'news'. I liked them and envied him his physical endurance. Khartoum is slowly atrophying me physically. Your picture of W.T. is very accurate. He now realizes he is a misfit, but a misfit only in a Government and owing to excess of certain ancient virtues and not because of any vices – a brave, awkward, attractive creature.

I was delighted to be going back to Kutum and immensely grateful to Gillan and Newbold. I felt in a sense reprieved; I should have hated to resign from a service that included such men. Now, assured of my future, I could look forward to the next four months with the Nuer, in what was here the most agreeable season of the year.

The floods were subsiding at last, the country was drying up, and soon the grass would be burnt off. Then visibility would no longer be restricted to a few yards on either side of the track; instead I should be able to see for miles across the plain. The Nuer, happy to escape from the confinement of their villages, would be gathered in their cattle camps. There would be plenty for me to do: disputes to settle, news to hear, and sick to treat. I should go hunting with them, and watch them dancing or singing to their favourite oxen. Just to be with them would be fun, and my very presence in the area would restrain the more turbulent from fighting each other.

I watched one dance at which five or six hundred people had assembled for the marriage of a 'leopard-skin chief', an oldish man above average height, who wore across his shoulders this exclusive token of his rank. I had seen many Nuer dances, usually small affairs in their villages and camps, but nothing like this. Many of the warriors wore feathers in their hair, while some had painted their bodies for this occasion with red and white pigments, bringing into prominence the lithe grace of their movements as they stamped and pirouetted. As I watched, I found myself enthralled by the massed singing and the mounting tempo of the dance. Suddenly two youths sprang forward, brandishing their spears, and challenged each other to mock combat. Others joined them and soon a score or more were leaping and parrying, stabbing at each other with potentially lethal thrusts, while the rest continued to dance around them unperturbed. I watched intently: it seemed incredible that no one was killed or even wounded. I was well aware that blood feuds sometimes originated from such mock combats, yet I could not possibly interfere.

In February Wedderburn sent me to the Kordofan border to find out whether the Humr, a tribe of Baggara Arabs from Kordofan, whose sheikh had agreed to stop them hunting giraffe in our district, were still doing so: having exterminated giraffe in their own country, they had been hunting further and further south into ours. When I got there the Humr had not yet moved south from their wet season grazing grounds. However, two months later when I went back, I found, as I expected, a large hunting party camped many miles across the border. I had already come across several carcasses of recently killed giraffe as much as a day's march south of this camp.

Accompanied by my Nuer, I surprised the camp at dawn, just as several Arabs were preparing to mount and go hunting. I found large quantities of dried meat and many ropes made from giraffe hide, all of which I confiscated. The Humr had obviously been here for some time, for they had already sent off a large consignment of dried meat, loaded on pack-oxen, the normal Baggara method of transport. I ordered them back to Kordofan and warned them that in future I would arrest any I found in our district.

These Humr were akin to the Bani Husain, with whom I had so often ridden down lion, and I would have enjoyed joining them on one of their hunts. The trouble was, they were all too successful: unless prevented, they would wipe out any giraffe within their reach. Two or three of them would ride a giraffe to a standstill, usually after a long gallop across broken wooded country; they would then dismount and spear it to death with their shovel-headed *shelegais* – a risky procedure, for a giraffe could kill or disable a man with a kick. They told me they sometimes killed elephant like this, too. As a boy I had read Samuel Baker's description of mounted Humran Arabs in the Eastern Sudan riding down elephant.

During my years in the Sudan the Government evinced little interest in conserving its wildlife: unlike Kenya and Tanganyika, the Sudan was seldom visited by European or American big game hunters. In East Africa hunting brought in a lot of money and was governed by elaborate regulations: professional white hunters booked hunting blocs for their clients in advance, then organized and conducted their safaris and safeguarded the hunters while they hunted. This I should have hated. In the Sudan you bought a licence and could hunt whenever you chose.

In April Wedderburn and I heard that some Nuba, with rifles, were in our district, just north of the Bahr al Arab, hunting illegally. They had apparently been camped there for some time and were killing a lot of animals. We decided to arrest them, and went there to do so. As we and our porters spread out to surround the encampment, a woman gave the alarm, and we saw several Nuba bolting into the bush. Wedderburn and I chased them on horseback and, with the help of the Nuer, eventually rounded them all up. One young man gave Wedderburn a long run before he was overtaken and brought back, grinning broadly, to join the others.

All seventeen were from the al-Liri; they had some women with them. In the camp was a quantity of dried meat which we gave to our Nuer, and seven antique Remington rifles, which Wedderburn confiscated. He sent the women back to their *jabal*, escorted by one of the men we had captured, and enrolled the rest among our porters – a token punishment, for they had little to carry and fed well. They were a cheerful crowd, more skilful hunters than the Nuer; they spoke Arabic and I enjoyed having them with me. Six weeks later, when we were in Malakal, they volunteered to remain with us, but Wedderburn gave them back their rifles and sent them home.

In early July 1939 I went on leave to England and, as I thought, on transfer from the Upper Nile Province. I was sad to part from Wedderburn, with whom I had always got on well, and was very sorry to say goodbye to Malo and my band of porters, but I sent

ABOVE A gathering of the Maidob in Northern Darfur.

BELOW Idris (with rifle) and other Zaghawa with a lioness notorious for killing cattle.

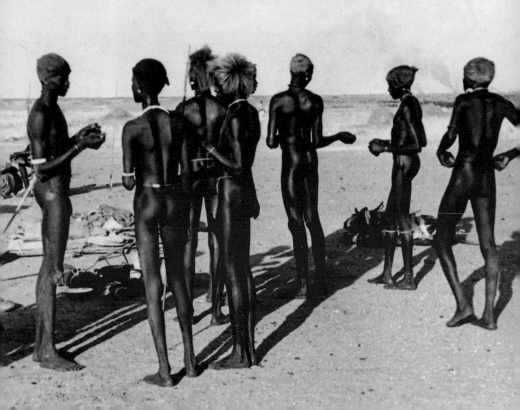

ABOVE LEFT Travelling with my porters during the floods in the Western Nuer District.

LEFT My porters.

TOP RIGHT The *Kereri*, the paddle steamer which was the Headquarters of the Western Nuer District.

CENTRE My trophies, 1938; Idris, left, Malo, my interpreter, right.

RIGHT Wedderburn-Maxwell with two Nile perch he had caught.

LEFT Nuba wrestling in the eastern jabals of Kordofan.

BELOW The Nanamsena Gorge, near Aouzou, in Tibesti.

OPPOSITE ABOVE The Mashakazy Gorge, on Emi Koussi, in Tibesti.

OPPOSITE BELOW My party on the Tibesti journey.

The Gojjam campaign, 1941–2:
LEFT Brigadier Dan Sandford, head of the 101 Mission.
RIGHT Colonel Orde Wingate, inspecting the 2nd Ethiopian Battalion.
BELOW Dedjazmatch Mangasha with his Patriot followers.

OPPOSITE ABOVE The Blue Nile Gorge at Shafartak.
OPPOSITE BELOW Prisoners who surrendered to me at Agibar.

ABOVE LEFT Faris Shahin, my Druze orderly, and his grandfather, at Malha.

ABOVE RIGHT A Druze cavalryman.

LEFT Druze elders among Roman ruins.

Opposite above David Stirling and an SAS patrol.

OPPOSITE BELOW Myself with Colonel Gigantes, Commander of the Greek Sacred Squadron of the SAS in the Western Desert.

The mountains of Northern Abyssinia.

RIGHT My caravan during a journey through Northern Abyssinia in 1960.

RIGHT A silver church drum at Lalibela.

BELOW A Fitaurari with his wife and family who entertained me during my journey into northern Abyssinia.

OPPOSITE The Tisisat Falls on the Blue Nile soon after its emergence from Lake Tana.

LEFT The monolithic church of Medhane Alam at Lalibela.

BELOW The cruciform rock-hewn church of Giorgis at Lalibela.

OPPOSITE ABOVE The palace built by Fasiladas in Gondar during the seventeenth century.

OPPOSITE BELOW The church of Imrahanna Krestos built in a cave during the twelfth century.

A signed photograph of Haile Selassie, taken during his exile in England, 1936–40, and presented to me.

them off contented with two cows and a bull apiece. My two years
with the Western Nuer were an unforgettable chapter in my life.
They gave me some idea of the Africa of the early explorers and
hunters, the Africa I had read about so avidly as a boy.

I had planned to spend the last half of my leave travelling with my
mother in Iraq and Persia, but each day war with Germany seemed
more imminent. I was therefore at The Milebrook when I received a
telegram ordering me back to the Sudan, and instructing me to
report immediately on board the liner *Montcalm* in the Clyde. On 3
September, two hours after listening to Chamberlain's uninspiring
declaration of war on Germany, we sailed in convoy escorted by a
battleship and several destroyers; after an uneventful journey
which took us far out into the Atlantic, we berthed at Alexandria.
Had we been torpedoed, promotion in the Sudan Political Service
might have been spectacular, for nearly half the officials, including
several Provincial Governors, were on board.

Because of the war, all transfers from Provinces had been suspended, so instead of going to Kutum, I was after all sent back to
Malakal. There C. L. Armstrong had taken over from Coryton as
Governor, not a happy appointment for such a province. He had
served with distinction in the First World War, won a DSO and an
MC, and ended as a brigadier. In the Sudan he was universally
known as 'Stuffy' Armstrong, a singularly appropriate nickname.
Inclined always to interfere, he had an insatiable desire for irrelev-
ant detail; he had already asked Wedderburn for a day-by-day
programme of his movements over the next six months.

Wedderburn was with his Western Nuer when I arrived in
Malakal on 2 October 1939, but Romilly was there and took me to his
headquarters at Nasir. Years before, this border area had frequently
been raided by well-armed gangs from Abyssinia, and the memory
of this was still fresh in the minds of the Nuer. Romilly and I spent
four days travelling by dug-out canoe along the frontier, wooded
country with tall trees, an agreeable change from the waterlogged
grass plains between Malakal and Nasir.

On 19 October I went back and joined Wedderburn in Malakal.
Armstrong had told him to take stores in the *Kereri* to Gambeila, a
Sudanese trading post on the Baro river inside Italian-occupied
Abyssinia: the concession for this post had been granted by the
Emperor Menelik to the Sudan Government. Both of us looked
forward to this seventy-mile trip up the Baro, but we did wonder

what would happen to us if Italy entered the war while we were in Abyssinia.

The Baro river, with a succession of stockaded Anuak villages along its banks and much cultivation, was well worth seeing. Groups of Anuak, most of them naked, watched the steamer go past. They gave me the impression of a formidable tribe, well able to look after themselves, as indeed they had proved in the past. Almost as soon as we entered the river from the Sobat, we could see in the distance the highlands of Abyssinia. They held my gaze; it was there that I hoped eventually to fight the Italians.

On my return to Malakal I was given a letter from the Civil Secretary's Office offering me a six-week course in Khartoum leading to a commission in the Sudan Defence Force as one of thirty new combatant officers. I accepted as it sounded promising: when Britain had gone to war with Germany, I assumed that Italy would shortly be involved and that back in the Sudan I should be despatched to Abyssinia; but the weeks had passed and to my frustration Italy remained neutral.

I went to Khartoum for the course. It was with the Cheshire Regiment, and twelve of us were on it, one from the Gezira Cotton Scheme, the others contemporaries of mine in the Sudan Service, among them two very agreeable companions, Paul Daniel and J. E. Kennett. It was a well-run and essentially practical course, and I enjoyed and profited from it. Now that I was destined for the Sudan Defence Force I was to go back as an administrative supernumerary at provincial headquarters in Malakal until I was commissioned in the Army. Newbold approved my returning there by way of the Nuba mountains, to enable me to see more of these remarkable people, and I spent four days touring the western *jabals*. I was surprised at the great difference in the appearance, dialects and customs of the Nuba. Some were short and stocky, others tall and well-proportioned; sometimes both men and women were naked; elsewhere the men might be naked and the women covered, or vice versa. Neighbouring communities of Nuba often spoke mutually incomprehensible languages and built dissimilar types of house. In most villages there were a number of pigs, foul-looking black animals, but useful as scavengers in the generally filthy environment.

One day I went to watch Nuba wrestling at the funeral games of a man who had died some months earlier. At midday I reached the village, situated in a natural amphitheatre among boulder-strewn hills. The villagers had slaughtered a dozen bulls and there was meat lying about everywhere, as well as pots of beer; people were sleeping under the trees. Eventually some young men began to hurl long heavy sticks at each other, while protecting themselves with round shields of elephant hide. I watched them for a time, then went into a hut where wrestlers were being got ready. There were only three: they were powdered with ashes until they were white all over, their eyes and lips the only dark things in the grotesque masks of their faces, and they were naked except for streamers of coloured cloth or bunches of feathers fastened round their waists above three rows of small brass bells, horrid things to be wearing in a fall.

Occasionally a drum was beaten outside, or someone blew a trumpet that growled like an angry lion. Under the trees people were still asleep and I could see no sign of activity: it looked as if the games were going to be a fiasco. An hour or so later, hearing a noise in the distance, I went outside to watch a couple of hundred men and women arrive, the women carrying on their heads more pots of beer. In the midst of this noisy throng six more wrestlers strutted and pranced. They were followed by other parties of wrestlers, each of which, as it arrived, circled the amphitheatre, stamping up clouds of dust, until a hundred and fifty wrestlers and a thousand or more others were assembled. For half an hour after the last party had arrived, while horns brayed and drums beat, the crowd continued to stamp and dance.

At last the wrestling began. The contenders were massively built, and conspicuously coated with ash; each individual group was distinctively adorned. They challenged their opponents by swaggering up to them, bending at the knees and thrusting a shoulder forward. Each pair then feinted and sparred while they tried to get a grip. A fall was usually achieved by heaving up an opponent's leg and throwing him off balance. The contests were watched by umpires who if there was a foul at once separated the wrestlers. A score or more contests went on at the same time, each surrounded by the wrestlers' partisans, who shouted encouragement and surged forward the moment there was a fall. Half an hour before sunset the wrestling ended. Then a bull was driven up, and the Nuba swarmed over it and hacked it to pieces; almost in minutes every vestige of meat, entrails, bones and skin had vanished from the blood-soaked earth. It seemed a brutal but fitting conclusion to an impressively African spectacle.

Six weeks later I was ordered to Khartoum, this time for an attachment with the Essex Regiment, which had replaced the Cheshires. This lasted till the end of April 1940, after which I was given a Governor-General's commission as a Bimbashi in the Sudan Defence Force. Bimbashi had been the lowest rank held by British officers who, as captains, were seconded before the Second World War to the Sudan Defence Force. This rank, among others of Turkish derivation, had been current in the Egyptian Army during Kitchener's reconquest of the Sudan; when the Sudan Defence Force was formed in 1924 from the Sudanese battalions of the Egyptian Army, all such ranks were retained. Though I wore an Egyptian crown and star, the insignia of a Bimbashi, my Governor-General's commission did not rate me in British Army terms as even a second lieutenant.

PART V

War Years

1940–4

CHAPTER 22

The Sudan Defence Force

A T THE BEGINNING of May 1940 I was posted to the Eastern Arab
Corps of the SDF, whose headquarters was at Gedaref, and
from there I was sent as second-in-command to Arthur
Hanks's company on the frontier at Galabat, where Emperor John of
Abyssinia had been killed fifty years earlier in the hard-fought battle
with the Dervishes. Our small Sudanese fort overlooked the adjacent Italian position at Metemma, across the dry water-course that
marked the frontier. Metemma covered a large area, surrounded by
thick belts of wire, and garrisoned by a battalion of Eritrean native
troops.

I had sent word to Idris and he now joined me at Galabat. He had
made his pilgrimage. It had been a tremendous experience, to sense
the inspiration of thousands upon thousands, Africans, Arabs, Per-
sians, Indians, Malays, Mongols, even Chinese, all dressed alike as
pilgrims, all assembled at Mecca, in ecstasy at this supreme moment
of their religious lives. Idris described it all and said, 'God reward
you for sending me.' He was a Hajj, but on account of his youthful-
ness he deferred assumption of that title. He now accompanied me
everywhere and I was glad to have him; with his easy unassuming
nature he was readily accepted by the troops. He was also a good
shot and Hanks issued him with a service rifle and bandolier.

A few days after I had arrived at Galabat, Hanks sent me with a
platoon to camp at a ford on the Atbara and patrol the frontier; for
transport I had four requisitioned merchants' lorries, all unreliable.
We dug in on the hills above the ford. I had no radio communication
and my orders, in the event of an Italian advance, were to delay it
long enough to get word back by lorry to Gedaref. I enjoyed being
on my own with the platoon. They were impressively smart and
enthusiastic, and I soon got to know them individually.

On getting back from patrol we often found Shukria and Lahawin
Arabs watering herds of camels near our camp, and I would go over
and sit with them on the riverbank, and listen to their news. Sometimes Rashaidah turned up too: these interested me, since their tribe

311

had only recently migrated into the Sudan from Arabia, and they still wore the traditional headrope, and Arabian-type dagger and sword. On patrol we encountered many Bani Amir, and some Hadendoa from further north in the Red Sea Hills.

There were many Bani Amir in Hanks's company but these Bani Amir and Hadendoa were the first Beja I had met in their tribal setting. I tried to talk to them, but disclaiming all knowledge of Arabic they remained aloof and unresponsive. With their handsome faces under great mops of hair, and their sparse, hard bodies gracefully wrapped in a single length of cloth, they were as challenging in appearance as the Danakil.

On 20 May Hussey de Burgh, commanding the Eastern Arab Corps, visited my outpost from Gedaref. Since arriving here I had been completely out of touch with what was happening in the war. Now I learnt with dismay that the Germans had overrun Holland and Belgium and penetrated deep into France, where the French armies were beginning to disintegrate. Mussolini was expected to enter the war at any moment, and Hussey de Burgh sent me back immediately to Galabat.

There Hanks was garrisoning the fort with a platoon, he himself and the rest of his company being dug in among the commiphora woods on some low hills a mile back from the fort. Ran Laurie, whom I now met for the first time, had been attached to the company as a Bimbashi; his task was to negotiate with the Abyssinian Patriot partisans who were arriving in our camp in increasing numbers. The Italian commander sent a protest to Hanks, that we were arming the Patriots. In response, Hanks sent me, as his second-in-command, to meet the Italian commander's representative, which I did in the bush near the frontier. He was a captain and seemed to be a gentleman. I assured him that we had not yet issued a single rifle to the Abyssinians but that we were ready, if Mussolini declared war on us, to pour weapons into their country; in that case, I said, the Patriots would exact a bitter vengeance.

Ran Laurie was my age; while on leave recently he had won the Diamond Sculls at Henley, but besides being a superb oarsman he was an outstanding personality, and I found his presence reassuring at this time of increasing anxiety. Daily the news from France grew worse: yet, inspired by Churchill's broadcasts, we never doubted we would ultimately win. It was with impatience that we awaited Italy's entry into the war. When at last on 10 June the BBC announced it as news, we greeted this broadcast by firing our machine-gun into the Italian positions. Some hours later we received and decoded a circular from HQ Khartoum to all units in the Sudan, informing us of Italy's declaration of war but ordering us under no (repeat no) circumstances, to take any offensive action without permission from Headquarters.

We never got a reprimand for our precipitate action, and it has always given me satisfaction that I fired the first shots in the Abyssinian campaign.

The Italians had at least a hundred thousand troops in Abyssinia with which to invade the Sudan. Confronting them were three British battalions, totalling fewer than 2500 men, and the Sudan Defence Force of 4500, with which to guard over twelve hundred miles of frontier.

On the other hand, ever since the Italians had occupied Abyssinia, much of that country had been in revolt, even as close to Addis Ababa as Manz, where the redoubtable Ababa Aragai was more than holding his own. In Gojjam, Walkait and Begemder and among the Gallas of Walega, the Italians found themselves confined to their forts except when travelling in convoy along the roads. This widespread hostility by the Abyssinian Patriots had thoroughly demoralized the Italians, and now, by tying up their forces, it saved the Sudan from invasion at a time when the Sudan was virtually defenceless; just as it later greatly facilitated the conquest of all Italian East Africa.

According to *The Abyssinian Campaign*, the official history of this war, 'Italian nervousness about an Abyssinian rising involved a severe drain upon their resources and a severe handicap upon their dispositions. At the crux of the campaign, when the Italians needed every man in the firing lines at Keren and Harar (and when they did indeed transfer the equivalent of seventy-five battalions to three fronts) the existence or the danger of an Abyssinian rising tied down the equivalent of fifty-six battalions in the Amhara and Walkait areas.'

Haile Selassie arrived in Khartoum on 27 June 1940. His arrival had not been welcomed by certain officials, who regarded his presence as an embarrassment. To conceal his identity, he was given the ridiculous and humiliating pseudonym of 'Mr Smith'. The fact is that the Italian conquest of Abyssinia had gratified not a few both in the Sudan and in Kenya, who hoped it would lead to a civilized administration in that country and mark the end of raids across the frontier. Now we were at war with Italy, they hoped that Britain would eventually take over and administer Abyssinia.

Across the border, however, news of the Emperor's arrival in the Sudan was greeted with rapture by the Patriots and with dismay by the Italians. Day after day the Patriots arrived at Galabat, sometimes in small parties, sometimes in hundreds as followers of some chief who had won renown as a fighter. All were starving, for the mountains they came from were far away beyond the empty intervening plains; some were so famished that after they had eaten the food we gave them they vomited.

Ran Laurie handed over rifles and ammunition. These rifles were single-shot Martini-Henrys, dating from before the reconquest of the Sudan, the only rifles locally available at that time. The Patriots naturally grumbled that they had come far, expecting to be given modern magazine rifles, not weapons such as these: but eventually they took them and went back. They were highly strung and excitable people, of a lightly built Highland race, fine-boned, with thin lips, high-bridged noses and small, shapely hands, very different from our cheerful, reliable and disciplined Sudanese troops. Most of them had great mops of hair, having vowed never to cut it until they had driven the Italians from their land. Hanks remarked, 'They're a cruel-looking lot. I wouldn't want to be an Italian who had fallen into their hands.' Laurie, I was glad to see, was in sympathy with them. To me they brought back a host of memories.

Hanks continued to maintain the fort at Galabat with one platoon. It was not protected by wire and if it was attacked, his orders were to withdraw from it rather than be overrun. His two Sudanese officers in the company and I took turns to command the platoon in the fort, and to patrol round Metemma with our mule-mounted section. On one such patrol soon after the declaration of war, Laurie watched another battalion of native troops arrive to reinforce the Italian garrison.

One night I occupied a hill behind Metemma with a platoon, and fired into the Italian positions soon after sunrise, withdrawing when the Italians counter-attacked with a battalion. Shortly after this, five of our Wellesley aircraft bombed Metemma, and one was shot down by heavy small-arms fire. On 27 July the Italians launched a full-scale attack on the fort at Galabat, and the platoon, commanded by Yusbashi Abdallah, withdrew after inflicting some casualties and itself suffering two killed and four wounded. On the same day the Italians captured Kassala, further north, after which they made no further attempt to invade the Sudan.

On 12 August Colonel Sandford with 101 Mission crossed the frontier near Galabat on his way to organize the resistance of the Patriot forces in Gojjam. Now fifty-eight years old, Dan Sandford was setting out during the rainy season on a journey that few younger men would have attempted at that time of year, even in peacetime. I was bitterly disappointed not to be with him. He had specially asked for me but General Platt, commanding the troops in the Sudan, had said he wished me first to gain experience of more orthodox soldiering.

Being short of mules, Sandford had left Arnold Wienholt at our camp, to follow as soon as he could raise transport. We suggested he should join us in the stockade we had built, but he preferred to camp nearby. Wienholt was Australian-born, and educated at Eton. In the South African war he had served as a trooper, and then spent years hunting in the Kalahari, where he was mauled by a lion. In the East African campaign against General von Lettow Vorbeck he had served as a scout, winning a DSO, MC and bar. Later he sat in the Australian Parliament. When Mussolini invaded Abyssinia, Wienholt went there to help the Abyssinians by working with the Red Cross. After Abyssinia's defeat he returned to Australia, but as soon as war was declared in 1939 he sailed to Aden and waited there for Italy to join in. When at last Mussolini did so, Wienholt went to Khartoum, was commissioned as a second lieutenant and attached to 101 Mission.

I often walked over to his bivouac, shared the 'dampers' he cooked and the strong tea he brewed. Quiet of speech and unhurried in movement, he had a spare body, steady, watchful eyes, a lined face and grizzled hair cut short. He reminisced most frequently about the time he had spent with the Bushmen in the Kalahari. To me he personified the great African hunters of the past; it was appropriate that he and Selous had served together in East Africa.

After he had been with us a fortnight he managed to buy three donkeys, and set off next morning to join Sandford in Gojjam. I recall, as if it was yesterday, my last sight of Arnold Wienholt. He had started down the path behind his two servants and the three donkeys. His rifle was slung over his shoulder and he had a long stick in his hand. At a bend in the path he stopped, turned round, and waved. I was reminded hauntingly of 'Rocky', in *Jock of the Bushveld*, gun on shoulder, stick in hand, starting with his donkeys on his last journey into the interior. Wienholt was ambushed and killed a few days later.

When Haile Selassie reached the Sudan in late June he expected to find preparations under way to raise a large Abyssinian force to help liberate his country. Four months later, all that had happened was that Sandford had entered Gojjam with a handful of men and a few mule-loads of rifles and ammunition. The Emperor did not realize how short of weapons and equipment the Sudan was; but he did know the Kenya Government had forbidden the many Abyssinian refugees there to go to the Sudan to be recruited. He had already been exasperated by attempts to keep him out of the Sudan, and now by having his movements restricted on security grounds. Justifiably, he felt ignored and humiliated. In early October 1940, while I was on leave in Khartoum, General Platt invited me to dinner. Someone asked him what part Haile Selassie would play in the liberation of Abyssinia. He answered, 'Haile Selassie will enter Abyssinia by the grace of William Platt, and with his baggage.'

Finally, Haile Selassie appealed to Churchill. As a result, Eden, who was visiting Egypt, flew to Khartoum and on 28 October held a conference attended, among others, by Field-Marshal Smuts, General Wavell, Generals Dickinson and Cunningham from Kenya, General Platt, and Michael Wright from the Embassy in Cairo. Anthony Eden accepted Haile Selassie's claim to be recognized as ruler of Abyssinia, and agreed to his demand that a regular Abyssinian force should take part in the campaign; he insisted that such a force should be raised as quickly as possible. Wavell, on his return to Cairo, sent Major Orde Wingate to Khartoum to organize it. I myself, isolated once more at Galabat, was unaware of these momentous decisions.

At Galabat the weeks had passed with frequent patrols that sometimes penetrated many miles into Abyssinia, and intermittent skirmishes and fairly regular bombing of our position. We had been reinforced by a Nuba company of the SDF under Bimbashi Camp-

bell. The 5th Indian Division had recently arrived in the Sudan, and
Brigadier Mayne visited us in October while Hanks was on leave. He
and I were having breakfast when the customary morning plane
came over. We got into the slit trench alongside my tent. Several
bombs landed nearby, one within a few feet of the trench, spattering
us with earth. Dusting his cap, the brigadier remarked reflectively:
'You'll find it doesn't get any easier as you get older.' I had been
envying him his composure.

At the beginning of November the woods round the camp suddenly and unexpectedly filled with troops, tanks and guns.
Brigadier Slim had arrived with the 10th Indian Brigade; it included
a squadron of tanks and a field regiment of artillery. We could
scarcely believe our eyes. We had hung on here throughout the
rains, conscious that there was nothing behind us and that the
Italians opposite us were being heavily reinforced. While I was on
leave they had tentatively attacked our position, which left Hanks
wondering if it was the prelude to an advance on Gedaref. Undismayed, he was preparing to do his best to counter any Italian thrust;
he was awarded a well-merited MC.

Soon after he arrived, Slim visited individually the two Sudanese
companies. Informally, he strolled round our position, asked Hanks
a number of questions and spoke a few friendly words to anyone he
met. There was a massive imperturbable quality about Slim that was
highly reassuring. I was sure nothing escaped him, and we were all
profoundly impressed. I count myself privileged to have served
briefly under this great man.

At 5.30 a.m. on 6 November 1940 the RAF bombed the Italian
positions and our guns opened up, catching the Italians completely
by surprise. As the shells streamed over our heads, our company
and the 3/18 Garwhal Rifles moved up to the starting line. Galabat
fort had consisted originally of a small stone-built building unpro-
tected by wire. After capturing it the Italians had extended the
fortifications by building massive stone *sangars* surrounded by a
dense belt of barbed wire, but even so the total area was comparatively small. Now it was obscured by smoke and dust, and it seemed
impossible that anyone in it could be left alive. The guns stopped
and we moved forward with the tanks.

The Eritrean battalion holding Galabat had suffered severely from
the bombardment, but they fought back magnificently, their
machine-gunners continuing to fire until the tanks ran over them.

THE LIFE OF MY CHOICE

Soon after we had recaptured the fort, the Italians counter-attacked, with two other native battalions from Metemma; but they were driven off by machine-gun fire, with heavy casualties.

Slim's next objective was Metemma, where the garrison included a battalion of Blackshirts, manning machine-guns and anti-tank weapons. Only tanks could have forced a passage through the belt of wire, but eight of the twelve British tanks had been put out of action by the rocky terrain. While they were being repaired, the Italian bombers and fighters came over and continued to do so throughout that day and the next. They shot down several British fighters, and thereby, despite losing five of their own, gained local air superiority, against which we had no anti-aircraft guns. The ground was stony; there was little shelter, and our casualties were heavy, especially among the Essex Regiment that had moved up for the assault on Metemma. After the lorry containing tank spares was blown up, Slim called off the attack, and withdrew his troops to the shelter of the woods, from which patrols could dominate Galabat.

A few days later I was ordered to Khartoum, having been personally selected by General Platt, to join Colonel Sandford in Gojjam as a replacement for Captain Critchley, his second-in-command, who was having to be evacuated with a serious eye injury.

On arrival two days later in Khartoum, I was told to report to Major Wingate. Although Wingate had served from 1928 to 1933 in the Eastern Arab Corps, I had not yet heard of him. In Khartoum I was to hear plenty about him. As I came into his office he was studying a map on the wall. He swung round, said, 'I've been expecting you,' and immediately launched into his plans to invade Gojjam, destroy the Italian forces stationed there, reach Addis Ababa before the South African Army from Kenya could do so, and restore Haile Selassie to his throne. While expounding his seemingly impossible plans, he strode about his office, his disproportionately large head thrust forward above his ungainly body; in his pale blue eyes, set close together in a bony angular face, was more than a hint of fanaticism.

I asked him what forces the Italians had in Gojjam: Intelligence estimated them at forty thousand, he said. Having seen Metemma, I could visualize the strength of their forts. I then asked how many troops he would have: he said he would have the Frontier Battalion of the SDF, raised and commanded by Colonel Hugh Boustead; a newly raised battalion of Abyssinian refugees; and half a dozen Operational Centres, each comprising one British officer, four British sergeants and fifty Abyssinians. It was obvious as he talked that Wingate never doubted he would be given command of the forthcoming campaign in Gojjam, even though Colonel Sandford, who was organizing Patriot resistance there, and Colonel Boustead, had both served with distinction in the First World War and were a rank senior to him.

Wingate, who was now thirty-seven, had served before the war under Wavell in Palestine. There he had organized and led Jewish night squads against Arab guerrillas with outstanding success and had won a DSO. So far this was the only active service he had seen. Although not himself a Jew, Wingate was a passionate believer in the Zionist cause, with which he identified himself completely. In Palestine he had been justifiably suspected by the military authorities of revealing information to the Jewish leaders, and of being involved in their intrigues.

His personal service file described him as a good soldier but a security risk, who as far as Palestine was concerned could not be trusted, since he put Jewish interests before British. It recommended that he should not be allowed into Palestine again, and he was sent back to England. There, as a Gunner, he served for two years in an anti-aircraft battery. However, he bitterly resented his expulsion from Palestine and continued to consort with Zionist leaders in England and openly to support their demands for a Jewish state. Always an arrogant and ill-disciplined officer, he now became increasingly aggressive and resentful of authority. He was an ambitious soldier, but had apparently wrecked his army career by the time war broke out.

Wavell, who had been appointed Commander-in-Chief, Middle East, had known Wingate in Palestine and recognized his potential as a guerrilla leader. He therefore sent for him. When Wingate reached Cairo in summer 1940 he soon made himself cordially disliked at GHQ, but in October Wavell sent him to Khartoum to organize the Abyssinian forces.

Soon after his arrival he met Haile Selassie. The Emperor was despondent, feeling that time was passing and nothing was being done. Wingate assured him he would raise a force that would take him back to Addis Ababa. This was a strange and eventful meeting, between the diminutive but indomitable Emperor and the uncouth, inspired soldier who was going to liberate Gojjam for him. Haile Selassie's legendary descent from Solomon and Sheba may have given him special standing in Wingate's eyes: certainly Wingate emerged from this encounter dedicated to the liberation and independence of Abyssinia.

Wingate took me round various offices at Headquarters. As he shambled from one to another, in his creased, ill-fitting uniform and out-of-date Wolseley helmet, carrying an alarm clock instead of wearing a watch, and a fly-whisk instead of a cane, I could sense the irritation and resentment he left in his wake. His behaviour certainly exasperated Platt, who anyway had little sympathy with irregular operations. I once heard Platt remark, even before Wingate's appointment, 'The curse of this war is Lawrence in the last.'

Wingate seemed to take pleasure in provoking people, and was often deliberately rude and aggressive. Once, breakfasting at the hotel with Dodds Parker, his staff captain, he gratuitously accused two young officers at a nearby table of cowardice, for taking staff jobs. He would make appointments with officers at his hotel, and then receive them lying naked on his bed; one of them described to me how Wingate had been brushing his body-hair with a tooth-brush as he gave him his instructions. Behaviour such as this made him disliked wherever he went.

Some weeks after he had arrived in Khartoum, Wingate was summoned by Wavell to a conference in Cairo on the forthcoming invasion of Abyssinia. Wingate was a major, whereas the other participants were generals and brigadiers. A story soon went the rounds of Khartoum that when a general questioned the feasibility of Wingate's plans for conquering Gojjam, which he had expounded for twice the time allotted him, Wingate said to him, 'You are an ignorant fool, General. It is men like you who lose us wars.' Wingate, who constantly referred to his superiors as military apes, was quite capable of saying this, but I suspect that if he had done so at this stage in his career he would not have got away with it.

Orde Wingate has often been compared with T. E. Lawrence, but in nothing did they differ more than in their personal relationship with others. Lawrence, despite his Arab dress and unconventional behaviour, won the confidence and friendship of Allenby and his staff; he consequently received all the help he asked for, in money, weapons and camels. Wingate, on the other hand, never received the support he could have expected during the Gojjam campaign, and when it was over received virtually no recognition of his achievements.

I myself found Wingate inspiring, realizing as soon as I met him that he did not regard the Gojjam campaign as just another step towards winnng the war. For both of us the liberation of Abyssinia and the restoration of Haile Selassie were in the nature of a crusade.

I had arrived in Khartoum on 12 November 1940, expecting to leave again almost at once to join Sandford in Gojjam, but Wingate kept me hanging about for six weeks. He took me with him to watch the Abyssinian recruits being trained, and to the lectures he gave to their British personnel. I was impressed by his passionate and ruthless drive, but unconvinced by his lectures. Again and again he emphasized his two cardinal rules for guerrilla warfare: never to employ a guide, since he might betray us, but to rely on our maps; and never to march on a road but always to make our away across country. Such rules might be applicable in Palestine, which had been meticulously surveyed, but I knew from experience that in the mountains of Abyssinia they were utter nonsense. However, Wingate repeatedly threatened to send back to Khartoum anyone who failed to observe them. I was left wondering how he would get on with Sandford and Boustead.

I became desperate to join Sandford, and was maddened by these pointless and endless delays. At first it was proposed to drop me by parachute in Gojjam. Parachuting or going in a submarine were my special nightmares, but to get to Gojjam I was willing to jump, even without training. I was glad, however, when that idea was abandoned and Wingate told me to find my own way to Sakela where Sandford was stationed.

During these six frustrating weeks I saw a certain amount of Douglas Newbold. He was dreadfully busy, but there was always a warm welcome in his house and the comfort of his kindly, wise and humorous presence: he had a great gift for friendship. Newbold was outstanding in a service that had produced not a few great men. He was devoted to the Sudanese, and despite failing health never spared himself, but worked ceaselessly on their behalf till 1945 when he died. Then all who knew him, whether Sudanese or British, realized the extent of their loss. One day when he and I were having

tea, Sayyah of the Maidob was announced. I was delighted to see
him again. Newbold poured him tea and handed him cakes, saying,
'Here in my house you must eat what we do.' Then, after the
customary exchange of compliments, Sayyah said, with his shy
smile: 'We Maidob realize what we owe to the British. Now you are
at war we want to help, but all we have are our sheep. My people
have sent you five hundred, which I have brought to Omdurman.
We hope they will help to feed the troops fighting to defend us.'
Newbold and I were much moved, and after Sayyah had left Newbold said to me, 'God, I do like that chap. I only wish I was like him.'

Before I left Khartoum I lunched with Haile Selassie in the villa
where he was living. He was courteous and welcoming as always,
showing no sign of the humiliations to which he had been subjected
on arrival, nor of the frustrations he had until recently felt. Next day
I watched him inspect the Patriot Battalion and the Operational
Centres. Wingate had kept his promise: the Emperor knew that the
day was approaching when he would cross the frontier. In Wingate,
who was destined to command his army, he had a dedicated champion; in Edwin Chapman-Andrews, his Political Officer, and above
all in Sandford, he had two other men devoted to his cause.

CHAPTER 23

The Invasion of Abyssinia, 1940–1

W HILE I WAS IN KHARTOUM, Idris received a message from his father saying he needed him at Tini to help with some family dispute. He was reluctant to leave me but I insisted he should go. I never saw him again, for I was unable to get in touch with him before I left for Abyssinia, going first by truck to Roseires with Muhammad, my Eastern Arab Corps orderly. During the ensuing months I would have given much to have had Idris with me.

At Roseires I found a guide and three camels waiting for me. I crossed the frontier at Umm Idla on 22 December 1940 and headed for Balaya. This isolated massif, about eighty miles away, had never fallen to the Italians. Our rough track ran through thick bush and the intervening country was almost waterless, so we averaged twelve hours' riding a day, and spent Christmas night without food or water at the foot of Balayia. Early next morning Muhammad and I set off on foot up the mountain, at first through thickets of bamboo and then through forest where, in the dim light, cold streams tumbled down the mountainside and bands of black-and-white colobus monkeys peered at us from among the lichen-covered branches.

Green meadows, stands of juniper, wild olive and a leafless tree covered with white blossom like a wild cherry, spread across the flat top of the mountain. Everywhere were flowers: wild roses and jasmine, delphiniums, yellow daisies and a variety of others, some of which I had seen on the hills near Addis Ababa and in the Arussi mountains. The air was refreshingly cool after the hot lowlands, and the view was immense. I looked westward towards the Sudan over an endless scrub-covered plain partly veiled in the smoke of many bush fires, and eastward to the Abyssinian escarpment that stretched in a seemingly sheer wall across my front.

A company of the Sudanese Frontier Force battalion was already

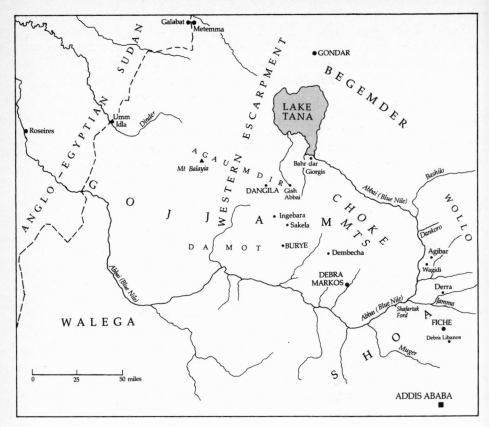

Gojjam, 1940–1

established on Balayia, preparing a forward base for the invasion of Gojjam and a temporary headquarters for the Emperor. I visited Peter Acland, the Bimbashi in command, and heard his latest news; then, after a welcome meal, I set off to find the local Fitaurari and arrange for mules to take me on my way. I stayed with the Fitaurari for two days and while I was with him he gave a *geber* for his men. His dim, smoke-filled house was crowded to overflowing with relays of armed men gorging on raw meat. The people here were Agaw, who spoke their own language. They were a handsome race and the great mops of hair that crowned the men's heads emphasized their untamed appearance.

I was joined at Balayia by a young Amhara from Sandford's

324

mission at Sakela who spoke good English. Then, on mules provided by the Fitaurari, we rode across the plain to the foot of the escarpment where Fitaurari Ayalew Makonnen, a renowned Patriot leader, was awaiting me with some twenty men. Ayalew was a tall, imposing figure and his bodyguard a formidable-looking group, all with the long hair that distinguished the Patriots. He led me up the steep mountainside to his hideout, concealed under trees in a gully. The long, rectangular shelter constructed of branches was divided by a partition behind which Ayalou's family lived; let into the main compartment was a small stall where he stabled his favourite mule and horse.

Except for the earthen platform on which we sat, the room was crowded with the Fitaurari's men, all armed with rifles, many captured from the Italians. As it grew dark, small boys with haloes of hair round their shaven skulls lit and held aloft torches of resinous wood that gave a wavering but somehow appropriate light. Food on woven grass trays was carried in: thin flaps of *injera*, made with flour from the seeds of *teff* (a small grass cultivated all over northern Abyssinia) and *wat*, a highly seasoned meat sauce. This constituted the staple fare of the Amhara and Tigreans. It was to be mine during the coming months; fortunately I enjoyed it. I now fed with the Fitaurari and his chiefs; like them, I used just the tips of my fingers to wrap the *wat* in a fold of *injera*. The slave woman who brought us our food was rewarded with a handful stuffed into her mouth by her master.

The others, packed shoulder to shoulder, ate in small groups below our platform, each man with his rifle in his left hand. Page boys, draping and redraping their *shammas* over their shoulders as etiquette demanded, filled our glasses with *tej*, an intoxicating honey wine, and poured *talla*, the local beer, into horn goblets for the soldiers. The young master of ceremonies stood in the entrance, quietly indicating to each man where he should sit and when he should leave. In a far corner some women tipped more *teff* paste on to iron griddles over open fires, and the mule poked its head into the room and whickered for its food. Sitting there and looking at these men who had fought for so long against the Italians, I felt supremely happy. I was here in Gojjam at last, with the opportunity to make amends now for my neglect to help them in the past.

Next day Muhammad and I, with the interpreter, two guides and three mules, started off in the early afternoon, and as it grew dark reached the top of the escarpment. Ahead of us was an extensive cultivated plain with many villages, traversed by a military road. Ayalou had warned me that a large body of cavalry from Dangila had been burning villages near our route the previous day. Fearing that the villagers might betray us to avoid further reprisals, he advised us to cross the plain in the dark so as to reach the broken country beyond before daylight. Our track in fact passed through several villages which we were unable to avoid: each time I felt apprehensive, as dogs barked and firelight flickered in doorways; but no one challenged us and before dawn we were safely across.

Two days later, when we were out on another open plain, an Italian fighter came over, flying very low. It changed direction to pass directly overhead and I fired two shots at it. It then swung round and dived at us; as it did so I got off three more shots and it made off without opening fire. I had possibly damaged it.

When I arrived at Sakela Sandford greeted me with, 'Hello, Wilfred. I must say you've taken a long time to get here.'

Rather disconcerted, I replied, 'I don't think I could have come any faster.' Then I realized he was referring to the interminable delays in Khartoum.

It was good to be here with him in the heart of Gojjam. Dressed in khaki shorts and bush shirt, he sat in a canvas chair and beamed at me through his spectacles. Short and stocky, swarthy, round-faced, rather bald and unfailingly cheerful, he looked indestructible, as indeed he had proved to be. Here was someone who from long experience really knew Abyssinia, knew the people, knew without prejudice or illusion their good qualities and their faults, and felt a great affection for them. I would have followed Sandford anywhere.

With him was Clifford Drew. I had known him in Fasher after he succeeded Maurice in charge of the hospital; and after war was declared we had sailed together from Glasgow on the *Montcalm*. I had always liked him and was delighted to find him here. I was often to watch him carrying out complicated operations in the open on wounded Patriots, assisted only by his Sudanese dresser. Several British officers would later owe their lives to his skill.

In the camp were two hard-working signallers, Sergeant-Major Grey and Corporal Whitmore; they were inundated with coded signals from Wingate, who with typical thoughtlessness dictated them without regard to length. There was also Azaj Kabada, an elderly Amhara, the Emperor's representative with 101 Mission.

Dedicated to his country's freedom and utterly fearless, he was giving invaluable assistance. Sandford described to me how indefatigable Kabada had been during the long march from Galabat, crossing and recrossing flooded rivers in pouring rain, to help to bring the loaded mules over.

101 Mission was camped in attractive country. On the nearby hills was the remnant of an ancient forest with some magnificent junipers; round the camp were meadows with trees, and along the streams bramble thickets, and everywhere wild flowers. It was cold in daytime, very cold at night. The day I arrived the weekly market was under way nearby. I was astonished at the crowd that attended it. Burye, with its large garrison, was perhaps fifteen miles away, and the Italians must have learnt that Sandford was camped here; yet they made no attempt to round him up. Except for that first night's march from the escarpment, I had travelled openly to Sakala, taking no precautions, and had been welcomed everywhere. Our immunity was convincing proof that, except immediately around their forts, the Italians had no control over the country.

Before the Italians had overrun Abyssinia, Ras Hailu was confined to Addis Ababa for his attempt in 1932 to reinstate Lij Yasu. He was head of the famous Takla Haimanot family, traditional rulers of Gojjam, and the Italians, anxious to gain support there, had reinstated him in Debra Markos with the honorary rank of general. In the past both Amhara and Tigreans had given their allegiance to regional overlords and been all too ready to follow them against whoever was Emperor. Hatred of the Italians, however, was stronger than loyalty to Ras Hailu, and Gojjam had developed into a main centre of opposition to them.

Sandford's arrival, accompanied by the Emperor's representative, had encouraged the war-weary Patriots, whose resistance was beginning to flag after six years of continuous warfare. Armed mostly with the rifles they had captured – and the large number of these was the measure of their success – they had to contend with aerial bombardment and with troops armed with machine-guns, artillery and tanks; if they were captured they faced inevitable execution. Sandford had distributed some rifles, but although the number he had been able to bring with him had been limited, Wingate later criticized him for doing so, maintaining that it was folly to give rifles to people who might never use them against the Italians. Wingate ignored the fact that the Patriots, on whom he depended for freedom of movement, might well have withdrawn their support unless given some weapons. But more important was the apprehension of the Italians when they learnt that the British were arming the rebels.

Sandford's first task had been to reconcile the various chiefs, who, even though in arms against the Italians, were often intensely jealous of each other. In these negotiations Azaj Kabada's support was essential. Of the chiefs in Western Gojjam, Dedjazmatch Mangasha Jambore and Dedjazmatch Negash Kabada were the most important, and both effectively controlled large areas. I liked Mangasha as soon as I met him; he was a large, dignified man with an agreeably open face and courteous manners, whereas Negash was small and unimpressive in appearance, looking ill-tempered, sensual and cruel. However, as a member of the Takla Haimanot family Negash had special standing with his followers.

Soon after I arrived at Sakala we heard that Lij Mammo, Ras Hailu's pro-Italian son, was harrying the Patriots in the country round Burye with a large force of cavalry. Sandford set off at once to co-ordinate resistance and left me in charge of the camp, until he sent for me a few days later. I then crossed the main road and ran into crowds of refugees driving animals and carrying whatever they had saved. To the south the sky was dark with the smoke of burning villages. When I arrived, Lij Mammo had withdrawn into Burye after some fierce fighting. A few days later he sallied out but was driven back by the Patriots once more into Burye.

Sandford now decided to confer with the chiefs in Agawmeder, a district inhabited by Agaw. We went together to the Gish Abbai where the Abbai, or Blue Nile, rises. We camped near the church, which, like many others in Gojjam, was circular, with mud walls and a thatched roof surmounted with a cross. It was surrounded by a grove of trees. Such groves are held sacred, a belief possibly introduced from Arabia by the early settlers; in many parts of Northern Abyssinia they are all that now remains of the ancient forests.

As soon as we arrived, the priests visited our camp and held out small silver crosses for us to kiss. They insisted that we must not drink from the spring until the morning, before we fed. Early next day I went to the meadow below our camp and drank from the clear water bubbling up from a small moss-ringed hollow, the fountain-head of the Blue Nile. James Bruce had come here in 1770. It had been the goal of his great journey, but despite his claim to have been the first European to achieve it, Pedro Paez, a Jesuit, had actually forestalled him by a century and a half. Even in Bruce's time the Agaw, who were still pagan, held this spring sacred.

The Emperor, accompanied among others by Wingate and Chapman-Andrews, crossed the frontier where I did, at Umm Idla, on 20 January 1941. There, in a simple but moving ceremony, he raised the national flag. In Khartoum Wingate had tried unsuccessfully to prevent him from having his own bodyguard, and was infuriated when the Emperor's advisers obtained for him a traditional state umbrella and war drums. Wingate said these were ridiculous in a modern campaign and insisted they be left behind. With singular lack of imagination he overlooked the impact that the reappearance of these ancient symbols of royalty would have on the traditionally minded people of Gojjam. I felt that the sound of the war drums, audible for miles, would have disturbed the Italian garrisons more than the loudspeakers Wingate used for propaganda.

Wingate's military status in the expedition was still invidious. He had been flown into Sakela to meet Sandford on 20 November to discuss the situation in Gojjam and the forthcoming operations. That was the first time they had met. Two days later Wingate, flown by Pilot Officer Collis, had left for Khartoum after a hair-raising take-off from an improvised runway. Sandford had been impressed by Wingate. One evening he said to me, 'You know, I'm not a soldier. It is true I was a regular before and during the First World War, but that's a long time ago. What interests me nowadays is the political side of this show. I don't want to be in charge of the military operations. Wingate, I think, is the man for that. I know that I should be more valuable as Political Adviser.'

The Emperor and Wingate reached Balayia on 6 February after an appalling journey. Wingate had insisted on marching on a compass bearing from Umm Idla. When he finally saw the mountain he was twenty degrees off course; and his route had taken him through dense bamboo jungle and across lava fields. Possibly he had been influenced by a sensational report which Captain Simonds, who had preceded him into Gojjam with one of the Operational Centres, sent back about the difficulties of the track he had followed. In fact it was the same track that I had used, to reach Balayia in four days from Umm Idla. In November, when he visited Sandford, Wingate had flown over the area, but this hardly constituted adequate reconnaissance before setting off into largely waterless country with the Emperor, lorries and many camels.

He had originally planned to use mules for transport, but these proved unprocurable and he had to make do with camels. In this mountainous country no animals could have been less suited: the last one died on reaching Entoto above Addis Ababa. Also, basing his judgements on experience with camels in Egypt, Wingate had overruled the camel-drivers and insisted on loading the camels far too heavily. Many of them died during this march. This incessant hacking through thickets of bamboo also wore out his men, and the lorries were soon abandoned. Wingate eventually went ahead to locate Balayia and having done so came back to fetch the Emperor. Being impatient to get a move on, he whacked the Emperor's tired horse, whereupon the Emperor is said to have turned on him and invited him to go in front, adding: 'I hope when we meet my subjects they will know which of us is Emperor.'

Wingate had already disconcerted his officers by his unseemly behaviour. He never washed now, and he grew an untended beard. Kenneth Anderson, Reuter's war correspondent, observed that on the march to Balayia, Wingate's only ablutions were to lower his trousers and cool his bottom in the occasional waterholes, from which, incidentally, others would have to drink. He apparently carried no change of clothes except for a dressing gown, and in this and his battered Wolseley helmet he was not, at first sight, a figure calculated to impress the Patriots, who expected their leaders to look the part. Yet I never heard him derided by them.

When Wingate reached Balayia he was promoted to lieutenant-colonel and given command of all troops, British and Abyssinian, serving under the Emperor. He learnt at the same time that Sandford, who had arrived at Balayia to receive the Emperor, had, as the Emperor's chief Political Officer, been made a brigadier. Wingate bitterly resented Sandford's promotion, which he felt threatened his own overall position. From now on he disagreed with Sandford on principle, to such an extent that General Platt sent him a caustic reprimand.

*   *   *

Captain Simonds, accompanied by Lieutenant Brown's Australian Operation Centre, arrived at Sakela a few days after Sandford had left for Balayia, and he sent me to join Dedjazmatch Mangasha, whose forces were investing Dangela. The town was said to be garrisoned by ten battalions, commanded by a Colonel Torelli. However, the Italian high command, who were under the impression that a British division was about to invade Gojjam, and were concerned by the resurgence of guerrilla activity, had ordered Torelli to evacuate Dangela. Sandford had received a copy of this order from Khartoum, where they had intercepted it and broken the Italian code.

I joined Mangasha just as Torelli was withdrawing from the town, which he left in flames. His troops were attacked, halted and temporarily driven off the road in a noisy battle that lasted three hours, with some heavy Italian bombing and artillery fire. The Abyssinians captured some prisoners, a number of machine-guns and masses of rifles, which indicated that the Italian losses had been severe. Torelli continued his withdrawal, and reached the fort at Piccolo Abbai in the evening. We could hear intermittent gunfire and bombing in the distance, and the following day Torelli retreated to Bahr dar Giorgis.

During the battle Mangasha had exercised no control, leaving its direction to his subordinate chiefs and remaining throughout at a distance from the fighting, regardless of my attempts to induce him to take a more active part. Although not a warrior, Mangasha had won acceptance from many of the Patriots as their overlord, and in establishing his authority over a large area round Dangela had successfully defied the Italians.

The evacuation of Dangela was the greatest mistake the Italians made during Wingate's campaign in Gojjam. Had they remained there, they might well have held the edge of the escarpment indefinitely and prevented Gideon Force, as Wingate now christened his command, from establishing itself on the plateau. Even without opposition, Gideon Force had the greatest difficulty getting its camel transport up the almost vertical face of the escarpment.

Once this had been achieved, Wingate advanced on Burye in a series of night marches with the Sudanese Frontier Battalion and the Abyssinian Patriot Battalion. This virtually defenceless column moved through the darkness with almost every soldier leading a loaded camel. Each night before dawn, the mass of men and animals had to be hidden from air attack. On the last night Wingate ordered small fires to be lit as guide marks; one fire spread out of control and the long column advancing on Burye was silhouetted against a blazing mountainside.

For my part, after the Italians had evacuated Dangela, Simonds had first sent me with Brown's Operation Centre to attack the fort at Ingebara. Brown had a three-inch mortar, and mortared the fort with remarkable accuracy, considering that the weapon had been improvised in the Khartoum railway workshops and had no range-finder. Two days later the Italians had evacuated Ingebara and withdrawn to Burye. There I joined Gideon Force outside the town.

Colonel Natale, who commanded the Italian troops in Burye, had been ordered to hold the place at all costs. It contained a large garrison and, like all the Italian positions, was strongly enough fortified to be impregnable to direct assault by Wingate's small force. Wingate's intention was to threaten the Italian communications with Debra Markos and, by a succession of night attacks with grenades and bayonets, to induce Natale to withdraw. He was helped by three Wellesley aircraft from Khartoum that came and bombed the town; this was the only occasion during the campaign when he received air support. Standing beside him as he watched the bombing, I was struck by the merciless, almost savage, expression on his face.

During this campaign I spent most of my time with the Patriots. I had a small 'bivvy' tent and my blankets, as well as some spare clothes, a few books and other personal possessions. These I loaded on a spare mule, but I carried no provisions, relying on the chiefs to feed Muhammad and myself. Since I liked Abyssinian food this was no hardship. All the same, when I joined the others, it was a pleasant change to be invited by Hugh Boustead to an evening meal. We would sit at a table with a tablecloth and cutlery lit by a red-shaded candle, and eat well-cooked food, and drink the Chianti he had acquired.

Wingate openly despised such luxury. He was accompanied by a civilian Jew called Akavia who had worked with him in Palestine; by an extraordinary arrangement, Akavia was now virtually his chief-of-staff. I once watched the two of them roast a chicken over a fire. They had no pots or pans, no plates or knives or forks, and when it was cooked, Wingate, squatting on the ground, tore it to pieces with his teeth, getting his hands and face smothered in grease. Having finished he said: 'Here, Akavia, catch!' and threw the remains to him. Yet only with Akavia did he seem to have a close relationship. If he went and joined a group of his officers sitting round a fire in the evening, conversation dried up and they would drift away. He appeared to live in a lonely world of his own making, driven by some perverse urge to alienate his fellows by his rudeness and eccentricity. In Khartoum he once asked me if I was happy. I answered that in general I was. He reflected, and said; 'I'm not happy, but I don't think any great man ever is.'

Personally I was fortunate in my relationship with Wingate, and he was never rude to me. Yet only once did I get past his self-imposed barrier. The two of us were sitting on a rock looking across a great sweep of mountain. Unexpectedly, he relaxed and began to talk. He told me of his stern, puritanical upbringing, his unhappy days at school, his unpopularity at Woolwich, his passion for fox-hunting and steeplechasing, and his dedication to Zionism. I asked why he became a Zionist, not being a Jew. He answered that his interest in the Jews dated from his prep school, where he had been mercilessly bullied and the boys had organized what they called 'Wingate hunts'. He had been brought up on the Bible by devout parents, and in those unhappy schooldays had found in the Old Testament a people who never gave in, though every man's hand was against them. He had accordingly identified them with himself. Perhaps in those early days Wingate's character had been permanently warped; yet, perhaps, it had been tempered too, and made resolute.

Hugh Boustead was very different, warm-hearted and sociable, a man who made friends wherever he went. He had spent most of his life abroad, usually in remote places, but as soon as he returned to England word went round that 'Hugh was back', and his friends would hurry to get in touch. Though he was now a colonel of much more seniority than Wingate, and had experience fighting on the Western Front during the First World War, and with the Russian White Armies, Boustead now found himself subordinate to an officer who had never commanded more than a Jewish night squad in action against Arab guerrillas. The position was difficult for both of them; Wingate's innate suspicion and jealousy made it all but intolerable.

Once, during the fighting round Burye, Wingate disappeared into the battle with a platoon, and to Boustead's fury was out of touch for the rest of the day. On another occasion Wingate accused Boustead of cowardice because he withdrew his battalion from an indefensible position: Boustead never forgave him. Later in the campaign, when we were fighting round Debra Markos, Wingate sent word to Boustead to move his battalion to another position. Time passed and nothing seemed to be happening. Wingate strode up and down, getting more and more impatient, then turned to me and said, 'Go at once to Colonel Boustead and tell him if he does not obey my orders and move his battalion at once I will send him back in disgrace to Khartoum.'

I went over to Boustead and told him Wingate was getting very impatient.

'Damn it!' Boustead exclaimed, 'if the man had ever commanded more than a platoon he would realize that it takes time to move a battalion.'

This was typical of the unhappy relationship which had developed between them.

While Gideon Force was fighting round Burye, Wingate sent me to the Choke mountains to persuade Haile Yusuf, a guerrilla fighter of renown, to attack the Italian fort at Dembecha on the road between Burye and Debra Markos. Muhammad and I arrived at sunset at Faras Beit, a cold, bleak spot in the mountains, and were relieved to find Haile Yusuf at home, and to shelter in his large *tukul*. We had not fed since the previous day so the excellent meal he provided of roasted meat, *injera* and *wat* was very welcome. It was cold during the night even by the fire, and, as they do in all these houses, the bugs came out of the mud walls and feasted on us. Typhus was not uncommon in these villages but I have always worked on the assumption that I shall not fall ill, so I eat whatever I am given and drink such water as comes to hand.

Haile Yusuf's circular room was crowded with his soldiery, most of them wearing captured uniforms, some with patched bullet-holes. All had the customary mop of hair. Sandford had told me that Haile Yusuf, unlike Mangasha and Negash, was a fighting leader. Though small in stature, delicately featured and quiet, he was nonetheless incisive and commanding, a typical Abyssinian aristocrat, dressed in a traditional black cloak. He agreed with my proposal, said he would start from Dembecha next morning, and sent off messengers to summon his troops.

The fort at Dembecha was held by a battalion of native troops, who were better fighters than most of the Italians; like all these forts it was surrounded by a wide belt of wire; a large village of thatched huts adjoined it. On his arrival Haile Yusuf occupied a steep-sided, flat-topped hill less than a thousand yards from the fort. The hill was partly covered with trees but soon after our arrival the Italian garrison, having evidently observed movement, first opened up with their machine-guns and then attacked us. After some confused fighting we succeeded in driving them back into their fort. Haile Yusuf's men then swarmed into the village, fired the houses and drove off cattle and mules. For the next two days this threat to their communications brought down on us repeated attacks by Italian fighter aircraft. In *Seven Pillars of Wisdom* Lawrence had described how he and his Arabs avoided casualties under Turkish air attack by squatting on the precipitous side of a hill. We copied them, and suffered no casualties.

I sent a report to Wingate and asked for a machine-gun, to rake the Italian position. Wingate had already sent Major Boyle's Patriot Battalion to cut the Burye–Dembecha road, and Boyle now sent me Lieutenant Rowe with a machine-gun. Rowe arrived in the afternoon and said Boyle was camped two miles away on the Burye road. That evening from the top of the hill we noticed in the far distance a dense, dark mass of men moving in our direction, and realized that the Italians had evacuated Burye and were now marching on Dembecha. I suggested that Rowe should rejoin his battalion, but he was anxious to shoot up Dembecha fort first, and said he would return to them at first light. This he did.

Boyle had camped beside the road without preparing defences or taking precautions against surprise. At about 8 a.m. on 6 March, the advance guard of the retreating Italians stumbled on his position. Boyle's camels had been turned out to graze, and when the first shots were fired his troops were busy preparing breakfast. On both sides surprise was complete. This was the first time the Patriot Battalion had come under fire, but the men did not panic, and fought back courageously. One of them ran forward with his anti-tank rifle and knocked out two armoured cars. The Italians halted in dense formations, and their battalions moved forward in turn to engage Boyle's troops. From our hilltop, the scene resembled a battle fought in Napoleonic times. The shelling was heavy, the small-arms fire continuous. To prevent the Dembecha garrison sallying to take Boyle's force in the rear, Haile Yusuf kept the fort under constant pressure; his men reoccupied the adjacent village and fired

from all sides at the defences. It took the Italians two hours to overrun Boyle's battalion. They then pressed on into Dembecha, leaving
more than two hundred dead on the field and taking hundreds of
wounded with them; but the Patriot Battalion had been destroyed
as a fighting unit. This battle was generally called Boyle's Blunder.

Wingate arrived at Dembecha during the day, with the Frontier
Force, the only effective formation he now had with which to capture Debra Markos. Intermittent fighting went on throughout the
day and Captain Harris, one of Boustead's company commanders,
was badly wounded; he owed his complete recovery to Clifford
Drew's initial treatment, carried out in the open under a tree. Next
morning the Italians abandoned Dembecha and withdrew towards
Debra Markos. They were harried for the first day of their retreat by
Haile Yusuf's men, but not very effectively. These men had been
fighting the Italians without support for six years: understandably,
they had no wish to be killed at the last moment when the enemy
was withdrawing from their land.

I watched the Italians depart and then went down to the fort
where I found Wingate trying to salvage some rations, and getting
filthy in the process. The Italians had set fire to their stores and
Wingate was scrambling about on a great pile of burst tins, mostly of
meat. I lent him a hand but with little success. He then rounded up
some Abyssinians to lay out a landing-ground and told me to come
and help. We managed to clear an adequate strip, but no plane ever
came to us, here or anywhere else. While we were supervising the
work Wingate lost his temper with the interpreter and slashed him
across the face several times with a stick.

Next day Wingate had gone off somewhere, and the rest of us
were having lunch, when we heard an explosion. 'Damn,' I
thought, 'they've booby-trapped the place.'

Going to the door, we were appalled to see four flaming figures
like living torches staggering about the yard, frantically beating at
their bodies with their hands. We threw them down and smothered
the flames with curtains torn from the room where we had been
eating, but by the time we had extinguished the last smouldering
vestiges, the clothes of all four were virtually burnt off; only their
puttees and bandoliers remained intact. Their bodies were marked
with deep burns, and great blisters wherever there was any skin;
charred bones showed through their hands. One of them went on
screaming 'Shoot me! Shoot me!'

Three were from the Frontier Battalion, the other was Wingate's interpreter. They had gone into a shed and when they lit a match to smoke, a leaking petrol barrel had exploded all over them. The previous day Clifford Drew had transported to Burye Bill Harris and the other wounded, held in the saddle on mules, and now we did not have even a medical orderly with us, and only the shell-dressings we carried. I hunted round the Italian dispensary, which fortunately had been neither burnt nor looted, and eventually found some morphia. The other officers had turned to me and I found myself in charge, though these casualties were not my men. I now told the officers what I was going to do, and they agreed. I then explained to the Sudanese who had gathered round that all four men were dying; they were in great pain, I said, and there was no hope for them, though they might last for hours. If I put them to sleep until they died, they would at least die unconscious of pain. I then gave each of the burnt men a lethal dose of morphia. Wingate's interpreter had been crying out for him, and that evening when Wingate returned I told him. He was silent for a while and then muttered, 'God, it makes me feel a brute.'

We now advanced on Debra Markos. I cannot remember how long it took us to get there. Taking part for the first time in these night marches, I realized how utterly defenceless we should be if attacked, with nearly everyone leading a camel; but Wingate judged, rightly, that the Italians would make no attempt to interfere with his advance, except perhaps by air attack. He attributed this with some justice to the moral supremacy he was fast acquiring, but again tended to overlook what he owed to the Patriots, whose widespread resistance over the years gave him his freedom of movement now.

On our last march, as we neared Debra Markos, Wingate called us to a halt at midnight. We were to start again at 4 a.m. Thankfully, we lay down to sleep. At 4 a.m. there was no sign of activity, so I went to look for Akavia. He said we were now to stay where we were till first light, since Wingate had received word that Ras Hailu, the Italian collaborator, was camped on the far side of the hill with a considerable body of men. I lay down again rather apprehensively; we were scattered along the track and in no position to withstand an attack. I joined Wingate at dawn. He seemed quite unperturbed and, as the

Emperor's commander-in-chief, was dictating a summons to Ras Hailu to surrender. He had some difficulty finding a messenger and by the time he had sent him off Ras Hailu had moved into Debra Markos.

Soon after we had taken up our position opposite that town we were ineffectively attacked from it. The initiative then passed to us and Wingate repeated the tactics he had employed so successfully at Burye, attacking a selected target each night with one of other of Boustead's companies. Colin Macdonald was killed during one of these attacks; I hardly knew him but he was a man with many devoted friends. Acland, whom I had known as a DC in Darfur and who had never shared my enthusiasm for the Abyssinians, was wounded in another night attack.

Belai Zeleka, who had proved the most formidable guerrilla leader in Gojjam, commanded the countryside along the Blue Nile, and was the only Patriot leader in a position to disrupt the eventual Italian withdrawal into Shoa from Debra Markos. Though of humble origin, among a people who set great store by lineage, he had nonetheless risen to his present commanding position because of his skill as a fighter, and his ruthlessness, that enabled him to impose on his troops a degree of discipline that Mangasha and Negash never achieved.

On 17 March, two days after our arrival near Debra Markos, Wingate sent me to contact Belai Zeleka and arrange with him to attack the garrison when it withdrew across the Blue Nile Gorge. I had with me my own bodyguard of fifteen Abyssinians who had over the past weeks attached themselves to me. They came from Shoa, Begemder and elsewhere and after deserting the Italians found themselves adrift in an alien countryside. With me I had Rowe, and some forty men from the now dispersed Patriot Battalion. I also had Tim Foley, a Sapper lieutenant: he was Irish, an individualist, a skilful improviser, and the best of company.

Hoping for great things, we joined Belai Zeleka, and spent a day at his homestead while he collected his troops and followers. Next morning we moved towards the road which led down to the Blue Nile crossing at Shafartak. Belai Zeleka, a slightly built man, pale in colour, narrow-faced, thin-lipped and unsmiling, rode a superb black mule; behind him pages led two war horses, caparisoned with red cloth emblazoned with white crosses, a touch of colour from the past. All round him moved a close-packed throng of men and animals. 'God help them', I thought, 'if a fighter comes over ...' Yet after years of bitter experience they still chose to move across country in this fashion.

Suddenly a shot was fired. Belai Zeleka halted and held up his hand.

'Who fired?'

Enquiries were made. A well-dressed woman was brought before him. She had fired her revolver by mistake.

'Flog her.'

She was flogged, and we moved on. All too often during the past weeks I had been exasperated by incessant fusillades fired off on the slightest occasion. I would think of Sandford, labouring across flooded rivers with boxes of ammunition from the Sudan, just to have it wasted.

We camped early that day and there we remained, spread over an open plain at the mercy of Italian aircraft. Each time I spoke to Belai Zeleka, he gave yet another reason for not moving: he was waiting for more troops, or for supplies, or for information. Finally he said it was his army, and he would move when he was ready. I feared the Italians might evacuate Debra Markos before we were in position, and was anxious to reconnoitre the road and select a place for an ambush; but I knew it would be a mistake to alienate Belai Zeleka by going on ahead. In any case, we carried no rations, relying on him for our food. I supposed he must know what he was doing: it seemed inconceivable that he would miss this chance of a decisive victory, one that would ensure him lasting fame.

Then, unbelievably, we heard on 5 April that the Debra Markos garrison had withdrawn, and crossed the Blue Nile into Shoa. Leaving Belai Zeleka to explain his treachery to his men, I went straight back to Debra Markos to report to Wingate. Boustead was furious with me over this missed opportunity, but Wingate was unexpectedly understanding.

We later learnt that Ras Hailu had suborned Belai Zeleka by offering him his daughter in marriage. To Belai Zeleka's peasant mind, the chance to marry into the Takla Haimanot family had proved irresistible. Four years later he and Lij Mammo, Hailu's son, were publicly hanged in Addis Ababa. Haile Selassie had imprisoned them for stirring up trouble in Gojjam. They killed a warder and escaped but were recaptured; they were tried for murder and sentenced to death.

After the Italians evacuated Debra Markos on 4 April 1941, Ras Hailu himself remained behind. Even before the Italian invasion in 1935 he had plotted time and again against Haile Selassie, and after it for six years he had assisted the Italians against the Patriots. In every occupied country in Europe after its liberation, collaborators were executed or imprisoned by their countrymen, many for offences less heinous than Hailu's. But the Emperor had proclaimed that past offences must be forgiven and forgotten so that all his countrymen could work together to rebuild their country. He therefore received Hailu's submission, but disdainfully and in public, and sentenced him to house arrest. Later he released him, only forbidding his return to Gojjam.

CHAPTER 24

Victory under Wingate

W INGATE'S OCCUPATION OF Debra Markos on 4 April 1941 was
only part of an overall military picture which was changing fast. General Cunningham had invaded Mussolini's
'Africa Orientale Italiana' from Kenya in February 1941. His forces
advanced through Italian Somaliland, and captured Mogadishu on
20 February, Harar on 26 March and Addis Ababa on 6 April: from
there he sent a division north to Dessie. Meanwhile, General Platt
had invaded Eritrea from the Sudan, and on 27 March, after weeks
of desperate fighting, his troops stormed the immensely strong
position of Keren. Then after occupying Asmara and Massawa, Platt
moved south on Amba Alagi, another strong mountain position
held by the Duke of Aosta with more than five thousand men.

The British military authorities, like almost everyone else, were
convinced that the Abyssinians, if given the opportunity, would
exact a terrible retribution on the Italians. Many instances of Abyssinian brutality, as witnessed for instance by James Bruce in Gondar
in 1771, seemed to warrant this assumption, and certainly the Abyssinians had cause enough for vengeance. Scattered over parts of the
country, especially round Addis Ababa, was a large Italian civilian
population which, the authorities believed, would suffer at the
hands of the Patriots, unless protected. For this reason if no other,
Platt cannot have wished Wingate to get to Addis Ababa before
Cunningham.

Soon after I arrived at Sakela I had discussed the likelihood of
reprisals with Sandford. I considered it a certainty that the Abyssinians, when afforded the opportunity, would exact retribution on
prisoners and civilians for the atrocities the Italians had inflicted on
them; Sandford, however, disagreed, insisting that the Emperor
would forbid it and be obeyed. Sandford must have been about the
only person who thought so, but, as often happened when he
disagreed with the majority, he was proved right.

Haile Selassie on his return to Addis Ababa on 5 May besought his
jubilant countrymen, by proclamation, not to spoil their name in the

eyes of the world by deeds of vengeance. I never came across, nor heard of, any single instance when he was disobeyed. His ability, on this occasion, to impose his own humanitarian principles on his subjects, was a striking indication of his authority.

The combined garrisons of Debra Markos, Dembecha, Burye and Injabara that had now retreated across the Blue Nile into Shoa on 5 April consisted mainly of native infantry, but also included some cavalry and artillery. Colonel Maraventano, who commanded this force, now turned north with the aim of joining the Duke of Aosta at Amba Alagi. If he succeeded, this would more than treble the size of the Duke's forces confronting General Platt. Wingate therefore sent Bimbashi Henry Johnson with his much-reduced company and Lieutenant Rowe with his platoon of Abyssinians in pursuit: in all, fewer than a hundred men after twelve thousand. Rowe had with him his heavy Vickers machine-gun, while Johnson had four Bren guns. I went with them. Johnson's orders were to harry the Italians at every opportunity. He knew he could expect no reinforcements, for Wingate was sending Boustead with the rest of the Frontier Battalion into northern Gojjam to capture Bahr dar Giorgis. Johnson had been in the Gezira Cotton Scheme in the Sudan before the war and, like me, had been given a Governor-General's commission. He had already proved himself a courageous and able officer, and as we set off to catch up with the Italian division ahead, he appeared unperturbed by his seemingly preposterous orders.

I had not previously seen the Blue Nile Gorge. Someone, who had seen both, once told me it was comparable with the Grand Canyon. Now, standing at its edge, I looked down on the river far below, a thread of silver at the bottom of this immense sheer-sided gash in the earth's surface. If only Belai Zeleka had ambushed the Italian column as it wound down the narrow road, few could have escaped.

The Italians had destroyed the bridge, but we waded waist-deep two hundred yards across the river and halted on the far side. For an hour or more the Italians shelled us, but the shells burst harmlessly on a cliff-face above. I was thankful they had not done this while we came down the road or were fording the river.

For the next month, across a dry, open plateau, cut up by occasional ravines, we followed this multitude of men and animals. Everywhere along its route the scattered native homesteads had been abandoned and the livestock driven off. The Italian column moved slowly, seldom more than a few miles a day, and often was static for days on end, probably out of consideration for the many wounded they had with them.

We usually camped a mile or more from their sprawling encampments. As it grew dark their fires resembled the lights of a town but as soon as Johnson's men, who had plenty of experience in this night fighting, started shooting, the fires were dowsed. On these flat bare plains we seldom found ourselves a defensible position, so we just camped in the open, and every morning I expected we would be attacked and annihilated. It seemed inevitable that sooner or later the Italians would be provoked into retaliation; they could perfectly well use a brigade or more if they thought it necessary.

After all these years, and without my diary which, when I flew to England in 1943 was taken from me and never returned, the exact sequence of those events becomes blurred in my mind. One day, Major Donald Nott joined us. Nott was a professional soldier; his presence was reassuring and I found him a stimulating companion. Soon after his arrival we reached broken country where we could afford to be more aggressive, shooting at the Italian camp even in daytime.

When the Italians eventually did attack us we were in by far the strongest position we had occupied. For several days we had been entrenched on a sheer-sided tabletop, connected by a panhandle a hundred yards long and twenty wide to a larger plateau occupied by the Italians. They attacked in the morning along this panhandle, and we shot them to pieces. Next day they resumed their retreat, and once again we resumed our pursuit.

Showers of rain had recently fallen and I wondered what would happen when the real rains broke in a few weeks' time; I had experienced the deluges that would then occur. The Sudanese had a groundsheet apiece, and their blankets, but no other protection against the weather. They came from the hot plains of the Sudan, a far cry from these cold, bleak Highlands. By now their clothes were in rags, their sandals worn out; the feet of some were already bruised and bleeding. Their rations were short, as was their ammunition, but under Johnson's magnificent leadership these superb troops remained as cheerful and disciplined as ever.

We intended to follow and harass the Italians for as long as possible, but I doubt if any of us, despite our recent victory, felt we could achieve solid success. Moreover, having no wireless, nor other communication with anybody, we felt cut off and forgotten.

Nott had brought the news that, in defiance of Cunningham's orders, Wingate had taken Haile Selassie into Addis Ababa on 5 May at the head of the remnant of the Patriot Battalion, and the Emperor had received a tremendous welcome from his liberated subjects. However, where Wingate was now Nott had no idea; perhaps detained in Addis Ababa for insubordination.

On 14 May we were camped above the small village of Derra, where the Italians had been stationary for two days, when suddenly one morning Wingate turned up, with three Patriot leaders from Fiche and four hundred of their followers. Akavia was also with him, and an English sergeant and three of the Australian sergeants from Brown's Operational Centre with a few of their men. Wingate had brought a wireless, and two mules loaded with tinned Italian meat for our hungry Sudanese. Unfortunately as the tins were marked with crosses, the Sudanese, as Muslims, refused to eat their contents and in their disgust threw the tins over a cliff.

So Wingate had come. He was a man I think we all disliked, but with his arrival the situation was transformed. Now for the first time I really appreciated his greatness. Bearded and unkempt, he had got off his mule, stared about him with searching eyes, set face and jutting jaw, then called us together. He wasted no time. He told us he intended to make the Italians surrender, and that within the next few days. As soon as the wireless was set up, he sent off an appreciation of the situation to Cunningham. The Italian force from Debra Markos was twelve thousand strong; it was now moving into country which, being both Galla and Muslim, inclined to favour the Italians; it was aimed to strengthen the Duke of Aosta's forces at Amba Alagi. Wingate intended to destroy or capture it within ten days.

The following day Wingate received a message from Cunningham ordering him to join Boustead in Gojjam, and ordering Nott to hand over the pursuit to whoever was next in command and to report to Addis Ababa. Wingate read this out with a grim smile, while we listened in disbelief. He said to Akavia, 'Send the following to the general from Wingate: "Read the appreciation I have sent you Stop." Then close down the wireless.' He got up, opened a tin of bully beef and stared north across the confusion of gorges, escarpments and isolated tablelands abutting on the Blue Nile as far as the eye could see.

'What stupendous country. It must compare with the Himalayas,' he said. Below us we could see the seemingly endless column of Italians evacuating Derra and moving off again on their way to Amba Alagi.

About nine o'clock that night Wingate sent for me.

'You will leave at once. Take Rowe and his men, the four sergeants and the three Patriot leaders and all their men with you. March without stopping until you get in front of the Italians, then engage them and make sure you inflict at least two hundred casualties. I shall follow them up and attack from this side. Their morale is bad and we're damned well going to make them surrender. Don't take any animals with you, they could delay you. Go off and get ready. Good luck.'

I don't remember what moon there was; there must have been some light. We descended the escarpment by a rough track to Derra, then followed a valley till dawn. After that I have a confused recollection of scrambling up and down the steep sides of mountains, of passing abandoned villages in valley bottoms and being fired on sporadically from cliff-tops by their inhabitants. I remember the heat in the valleys, the occasional welcome stream, the incessant strain of keeping up with these nimble mountaineers, and the disquiet of frequently looking down the barrels of their rifles, all of which were loaded, most with the safety-catch off. I remember Muhammad beside me, silent as usual, attentive and helpful as always, and my personal bodyguard always close at hand. We continued till the late afternoon, with only the briefest of halts. Then Ayalew, one of the Patriot leaders, told me that he had just heard from some villagers that the Italians were encamped on a mountain behind us.

Down the valley ahead was a typical feature of this broken landscape, another sheer-sided plateau, Ayalew said there was a track up it, with a small guard-post at the top, and a fort called Wagidi on another adjacent and connected plateau. The three Patriot leaders were agreed that our Italians must be making for Wagidi on their way to Agibar, a day's march further on, where there was apparently a large Italian garrison. Even the Abyssinians, accustomed to this sort of going, were weary, and we decided to rest where we were. Then, before dawn, we would climb the precipice ahead and surprise the guard-post.

345

This we did. The guard-post was a hut, and in it we found an old man and his five sons, asleep. When we roused them they were clearly terrified, though we assured them we intended them no harm. Muhammad made them tea and the old man told his wife to cook us some food. He informed me that another of his sons was with the twelve hundred *banda*, or local levies, holding the fort at Wagidi that we could see: it was across a gorge spanned by another panhandle. I told him to go there at once and advise the *banda* to make their escape before it was too late. Ayalew had already let him know that the Emperor was back on his throne, and he warned him that behind us followed a great army.

He went off with one of his sons, and we spent the day lazing in the sun; it was cool at this altitude. Soon after dark a rocket soared up from the fort, and later the old man came back and said the *banda* had duly deserted and the fort was now empty. We occupied it in the morning, while the Italian force from Debra Markos trailed up on to the Wagidi plateau and camped some miles away.

Next morning, the 19th, scouts from my bodyguard reported that the Italians had struck camp. Not wishing to be penned in the fort, I moved out to fight on a low ridge near the edge of the plateau we were on; if dislodged from there we would withdraw across the panhandle to the other plateau, and then hold that. As we reached our position we saw the Italians advancing across the open plain towards us in dense formation. They halted, and their first shell burst beside me, knocking me down. When I stood up my leg felt rather numb; I assumed a stone had bruised my knee, which looked grazed; however, I could hobble. Twenty-five years later, before I had a cartilage removed, the surgeon looked at the X-ray and said, 'You have a nice piece of shrapnel in your knee.'

Rowe's Vickers machine-gun was so heavy that we had left it with Wingate, but the Australians had brought their Hotchkiss automatic, a lighter weapon likewise dating from the First Word War, with drum magazines. It was often unreliable but this time served us well, while the rest of us opened fire with our rifles. What appeared to be an attack in battalion strength was by this means brought to a halt. The Italians then made a rather half-hearted charge with their native cavalry, some of whom got close enough for us to throw Mills grenades among them. Realizing that we should be surrounded if we remained here, I decided to withdraw to the panhandle.

Hobbling back with my arm over Muhammad's shoulder, I felt

the two of us offered an obvious target as the enemy occupied successive crests behind and opened fire. Having crossed the panhandle I knew we could beat off any attack, but beyond shelling us the Italians left us alone, and we watched them making camp round the fort. I now learnt that during our rather disorganized retreat Rowe had been wounded and captured: he died later in Addis Ababa. Rowe's Abyssinians had high regard for him; at Dembecha he had fought like a lion, they said. The Patriots had lost some thirty killed or missing. As for the enemy, when I eventually rejoined Wingate he said, with his grim smile, 'Well, you got your two hundred, indeed rather more, I think.'

I was surprised we had killed so many, but the fighting had been scattered and it had been difficult to see what was going on. Two days later Bimbashi Riley turned up with an Italian lieutenant and a message from Wingate. Colonel Maraventano had agreed to surrender his force, and I was now to go on to Agibar and demand the surrender of its garrison. Riley told me how Wingate had harried the Italian force during their retreat and attacked their rear while we were fighting them in front.

Soon after sunrise on 22 May we started down yet another escarpment. As we neared its foot we heard explosions, which I later learnt were from hundreds of hand-grenades back at Wagidi. The Abyssinians, convinced the Italians had treacherously attacked Wingate's force, clustered round urging me to go back and find out what had happened. I refused, and after some argument we went on. After climbing another precipice, we came to Agibar.

I sent Riley and the Italian officer into the fort under a white flag to require its commanding officer to come out and meet me. Meanwhile several hundred locals had assembled nearby under their Dedjazmatch. They shouted insults at my Abyssinians, and someone fired a shot, and then everyone started to fire their rifles. Too furious to feel frightened, I advanced on them with my interpreter and with one of my bodyguard, carrying the Abyssinian flag. I yelled at them till they stopped firing, then demanded to speak to the Dedjazmatch. When he came forward I told him that if he fired on the flag of his country he would hang, and he was to remove his rabble forthwith. He did so.

Riley emerged from the fort shortly afterwards with the Italian commander, accompanied by his medical officer who spoke English. The colonel said he was prepared to surrender the fort provided

I awarded his troops the honours of war, and provided I hoisted the British, not the Abyssinian flag in place of the Italian one. I told him that my only terms were unconditional surrender; since I was serving in the Emperor's army I should raise the Abyssinian flag over the fort. He immediately replied that his officers would never accept such terms.

'Very well,' I said. 'I admire their resolution but I hope they realize what their refusal to surrender to me will entail. Ras Kassa with his army from Shoa, Ras Ababa Aregai from Manz and thousands of Gojjam Patriots are on their way. In a few days' time they will be here. When they storm the fort, expect no mercy. This is your last chance to save your lives. If you surrender now I will escort you to Fiche. If you refuse you will have to fight it out.'

The medical officer interrupted me: 'No, no, that is not at all what we want!'

The Italian flag came down over the fort, and the Abyssinian flag rose in its place. Ayalew, Makonnen and Birru, the three Patriot leaders, were present at the ceremony, but I insisted that none of their followers should enter the fort without my permission. Shortly afterwards I found one of their men making off with a carpet; I had him taken to the gateway and flogged in front of his compatriots. I had accepted responsibility for the safety of the garrison and had only a handful of men on whom I could rely. All too easily things could get out of hand and my prisoners be massacred. A little later I heard shouting, and found another Abyssinian had been trying to steal an Italian's watch. He too was flogged. I then told Ayalew and the two other chiefs that I would hang the next unauthorized person I found inside the fort, and ordered them to warn their men again. This put a stop to it.

Meanwhile Riley and the sergeants were collecting all the rifles and machine-guns and removing their bolts, which they packed in boxes: I intended that the garrison should carry their weapons back to Fiche for us like this. We also found in the fort an enormous amount of ammunition. I saw no reason why this should fall into the hands of the locals, after their earlier demonstration, so I told the Patriot leaders they could send their men, in small parties under guard, to remove it. They, I felt, did deserve it.

I had already sent a runner to Wingate informing him that the fort had surrendered, and he replied, telling me to march the garrison to Fiche. They numbered some two thousand five hundred. Wingate's messenger described to me how Wingate had received Colonel Maraventano's surrender standing in front of the much reduced company of the Sudan Defence Force, a handful of men confronting an army; it was exactly ten days since he had sent his appreciation to Cunningham. Before they surrendered, some of the Italian troops had thrown their grenades over the cliff, and only stopped when Wingate threatened to open fire on them: those were the explosions we heard as we went down the escarpment.

I think it took us four days to reach Fiche; it may have been longer. To me the march seemed interminable, worried as I was that the locals might attack our mile-long column of unarmed men, cumbered with women and children. All would be tempted by prospects of loot; many had scores to settle. Indeed they followed us on the march, and hung about when we camped. All carried rifles. Before we left Agibar I had impressed upon the Patriot leaders their responsibility to help me get the Emperor's prisoners safely to Fiche; and they undertook to do so. Each day I went in front with my own men, while Riley and the sergeants shepherded the rear.

At Fiche I thankfully handed them over to Wingate, who arranged for them to join his other prisoners. These would now total 282 Italian officers, 800 Italian other ranks and 14,500 native troops. He had captured 4 field guns, 8 pack guns, 4 mortars, 60 heavy machine-guns, 161 light machine-guns and 12,000 rifles. This success marked the climax of his achievements. He had set out from the Sudan with two battalions, one Sudanese and one Abyssinian, armed, in addition to their rifles, only with a mortar, a Vickers machine-gun and a few Brens; with the help of the Patriot forces, he had fulfilled his promise to the Emperor and liberated Gojjam.

When I reported to Wingate in Fiche I felt I had redeemed my failure at the Blue Nile Gorge. I realized that I owed my success to him. He could easily have denied me another chance, but he had always appreciated my passionate involvement with the Abyssinian cause. Months later I heard that he had recommended me for a DSO. In due course I received this award which, for a subaltern, was far beyond my expectations.

Unfortunately, on almost the last occasion I was with him, Wingate behaved in a typically brutal fashion. I mention the incident because it helps to assess the character of this controversial figure.

Wearing his dressing gown, he went to the compound where the captured weapons were stored; they were held on behalf of the

Emperor, under the guard of a Dedjazmatch. The Dedjazmatch held up his hand and said, 'No one is allowed in here.'

'Don't you know who I am ?' Wingate snarled, and struck the old man across the face with his cane. There was a rattle of bolts as the guard loaded their rifles, and I was convinced we would both be shot, but Wingate paid no attention. He strode past, selected a revolver which he intended to give to someone, and walked out.

Shortly after this Wingate was ordered to report to Cunningham at his headquarters in Harar. The general was anxious to get him out of the country: Wingate had already defied his orders by conducting the Emperor from Debra Markos to Addis Ababa, and Cunningham was determined that, with his pre-war reputation for political intrigue in Palestine, he should not further complicate the difficult relationship between the military administration and the Emperor. He now sent him to Cairo at the first opportunity. On his departure from Abyssinia many people must have felt, 'Now, thank God, we're rid of Wingate.' When he went on to even greater things in Burma he provoked the same antagonisms.

Orde Wingate, with T. E. Lawrence, has an established place in British history. The exploits of both men have the dramatic quality that ensures lasting fame: today, although his contribution to final victory was negligible, Lawrence's name is more generally known than that of any general in the First World War. In time the same may apply to Wingate. In both cases it was their character rather than their achievements that made them unique. Much has been written about Lawrence, almost nothing at first hand about Wingate; and many of the people who knew him in his Abyssinian campaign are now dead. Christopher Sykes, who wrote the best biography about him, never met him. Sykes spent several hours with me discussing Wingate, and I told him everything I remembered. In his biography, he chose to omit two incidents that I have described which illustrate Wingate's ungovernable temper. I think he was wrong to do so, and have included them not to denigrate Wingate, but because I consider he was of sufficient historical importance for every incident that reveals his character to be worth recording.

Wingate was ruthlessly ambitious, yet his aims transcended personal ambition. He was an idealist and a fanatic. He needed a cause with which he could identify himself, but his intolerance and arrogance required him to be in command. He should have lived in the time of the Crusades. I can picture him in that brutal age, fighting with a mad gleam in his eye to liberate the Holy City, but equally determined, when it fell, to be crowned King of Jerusalem.

Just after Wingate left Fiche the Emperor announced that he intended to come there and hold a parade of his prisoners. Nott sent me to Colonel Maraventano to tell him of the Emperor's decision.

'It's not civilized,' the colonel protested. 'It's barbarous to humiliate prisoners so.'

I felt no vestige of sympathy.

'Don't dare to speak to me about barbarous treatment of prisoners,' I replied. 'You Italians shot Ras Desta, the Emperor's son-in-law, who commanded the armies in the south, after he had surrendered to Marshal Graziani. You Italians shot Ras Kassa's sons after they had surrendered to you. You shot four hundred priests near here in the monastery of Debra Libanos. Your blackshirts massacred ten thousand men, women and children in Addis Ababa after you took the town. Now you have the effrontery to stand there and talk about barbarous treatment of prisoners. A few days ago in Agibar I found photographs of your officers holding by the hair the severed heads of Abyssinians, with their feet on the corpses. Perhaps you yourself took part in the Roman triumph which Mussolini held in Rome at the end of the war, when Abyssinian prisoners were paraded. Now it's your turn. Tomorrow at ten o'clock you will march past the Emperor or be driven past him by Ras Kassa's men. I don't care which.'

The parade next day was quiet and orderly. Guarded by Johnson's Sudanese, their Bren guns manned, the Emperor sat in an open-sided tent with his son Asfa Wossen, Chapman-Andrews and a few retainers. The presence of this small, indomitable man endowed the proceedings with a strange dignity and significance. For him, as ruler of a warrior race, the parade may well have been a necessary manifestation of victory, but no hint of triumph showed on his face; he watched in silence, his expression sombre and rather sad. Ras Kassa, old and heavy, sat his mule between Johnson and myself, and watched with an impassive face the parade of the men who had murdered his sons. Nor did the assembled crowds, women as well as men, give vent to their feelings, though the relatives of many had died at Italian hands.

351

When the parade was over I motored with Chapman-Andrews to
Addis Ababa where we stayed with Sandford in his old house. I
attended a banquet given by the Emperor in his palace for the British
officers who had served in his army. Wingate was not there; otherwise the occasion was a fitting and memorable conclusion to the
Gojjam campaign.

I heard later that Wingate had arrived in Cairo in early June to find
himself without a job and with instructions to revert to the rank of
major. Disasters in Greece and in the desert absorbed everyone's
attention. Few people had heard of his exploits in Gojjam. He was
already feeling bitter and resentful at the lack of support he had been
given during the campaign, at the attempt to recall him before his
victory at Wagidi, and at his summary dismissal from the country.
He wandered about Headquarters but no one wished to employ
him.

Finally he was instructed to write a report on the operations in
Gojjam. When he wrote it he was suffering from recurrent attacks of
malaria and the accumulated strain of the past months. The report,
as was to be expected, was extremely controversial, expounding a
new theory of guerrilla warfare, but also containing critical and
unflattering passages about his superiors. To disparage some of
them he used his favourite expression, 'military apes', and he
described some of the officers who had served under him as 'the
scum of the cavalry brigade'.

General Wavell read the report and recorded that it would almost
justify placing Wingate under arrest for insubordination. At first he
was inclined to suppress the report, but eventually decided to
circulate a limited number of copies after the most offensive passages had been deleted. He did, however, order enquiries to be
made into a number of Wingate's complaints. The report caused
great resentment, and the enquiries which resulted from it even
more.

Wingate must by now have realized how intensely he was disliked, and have felt concerned whether he would be given any
further worthwhile employment. He had as yet received no award
for his services in Abyssinia and little sign of approbation, though
he was later awarded a bar to his DSO.

He had fought his campaign in Gojjam to restore Haile Selassie to his throne and to right the wrongs done to him and to his people. Now he became obsessed by the conviction that the British intended to deprive Abyssinia of her independence. He viewed the Enemy Occupied Territories Administration, which had been set up in Abyssinia, with profound mistrust; it had certainly been extraordinarily inept in its dealing with the Emperor.

Wingate's conviction that we were going to let down the Abyssinians affords an interesting analogy with Lawrence and the Arabs. Lawrence's apprehension was justified; Wingate's was not, as he could have discovered by making a few enquiries from Chapman-Andrews, who was in Cairo. But by now Wingate was past the stage of rational behaviour. He was treating his malaria with massive doses of Atabrin, and physically was in a state of near collapse. Frantic with worry and despair, he one day cut his throat in his hotel, but unaccountably did not do it thoroughly. His odd behaviour as he went to his room had attracted attention; he was found collapsed on the floor and was taken to hospital. Later he recorded, 'I thought our treatment of Ethiopia cold and tyrannical, and our talk of liberation miserable cant. I thought my death at my own hand would make people pause and think.'

When I heard the news I was haunted by the thought of Wingate alone in his hotel bedroom, desolate and devoid of hope. The tragedy was deepened by the fact that someone as magnanimous as Hugh Boustead could have been so provoked that he now felt impelled to visit Wingate in hospital and say to him, 'You bloody fool, why didn't you use a revolver?'

Some of Wingate's detractors have since claimed that Boustead could have accomplished as much in Gojjam with none of the antagonism and disorganization which Wingate created. Boustead had indeed had considerable and varied experience of war, but he lacked Wingate's originality of thought, bold imagination and ruthless single-mindedness. In my opinion, no other officer in Platt's or Cunningham's army could have achieved what Wingate did, with the force at his disposal.

Wingate was sent back to England as soon as he was sufficiently recovered. Mentally he was still a very sick man and owed his recovery in large part to the treatment he received from a great physician, Lord Horder. Typically, his first remark to Horder was, 'You know, I am not the only great soldier who has tried to commit suicide. There was Napoleon, for instance.'

Eventually Horder was able to assure the War Office of Wingate's mental fitness; this saved him from compulsory retirement, and enabled him to go on and win lasting fame with his Chindits in Burma.

CHAPTER 25

The Druze

THE DAY AFTER Haile Selassie's banquet in Addis Ababa I was given orders to report to GHQ in Cairo because I was to join Glubb Pasha's Arab Legion in Trans-Jordan. This meant that I had to catch a ship at Massawa, so there I went by way of Asmara in a civilian car which I commandeered, driven by an Italian. We passed through Dessie, capital of Wollo, and under the bastion of Amba Alagi, which had recently fallen to General Platt. Everywhere were detachments of South African and, further on, British and Indian troops, camped along the road or moving in convoy. It was my first sight of a modern army on active service, and I found it impressive and exciting.

From Massawa I sailed to Port Said in a troopship filled with South Africans. On reaching Cairo I reported at Army Headquarters, but was told that the Arab Legion post had been filled and that I was to go back to the Sudan Defence Force in Abyssinia.

It was June 1941 and British forces that had recently invaded Syria were meeting with unexpected and bitter resistance from the Vichy French. Since the major interviewing me in Cairo was obviously sympathetic, I suggested he should find me a job in Syria; I mentioned that I had travelled in that country and was familiar with Jabal Druze. This proved to be a fortunate remark. He told me that the British advance on Damascus was being held up at Deraa, a name with which I was familiar from a well-known episode in Lawrence's *Seven Pillars*, and that General Wilson believed that the French withdrawal would be hastened by a threat of insurrection in Jabal Druze. To this end Colonel Gerald de Gaury was raising a Druze Legion. Would I like to be his second-in-command? I jumped at the offer, was given a King's commission this time, with the rank of major, and was sent next day to join de Gaury at Mafraq in Trans-Jordan.

When I arrived there de Gaury was busy recruiting Druze; some were deserters from the French forces, others were civilians. Since there were no British rifles to spare, we gave them Italian rifles

355

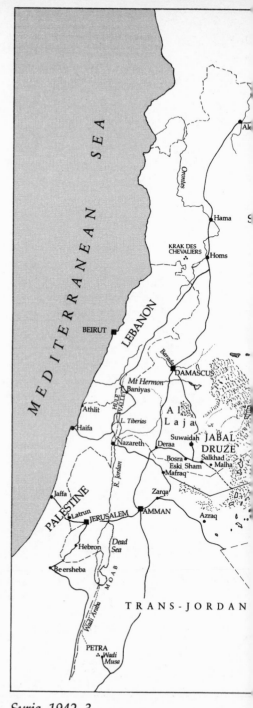

Syria, 1942–3

captured in the Western Desert. Four days later I crossed the Syrian frontier into Jabal Druze with the equivalent of a squadron of mounted Druze, all armed but utterly disorganized. After an hour or so I stopped, and told them to hold a meeting and select two men as officers and others as NCOs. This unorthodox method worked well, and while I was with this unit I never had cause to take any disciplinary action. Admittedly, when I next met de Gaury he remonstrated with me for commissioning officers without authority, but it was the only disagreement I ever had with him.

Jabal Druze was in no sense a real mountain, but consisted of high ground rising in places to small hills, none of them steep. At this time of year, the crops having been gathered, the countryside in general gave the impression of a desolate volcanic waste. Its many vineyards, however, produced the best grapes I have ever eaten. I made my headquarters at Malha, which we reached in a day from Mafraq. Here we were welcomed by the villagers and feasted by the elders. Like other Druze villages, Malha consisted of massively built, flat-roofed houses. I occupied a spacious room built of basalt blocks with two solid arches supporting the roof; a stone bench ran round three of the walls; as in all these houses, the only furnishings were rugs and cushions. The rest of the squadron found quarters in the village with relations or friends.

I had an orderly, Faris Shahin, who looked after me and shared my quarters; he had been selected for me by Captain Fawwaz, who had been chosen as my second-in-command; Faris was related to him by marriage and belonged to the highly respected Hanawi family. He was intelligent, literate like all the Druze, well informed and universally popular, but was only about sixteen, with the almost girlish good looks that characterized many Druze boys. Yet any impression of gentleness was misleading; he had a fierce pride in himself and his family. I once saw him roused when someone referred slightingly to the Hanawis: his hand was close to his dagger and he looked really dangerous.

The more I saw of the Druze the more I liked and admired them; I was delighted by their spontaneous friendliness and hospitality, and was always conscious of their pride as a warrior race. My relations with my squadron were deliberately informal: I saw myself as their leader rather than their commanding officer. Their value to us was as an irregular force closely associated with their kinsmen in the surrounding villages, so I wanted no nonsense with orderly-room, parade-ground drill or saluting. I asked only for the respect they gave their own leaders, and this they accorded me.

The Druze are not Arabs, nor Muslims. They derive from the inhabitants of the Lebanon, among some of whom the Druze cult took root in the eleventh century. This esoteric cult confirms the divinity of al-Hakim, sixth of the Fatimid rulers of Egypt, who came to the throne at the age of eleven in AD 988 and ruled for twenty-five years. He was an unbalanced, cruel and tyrannical man whose pretensions knew no bounds, and who went on to proclaim himself divine; he was eventually murdered in Cairo.

Shortly before his death he had despatched Durazi, one of his disciples, to proselytize the inhabitants of the Lebanon: Durazi's converts were the original Druze. Their numbers multiplied, but until the second half of the nineteenth century they remained based on the Lebanese mountains. In 1860, incited by the Turks, the Druze were largely responsible for an indiscriminate slaughter of Maronite Christians in this corner of the Turkish Empire. However, when a French force landed to avenge the massacre, the Turks disowned them, whereupon many left the Lebanon, migrated to Syria and settled in that part of the Hauran which came to be known as Jabal Druze. When they arrived, it was a volcanic wilderness inhabited only by Arab nomads, but the area had once been a flourishing outpost of the Roman Empire and the Druze found ruins of ancient towns and villages there. They repaired some houses, built others of similar design, and began to cultivate the fertile volcanic soil.

After the First World War, the French were given a Mandate over Syria and the Lebanon, but their rule was universally unpopular and in 1924 the Druze rebelled. I was several times told by elders in Malha of the dramatic event that had roused the Jabal. A man who was wanted by the French authorities had sought sanctuary with the most renowned of the Druze, Sultan Pasha al-Atrash. A few days later a French officer with an armed escort arrived at Sultan Pasha's house and ordered him to hand the man over. Sultan Pasha refused, since to hand over someone who had asked for and been granted asylum would be a shameful violation of tribal custom. The officer thereupon removed the man by force and drove off. Sultan Pasha and his followers mounted their horses and waylaid the car on its way back to Suwaidah. Sultan Pasha cut off the officer's head with one blow of his sword, so my informants insisted, and his followers killed the escort. That night beacons blazed on the roofs throughout the Jabal and the Druze gathered for war.

Under the leadership of Sultan Pasha they destroyed a French force three thousand strong sent from Damascus to relieve the beleaguered garrison in Suwaidah. They then advanced on Damascus and occupied part of the city, which the French shelled from the nearby hills. The rebellion, supported by Druze in the Lebanon, spread across most of Syria and was only suppressed two years later, after the French had poured troops into the country. The Druze were the last to submit.

From Malha I visited the neighbouring villages with my squadron. In each of them I listened to interminable speeches of goodwill for the British, and had to make a suitable reply to each; no easy task, for the Druze spoke a classical Arabic very different from the Arabic I had learnt among the Zaghawah and Maidob in the Sudan. In every village we were given a banquet which, even if we had arrived in the early morning, would never be ready till the late afternoon. Meanwhile we would be served in turn, again and again, with a few drops of bitter cardamom-flavoured coffee in the bottom of a small cup.

This endless feasting seemed an odd way to wage war; yet it was effective. From most of the surrounding villages we could see the fort on the hill above the little town of Salkhad, garrisoned by the only French troops nearer than Suwaidah. Once when we got too close they shelled us; otherwise they took no action, and we were content to keep out of range. It was our mere presence, rather than our numbers or military effectiveness, that constituted the threat; as a hostile Druze force we might well instigate widespread rebellion in the Jabal; and the Jabal lay on the flank of French communications between Deraa and Damascus.

I was convinced that the French in Salkhad must know of the deputations of elders from all parts of the Jabal who were visiting me in Malha to affirm their allegiance to the British. Among these visitors was Sultan Pasha al-Atrash himself, who had been one of my boyhood heroes. Now, when I met him, he did not disappoint me; though utterly without ostentation, his presence commanded immediate respect. His face, framed in a white headcloth, was austere and authoritative; his body, wrapped in a black cloak of finest weave, was lean and upright. His was a social call, however;

alone among my visitors he professed no allegiance to the British. The French had allowed him to return to the Jabal from exile on condition that he would engage in no further action against them, and now he kept his word.

Most evenings Faris and I were invited with the rest of the squadron to one or other of the houses in Malha for the customary Druze *mansaf* of mutton and boiled wheat, heaped on a large circular dish and drenched with liquid butter. I liked the food and always enjoyed these evenings. After everyone had fed, the young men and boys danced to the music of their pipes, the assembly sang rousing war songs, someone recited poetry to a hushed audience, or we just sat and talked. The elders remembered the days of Turkish rule and the Arab Revolt. They described Faisal's entry into Damascus, the frenzied excitement, the press of armed men on camels and horses, the banners and the massed tribal singing. They spoke, too, of their rebellion under Sultan Pasha against the French, when even young boys and old men had fought on the lava fields around Suwaidah.

At Malha we were joined by Faris's father, Shahin, a blind and gentle individual whom Faris treated with devotion. Shahin was a well-known poet, and in the evenings was sometimes persuaded to recite. He had a fine voice, and when he declaimed he was transformed, and swept his audience into the past with him, while I, understanding little of his verses, had to be content with their rhythm. Faris's grandfather also visited us, a striking figure, white-bearded but alert, wearing the small compact white turban of a religious elder; he had considerable standing in the important Hanawi clan.

The Druze, with their secret religion, were regarded with misgiving by their Muslim neighbours, so young Druze men tended to stay in their villages instead of drifting off elsewhere to find work. Druze society was therefore close-knit and exclusive. Here at Malha I encountered for the first time a civilized community that observed the traditional Arab code of behaviour, but held to their own ancient customs and dress. I found their way of life, little affected by change elsewhere, satisfying as a reminder of an Eastern world of fifty years before.

Gerald de Gaury had moved from Mafraq to Bosra eski Sham,

where he had established his headquarters in the massive castle built by the Saracens round a well-preserved Roman amphitheatre. He sent for me and I rode there with my squadron across the Jabal; as we approached we could see the castle from afar. As well as commanding the Druze Legion, de Gaury was Political Officer to Brigadier Keith Dunn, who commanded the 5th Cavalry Brigade; accordingly many Arab sheikhs and their retainers visited him; some, like the grandson of Audah Abu Tayyi of the Huwaitat, bore famous names. I was struck by the constant coming and going of these impressive figures.

Gawain Bell, whom I had met for the first time at Mafraq, commanded another Druze squadron. He too was from the Sudan Political Service, but unlike myself was a brilliant Arabic speaker. De Gaury sent us both with our squadrons to patrol towards Suwaidah, but all we encountered was some long-range rifle fire.

I liked de Gaury, an eminently civilized man, courteous, well-informed and always impeccably dressed. However, he was then transferred to Cairo, and I found myself temporarily in command of the Druze Legion until the arrival of Colonel Buller from the Trans-Jordan Frontier Force. Buller, unlike de Gaury, was a professional soldier and even now in wartime showed exasperating preoccupation with the formalities and ceremonial of peacetime soldiering. After the French forces in Syria had surrendered on 14 July 1941 he remarked to Jack Collard, his adjutant, 'Now we can get down to some proper soldiering.' Foreseeing that he would expect me to remain with him at his headquarters, I suggested he should appoint another officer second-in-command, and leave me with my squadron. He readily agreed.

After the Vichy French surrender the British assumed the administration of Syria, with the Druze Legion as part of the occupying force. At Malha my cavalry squadron was replaced by a newly raised Druze camel squadron, more suited to patrolling the lava desert to the east. At my request Buller agreed I should stay and take it over.

I was sorry to part from my old squadron but I was soon even happier with the new one. I was more interested in camels than in horses, and I bought a particularly fine thoroughbred for my own use; with her coloured, woven saddlebags and tasselled trappings she looked splendid. Faris remained as my orderly, and I was lucky to have Salih Ma'z as my second-in-command, a very capable officer who had served under the French and was much respected by the people of Malha. I had already met him, in 1936, when he had been in charge of the party that took me from Suwaidah to Azraq.

Life in Malha went on much as before but now, instead of keeping watch on Salkhad, we patrolled the lava fields and kept an eye on the scattered encampments of shepherd tribes. These were dependent on pools of rainwater and on patches of grass that grew in hollows among the lava. Such was my introduction to the black tents of Arabia. These shepherd tribes ranked low in the hierarchy of the desert, but we found them embarrassingly hospitable, reluctant even to use our rations despite their evident poverty.

In November 1941 it was decided that the Free French should administer Jabal Druze, and the Druze Legion should move to Palestine. By now, much as I enjoyed my time with the Druze, I was getting restive, and anxious for a more active part in the war; I hoped to get to the Western Desert

The snag was that I belonged to no established army unit. The Druze Legion came under Special Operations Executive, generally referred to as SOE, and it was to them that I applied for a transfer. Since it now seemed very possible that the Germans, who had invaded Russia in June, would overrun Syria by way of the Caucasus, SOE instructed me to make plans to stay behind in Syria should this happen. I was glad to do so, knowing I should have an interesting time preparing for this eventuality, and plenty of excitement if the Germans did arrive. In the meanwhile, SOE arranged for me to take an explosives course in Palestine, but gave me a week's leave before the course started.

This leave I spent visiting Petra in Trans-Jordan, at a time when, owing to the war, there were no tourists to deprive me of my sense of discovery. Accompanied by an Arab legionary from the fort in the Wadi Musa and a shepherd from a neighbouring encampment, I rode down the long, narrow, sheer-sided gorge that leads to Petra. Suddenly, unexpectedly, twenty yards ahead, framed by the cliffs on either side, I saw part of the Khaznah, the Treasure House. A few paces further, the whole monument was visible, rose-coloured in the reflected light, carved into the cliff that faced me. This astonishing edifice, built in the fourth century BC by the Nabataeans, was more than sixty feet high. Its lower storey consisted of a six-columned Corinthian portico; above this six more columns supported a broken pediment and a circular structure surmounted by a conical roof and urn. I could imagine Burckhardt's awe on first seeing it in 1812, his excitement as he wondered what further marvels awaited his discovery.

After spending the night in one of the man-made caves, we climbed to the Dair soon after sunrise, by a staircase cut in the face of the mountain. The Dair resembled the Khaznah, and of all the monuments in Petra these two, seen from outside with their bizarre classical façades, are the most impressive. Inside, by contrast, they are cramped and uninteresting. From the Dair I looked over a chaos of rock pinnacles, precipices and gorges, where the green of an occasional bush only emphasized the landscape's desolation. We visited many other monuments, which varied in design and appearance, some rough-hewn and some unfinished; I remember in particular the Palace Tomb, the Tomb of the Lion and one other, where bands of different coloured rock gave a striking impression of watered silk.

From Petra I went to Latrun in Palestine where, incongruously housed in the monastery, some twenty officers, including several Australians, were to attend the explosives course. Here, for a month, we were taught about demolition, sabotage, armed and unarmed combat, ambushes and night operations. I found the surrounding countryside very lovely, with the same weathered beauty that can be seen in Greece; during our scant time off I wandered happily among these Judaean hills. I still remember coming across some cyclamens among the rocks, promise of a spring as yet far off.

Towards the end of our course we ran short of things to blow up. One evening our chief instructor returned from Sarafand with a sea mine in the back of his lorry: since it had been too bulky for the blast furnace at Sarafand he had been given it to play with, on the understanding that he returned the pieces. Next morning, after we had taken the mine in the lorry to a nearby field, the assistant instructor detailed me to cut a panel a foot square in the side of it. I suggested a method using gelignite and a short fuse. He approved and I attached the charge. We withdrew about fifty yards.

'We'd better get down behind that rock in case pieces fly about,' he told the course.

A minute later the mine went up. I noticed some Arabs, who were ploughing on a nearby hillside, take off across the fields. Our chief instructor, who was away in Sarafand, heard the explosion, saw the resultant column of smoke, and raced back to Latrun, convinced we had blown up the explosives store.

I enjoyed the course but I did wonder if I should ever have occasion to put into practice the skills I was learning. It was here at Latrun in December 1941 that we heard one evening that the *Repulse* and the *Prince of Wales* had been sunk. No other disaster during the war seemed as shattering.

As soon as the course finished I went to Damascus, to be joined by Lieutenant Edward Henderson, sent from Cairo to collaborate with me. For me this was a happy choice and the beginning of a lasting friendship; for Henderson it was his introduction to the Arab world, where he was later to make his name in the Gulf States. Our plan was to travel widely over Syria, familiarize ourselves with the lie of the land, and get to know as many townsmen, villagers and tribesmen as possible. We should then be able to select suitable areas from which to operate when the Germans arrived. We decided to start with Damascus and its surroundings.

In 1936, on my way back to the Sudan, I had spent a day or two in Damascus and been rather disappointed by the city. Both the Turks and the French had disfigured it; the Turks with a large tarmac square, past which they had channelled the Barada river in a concrete ditch, and the French with incongruous concrete buildings; even the 'street called Straight' had been roofed with iron sheeting, probably as a result of the French bombardment in 1924. But the great Omayyad mosque, built at the beginning of the eighth century, was magnificent, and Henderson and I soon found that the remoter parts of the city were still unspoilt. On the outskirts was a paradise of orchards, gardens and flowing water, particularly beautiful in spring when the almond and peach trees were in blossom.

One night Colonel Elphinstone, who had responsibility for British relations with the Arabs and was always helpful to us, took us to see the Whirling Dervishes. We went first to the palace of Abd al-Qadir in the heart of the old city. The Amir was the grandson of the renowned Abd al-Qadir who had fought so valiantly against the French in Algeria from 1832 to 1847. He had been captured, imprisoned and eventually released, and he spent the rest of his life in Damascus. There, during the massacres in 1860, this chivalrous man rode into the city, outfaced the frenzied, murderous mob and rescued such Christians as he could.

We walked down a silent, empty street to the Amir's palace. As with all those old Arab houses, the front facing the street was blank except for the entrance. We knocked, the door opened and the Amir came forward, greeted us and led us inside. He himself made little impression on me: I cannot now remember what he looked like nor what he wore; but his palace delighted me. The spacious rooms were built round an inner court where a fountain played among fruit trees, and through a window I saw and heard the Barada, here free of its canal, flowing against an outer wall. The ceiling was carved and richly painted; on the floor were beautiful old rugs. There were some couches, a few small tables, but no other furniture. Here was simplicity combined with splendour, the bareness of the nomad's tent blended with the refinement of town life.

After we had drunk coffee and eaten some sweetmeats, our host escorted us to the Dervish monastery. These Dervishes belonged to the Mevlevi order founded in the thirteenth century by Jallal al Din al Rumi. Their headquarters had been at Konya in Turkey, where their founder was buried, until Atatürk, in his determination to modernize the country, had closed the monastery in 1925. Here in Damascus the Dervishes still performed their traditional cere-monies.

When we arrived they were praying, and we were ushered into a room to be served coffee; half an hour later we were conducted to a court where we joined the congregation sitting along the walls. I was very conscious that for them this was a significant religious occasion, not just, as it was for us, an interesting spectacle.

The Sheikh of the Dervishes beat on a tambourine, a boy sitting beside him kept time on cymbals, and the Dervishes lining two sides of the court chanted in unison, a surging hypnotic rhythm of devo-tional Arabic. Then, slowly and impassively, three men and a boy moved forward to the centre of the court. The men were dressed in white, the boy in emerald green; all wore long full-skirted robes, tight-fitting at the waist, and tall, conical, brown felt caps. They stood for a while, silent and motionless, then clasped their hands on their chests and began to rotate, using the right foot as a pivot. Very slowly they raised their arms above their heads, then lowered them horizontally with open, drooping hands. As they spun round and round they appeared utterly oblivious of their surroundings.

Ten minutes later the chanting stopped, and they ceased rotating. After a pause the chanting was renewed, and the three men, but not the boy, took up their positions again. The music grew louder, even more urgent and compelling: I seem to recollect the sound of pipes and the beat of a drum in addition to the clash of cymbals and the thud of the tambourine. The three expressionless white-clad figures spun for half an hour, their skirts rising in hoops around them. Another pause, then once again they took the floor. When the ceremony ended, the Sheikh invited us to remain while the congregation and Dervishes prayed. Even as a spectator I had been carried out of myself. Now I came slowly back to earth.

During the ensuing months Henderson and I travelled over much of Syria. We visited Homs, and the strangely sinister town of Hama where enormous waterwheels creaked day and night, and Aleppo, that had once been Saladin's capital; his massive citadel, though damaged by earthquakes, still dominated the town. There we wandered for hours in the *suqs*, shadowy alleyways crowded with visiting Bedu.

I was familiar with Doughty's *Arabia Deserta* and Lawrence's *Seven Pillars* and I had read a number of other books about the desert Arabs. Now, for the first time, I encountered the great tribes of northern Arabia. Henderson and I watched the Shammar migrating, a nation on the move. We visited the Ruallah in their summer camp near Damascus, a city of black tents spread over the desert. There we met Nuri al-Shalan, their famous Amir. A quarter of a century earlier, when Nuri brought the Ruallah to join Faisal's army for the final advance on Damascus, Lawrence had described him as an old man. Now he must have been old indeed; yet he did not give that impression, for though his face was lined, his hair was dyed black and he moved without difficulty and sat very upright, alert to all that went on around him. He was still undisputed ruler of his tribe; his merest glance commanded immediate attention.

With his kinsmen and his guests, in his distinctive white open-fronted tent that was supported on as many as ten poles, we feasted, feeding in relays from an enormous platter, brought in by slaves, on which a dismembered camel colt rested on a mountain of rice soaked in liquid butter. After so greasy a meal the bitter black coffee was welcome. Sitting there, I watched the camel herds being driven to

367

the wells; Arabs riding past on their thoroughbred mares; all the coming and going around the tents. We spoke of Lawrence, after whom Nuri had named a son. I asked how good Lawrence's Arabic had been, and the answers varied: some said nearly perfect, others said indifferent, but all spoke of Lawrence with great respect.

We stayed in all the cities of Syria and the Lebanon, and in villages, and in the tents of the Bedu, and we visited several Christian monasteries. We met a great variety of people, Arabs, Turks, Circassians, Alawites and Druze, and took the opportunity to see something of the Crusader castles. Of these, Krak des Chevaliers was the most impressive and best preserved. Some Arab families were then living within its walls; when I went back after the war they had been turned out, and with them the last sense of continuity had gone; Krak des Chevaliers had become yet another ancient monument for tourists.

Eventually Henderson and I decided that the lava fields of the Laja in the Hauran would afford the most satisfactory hideout. Here there were numerous caves between the lava and the underlying rock, and for centuries these had provided a safe refuge to outlaws and other wanted men. Even from close at hand they were difficult to locate. Moreover, they were within reach of the main road south from Damascus, which would enable us to watch and report on the traffic using it, and perhaps do some sabotage; they were also close to Jabal Druze where I had many friends. From this base, our by now extensive knowledge of Syria and the Lebanon would enable us to travel about the country, and then our many contacts should prove useful.

However, the German threat to Syria vanished when their army became bogged down in Russia; and as time went by I was transferred to Cairo at my own request, still hoping to operate behind enemy lines in Libya.

CHAPTER 26

With the SAS
in the Western Desert

I N Cairo I stayed in a hotel and went each day to Grey Pillars, the massive building where SOE had their headquarters. There I found myself sharing an office with Pat Domville, a rather unconvincing Wing-Commander who had spent years as a Staff Officer in Iraq. He seemed to have little to do but gossip. I was given vague assurances that I should shortly be dropped behind the enemy lines in Cyrenaica by the Long Range Desert Group, but there was no sort of briefing for the job I was to do. The days ran into weeks and I was still hanging about Grey Pillars.

With plenty of spare time, I explored Cairo's Old City, where the Citadel, surmounted by the Muhammad Ali mosque and its tapering minarets, stood out sharp against a cloudless sky. Mosques of different periods and designs, minarets, vaulted tombs, massive gateways in fragments of walls, ancient latticed houses, were all scattered unpredictably throughout a maze of narrow streets.

Of the Eastern cities I had seen, medieval Cairo impressed me as the most authentic, the least affected by contact with the West. The crowds still wore native dress, the men in long white gowns and turbans, the women swathed in black; I thoroughly enjoyed wandering among them. As a member of SOE, I was entitled to wear civilian clothes instead of uniform; this made me less conspicuous, and speaking Arabic helped. I liked to sit sipping tea in one of the many open-fronted booths that lined the streets, and to watch the passing crowd, while I bargained for a carpet, an old Turkish dagger, a length of silk, an amber rosary, or a piece of silverwork: anything could be found here if one knew where to look. Porters, bowed under heavy loads, shouted 'Balak! balak!' to clear a passage; donkey carts, piled high, moved forward through the crowd a few paces at a time; small boys dodged about carrying trays of tea; a group of bearded, turbanned *mullahs*, wrapped in cloaks and sanctity, entered a mosque; a *muezzin* gave the long, lingering call to

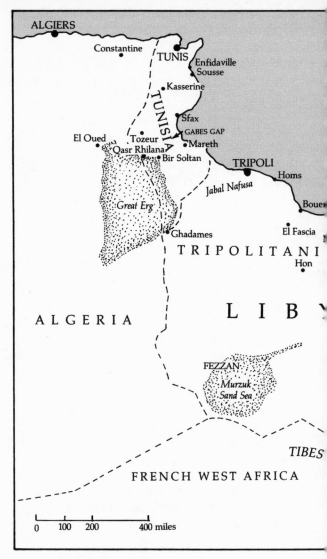

Western Desert, 1939–42

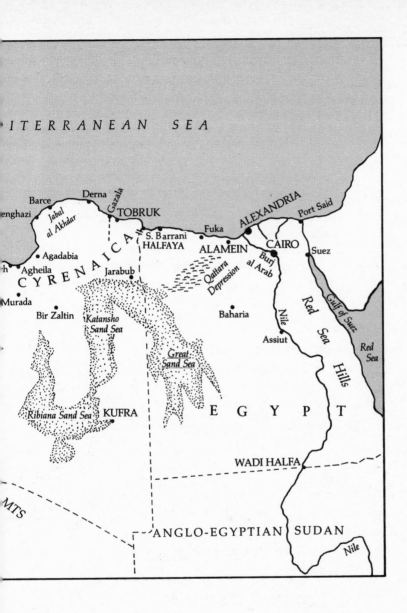

MEDITERRANEAN SEA

Benghazi
Barce
Derna
Gazala
TOBRUK
Jabal al Akhdar
Agadabia
Agheila
CYRENAICA
Murada
Jarabub
Bir Zaltin
Katansho Sand Sea
Great Sand Sea
Ribiana Sand Sea
KUFRA

S. Barrani
HALFAYA
Fuka
ALAMEIN
Buri al Arab
Qattara Depression
Baharia
Assiut

ALEXANDRIA
Port Said
CAIRO
Suez

Nile
Red Sea Hills
Gulf of Suez
Red Sea

E G Y P T

WADI HALFA

MTS

ANGLO-EGYPTIAN SUDAN

Nile

prayer. Here was colour, squalor, dirt, poverty, with good humour swiftly erupting into sudden brawls, and a variety of pervasive smells.

While I was in Cairo there had been heavy fighting in the desert and it was soon evident that things were going badly for the Eighth Army. On 26 May 1942 Rommel had attacked the Gazala Line. General Ritchie, commanding the Eighth Army, failed to drive Rommel from the Cauldron and suffered heavy losses, especially with his armour: by 12 June he had withdrawn and on the 21st Rommel captured Tobruk with thirty-three thousand prisoners.

General Auchinleck, Commander-in-Chief in the Middle East, dismissed Ritchie, took personal command of the Eighth Army and withdrew to the Alamein position, which he reached on 30 June. There, only sixty miles from Alexandria, he halted Rommel's advance; but in Cairo everyone was wondering how long he would manage to hold the Alamein Line. The whole of Egypt seemed to be at risk and the Canal was threatened. Headquarters and the Embassy burnt their files, and young officers flippantly referred to Ash Wednesday.

Domville now asked me to stay behind in Cairo if the Germans occupied the city, an assignment I accepted without enthusiasm. Despite my rambles in the Old City, I knew Cairo only superficially. I felt little real affinity with its inhabitants, had no friends among them, and indeed had never been inside an Egyptian house. Domville now introduced me to three sophisticated Egyptians, assuring me that they were devoted to the British cause and would give me every help. I found it difficult to believe they would be prepared to risk their lives to assist an Englishman they did not know, taking into account the nationalist feeling against the British.

Domville also put me in touch with a British wireless operator and gave me a belt full of sovereigns and a packet of uncut diamonds. Realizing that I should be here for a long time, unless I was soon arrested by the Germans, which seemed more than probable, I bought a quantity of things at the NAAFI, and then set about looking for a safe house. It all seemed highly unprofessional, as I had learnt to expect from the set-up in Grey Pillars.

When it became evident that Auchinleck was holding the Germans at Alamein the panic in Cairo died down: the future was still uncertain, but the immediate urgency was over. I now proposed to Domville that he should find someone better qualified to stay in

Cairo if the necessity arose, and send me into the Red Sea Hills. From there, with the cooperation of the Ababdah tribe, I would be in a position to interrupt German communications if they took Cairo and advanced up the Nile valley. This, I maintained, was the sort of job for which I was best qualified. He agreed and a few days later sent me off, glad no doubt to be rid of me.

Tim Foley, who had been with me in Gojjam, was mining wolfram in the Red Sea Hills. I joined him there and together we worked out our plans. With his gift for improvisation, his technical skill and his friendly and accommodating nature, I could not have found a more ideal collaborator. He was also on good terms with the Ababdah, some of whom worked for him. These were one of the four great Beja tribes; with the Bisharin, the Hadendoa and the Bani Amir, they occupied the entire range of Red Sea Hills from Egypt to Eritrea. I had encountered some of the Bani Amir near the Eritrean border at the beginning of the war and been impressed by those virile, handsome people: the Ababdah resembled them.

Obviously we could not suggest to them that the Germans might occupy Egypt; all we could do was to make friends with as many as possible and earmark those we felt would be most suitable. Meanwhile, I reconnoitred the approaches to the Nile and selected targets on the railway line, while Foley went on mining wolfram, which was badly needed. He had masses of explosives and I secured weapons, ammunition and specialized explosives, such as limpet mines, from Cairo. However, after the battle of Alamein in late October, with Rommel now in full retreat towards Libya, the threat to Egypt was obviously over. I therefore borrowed a car and driver from Foley and went up to Cairo to apply for an active posting.

Back at Grey Pillars I found myself once more hanging about with nothing to do. Feeling fed up, I asked to see the brigadier, whom I had not previously met. He kept me standing, said he was very busy, and asked what I wanted. I said I had originally been brought from Damascus to be dropped behind the enemy lines. Now I asked for an assurance that I would be actively employed in the desert. When he would give me no such assurance, I said in that case I wished to try and join the Long Range Desert Group, and I asked to be released by SOE if the LRDG accepted me.

'The LRDG would not take you as a major.'

I answered rather shortly: 'I would be content to be a captain, even a lieutenant, if I was with them.'

He replied, 'Anyway, I'm not releasing you. You should not have come up to Cairo without my permission.'

I went straight round from his office to see the Military Secretary, who was sympathetic and said he would take up my case with the brigadier. Next day when I went into Grey Pillars I heard that the brigadier was threatening me with a court martial for insubordination.

Luckily at this moment someone advised me to get in touch with David Stirling, who was setting off with his SAS in a few days' time on one of his raids behind enemy lines. I had heard of neither Stirling nor the SAS, but I took immediate advantage of this information. I found David Stirling in his brother Peter's flat. Six foot three, dark-haired and immaculately dressed he listened courteously while I explained my frustrations with SOE. I told him I had been with Wingate in Abyssinia, was familiar with desert life, and spoke Arabic. I asked him to take me with him. He enquired how I knew he was going on a raid.

'I don't really know, but these things get about.'

'All right. Get down to SAS headquarters at Kabrit on the Canal as quickly as you can. I'll give them a ring and tell them you're coming. I'll be down there tomorrow.'

'What about the brigadier?' I asked.

He picked up the telephone and asked to speak to him.

'Colonel Stirling here. I've got Major Thesiger with me. I'm taking him on a forthcoming operation. So please release him at once.'

Thus I joined the now famous Special Air Service, which Stirling had founded at the age of twenty-five, and commanded.

David Stirling had joined the Scots Guards on the outbreak of war and then transferred to the Commandos. At the end of 1940 he went with a Commando force of two thousand men to the Middle East but the unit was disbanded when the Navy, after its losses in the evacuations from Greece and Crete, could no longer spare ships for commando operations.

Stirling, then a lieutenant, was convinced that small, highly trained parties, dropped in the desert behind enemy lines, could cause much damage by attacking airfields. No one took him seriously until he met Auchinleck: the Commander-in-Chief approved his plans and authorized him to select six officers and sixty men. To

374

mislead German Intelligence that the British had a parachute brigade in the Middle East, Stirling's unit was named 'Detachment L of the Special Air Service Brigade'. This was the birth of the SAS. Stirling designed a winged dagger as its badge with the now famous motto, 'Who Dares Wins'.

At that time, as a result of the recent disasters, equipment of all sorts was hard to come by, but Stirling managed to get hold of a tent and appropriate some parachutes that had been off-loaded on their way to India by mistake. After an initial and unsuccessful parachute operation, wrecked by high winds, Stirling's small unit operated on the ground, at first with the help of the Long Range Desert Group, but later with its own transport.

In small groups with two men to a jeep, each jeep fitted with three Vickers K machine-guns, the SAS would emerge unexpectedly out of the desert, attack German communications, and blow up petrol dumps and ammunition depots, or mine roads. In fourteen months they destroyed two hundred and fifty-six aircraft. On one notable raid on Fuka aerodrome, the SAS probably destroyed fifty planes, though Stirling claimed only forty; these included fourteen Junkers 52 transports.

By 1942 Stirling had been promoted Lieutenant-Colonel, and General Alexander, who had succeeded General Auchinleck, had given orders for the SAS detachment to be raised to a full regiment. In just over a year, Stirling had added a new regiment to the British Army, and devised a new and effective method of warfare.

By treating his officers and men with consideration and respect, he gained their friendship as well as their admiration. When he visited Army Headquarters, though determined to get whatever he required, he remained patient in the face of opposition, and achieved his end by reasoned argument. He avoided all self-advertisement. Once, when we were discussing his plans to develop the SAS to brigade strength, I suggested it would help if he was given promotion. He answered, 'I think I feel sufficiently inflated as it is.'

I left Kabrit with Stirling on 20 November 1942. He had with him ninety men, mounted in jeeps and in the dozen three-ton lorries that carried rations, ammunition, petrol and water. These men comprised the newly raised 'B' Squadron of the SAS and reinforcements for 'A' Squadron. We skirted Alexandria and entered the desert; then, passing Burj al Arab, we arrived at Alamein. The battlefield was littered with destroyed tanks and guns, burnt-out lorries, crashed aircraft, all the debris of modern war. We overtook endless lorries filled with troops, others loaded with supplies, signal vehicles, staff cars, ambulances, mobile workshops, Sherman tanks on carriers, batteries of guns, all of them bumping and grinding across the desert under clouds of dust. Day after day we passed through this moving mass of vehicles, camping among them in the evenings.

I found it immensely exhilarating. At Alamein the tide had turned: we now sensed that even Tripoli was within our reach. But I was a newcomer to the desert war, very conscious that I had played no part during the past three years in the victories and defeats that had culminated at Alamein. I had been serving apart from my countrymen, and had never experienced the close-knit comradeship of regimental life, never known at first hand the traditions of a regiment. Regretfully, I could never boast that I had been one of the Desert Rats.

We climbed Halfaya Pass, entered Libya, and halted briefly in Tobruk to collect petrol and rations. The harbour was filled with wrecks which the Navy were busy clearing. Everywhere was a sense of urgency. More and more convoys poured westwards. Aircraft passed overhead, flights of heavy bombers and graceful, glittering Spitfires; we barely glanced up when we heard their engines, confident that they were our own. Travelling long hours, we crossed the Jabal al Akhdar or Green Mountain. Here, among its gorges and wooded slopes, Umar Mukhtar and his Senussi tribesmen had fought valiantly but unavailingly against the Italians in the 1920s. During the past three years, these same tribesmen, undaunted by Italian repression and brutality, had often helped the British. It was on them that SOE agents had relied when they were dropped behind the enemy lines. Now they had occupied many abandoned Italian farms; they themselves still camped in their black tents, but they penned their sheep and goats in the houses. Seeing this, some of our troops would remark despairingly, 'Could you believe it?' Yet it seemed to me a sensible arrangement.

At Agadabia we left the coastal road and turned south into the desert, to get round the German positions at Agheila, which was a hundred miles on down the coast and the furthest point the British had reached on their two previous advances. The desert through which we now passed was as barren as any I had seen: sand, gravel and occasional rocks, but never a tree or bush. Our constant apprehension, mine at any rate, was that we should be spotted from the air and bombed or strafed. Stirling had told me that General Montgomery had originally turned down his proposal to get behind the German lines at Agheila on the grounds that his tracks would inevitably be seen by patrolling aircraft. However, all went well and on 29 November we joined 'A' Squadron under Major Mayne at Bir Zaltin, a hundred miles south of Agheila.

'A' Squadron had a quiet self-confidence that was impressive. In the past year these men had mastered the desert and learnt to use its vast emptiness as their hideout. Many of them had grown up in towns; few of them had been out of England before the war. Yet now they were equally at home among the giant dunes of the Sand Sea or on the limitless gravel flats of the Hammad. Fortunately, the Germans never evolved units like the Long Range Desert Group or the SAS to operate behind our lines. This partiality for operating in small, isolated groups, whether in the desert, the jungle, in mountains or on the sea, was a peculiarly British trait.

Stirling intended 'A' Squadron to attack transport by night on the road between Agheila and Bouerat, and 'B' Squadron to operate along the two hundred and eighty miles of road between Bouerat and Tripoli. These attacks were to synchronize with General Montgomery's offensive against Rommel's position at Agheila, due to start on 13 December. Stirling's intention was to stop all movement along the coastal road after dark; during the daytime German transport would be at the mercy of the RAF.

'B' Squadron, to which I had been attached by Stirling, was divided into eight patrols, each consisting of two or three jeeps. I shared a jeep with Lieutenant Gordon Alston and we had with us two signallers in a wireless jeep. Stirling was returning to Kabrit to supervise the build-up of the SAS Regiment but he intended before doing so to accompany 'B' Squadron as far as El Fascia, an old Roman cistern forty miles south of Bouerat.

El Fascia was four hundred miles west of Bir Zaltin, but to avoid detection we made a circuit far south through an area marked 'impassable' on the 'going' maps made by the LRDG. We lay up by day and then, moving off in the late afternoon, travelled through the night; the going was appalling and after dark we used our headlights. The squadron was brilliantly guided by Mike Sadler, a young Rhodesian with uncanny aptitude for keeping his direction by night, even over ground strewn with rocks, cut up by steep-sided wadis or interspersed with areas of soft sand. To fix his position he took bearings on the stars.

Alston and I drove in turn; it needed unfailing concentration to avoid getting stuck in a sand drift or damaging the sump on a rock. I had never derived any satisfaction from driving a car and was consequently a bad driver, and I found these night drives interminable, exhausting and bitterly cold, though luckily it did not rain, which it did heavily elsewhere. The going proved even worse than Stirling had expected and as we were falling behind time he decided to take a chance and travel by day. One afternoon, crossing the road between Bouerat and Hon, we were fired on by two Italian armoured cars. They did not pursue us, but I expected that now we had been sighted we should be attacked by aircraft, and was relieved when night fell.

We arrived at El Fascia on 13 December, the day Montgomery's offensive was due to start. The other seven patrols of 'B' Squadron left us here to take up their positions. Our target was the road to the west of Bouerat. We decided to lie up in daytime at El Fascia: there were bushes along the various wadis where we could camouflage our jeeps against air observation, and water in the cistern, but with no evidence that it was being used by others. We should be within striking distance of the road at night but far enough from it, we hoped, not to be stumbled on inadvertently.

Stirling was determined to have another go at the Germans before he went back to Egypt, so he and his driver, Sergeant Cooper, went with us on our first raid. We left the two signallers and their jeep at El Fascia and set off as it grew dark, separating when we reached the road, Stirling to shoot up a camp, while Alston and I waited for a convoy.

Shortly afterwards, with Alston driving, we saw the lights of a large convoy coming from the direction of Agheila. We waited until it was close, when I enfiladed it with a pair of our machine-guns, emptying both drums into it. We then drove off down the road, blew up some telegraph poles, cut the wires and laid some mines.

Further on we came to a large tented camp where cars were driving about with their lights on. We switched on our own lights and motored into the camp, raked a line of tents and drove out on the far side. Again no one fired at us but almost as soon as we left the camp, one of our tyres went flat. We stopped and tried to get the wheel off, but the nuts would not move. We hammered away, unable to make any impression on the nuts and very conscious of the proximity of the camp we had just shot up. Eventually we drove back to El Fascia on a flat tyre. In the morning Cooper pointed out that we had been tightening instead of undoing the nuts. I had never changed a wheel before.

As it got dark Stirling set off with Cooper on his long journey back to Egypt, and Alston and I went back to the road, again leaving our signals jeep at El Fascia.

Each night we found more parked vehicles and more tents, but now less and less traffic on the road. On one occasion I saw a large tanker driving towards us, and at the same moment a Staff car coming from the opposite direction. I decided to take the tanker; as it blew up the Staff car skidded to a halt and its occupants scrambled for cover. During these nights we shot up camps over a wide area, including one which turned out later to be a Divisional Headquarters. We would drive into a camp and stop to select a target. We often heard men talking in their tents, and sometimes saw people moving about in the moonlight, but I had a comforting delusion that we were invisible, for we were never challenged or shot at. Once we drove up to a group of tents and found ourselves among a number of tanks; we were evidently in a tank repair workshop. When I tried to open fire on the tents the guns jammed. I changed the drums as quietly as possible, conscious even so of the rattle, but the guns still refused to fire, so we drove into the desert, put them right and found another target. One night we motored up to a canteen with a dozen lorries parked outside the large tent; inside men were talking, laughing and singing. I fired a long burst into the tent, and short bursts into the engines of the lorries as we drove off.

During these operations we must have killed and wounded many people, but as I never saw the casualties we inflicted my feelings remained impersonal. I did, however, begin to feel that our luck could not last much longer. It seemed inevitable that sooner or later a sentry would identify us and fire a burst into our car. Even if he missed Alston and myself the land mines in the car would probably go up.

Several times while lying up at El Fascia, we heard the sound of engines and suspected that patrols were hunting for us.

One morning Alston took the two signallers in our jeep to fetch water. Shortly after he had left I noticed a small reconnaissance plane flying towards the cistern; it circled and went off. A little later I heard the sound of several heavy vehicles coming along the wadi towards me. We had carefully hidden the wireless jeep under a camouflage net among some bushes. I took a blanket, went some distance away into the open, where there was no apparent cover, and lay down in a small hollow, covering myself with the blanket on which I scattered earth and bits of vegetation. Peeping out from under it, I saw two armoured cars; I thought I heard others on the far side of the wadi.

The cars nosed about but failed to find the jeep. One of them passed within a couple of hundred yards of where I lay. I heard it stop; my head was under the blanket and I wondered if they had seen me and were about to open fire; then it went on. It seemed ages before they finally drove off. Soon after they had gone I heard several bursts of machine-gun fire. I felt certain they had either killed or captured the others, and that I was now on my own.

Thinking things over under my blanket, I decided the best thing would be to remain at El Fascia and hope the Eighth Army would eventually turn up; there was water in the cistern, food in the wireless jeep and some petrol, but I had no idea how to work the wireless. I felt that the Germans, having searched the place once, would probably not come back another day; meanwhile I stayed under the blanket in case they came back now. I had Doughty's *Arabia Deserta* in my haversack but felt little inclination to read.

Some hours later I spotted Alston moving about cautiously among the bushes and startled him by calling from cover, 'Hello, Gordon. I thought they'd got you.'

'I thought they'd got *you* when I heard the firing. I just hoped they hadn't found the wireless jeep. I came back to look for it. The plane came right over our heads. Luckily our jeep was in some bushes and they didn't spot it. The armoured cars never came very close.'

'Well, they came damned close to me!'

Alston went off and fetched the jeep and the other two. Later that afternoon Lieutenant Martin and his driver, both of them Free French, turned up in their jeep. They had been with one of the patrols in 'B' Squadron and had been surprised by the Germans, but had managed to escape. When they got near El Fascia they had again been chased and shot at by armoured cars. This accounted for the firing we had heard.

We now decided that after dark we would move to another wadi some distance from the well, and lie up there to await the arrival of the Eighth Army. Our petrol was very low; we had not enough left to go on raiding the road. Martin was also short of petrol and decided to remain with us. In the late evening several armoured cars arrived and laagered nearby. They must have heard us when we eventually motored off; it looked as if, having found our tracks, they intended to deny us the cistern, and go on searching for us.

Our new hiding place was in a delightful wadi full of trees and carpeted with green grass and flowers. Some Arabs turned up in the morning. Like all these tribal Arabs, they wore white blankets wrapped round their clothes. They were very friendly and I found their Arabic comparatively easy to understand. We made them tea and later they fetched us a goat and spent the night with us. They hated the Italians, who during the pacification of Libya had treated the inhabitants with incredible brutality. I was confident that as the Germans were helping the Italians these Arabs would not betray us. On Christmas Day, two days after we had left El Fascia, we again heard armoured cars; they sounded fairly close but did not enter our wadi. I was certain that they would not be able to follow our tracks over the rocky ground we had crossed to get there.

Stirling had given El Fascia as the rendezvous for 'B' Squadron, and we expected some of the other patrols to arrive shortly in our neighbourhood. We had no idea that all the others had actually been killed or captured; but we were aware that our combined raids had brought night traffic more or less to a halt during the critical days of Montgomery's offensive.

Rommel had been very concerned by these SAS raids on his communications. He wrote in his diary, which was later edited in English by B. H. Liddell Hart:

They succeeded again and again in shooting up supply lorries behind our lines, laying mines, cutting down telegraph poles and similar nefarious activities ...

On 23 December we set off on a beautiful sunny morning to inspect the country south of our front. First we drove along the Via Balbia and then, with two Italian armoured cars as escort, through the fantastically fissured Wadi Zem-Zem towards El Fascia. Soon we began to find tracks of British vehicles, probably made by some of Stirling's people who had been round here on the job of harassing our supply lines. The tracks were comparatively new and we kept a sharp look out to see if we could catch a 'Tommy'. Near to El Fascia I suddenly spotted a lone vehicle. We gave chase but found its crew were Italian. Troops from my Kampfstaffel were also in the area. They had surprised some British commandos the day before and captured maps marked with British store dumps and strong points. Now they were combing the district, also hoping to stumble on a 'Tommy'.

When I read this after the war I realized that Rommel himself must have been with the armoured cars that I had seen searching for us at El Fascia.

Stirling arrived back from Cairo, and Alston, Martin and I joined him near our hideout, which was still some forty miles behind the German lines. He intended to establish a forward base at Bir Soltan, some thirty miles from the Mareth Line, and from there with a small party to make contact in Tunisia with the First Army, which had landed in North Africa in November. To reach Bir Soltan involved us in a journey of more than two hundred miles, the last part along the edge of the Great Eastern Erg or Sand Sea, where we found the high steep dunes very difficult to cross.

Stirling had intended to take me with him from Bir Soltan to Tunisia, but before he started one of his jeeps gave trouble and he exchanged it for mine, leaving me to await the arrival of reinforcements. After successfully outflanking the Mareth Line he was captured near the Gabes Gap, and despite three attempts to escape remained a prisoner till the end of the war.

I now find myself uncertain over the sequence of events after Stirling left. I did not keep a diary and some of the letters to my mother, describing those days, have gone astray. I remember that Alston and I lay up for a time in the Jabal Nafusa to the south of Tripoli and kept watch on the Italian positions.

On one occasion we were short of water, but reluctant to go to the well where Arabs were watering their herds, in case the Italians got word of our presence. We had made friends with two young Arabs and I asked them to fetch us water. They promptly started a heated argument among themselves. Alston asked me rather apprehensively what had gone wrong: I was able to reassure him that they were only arguing whether to use their donkey or their sister to carry the jerry cans.

After the Italian troops had withdrawn, I went into one of their dug-outs. When I came out I noticed that the bottom of my trousers was black with a solid mass of fleas, not hopping about but moving slowly upwards. I scraped them off with a bayonet.

Having made contact with the reinforcements from Kabrit, Alston and I crossed into Tunisia on 23 January 1943, the day Tripoli fell, and established a base to which raiding parties could return. We then went to Tripoli by way of Nalut and Garian and reported to the Eighth Army. Alston was recalled to Cairo and I was attached to the newly formed Greek Sacred Squadron of the SAS. This remarkable unit, composed entirely of officers and commanded by Colonel Gigantes, had been formed to emulate the Theban Band of Hellenic times.

Rommel had meanwhile withdrawn to the Mareth Line, originally erected by the French along part of the Tunisian frontier to guard against an Italian invasion from Tripolitania. The French had assumed the country to the south of the Line would be impassable to mechanised vehicles, a misapprehension which enabled the SAS to operate there, and Montgomery eventually to outflank the Mareth Line.

The Greek Sacred Squadron was sent south to Qasr Rhilana near the Great Erg Sand Sea to await the arrival of the Free French under General Leclerc. Months earlier, this force had started its great odyssey from Fort Lamy in French Equatorial Africa; after crossing the Sahara by way of Tibesti and the Fezzan it had recently arrived in Tunisia.

When we made contact with Leclerc's force, it was very much to their surprise and ours. We were resting and brewing up at midday near our destination when we heard the approach of many vehicles; having no idea what this portended, we took off. A French officer later described to me how he suddenly saw *'un tas de petites voitures qui courait à travers le désert'*. We were Leclerc's first contact with the

Eighth Army, and we remained with the French for the next six weeks.

On 10 March the Germans, anxious about their exposed flank, attacked the French at Qasr Rhilana but were driven off. Spitfires came to our assistance and saw off the German bombers, one of which jettisoned two bombs that fell in the sand within a few yards of me, but did not explode.

The New Zealand Corps, under General Freyberg, VC, arrived at Qasr Rhilana on 19 March after a remarkable march across reputedly impassable country. The Greek Squadron was now attached to these superb troops, whom Rommel rated the finest in the Eighth Army. On the 20th Montgomery's frontal attack on the Mareth Line failed. He therefore reinforced the New Zealand Corps, which was advancing towards the Hamma Gap, with the 10th Corps under General Horrocks.

At four o'clock in the afternoon of the 27th the New Zealanders and the 8th Armoured Brigade attacked the Gap. We were on high ground and had a superb view of the battle. Wave after wave of light bombers and fighters, flying very low, roared over the German positions, and under this umbrella the tanks moved forward down the corridor between the steep hills. By nightfall the Germans were in full retreat. The next morning we followed them through the Gap. The battlefield was littered with corpses and destroyed or captured tanks, guns and transport. Seven thousand Germans had been captured. This battle was decisive. Rommel abandoned the Mareth Line and withdrew to the Wadi Akarit, which Montgomery attacked on 5 April.

Back in 1940 at Galabat I had been impressed when just one battery opened fire on the Italian positions. The bombardment at the Wadi Akarit now appeared to me unbelievable. Exactly at four o'clock in the morning of the 5th the night behind us burst suddenly and instantaneously along the entire horizon into a lasting, flickering sheet of flame. We took no part in the battle but as soon as it was over pushed forward with the New Zealand Divisional Cavalry who, in their light tanks, led the advance. We passed masses of Italians, all anxious to surrender, and a few Germans. Then we were held up by German anti-tank guns.

I drew up alongside the tank belonging to the Intelligence Officer, who was sitting on the roof, busy writing. Some New Zealanders came towards us with yet another prisoner. The Intelligence Officer had already interrogated a number. He looked up and called out, 'Don't bring me any more, I've got all the information I want. I'm busy writing to my mum. Tell him to fuck off down the track and someone will pick him up.'

However, they came over to us and one of them said, 'I think you'd better have a look at this one, sir.'

The Italian, an elderly, much ribboned and braided officer, looked up at the Intelligence Officer and said despairingly, 'For an hour I have been trying to surrender and everyone tells me to fuck off down the road.' After a pause he added, 'And after all, I am an Italian general.'

He was in fact the general who commanded the Saharan Corps. I felt immensely sorry for this tired old man in his ultimate humiliation. I had hated the Italians ever since they had invaded Abyssinia, but this pathetic scene purged me of my hatred. We took him over to General Freyberg and while they were talking a Spitfire shot down a German plane immediately overhead.

It was exhilarating to be heading the advance of the Eighth Army, to be sweeping forward irresistibly to what we knew was final victory in Africa. We were now on the Tunisian plains. I remember vividly the profusion of wild flowers: for days we drove through scarlet poppies, yellow marigolds, white daisies, irises and gladioli. Every time we brewed up, a patch of flowers shrivelled and collapsed as the petrol we poured into the sand blazed up. We now passed French farms, and plantations of olives in ordered rows. The others were delighted to be out of the desert at last and back in civilization; for my part I subconsciously resented this evidence of European occupation.

We entered Sousse some five minutes after the Germans had left. It was a strange and moving experience. At first the townspeople thought we were the last of the retreating Germans. Then they assumed we were Americans, and waved American flags. Most of the French were in tears. The town was full of hysterical Tunisian Jews with the Star of David sewn on their clothes. Finally, at Enfidaville, against the mountain bastion of the Tunisian peninsula, the Eighth Army's long advance came to a halt, while from the other side the First Army moved in for the kill. My brother Roddy was with them in the First Parachute Brigade, though I did not know this at the time. He was later to be dropped at Primasole Bridge in Sicily and again at Arnhem, where he was wounded and captured.

David Stirling's material contribution to the victory in the desert was certainly comparable with Wingate's in Burma, and was achieved at a trifle of the cost. Stirling employed a handful of men, whereas Wingate's second Chindit expedition withdrew a division from General Slim's main thrust into Burma, where it might perhaps have been more effectively employed. However, when Wingate had gone into Burma with his first Chindit expedition the Japanese seemed invincible in jungle warfare; when he returned, he had proved that man for man British soldiers could defeat Japanese in the jungle. This achievement, effectively publicised, did much to raise morale throughout the Fourteenth Army.

Both Stirling's and Wingate's concepts of operations were original, and both men were equally resolute and daring in carrying out their plans. But no two men could have been more dissimilar in character. Unlike Wingate, Stirling shunned affectation, and invariably dressed and behaved in the civilized manner expected of his background.

During these months in the Western Desert I had missed the sense of involvement with the country and its inhabitants which had been so important to me during Wingate's campaign in Gojjam. There we had used animal transport and fought on foot. Here the jeeps in which we operated were marvellously suited to the role of the SAS; but we carried in them everything we required and our only concern with our surroundings was whether the going for our vehicles was good or bad. In these circumstances, I personally could derive no pleasure from the desert itself; even the enormous sand dunes of the Erg left me unmoved; they were but another obstacle to be mechanically surmounted.

In May 1943, the Greek Sacred Squadron was recalled to Egypt from Enfidaville. We motored back along the North African coast through Tripoli, Benghazi and the Jabal al Akhdar, past Tobruk and Alamein, and from Cairo we drove to the new SAS headquarters in Athlit in Northern Palestine.

The Squadron was housed a mile or more from the others; it was virtually independent, and under Colonel Gigantes led its own existence. Many of these officers had fought valiantly when the Italians invaded Greece. Now they tended to be dilatory over their training, insisting that when the occasion arose they would know what to do. They spent most of their time bathing, or arguing about politics in a nearby café.

In July 1943 I went with the Squadron to Janin on a parachute course. Many of them looked forward to this course, whereas I dreaded it: I had a particular horror of jumping into space. However, having joined the SAS, I was committed to doing so. The night before my first jump I had a nightmare; I dreamt I was a prisoner, and was to be shot at dawn. I woke sweating to find that all I had to face was a parachute jump. After a week's strenuous training, during which we had several serious injuries, we did eight jumps, two at night and the last six at low level. I made a point of never looking down before I jumped. Half way through the course one of our group was killed: his parachute failed to open and he went into the ground near where I was standing, but this shook me less than I would have expected. When the course was over I had a satisfactory sense of achievement but no desire to jump again. Back at Athlit we continued to train for the invasion of Europe, expecting to be used in the Balkans.

I often visited the Arab villages situated nearby in the hills along the border, where the villagers, courteous and hospitable despite their resentment with the British over Jewish immigration, made me welcome. For untold centuries their ancestors had lived in Palestine. A few years later, with the virtual connivance of Britain and America, they were to be driven from their homeland or subjected to the intolerable rule of the Israelis, who claimed the right to a country from which they had been expelled two thousand years earlier. Seldom can a greater wrong have been inflicted on an innocent people with such general approbation, and the seeds of such catastrophic and widespread hatred been sown with so much complacency.

I had learned soon after I arrived at Athlit that a Druze squadron was stationed nearby. I visited them at the first opportunity and the first person I saw as I drove into their camp was Faris. I called to him from the car and he rushed over, shouting to the others that I was back: by happy chance, this squadron was the camel squadron I had commanded at Malha, with Salih Ma'z now in command. He took me to the mess tent with Faris at my side and the others pressing about us. One and all pressed me to stay for the evening meal, Salih apologising that they had only Army rations to offer me. I must, he insisted, come back on Sunday, in two days' time; then they would prepare a traditional Druze *mansaf*.

I was delighted to see them all again, to be greeted with a welcome so spontaneous and genuine. They told me they were now infantry, and had been here for six months. 'If only we were back at Malha ...,' they said; and they reminded me of patrols we had made in the lava desert, and how we had tried to shoot gazelle, and camped near a certain pool of water, and slept in the tents of the nomads. They recalled Druze villages we had visited, the feasts we had had in Malha and elsewhere, the grapes we had eaten in their vineyards, all sorts of incidents I had almost forgotten. When I went back there for the *mansaf* on the Sunday I took two Greek officers with me. After we had eaten, Salih called for the pipes and they sang the Druze war songs, the same songs to which I had ridden into the Jabal from Mafraq during the Syrian campaign.

After that I visited them whenever I had a chance. One weekend Salih, Faris and I went to Majdal ash Shams, a large Druze village in the Lebanon on the slopes of Mount Hermon, intending from there to climb the mountain. We motored to Majdal by way of Tiberias and the Hule valley, passing through Baniyas, Pan's garden of olden days, an enchanting little village. The whole valley, lit by the evening sun, was extraordinarily beautiful. They were expecting us at Majdal, for Salih had sent word to a relative who lived there. That night we were very late to bed, but we were up again at dawn.

We motored to Arnah, another Druze village, the highest on the mountain. Everywhere ice cold water trickled down the mountainside through tall green grass, among the willows and poplars, the peach and almond trees; reputedly there were three hundred and sixty springs at Arnah. From there to the summit of Hermon it took us three hours on foot. Near the top we met an aged Druze with his flock of goats. Like most Druze in those mountain villages, he wore a red coat, baggy blue trousers and a white headcloth. He brought us a wooden bowl of milk cooled with snow, which was welcome, and then sat with us and talked while his goats wandered among the drifts of snow to the music of their bells, and we looked out over Syria, Palestine and the Lebanon.

Since joining the Sudan Defence Force in 1940 I had had one week's leave in Khartoum and then only that other week which I had spent visiting Petra. This lack of leave had been no deprivation: almost all the time I had been doing interesting jobs in places I had long wanted to see. I was well aware how lucky I had been. Now, however, I did take a fortnight to visit northern Syria.

I had never previously crossed the Euphrates into the Jazirah; now I motored along two hundred miles of the Turkish frontier to the Tigris. This frontier marked the limit of the ancient Arab conquests: beyond it the wave of Arab invasions beginning in the seventh century had at last lapsed and broken against the foot of the mountains.

I passed through Qamashlia, a squalid settlement composed largely of mud buildings roofed with zinc sheeting, but redeemed by a fascinating variety of races: Arabs, Kurds in colourful turbans, Circassians in large black sheepskin *kalpaks*, Armenians, Assyrians, Turks and Turkomans. Some hundred miles further on I reached Ain Diyar and looked across the gorge of the Tigris to the Kurdish mountains rising to twelve thousand feet, an immensely impressive confusion of peaks and precipices. Behind them I could see others, range after range, extending north to Van, and far beyond to Georgia and the Caucasus.

The villagers danced that night by moonlight in the square of Ain Diyar, a line of men swaying to the beat of drums and the rhythm of their songs. They were Kurds, in all the finery of national dress: tasselled turbans wound round tall felt caps, embroidered jackets, wide trousers woven in broad stripes of variegated colours. In their waist sashes they carried large, curved silver-sheathed daggers. They were the first Kurds I had seen. I was enthralled, realizing too that it was among such people that my father had worked at the end of the last century, in Van. Now, only a few miles away, across the Turkish frontier, Kurds were forbidden to wear their national dress; Atatürk had decreed that they were just 'Mountain Turks'.

I went on beyond Ain Diyar and crossed the Tigris into Iraq. I motored south past encampments of Shammer Arabs, one of the great Bedu tribes, and reached Jabal Singhar, an isolated mountain inhabited by the Yazidis. Misnamed 'Devil Worshippers', because they propitiate Shaitan, they have on this account been much persecuted by Muslims. The Yazidis observe a number of curious prohibitions; among others they will utter no word beginning with 'sh', will never wear blue, nor a shirt open at the neck, will not defecate into water, nor eat lettuces. I was much impressed by their good looks, their dignity and the cleanliness of their dwellings. Time was now short and I could only stay in Jabal Singhar for a day, but I made up my mind to come back some day. Eight years later I did so during a long journey with animal transport through Iraqi Kurdistan.

At the end of my leave I returned to the Squadron at Athlit and there, quite unexpectedly, ended my military service, in order to return to civil duties in Abyssinia at the personal request of Haile Selassie.

PART VI

Return to Abyssinia
1944–5;
and Later Travels

CHAPTER 27

With the Crown Prince
at Dessie

I N OCTOBER 1943 Haile Selassie asked for me to be sent as adviser
to his eldest son, Asfa Wossen, whom he had appointed ruler of
the province of Wollo. This was a request which, despite my
reluctance to leave the SAS at this juncture of the war, I felt unable to
refuse. I flew to Addis Ababa for an audience with the Emperor,
motored to Dessie to see the Crown Prince, accepted the job and
flew back to Cairo. The authorities there then gave me permission to
go to London before taking up this two-year appointment.

I had a low priority for a seat on a plane. Every morning for a
fortnight I went to Movement Control to make enquiries. One day
the officer in charge said, 'Where did you get to last night? We had a
cancellation and a seat for you: we rang your hotel but you were out.
It was just as well,' he continued, 'we've just heard the plane was
shot down.' A few days later I got away and in London I was
demobilized.

For the next two months I stayed with my mother who was now
living in the sunny, top-storey flat in Chelsea which thirty years
later became mine, with a view over the Physick Garden and away
up the river. Her second husband, Reggie Astley, had died at The
Milebrook, and my brother Dermot had been killed in the Air Force.
Of the four of us, Dermot had been closest to my mother, and after
his death she could no longer bear to go on living at The Milebrook.

In January 1944 I returned to Egypt in a convoy that sailed far out
into the Atlantic before passing through the Straits of Gibraltar.
From Cairo I travelled up the Nile to Khartoum, where I stayed with
Douglas Newbold. He was desperately busy with the problems the
war had brought to the Sudan, very conscious of changes that
would be necessary in the future; yet he remained as imperturbable,
relaxed and entertaining as ever. I treasure the memory of those

393

days. I never saw him again, for while I was in Abyssinia he died, working to the end, despite ill health, for the Sudanese he loved.

I went to Addis Ababa by way of Asmara and Dessie, travelling by motor coach down the road the Italians had built. In Addis Ababa I stayed with the Sandfords; he was now Adviser to the Minister of the Interior. I enjoyed being with them but was impatient to get to Dessie and start work. Asfa Wossen, the Crown Prince, was in Addis Ababa and was expected to leave any day for Dessie; but his departure was constantly postponed. At last he told me to go on ahead.

Dessie is situated at eight thousand feet on a shelf of a tremendous escarpment that falls to the lowlands and the Danakil desert; twenty years later I was to see the equally spectacular escarpment in the Yemen, on the opposite side of the Rift Valley. Despite some jerry-built Italian villas, in one of which I lived, Dessie was an attractive place, consisting largely of thatched *tukuls* among groves of eucalyptus. Here I often watched lammergeyers at the town rubbish tip; half a dozen of these great bearded vultures, with their nine-foot wing span, might sail past, sometimes close by my head.

After I had been at Dessie a fortnight, the Crown Prince arrived and the following evening gave a dinner party. During the Italian occupation he had been educated in England, so he spoke fluent English. To me he was invariably welcoming and friendly, and was well aware that twenty-seven years earlier, during the critical days of the Revolution, my parents had sheltered him in the Legation.

Dessie was his first administrative appointment. Unfortunately, his relationship with his father was strained. The Emperor, who preferred the younger Prince Makonnen of Harar, kept Asfa Wossen in the background; this had undermined his self-confidence so that he consulted his retainers unduly and made no important decision without reference to the Minister of the Pen, who was also Minister of the Interior.

Abyssinia had a real need both for outside advisers to help organize the financial, legal, educational and administrative departments, and for technicians to maintain the services which the Italians had installed in the larger towns. In the capital, some officials recognized the necessity for such specialized assistance; but in the provinces few could see any need for political or administrative advice. They were conservative by nature, holding instinctively to the methods of the past and mistrusting innovation. The Abyssinian officials at

Dessie certainly did not want an Englishman interfering in their administration, suggesting land reforms or new methods of taxation: they felt there was too much of this going on in Addis Ababa. Since I had been appointed by the Emperor himself they tolerated my presence, but they were determined to limit my influence with the Crown Prince. Consequently, I only saw him about once a week: our meetings tended to be purely social; rarely did we have any serious discussion.

I had no previous experience of Wollo, which was unlike any other province in the Empire and had its own particular problems. I had expected to go on tour, being convinced that until I had done so my advice could be of little practical value; however, each time I proposed it I was put off, with one excuse after another, and I felt a growing sense of frustration and failure. One improvement I did achieve concerned the overcrowded prison, where conditions were appalling. It was in the centre of town, but had no proper sanitation, and the overflow from its shallow pit-latrines poured down the hillside. I managed to get the prison moved outside the town; I accomplished little else.

During the campaign in Gojjam I had lived among the Patriots, feeding with them and sleeping in their houses. It had been an enthralling experience to take part in their archaic life, and to witness the customs and courtesies of a bygone age; I often thought how much I should have missed had I been serving with the Frontier Battalion. However, here in Dessie I had my own house and servants, and I found I was never invited out, except by Asfa Wossen himself. Actually, this was normal behaviour towards Europeans on the part of Abyssinians in the larger towns: even the Sandfords in Addis Ababa were seldom invited to a meal. I inevitably contrasted this treatment with my experience of the Druze and Arabs in Syria. They had welcomed me to their homes, overwhelmed me with hospitality; even strangers, whom I just chanced to meet, had insisted on entertaining me.

After my arrival Asfa Wossen had presented me with a splendid Arab stallion, and almost every day I rode out into the country; sometimes I went shooting for snipe or duck. I was in Dessie throughout the 'big rains', which normally start in June and are expected to end in mid-September, in time for Mascal, the Feast of the Cross. During the rainy season the mornings were usually fine, but by midday the clouds had banked up and then the rain deluged down, often continuing late into the night. When the rains were over the landscape was yellow with Mascal daisies. In Abyssinia individual flowers are of course beautiful, but only these daisies provide an overall effect comparable with the massed colour of the anemones, poppies and tulips in Iraq and Persia.

That year at Dessie was the most frustrating of my life. Elsewhere tremendous events were taking place. In Europe and the Far East, great battles were being fought. The SAS were engaged in the Mediterranean, Wingate was leading his Chindits into Burma, while here was I, stuck in Dessie, achieving nothing. Yet, such is the fortuitous nature of events, had I been anywhere else I should never have been offered the chance of exploring the Empty Quarter of Arabia, which was to prove the most important experience of my life.

Though my appointment at Dessie had been for two years, I resigned at the end of the first. Then, in Addis Ababa, at dinner in a friend's house, while I was waiting to leave the country, I happened to meet O. B. Lean of the Desert Locust Research Organization. During dinner he offered me a job, to look for locust outbreak centres in the deserts of Southern Arabia. I accepted at once, without asking about pay or anything else. Lean assured me that his organization could get me the Sultan of Muscat's permission to travel into the desert from the south coast of Arabia. That meant Dhaufar: and Dhaufar was the threshold of the Empty Quarter.

CHAPTER 28

Desert, Marsh and Mountain, 1945–58

Asa BOY I had longed to be an explorer. Early childhood in
Abyssinia, and the books I later read, predisposed me to
African adventure. Haile Selassie's invitation to his coronation had given me the opportunity to travel in the Danakil country;
this had been my introduction to the desert, and my first experience
of exploration. Later, during my two years in Northern Darfur and
my subsequent journey to Tibesti, I had become increasingly drawn
to the desert and to desert peoples. By then, however, the Sahara
had been explored, its tribes pacified and administered.

During the war the LRDG and SAS, profiting by the previous
experience of Bagnold who had explored the Libyan Desert by car,
had penetrated into its remotest areas: accordingly, there was
nothing left for me in the deserts of North Africa. Only in Arabia did
an enormous tract of desert, which even Arabs call Rub al Khali, the
Empty Quarter, remain largely inviolate, offering the final challenge
of desert exploration.

Thomas and Philby had crossed the Empty Quarter in the early
1930s but no other European had been there since, no aeroplane had
ever flown over it, and no car had been nearer than the RAF camp at
Salala, on the shore of the Indian Ocean, or the townships on the
Trucial Coast. In contrast with the Sahara, vast areas of the Empty
Quarter were still unexplored and it was surrounded by a no-
man's-land of warring tribes. Hitherto I myself had regarded it as
inaccessible; now, suddenly, utterly unexpectedly, it was within my
reach.

In the event, I worked for the Locust Research Organization for
two years. During that time, with a few chosen Bedu companions
from the Rashid tribe, I made the first of my two crossings of the
Empty Quarter, in late 1946, making my way back circuitously to
Dhaufar through the desert borderlands of Oman, a region at that
time ruled by a xenophobic Imam and consequently more inaccess-

ible to Europeans than Tibet. The Locust Research Organization were satisfied with the information I had collected, and offered me employment elsewhere. This however I declined. I was now determined to remain with the Rashid, and with them to continue my exploration of the Empty Quarter and of the interior of Oman. Already I was the first European to have visited the extensive Liwa Oasis, which though only sixty miles from the Trucial Coast had been unexplored as yet, and to have seen the legendary quicksands of Umm al Sammim. Accordingly I stayed in Arabia till 1950.

In *Arabian Sands* I have described my five memorable years with the Bedu, and have tried to convey the clean beauty of the sands and the sculptured shape of dunes that rise to seven hundred feet and extend a hundred miles. There, distances were measured in hours on camel-back, and over all lay a silence that we have now driven from our world. In the Empty Quarter we endured almost incessant hunger and, worse still, thirst, sometimes for days on end rationing ourselves to a pint a day; there was the heat of a blazing sun in a shadeless land; the bitter cold of winter nights; incessant watchfulness for raiders, our rifles always at hand; anxiety that our camels, on which our lives depended, would collapse.

It is difficult to analyse the motive that induced me to make those journeys, or the satisfaction I derived from such a life. There was of course the lure of the unknown; there was the constant test of resolution and endurance. Yet those travels in the Empty Quarter would have been for me a pointless penance but for the comradeship of my Bedu companions. All they possessed were their camels and saddlery, their rifles and daggers, some waterskins and cooking pots and bowls, and the very clothes they wore; few of them even owned a blanket. They possessed, however, a freedom which we, with all our craving for possessions, cannot experience. Any of them could have found a job in the towns and villages of the Hadhramaut; but all would have rejected that easier life of lesser men. They met every challenge, every hardship, with the proud boast: 'We are Bedu.'

When I joined them I asked for no concessions; I was determined to live as they lived, to face the hardships of the desert on equal terms with them. I knew I could not match them in physical endurance, but, with my family background, Eton, Oxford, the Sudan Political Service, I did perhaps think I would match them in civilized behaviour. When the test came, with near-starvation, thirst that clogged the throat, weariness and frustration, it was humiliating to fall short. All too often I would become withdrawn and irritable when they entertained chance-met strangers on our dwindling rations; highly resentful when we stood aside, pressing them to eat more, insisting that they were our guests, and that for us this was a 'blessed day'.

There were of course other occasions when someone whose encampment we happened to pass would hail us, would insist on entertaining us, would slaughter a camel to feed us, and would send us off in the morning having half-convinced me that we had conferred a kindness on him by accepting his hospitality. I have never forgotten the open-handed generosity of the Bedu with any money they had acquired, no matter if it left them penniless; their total honesty; their pride in themselves and in their tribe; their loyalty to each other and not least to me, a stranger of alien faith from an unknown land, a loyalty tested more than once at risk of their lives.

Inevitably these Bedu had little veneration for human life. In their frequent raids and counter-raids they killed and were killed, and each killing involved the tribe or family in another blood-feud to be settled without mercy – though in no circumstances would they have tortured anyone. I soon acquired the same attitude, and if anyone had killed one of my companions I would unquestionably have sought to avenge him: I have no belief in the 'sanctity' of life.

I would have remained with the Bedu indefinitely, but political circumstances beyond my control finally barred me from further access to them. Then I learnt what exile felt like. *Arabian Sands* is my tribute to my companions; a memorial to a way of life now gone for ever.

Next, in mid-1950, in search of an alternative to the desert, I travelled for three months on horseback among the mountains of Iraqi Kurdistan. The scenery was magnificent, but, after the years I had spent among the Arabs, I felt less compatibility with Kurds.

In the autumn of 1950, I went for a fortnight's duck shooting in the Marshes of Southern Iraq. In the event I spent much of the next eight years there, until I was excluded from Iraq after the revolution of 1958. This passage from *The Marsh Arabs*, the book in which I described those years, expresses something of the appeal which that remote area held for me:

> Memories of that first visit to the Marshes have never left me: firelight on a half-turned face, the crying of geese, duck flighting in

to feed, a boy's voice singing somewhere in the dark, canoes moving in procession down a waterway, the setting sun seen crimson through the smoke of burning reedbeds, narrow waterways that wound still deeper into the Marshes. A naked man in a canoe with a trident in his hand, reed houses built upon water, black, dripping buffaloes that looked as if they had calved from the swamp with the first dry land. Stars reflected in dark water, the croaking of frogs, canoes coming home at evening, peace and continuity, the stillness of a world that never knew an engine. Once again I experienced the longing to share this life, and to be more than a mere spectator.

In the desert I had lived month after month in a close-knit relationship with my five or six companions, two of whom, the dearest to me, remained with me throughout the five years I was there. During our journeys we seldom encountered anyone else, and almost never saw a woman. In the Marshes, on the other hand, I fed and slept in the villages of the Madan, as those Arabs were called, sharing to the full their communal life.

At first I met with some suspicion, but once I had gained their confidence I was welcomed wherever I went. My medicine chest helped me win acceptance, since there was no one else to treat their ailments. I was also of use to them by hunting the innumerable wild boar that posed a danger to them in the reedbeds. I acquired my own beautiful thirty-six-foot long canoe, and was joined by four lads who served as crew and remained with me all the time I was in the Marshes: in a very real sense I accepted their families as my own. I was happy with these cheerful, forthcoming Madan, whether paddling across the seemingly endless Marshes, or sitting in the evenings in smoke-filled reed houses where a crowd had gathered to watch the dancing and singing of talented boys. In these circumstances of a shared way of life, drawbacks like mosquitoes or fleas or the smoke that made the eyes smart were unavoidable and seemed scarcely troublesome.

For several months of the year, during most of the years from 1951 to 1958, the Marshes delighted me with the timeless, untroubled beauty of an unspoilt land. Autumn was when the wildfowl arrived from Siberia, duck of many kinds and skein after skein of grey geese. Winter days were exhilarating, with chill winds off the snow of Luristan, and everywhere an unbelievable wealth of wildfowl. In spring, the lagoons were carpeted with white ranunculus and flowering water-lilies. Only summer, with its torpid, dripping humidity, seemed intolerable, and I went elsewhere.

For instance, in May 1951 I returned to Kurdistan, where gentians, uncovered by the melting of snow drifts, were in flower, and whole mountain-sides blazed scarlet with tulips. I rode the length and breadth of Iraqi Kurdistan on horseback; there can have been few villages I did not visit, hardly a mountain I did not climb. Then I spent two summers, of 1952 and 1953, in Pakistan, travelling with three or four porters among the stupendous mountains of the Hindu Kush and Karakorams. From Chitral I looked out over Wakhan, and from the Baroghil Pass saw far below me the headwaters of the Oxus. On my way to Hunza, I skirted Nanga Parbat, passed beneath that superb mountain Rakaposhi, and reached the borders of Sinkiang. There one day at dusk we encountered a party of Kirghiz, quilted Mongolian figures on yaks, who had come down from the passes of the north and embodied for me everything that I imagined to lie beyond that forbidden frontier of Inner Asia.

The summers of 1954 and 1956 I spent in Afghanistan. In the first I visited the uplands west of Kabul, and saw Pathans in their black tents and also the Hazaras in their villages, a people whose Mongol ancestors had probably been established there by Genghis Khan. The second summer I spent among the Nuristanis in their remote valleys bordering on Chitral and in those days barely known to the outside world.

My travels in Persia, Iraqi Kurdistan, Pakistan and Afghanistan are recounted in my book *Desert, Marsh and Mountain*. I also went back one summer to Morocco, and there, under the aegis of Hajj Thami al Glawi, was escorted from one magnificent *kasbah* to another through the High Atlas. Only in late 1958, after the revolution in Iraq had made it impossible for me to resume my life in the Marshes, did I decide, after an interval of almost fourteen years, to return once again to Abyssinia.

CHAPTER 29

Lalibela;
and South to the Kenya Border

I FLEW TO ADDIS ABABA in early January 1959 and was met at the airport by Dan and Chris Sandford, who motored me out to their farm. Their elder son, Dick, and their daughters Eleanor and Philippa were there; all three were married, so with their families there was a whole clan of Sandfords to welcome me back to Mullu.

I was happy to be in Abyssinia again. Outside Addis Ababa every sight, sound and smell recalled the past: circular thatched churches in groves of trees; villages with cattle grazing on dry hillsides; crowded open-air markets, with people still wearing the customary white *shamma*; the outline of familiar mountains.

A fortnight later I went to stay with the Mansfields at the British Embassy. Both Philip Mansfield, a First Secretary, and his wife Elinor, had been in the Sudan; he in the Political Service and she as an anthropologist. This, though I had not previously met them, gave us much in common. I quickly realized they were extremely interested in Abyssinia and all its diverse races; both had learnt Amharic, an unusual accomplishment. I met several eminent Abyssinians dining with them, including the Emperor's granddaughter Princess Ruth, a charming cultured lady with faultless English.

Soon after my arrival in Addis Ababa I was summoned to an audience with the Emperor, a rare distinction for an unofficial visitor.

'As you came in you reminded me at once of your father,' he said. Then, after enquiring how my mother was, he asked about my plans. I told him I wanted to travel south with mules as far as the Kenya border, but first I hoped to visit Lalibela in Northern Abyssinia with Philip Mansfield. The Emperor replied that his secretary would provide me with letters to the officials in the south, and Asfa Wossen would make all arrangements for our journey to Lalibela. Before withdrawing I said how honoured I was to have attended his coronation and also to have served under his flag in the liberation of Abyssinia. With his gentle smile he replied, 'I owed much to you British who served with my countrymen during the campaign in Gojjam.'

Next day I called on the Crown Prince; he too was very friendly and we had a long talk; he asked many questions about Arabia and other countries I had been to since leaving Dessie, then assured me that he would arrange everything for the journey to Lalibela.

We left Addis Ababa by car on 15 February 1959, spent the night at Dessie in Asfa Wossen's guest house, and motored next day to Waldia. There the Dedjazmatch had been one of the Patriot leaders with me during the last stage of Wingate's campaign. He gave me a warm welcome, and feasted us on excellent *injera* and *wat* and much *tej*. Mansfield, unlike most English people, appreciated this highly spiced food as much as I did.

We left Waldia the following morning with seven mules and an escort of armed *zabanyas*. We had two servants with us: Bogale, a thirty-year-old Amhara who had been my cook's boy while I was at Dessie, and Gasha, a Galla who worked for the Mansfields; both spoke some English.

It was cloudy and threatened rain as we set off, and we camped that night in thick mist high on the southern face of the Lasta mountains. In the morning, after a steep climb to twelve thousand feet, we crossed them, and left the clouds behind. As we went down the valley on the far side the bare mountains towered above us. High up on their slopes, men and boys, dressed in skins, were ploughing with oxen; preceding us down the path were several caravans, their donkeys loaded with bars of salt from the Danakil country. Aloes in flower flamed red along the hillsides, the chill air smelt agreeably of herbs, while overhead, against white cumulus clouds in a deep blue sky, lammergeyer and griffon vultures circled on motionless wings. Lower down the valley we passed homesteads and villages, with churches in groves of juniper.

We marched for eight hours that day and seven the next, before arriving at Lalibela. The extensive village was set among massive junipers at 8500 feet, on a shoulder of the high mountains to the north. The thatched houses, unlike the circular *tukuls* I knew, were stone-built, rectangular, and in many cases two-storeyed. At that date only two were roofed in the corrugated iron which has become so incongruous and unsightly a feature of Abyssinian villages.

Lalibela's weekly market, a scene unchanged over the years, was under way when we arrived. Of the famous monolithic churches we had come to see there was at first sight no sign, for they were below ground level and only visible from close at hand.

We were courteously received by the chief priest, a refined and informative man who invited us to pitch our tent in his compound. While we were in Lalibela he entertained us lavishly, and personally showed us round the churches. There were twelve of these, all quite different. The most spectacular had been chiselled out of enormous blocks of tufa, and separated by deep trenches from the surrounding rock. Some of the others were detached on all sides except from the rock overhead; others again had been excavated into rock faces. One called Beta Medhane Alam (Saviour of the World) was over a hundred feet long, seventy-two wide and thirty-six high, with external and internal columns precisely aligned: another, Beta Giorgis, was in the form of a Greek cross. Both were monolithic.

All these astounding rock-hewn churches were created in the thirteenth century at the instance of King Lalibela of the 'usurping' Zagwe dynasty; they are supposedly modelled on then existing churches, which were mostly destroyed in the sixteenth century by Muslim invaders under Ahmad Granj. Seeing them, I was amazed by the inspiration that had visualized them, and the craftsmanship and labour that had created them.

Lalibela, inaccessibly situated in the mountainous heart of Abyssinia, symbolized for me the history of this ancient land; it represented to its people, with their deep religious faith and veneration for the past, something of what the monasteries had represented to the English before the Reformation. Perhaps no other place in the world has so profoundly impressed me.

Alvares had visited Lalibela in about 1521; Rohlfs, a German explorer, had done so in 1865. Since then comparatively few Europeans had been there. I was horrified to hear in Addis Ababa of plans to fly tourists to Lalibela; in such a place large groups of ignorant visitors, with both sexes often dressed alike, would have had a disruptive effect. One could imagine importunate crowds following the tourists, demanding money to be photographed, and learning to beg and pilfer.

At 5 a.m. on the Sunday of our visit, under a full moon, we went with the chief priest to a service in Beta Mariam, the church that was most generally used. As we approached, the sound of chanting and drumming rose apparently out of the ground ahead of us. The service lasted until ten, and we stood throughout; no one sits. On arrival we had been handed armrests resembling crutches, and after a time were thankful for them. I was inspired by the extraordinary high-pitched chanting; one boy, who did most of the singing, had a really lovely voice. When we came out the *debtaras*, or deacons, performed a traditional slow dance to the beat of their drums.

While we were at Lalibela we visited an eleventh-century church called Imrahanna Krestos, four hours away on Abuna Yosef, a mountain in the province of Wag. It was concealed in a cave in a ravine, surrounded by forest, and was one of the churches that survived the Muslim incursion. One of the others was Debra Damot in Tigre, which could only be reached by a rope up a sheer cliff. Imraha was built of alternating layers of dark beams and of stones faced with smooth plaster. Situated as it was in the cave, with darkness behind it, the church looked extraordinarily impressive, though I thought the outside was more so than its gloomy interior. We camped nearby in the forest among magnificent junipers, lit all night by the moon: to me, Imraha conveyed a rare quality.

I have heard Europeans condemn the Abyssinian clergy as ignorant, superstitious, and dissolute. This was not the impression I formed of the priests at Lalibela and Imrahanna; I was struck by their courtesy, kindliness and evident piety, and they personified 'the gentle Ethiopian'. In fact I would attribute the lack of vindictiveness, traditionally so marked in the Abyssinian character, to the teaching of their church.

Leaving Imrahanna in the morning, we rode back to Lalibela; the whole way was a succession of breathtaking views, half across Abyssinia, it seemed. The next day we left Lalibela, and travelling by Waldia and Dessie reached Addis Ababa on 1 March.

I left Addis Ababa again on 26 March, this time with Bogale and Gasha on a bus for Soddu; there I intended to hire mules and start my journey through Southern Abyssinia to Moyale on the Kenya border. However, the road to Soddu was so appalling as a result of recent rain that the driver insisted on turning back. Eventually we got a lift on a lorry loaded with tins of kerosene. That night it poured again, but though we often stuck axle-deep in mud, we managed to reach Soddu in the evening of 29 March.

405

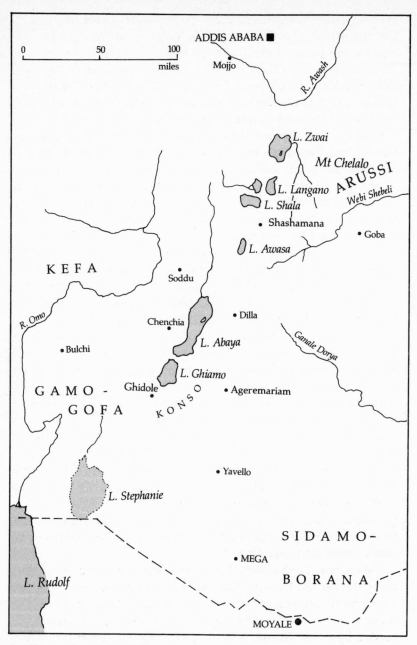

Southern Abyssinia, 1959

I went to an American mission station and they gave me a room. Despite their hospitality, these missionaries particularly exasperated me; they constantly referred to themselves and their few converts as 'The Elect', and seemed to be chiefly concerned with endeavours to make the local Christians discard the blue or green threads that all adherents of the Abyssinian Monophysite Church wore round the neck. Understandably, they met no success.

Mules in Soddu were hard to come by, but the Governor was helpful and found me two riding mules and four for baggage. I expected that at this season we would have a wet and uncomfortable journey, but it did not worry me. What I should have hated was the prospect of travelling any further by motor transport, which even under favourable conditions I dislike; with mules I felt the next two months should be rewarding.

Leaving Soddu on 1 April we visited Lake Abaya in the Rift Valley, then headed back to the mountains, arriving three days later at Chenchia, a small town high up in open country. Below it, in downward succession, were belts of giant heath, thickets of bamboo, and forests of juniper and hagenia. My route to Konso, which I was particularly anxious to visit, would take me through Bulchi, and the Governor at Chenchia assisted me by ordering fresh mules for the onward journey. In the past it had been possible to hire the same animals for an entire journey; now, thanks to the introduction of motor transport, the old system had broken down and it was necessary to replace the mules every few days.

It took seven days, travelling five or six hours a day, to reach Bulchi. Sometimes we camped near a village in the mountains, sometimes in the thorn bush country below. The 'little rains', always heavy in the south, were now really under way, and for the next week we had torrential rain every day, with thunder and gale-force winds, though fortunately the worst of it was after dark. When the sun came out after a storm the world looked beautiful, rain-washed and sparkling.

Bogale and Gasha were both hard-working, never grumbling about the wet, and always ready to help with the mules. Bogale was a forceful character and assumed control of the caravan; but unfortunately he was subject to unpredictable bouts of ill temper succeeded by sulks. Gasha, however, accepted his tantrums uncomplainingly and cheerfully produced meals, sometimes under seemingly impossible conditions.

During the next few days we several times came across tracks of
lion and once we sighted a small herd of buffalo, but altogether
during this journey I saw few wild animals. Game had once been as
plentiful as in Kenya, but the well-armed Abyssinians had nearly
wiped it out.

It was market day in Bulchi when we arrived there after a climb of
over three thousand feet. The little town consisted almost entirely of
grass-thatched *tukuls* among scattered junipers and eucalyptus. We
camped nearby on the edge of the escarpment, with a tremendous
view across the Rift Valley to distant mountains; this was the most
spectacular view that I had yet seen in Abyssinia.

We left Bulchi on 16 April and travelled through the mountains,
reaching Garaisi five days later. From there, at ten thousand feet, I
looked down on Lake Ghiamo in the bottom of the Rift Valley. Two
days further on, at Ghidole, I had another immense view, north
along the length of the lake with continuous ranges of mountains on
either side, and south across the desert towards Mega and the
Kenya border.

We spent two days at Ghidole negotiating for other mules, then
descended gradually to the hot, bush-covered lowlands, and when
we reached the village of Bakalawi we were in Konso country. We
camped near an Icelandic mission at Bakalawi; there had been a
Norwegian mission at Ghidole, and an Australian couple were
starting one at Bulchi. These particular missionaries happened to be
simple, friendly people; nonetheless I did resent their presence.
How many missionaries, I wondered gloomily, representing rival
denominations from Catholics to Nonconformists, Baptists,
Seventh Day Adventists and others, were now at work in Southern
Abyssinia, gratuitously disrupting the life of these tribal people?

The Konso, however, numbering about thirty thousand, were
still pagan and, as yet, little affected by outside pressures. Their
villages were set among stony hills some five thousand feet high,
the hillsides carefully terraced and cultivated. Each village, and each
group of houses, was enclosed by a well-constructed stone wall.
Flowering acacias and tall *Euphorbia candelabrum* dotted a landscape
greened by recent rain; later in the season water would be scarce.

Konso women wore leather caps and leather aprons; the men
affected a variety of hairstyles, carried spears and wore long knives
hung in sheaths from their necks. One eighteen-year-old boy had
two ostrich feathers in his hair, to show that he had lately under-

gone some form of initiation. I was told that the aged Konso chief lived in seclusion in a grove of trees on a hill. The most remarkable things I saw here were the Konso monuments commemorating famous warriors: the statue of the warrior himself would be flanked by others representing the men, or even lions, he had killed. These figures were up to four feet high; some were painted red. One of them had a phallic symbol sticking from the forehead, which meant that this particular victim had been of the Boran tribe, some of whose men will ceremonially wear a metal phallus on their forehead.

After three days among the Konso I left for Teltale. Though little more than a big village, this was an administrative centre for the Boran, a large Galla tribe who owned camels as well as cattle; many Boran had migrated into Kenya to escape from the Abyssinians after they had been conquered by Menelik. The Governor of Teltale was away, but his wife, a masterful old lady, entertained me and procured for me two camels and two mules.

We left for Mega on 4 May and travelled for five days across semi-desert country, camping each night near Boran villages, temporary mat-roofed structures whose inhabitants were generous with the fresh and sour milk that was an important part of their diet. I liked these people. Pastoralists have always appealed to me more than agriculturalists, and these pagan Boran recalled the Arussi I had encountered on the Webi Shebeli twenty-five years before.

Then we arrived at the British Consulate at Mega. Close by, an escarpment crowned with dying juniper forest fell away to the hot plains far below. There were a few greater kudu in Mega, survivors from a large herd that rinderpest had practically wiped out the previous year.

John Bromley, the Consul, was on leave when I arrived, but a Vice-Consul, young Ian Reeman, was there acting for him. Reeman was a good host and I was happy to spend a few days here in comfort. My shoes were now worn out and Reeman offered to motor me to Moyale, a British District Headquarters on the Kenya border, where he thought I might get others. It was thanks to these worn-out shoes that I thus met George Webb, District Commissioner at Moyale, a good linguist speaking Boran as well as Swahili, a widely read man, humorous and eminently civilized. George sent for the local cobbler and arranged for a pair of leather *chapli* sandals to be ready by breakfast time next day – which they were. Meanwhile he and his wife Jo put Reeman and myself up.

George Webb had a gift for lucid exposition, and that evening I learnt much about his Boran and Somali tribesmen, as well as the Turkana, Samburu and other peoples of northern Kenya, with whom a few years later I was to become familiar. Next morning he motored me round Moyale township: just outside it we passed fresh droppings of an elephant; across the border none now survived. Reeman and I went back to Mega in the afternoon. As I left, George said to me, 'My heart sank when I saw you. I thought, "Oh God, another poor white come to bounce a cheque."' I met the Webbs again when I went to Kenya two years later and since then they have become my closest friends.

On our way back to Mega, we encountered a migration of Degodia Somalis; men, women and children with a mass of camels advancing on a broad front far across the 'Somali Line' that had been drawn by the Abyssinian authorities in an attempt to prevent any further intrusion into other tribes' territories by these ever-encroaching Somalis.

Reeman also took me, with Bogale and Gasha, from Mega to Yavello, where he left us. Like all the towns that had sprung up along the main Italian motor roads, Yavello was an unattractive collection of tin-roofed shacks, many of them squalid, noisy drinking-houses. After leaving Yavello I travelled for four days among the Guggi, a pastoral people similar to the Boran. I was glad to see that they too were little affected as yet by the Abyssinian administration, or by the efforts of missionaries to convert them. One day we camped by a village, near a deep pool by a cliff, under a grove of large acacias hung with orchids. No one, the Guggi told me, was allowed to cut these trees, since here lived a sacred python, twenty-five feet long they said, to which they offered sacrificial sheep or goats.

We arrived at Ageremariam next day. We had been travelling through thorn bush since leaving Yavello, but near Ageremariam we entered a forest of tall, dark, lichen-hung *podocarpus*. From here we sent back the two camels and two mules and took on five other mules. We were now back in the highlands, and the scenery should have been magnificent, but all I can remember is heavy rain and low cloud. Luckily I had bought three mackintosh capes in Addis Ababa; wrapped in these, we plodded along the road, while one torrential

410

downpour after another turned it into a river. Four days later we reached Dilla, where we found a bus to take us to Shashamana, and thence next day to Addis Ababa, where we arrived on 27 May.

Later, on my way back to England I stayed for a week in Khartoum with Chapman-Andrews who was now our Ambassador there. Khartoum had already changed greatly since the Sudanese independence in 1956; the town now extended into what had been desert; it was there that the Embassies and houses of senior officials were situated. The former residences along the bank of the Blue Nile, where the senior British officials had once lived and where, when I first arrived in the Sudan, I had done my round of duty calls, were now offices or even stores. However, I felt no regret: with independence an era had ended. For years men like Douglas Newbold, Angus Gillan, Charles Dupuis and Guy Moore had given of their best to this country. Now it was back in the hands of its owners, perhaps the most likeable people in all Africa, the Sudanese.

CHAPTER 30

North to the Simien; and Magdala

AFTER VISITING EUROPE I was back in Addis Ababa again at the end of December 1959. During my journey in Southern Abyssinia earlier in the year I had been travelling through country that Menelik had annexed to his Empire only at the end of the last century. It bore no resemblance, whether in landscape or inhabitants, to Northern Abyssinia. This time I planned to take a different direction and follow the Abbai, or Blue Nile, north to Lake Tana; thence I would go to Gondar, on my way to the Simien mountains; from the Simien I would return by way of Lalibela again, and Magdala, to Addis Ababa.

When selecting my route, I bore in mind that the way the regular caravans went from Addis Ababa to Tana and beyond took them across the Abbai at Shafartak, then north through Gojjam to Bahr dar Giorgis, and from there to Gondar; it was of course well known and presented no difficulties. On the other hand, the route along the east side of the Abbai had to traverse very broken country indeed, across several formidable gorges. Moreover, whereas I was familiar with Gojjam, this eastern route passed through little-known country; it was the obvious choice for me.

Though the Emperor provided me in January 1960 with letters to the Governors I would meet on my route, so that I had hopes of leaving almost at once, I now encountered maddening delays before Customs would release a new tent I had had sent out from England. This hold-up was thoroughly typical of Abyssinian bureaucracy. When I had at last obtained my tent, the Mansfields drove me to Mullu, the starting point for my journey. With some misgivings I again employed Bogale; on my last journey he had been efficient, but had too often proved quarrelsome and aggressive; he promised, however, to mend his ways, and entreated me to take him. As cook I took an elderly Amhara, Walda Hanna, whom the Sandfords recommended; and he produced a boy called Ababu to help him.

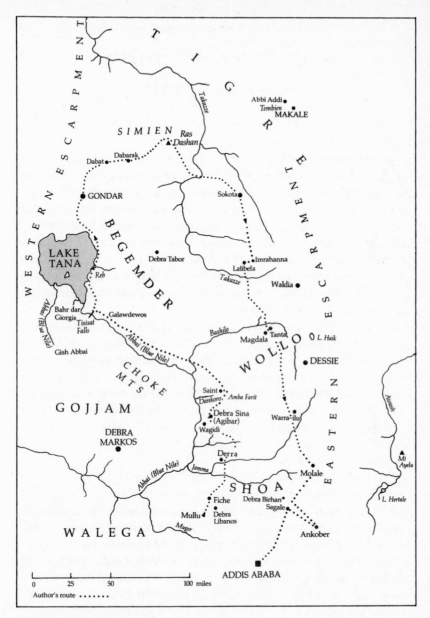

Northern Abyssinia, 1960

413

After last year's delays and difficulties in hiring animal transport, I decided this time to buy my own. I engaged three muleteers, one a Tigrean called Mabratu who spoke some Arabic, and sent them with Bogale to a nearby market to buy three riding mules and five baggage mules; the Sandfords took me there by car on 26 January, and we found Bogale had already bought the animals. They looked in good condition, and certainly proved it next morning by bucking off their loads as fast as we could put them on; one mule broke free and bolted for several miles before Bogale caught it. However, once we got them under control, they went well.

In two days we reached Fiche: this was the place where in 1941 I had brought the Italian garrison from Agibar to join the main force that had surrendered to Wingate at Wagidi. The Governor at Fiche now provided me with letters to his deputies, and an escort to accompany me as far as Derra, since the country ahead had a bad name for *shifta*, brigands. We skirted the mountains near Fiche, crossed the Jamma river and arrived at Derra on 7 February; it was from there that Wingate had sent me ahead to outflank and hold up the retreating Italian army near Wagidi.

This time it took me three days to reach Wagidi. On the way there I visited an abandoned rock-hewn church, Debra Karbi Giorgis, hollowed out of the cliff below Wagidi: it was cruder than the Lalibela churches, and was one of four such in this neighbourhood. Then, after a stiff climb up to the plateau, we passed the scene of my little battle and camped inside the walls of the now tumbledown fort that I had occupied in 1941. Next day, after a steep descent and another hard climb on to the adjacent tableland, we reached the other fort that had surrendered to me. A village had since been built nearby, and we camped there: the place was no longer called Agibar, but Debra Sina.

We now set off to cross Amba Farit, the 1300-foot mountain above the village. Apparently someone had been waylaid and robbed there on the previous day by a band of *shifta*; however, with my escort of four police I felt secure, though my only weapon was a single-barrelled shotgun. The uphill track, first through giant heath, then giant lobelia, was nowhere unduly steep. Beyond the bare mountain-top we crossed the head of the Dankoro valley: we could see it was forested down to the Dankoro's confluence with the Abbai; it was an unexpected sight in a treeless region, where such few trees as had survived were usually only around churches.

414

We camped at a village in Amara Saint, in one of the many deep valleys we had crossed that day. It rained throughout the night and the crest of Amba Farit gleamed white with hail next morning. In the morning, accompanied with three headmen, two police and a dozen armed men, we climbed to what had in a geological timescale been a vast plateau, now sliced into separate tables by precipitous thousand-foot gorges. We crossed a series of these tables, typically up to half a mile wide, each linked with the next by a narrow ridge of rock, dropping sheer on either side to the gorges at our feet. On shelves near the foot of the cliffs were occasional small villages but on the remnants of this waterless plateau no habitation.

Towards evening we worked our way down a spur and passed a small spring where some men and boys, clad only in leather aprons with skins about their shoulders, were watering a small herd of cattle. From here, after a further short but difficult descent, we came to the village of one of our headmen; he generously killed a goat for us and lent me his house to sleep in.

Next morning, after scrambling down for two more hours, we forded the Bashilo, a fast-flowing river that joined the Abbai. We were now in Begemder and that evening, after we had made a hot climb to a village on a shelf across the valley, an old man sat with us and recited the names of illustrious ones whom he had seen pass this way over the years: Ras Kassa, Negus Walda Giorgis, Ras Hailu, Ras Gugsa Wale, Ras Imru and several more. His reminiscences brought vividly to mind events dating from my childhood and youth. Astoundingly, one of the headmen had enquired on the previous day if Lij Yasu – dead for a quarter of a century – were still alive. I realized then how remote and out of touch this region was.

The local Kenyazmatch arrived at sunset, and was angry that the villagers had not done more for me, though in fact they had provided *injera*, eggs and *talla*, and had brought wood, and grass for the mules. He accompanied me next day on a steep, seemingly endless climb to the plateau above, from which I could see the Blue Nile not more than three miles away. From now on the going was easy across bare, gently undulating country.

Five days later, on 29 February, we arrived at Galawdewos, where I was hospitably received in his rather dilapidated house by the Fitaurari, a delightful old man of seventy-five, with a fringe of white beard, still active and alert. He had seen much fighting during his life, had marched to defeat at Zebit under Ras Gugsa Wale, had taken part in the desperate hand-to-hand fighting against the Italians in the Tembien, and had helped the British at the capture of Gondar.

In the morning I visited the stone-built rectangular church of Merka Samait Galawdewos. It stood on the hill above the Fitaurari's house, among ancient junipers in a walled enclosure with a gatehouse over the entrance. From there I had my first sight of Lake Tana. The church had been burnt by Ahmad Granj in the sixteenth century, and its roof had been replaced by thatch supported on external poles. The priests took me to the gatehouse and from a jumble of stuff unearthed a moth-eaten burnous of red wool with a tasselled head-covering, like ones I had seen in North Africa. They assured me it had belonged to Ahmad Granj, and reached only to his waist. I knew he had been killed in battle near Lake Tana. The site might well have been near here; Galawdewos was the Amharic name of the Emperor Claudius who had defeated him.

As we approached Galawdewos the bare dry landscape gave place to streams lined with jasmine-scented thickets, and scattered junipers and olive trees, remnants of ancient forest with villages and herds of cattle and many churches on the high ground. By now our mules were in a sorry condition: they had been lightly loaded, but much of our route had been exacting, and there had been a constant shortage of grazing; even here the land was badly over-grazed.

Three days later, from our camp nearby, I was able to go with a local guide to admire the Blue Nile Falls. These are known as Tisisat, 'Smoke of Fire', and are twelve miles from where the Big Abbai emerges from Lake Tana. At this dry season they comprised three separate falls with a hundred and fifty foot drop, the central one the widest and most impressive. Even now there was much spray and a rainbow, but with their total width of some six hundred yards the falls must be a tremendous spectacle when the river is in spate.

From our viewing point we went down to what remained of a small sixteenth-century Portuguese bridge which the Italians, in an act of sheer vandalism, had dynamited during the war. At this point the entire river converged to rush through a crevice in the basalt rock, less than eight feet wide. Our guide said men had been known to jump across. It was now bridged with tree trunks.

On our way back we stopped in the guide's village, where they gave us coffee, *talla* and *injera*; as soon as we left his house we were asked into another for more coffee. I enjoyed lingering among these hospitable people.

416

We arrived at Lake Tana after three days in which we first traversed a ridge of hills through hot, dusty, uninteresting country, then crossed the Gumare river, and eventually came on to a flat plain that extended to the lake. A friendly *balambaras* gave us lunch in his village and then accompanied us to the lakeside; on the way we passed other villages, and larger herds of fine cattle than I had previously seen anywhere in Abyssinia. The ground was densely cultivated, in places to the water's edge. We followed the lake shore for a couple of hours until we came to the Reb, a broad river flowing into it, and there we camped. In the evening the colours were lovely, pale shades of gold and straw, with the misty blue of distant mountains; in the morning, as the sun rose, the light on plain and mountain was very beautiful.

The people here were the Waito, a distinctive type, dark with high-bridged noses; men and boys wore only a thick *shamma,* flung round them to leave a shoulder bare. The *balambaras* took me down the Reb river and out on to the lake in a *tankwa*, a papyrus canoe with a pointed prow and a raised deck: the Waito built these *tankwas* and acted as boatmen on the lake. As we drifted peacefully along I could listen to the constant cry of many birds: Egyptian and spur-winged geese, crowned cranes, larger grey cranes which I did not recognize, and along the shore sacred and glossy ibis, egrets and many sorts of wader. When we got back the villagers netted some small perch for our midday meal; the *balambaras* mentioned that there were hippo in the lake, and that the Waito hunted and ate them.

Later we ferried our luggage over the river and swam the mules across. The *balambaras* had exchanged his mule for the two weakest of mine, which would soon recover here. I was sorry to say goodbye to him, for he was a kindly man who had gone out of his way to help me. We now headed back to the hills we had left when we approached the lake and the next day travelled along below them for an eight-hour march till they met the lake again. In the evening Bogale had a silly row with Walda Hanna and Mabrutu over a piece of *injera*, and spent the following day in a state of near-hysterics. When we reached Gondar a day later I sent him back to Addis Ababa on a bus. By now we were all glad to be rid of him.

We spent five days in Gondar to rest the mules and buy grain for them in the market. I camped just outside the town in the British

CMS Protestant missionary compound. Stokes, who ran the mission, was away in Fiche, and I was sorry to miss him, for he was a scholar who was knowledgeable and deeply interested in the indigenous Abyssinian Christianity. However, his wife was there and I appreciated her hospitality. But Gondar I disliked. To me the town typified the least attractive aspects of Abyssinia's recent development: ubiquitous tin roofs, ramshackle modern buildings, noise and fumes of motor transport; its inhabitants forfeited any distinction of appearance by wearing shabby European clothes. I was left with an impression of squalor which would not have been there thirty years earlier.

In this shoddy setting even the castles I had come to see lost something, but the two most attractive, which alone had escaped indifferent restoration by the Italians, were outside the town. In fact, all these castles, erected in the time of Fasiladas and his immediate successors, were singularly impressive. They are of various designs and lack any apparent affinity with buildings elsewhere. So their derivation is disputed. In my view, though they were built after the Portuguese had been expelled from Abyssinia, they must owe something to Portuguese influence. Buxton, in his *Travels in Ethiopia*, suggested that they derived from southern Arabia, but during my wanderings there I saw nothing like them.

After Gondar we spent two days at Dabat, where I sold two of my mules and bought three others. Here there was an English Protestant mission to the Falasha: these people now claimed to be Jews, but their pre-talmudic beliefs differed from orthodox Judaism. As so-called Abyssinian Jews they were superficially indistinguishable from their Christian neighbours, among whom they lived amicably.

A week after leaving Gondar we reached Dabarak: all this time our way had lain across cold, bare country along the edge of the western escarpment. Now, head of us, stretched the Simien range, including one of the highest peaks in Africa. This was hard to believe when viewing it from the south: it was obviously higher than the high ground across which we were travelling, but neither spectacular nor impressive.

We left Dabarak in the morning and climbed steadily up on to Simien through giant heath, some of it as large as fair-sized apple trees. It was interspersed with tall clusters of St John's wort, heavy with bright yellow flowers; there were also occasional wild roses and a few small purple irises. I saw many birds of prey during the day, lammergeyer, augur buzzards, griffon vultures, as well as bald-headed and fan-tailed ravens. In the evening, we camped beside a village in the open country near the crest of the mountain, and I walked over to its northern face.

A staggering sight, unmatched anywhere else in Abyssinia or possibly even in Africa, met my eyes. A precipice miles long fell sheer for thousands of feet before easing imperceptibly into heath-covered slopes and lower still forest. Eight thousand feet below me, the Takazze river half-circled the mountain and flowed on towards the Sudan.

We next followed the escarpment eastwards in the direction of Ras Dashan, at 15,750 feet the summit of Simien. For a short way the ridge narrowed to a few yards, with the great precipice on one side and the abrupt heads of valleys on the other, then it widened again into an expanse of downs and valleys. There were several small villages up here, of circular stone-built houses roughly thatched with grass. Even in the daytime it was cold and at night it was bitter; the men and boys had wrapped skins over their clothes, and the boys wore distinctive knitted woollen caps. Much of the land, however steep, was ploughed, and on the slopes were large herds of cattle and flocks of sheep and goats. There were donkeys too but no mules, and since our own mules were now in very poor condition I bought two donkeys to carry much of our baggage, which allowed our more exhausted mules to go unburdened.

After three days of short marches between villages, we camped under Ras Dashan, at the highest village on Simien, and rested the mules for a day. The villagers gave them straw, which was plentiful, and I bought them some barley. They had had a hard time. We had tried to cross valleys near the valley head, but had sometimes been forced to go lower down, which then gave us another steep climb up the far side. On one such ascent, to about fourteen thousand feet, the mule Ababu was in charge of collapsed, and we had to leave it lying. Ababu was in tears. The headman accompanying us promised he would rescue it on his way back to his village.

Here the northern precipice, spectacular enough where I had first seen it, was even more so. It was cut through by tremendous sheer-sided gorges. Those cliffs, the most impressive in Simien, were also the last stronghold of the walia ibex; this magnificent animal, always confined to this range, was now on the verge of extinction, though the villagers said a few could still be found in fours and fives on the Ambaras and Buahit cliffs. Here I also saw and heard some choughs.

It took us three hours next day, on a steep but easy path, to reach the pass, near the summit of Ras Dashan. It was guarded by a loopholed breastwork which the headman said, rather improbably, had been built at the time of the battle of Adua. Here were giant lobelias and everlastings; lower down some red-hot pokers grew among the grass; cattle and sheep grazed almost up to the pass. From the last village I had observed small white patches on the topmost slopes and wondered if they were snow, which I had not heard of on Simien; in fact they turned out to be ice.

We would now be beginning to head back towards Addis Ababa. On my way, I wanted to revisit Lalibela, and then to go and see Magdala, where the capture of that mountain and the death of the Emperor Theodore had marked the end of Napier's campaign of 1868. Finally, I intended to inspect the battlefield of Sagale where Ras Tafari and the Shoan army, by defeating Negus Mikael in 1917, had ensured the deposition of Lij Yasu. My immediate concern, however, was to reach Sokota, the capital of Wag, and replace my mules: the two donkeys had gone well but only three of the mules were now able to carry any load at all.

After three hours' descent of an easy grassy slope covered with lobelias, we reached a village; the Fitaurari was away so we camped in the shelter of some nearby rocks. No heath grew on this side of the mountain and Walda Hanna had to burn cow dung for his fire. Though we met a sharp hail storm as we reached the village, we had been fortunate: it would have been singularly unpleasant to have experienced it on Simien. I did later watch a tremendous storm raging over Ras Dashan, and now, nearly every night, we were subjected to violent gales, one of which blew my tent flat.

After resting the mules for a day and buying them some oats, we set off on 26 March for Sokota, a fortnight's march away. Luckily, two police went with us; without them we should not have got through, since it was they who secured for us donkeys to carry our loads from village to village. Often this was only achieved by overriding the vociferous protests of their owners, though I did compensate them when we exchanged their donkeys for others. On this journey I gained no impression of a downtrodden peasantry pauperized by feudal landlords. On the contrary, though the villagers I encountered were invariably hospitable they impressed me as independent-minded and quick to assert their rights. Nor was I conscious of real poverty.

We travelled for two days through low, hot country inhabited by Agaw. At one midday halt Agaw from nearby villages brought us enough *injera* and *wat* for a huge meal, no doubt instructed by their chief, who was an effectual and helpful man.

On 30 March, a day when we met several donkey caravans carrying salt to Simien, we crossed the Takazze, a fair-sized river bordered with tamarisk, flowing here at the foot of a steep mountain. Somewhere in this neighbourhood the Italians had bombed and gassed Ras Kassa's and Ras Seyum's armies as they forded the river on their retreat from Abbi Addi. As we were crossing by a ford I saw a crocodile; the locals were evidently scared of them.

For the next seven days, trying to nurse our mules as much as possible, we struggled along, doing two or three hours in the morning and another short march in the evening. Much of the route was exacting, with frequent steep ascents and descents; nearly everywhere water was hard to come by, which made it difficult to water the mules. However, the villagers were always helpful and kind, and fetched water for ourselves and provided us with food. There were impressive views across Tigre and back towards Simien, but the country we were passing through was not spectacular. Still, I should have enjoyed travelling here had I not been anxious about getting to Sokota, where we arrived at last on 6 April. It was an attractive little town, in a hollow among pepper trees with an escarpment to the north. Many of the houses had two storeys, and all had thatched roofs. It was the capital of Wag, governed by the hereditary Wagshum. The present incumbent was very friendly and spoke good English. Hearing I was having trouble, he had sent his representative to the last village to ensure I was provided with transport.

Two miles south of Sokota I visited a church that had been meticulously carved into a face of rock, from which it was separated by deep trenches. The mausoleum of the Wagshums was in an adjacent cave, the body of each in a coffin with his name on it.

I had left one mule in the last village and I now sold two more for a nominal price and bought four to replace them. I still had my own riding mule; he was thin from lack of grazing but otherwise fit for the

421

journey back to Addis Ababa. For choice I had walked most of the way from Fiche, and I intended to do the same from now on. It was only as a matter of prestige that I needed a riding mule: in Abyssinia no one of standing travelled without one. My two donkeys, though they had been heavily loaded, were still in good condition.

When I left Sokota on 9 April it was with a sense of relief to be travelling again with sound transport. Watching our exhausted mules carrying loads on Simien had distressed me, and there was the added anxiety that if they collapsed we should be stranded. Now I was happy to see Walda Hanna riding once more. After I had got rid of Bogale he had taken charge and now the five of them worked contentedly together. The Wagshum had provided me with two fresh police to go as far as Lalibela, and I now parted regretfully with the others, who had done all they could to help me.

We climbed two mountains and from the jagged rocky crest of the second we could see Abuna Yosef, the fourteen thousand foot mountain above Lalibela. After a laborious traverse of a series of steep ridges, we eventually camped on the edge of the forest near Imrahanna Krestos. An early start next day brought us to Imrahanna as the sun was lighting the trees; the countryside here was green after recent rain. Having unloaded among the junipers and olives where Philip Mansfield and I had stayed the previous year, I followed a path bordered by aloes in flower along the foot of the cliff, to the large cave that housed the church. The early sun shone in, on to the alternating bands of dark wood and plaster. The priests remembered me, welcomed me and conducted me round. I was glad to find that this singular and very ancient church in its superb environment retained for me the same magic that I had felt on first seeing it.

I left Imrahanna at midday so as to be in Lalibela for Easter; this year Ethiopian Easter coincided with our own. On our way there we crossed a shoulder of Abuna Yosef and camped on a shelf of the mountain. We arrived at Lalibela early next morning, the day before Good Friday.

The head priest let me camp once more in his compound, and later invited me to accompany him to the Easter Service in Beta Mariam, which would begin at nine at night and go on till five on Easter morning. I shall never forget that service in the dimly lit, rock-hewn church, with the dark devout faces of the white-clad congregation standing massed around me, the drifting fragrance of incense, and above all the compelling music of those alien chants, and the clear beauty of a boy's voice, unaccompanied. The singing alternated with passages from the liturgy in ancient Ge'ez; whenever the reader mispronounced a word he was corrected by the congregation. At midnight we processed round the outside of the church, each carrying a lighted candle; perhaps symbolically we were looking for the body of the risen Christ. The service ended with the dance of the *debtara* to the slow beat of church drums which hung round their necks.

Later the head priest feasted his priests and *debtaras*, some one hundred and fifty strong, under a canopy of branches on the terrace below his house. The feast lasted from eleven till six in the evening on a fine and sunny day. I was called on to make a speech, which my host translated. At the end of the festival, boy deacons came with a drum and danced and frolicked.

Next day the head priest took me to Medhane Alam, where he showed me a large processional cross, reputedly of gold, which had been found some years ago in a hole over one of the arches, perhaps concealed at the time of Ahmad Granj's invasion, and he also brought out their oldest book, partly glossed in Arabic script, for me to see. We then went to the three adjacent churches of Debra Sina, Golgotha, and Selassie The Trinity. On the walls of Golgotha were four carved reliefs, three quarters life-size, of St John, St George and two Ethiopian saints. This church contained the tomb of King Lalibela, draped with cloth, and the requisite *tabot*, a sanctified slab of wood representing the Ark, on a covered stand of the same size and shape as the tomb. Behind Lalibela's tomb was a relief of Christ in the tomb with a guardian angel at His feet. I was shown a small hand-cross of good design, an arm-rest and a stool, all said to have belonged to Lalibela. We then entered the sanctuary of Selassie; it contained three large stone altars of equal size and another small altar between the middle and left-hand one. The large central altar had carved on it a winged figure, which the priest told me represented man, lion, eagle and bull. This sanctuary was the holy of holies. An Italian had apparently forced his way in during the occupation; otherwise no European before me, the priest assured me, had set foot in here.

From here we went to the other group of churches, Emanuel, Merkurios, Abba Libanos and Gabriel: no two at Lalibela were alike.

To reach Merkurios we followed a pitch-dark tunnel through the rock. After these we went to Giorgis, which stands apart from the others and was my favourite. Once again I stood amazed at the vision of the man who had conceived these churches, had visualized them carved from the rock beneath his feet, and had then been able to instigate what must have seemed an impossible task. The labour had been immense, to hew out the trenches and courts, to excavate and fashion the churches, and to dispose of thousands of tons of debris. Much of the craftsmanship was superb and it had been achieved with primitive tools in a sparsely peopled district. During the five days I remained at Lalibela, I was always conscious of the peace, and of the spirit of gentleness, that permeated this ancient sanctuary.

On 19 April we left Lalibela for Magdala, and after looking at two more rock churches, Nakatola and Gannata Mariam, we re-crossed the Takazze, here only a shallow stream, and camped by one of several villages under yet another escarpment. Next day, from ten thousand feet, I could see Magdala in the far distance, but it took us six more days, travelling some five hours a day, to reach it. At times we had to go almost due east to skirt the heads of ravines that ran down to the Blue Nile, and then had to make wide westward detours to avoid the canyons on our left.

On 23 April we arrived at the attractive little town of Ugualtiena. Among rocky tables around it I saw some of the maned gelada baboons that are only found in Abyssinia; lammergeyer were to be seen throughout the day.

Next we crossed the Bashilo: fortunately the river, which had been in flood, was down again when we reached it. We had had heavy rain and gales at night during the past four days, but only once while we were on the move. On the following day, we passed a church built by Negus Mikael, and a little further on the site of his *gibbi* or palace, which was connected to the plateau beyond by a neck eight yards wide; a deep ditch had once been cut across this neck, but had been filled in again. We continued across this plateau till we came to another pleasant, unspoilt little town, Tanta.

Opposite us was the sheer-sided plateau of Magdala, connected to the Tanta plateau by what looked like an impassable ridge. The Governor of Tanta, however, told me that Magdala could indeed be reached by a narrow track along this ridge. The Governor, Lij Faris, was a son of Dedjazmatch Gabra Mariam; he was related to the Empress Zauditu, and by marriage to Negus Mikael. He lived in some state and was outstandingly hospitable, and spoke excellent English.

I set off early next morning to visit Magdala with Walda Hanna, Ababu and Mabratu. We found that we were forced to descend from the connecting ridge into the valley, and from there we scrambled up the southern face of Magdala by a barely passable track. It took us three hours from Tanta to the top. It occurred to me that possibly Lij Yasu and Ras Yemer had used this track to escape when they were besieged on Magdala by the Shoan army after the battle of Sagale.

On Magdala's grassy plateau were some junipers, a hamlet of a dozen huts, and the church built by the Emperor John, who after an interval had succeeded Theodore. Otherwise, apart from a solitary man ploughing in the distance, a flock of sheep and goats, and a troop of baboons on the cliff's edge, there was nothing.

After a while an old man, grey-headed, stiff in his movements, wrapped in his *shamma*, emerged from one of the huts and greeted us. He was Alaqa Dessie, headman of this small community. Learning that I was English, he told me that his father had been here in Magdala when the British captured it in 1868. It was entirely probable, I thought, that his father had seen my grandfather in this place. On an empty mountain-top, where absolutely nothing from the tragic time of Theodore now survived, one dignified old man brought past and present together for a moment.

He showed me some faint traces in the ground where Theodore's church had once stood, and pointed out the spot where his father had told him Theodore was buried; not even a mound marked the grave. Then he conducted me to the site of Theodore's *gibbi*; it had stood on the edge of a precipice, from which Theodore had on occasions thrown his prisoners. From here a built-up path led down a steep slope to another plateau below. This, the only feasible access to Magdala, was the route by which Napier's army had gained the summit; elsewhere the cliffs were sheer, or nearly so.

A strong gateway had once guarded the entrance to Theodore's *gibbi* and it was here, refusing to surrender after the rout of his army, that the Emperor shot himself as the British troops stormed forward. Napier, I felt, would have had serious difficulty in taking Magdala if Theodore, instead of fatally giving battle below the mountain, had waited and defended this position; but it was always the custom of

Abyssinian armies to fight in the open, hand-to-hand. Years later Negus Mikael, Lij Yasu's father, had fortified Magdala and some of his stone walls could still be seen on the site.

We next visited the charming little church. It was built of mud with a thatched roof, and was surmounted by a fine cross presented by the Emperor John. Inside were striking paintings on cloth, depicting biblical scenes such as the Crucifixion, the Virgin suckling the Child, the raising of Lazarus, the entry into Jerusalem, Judgement Day and Hell. There was also a remarkable picture of the Emperor John with war drums and national flags, escorted in procession by Menelik of Shoa, Tekla Haimanot of Gojjam, Mikael of Wollo and Mangasha of Tigre.

Alaqa Dessie now led us back to his house, where he gave us coffee and insisted on our having lunch. On our way he pointed to the empty plain, saying, 'All this was once covered with houses.' I had always wanted to see Magdala and I thoroughly enjoyed the day, not least for Alaqa Dessie's company. He was a fine old man, with the innate dignity and courtesy of his race.

Back in Tanta I spent the next day enjoying the lavish hospitality of Lij Faris. We left again on 29 April, heading towards distant mountains across a plain intersected by deep gorges. It was a landscape dotted with small villages, their crops bright green after recent rain. Our host that day was the *balambaras* Ali Imam; he was Christian despite his Islamic name but many of the villagers here were Muslim. I had meant merely to rest in his village and then press on but he slaughtered a sheep for our midday meal and insisted we must stay for the night. We continued to meet with hospitality like this until we reached Addis Ababa, nineteen days later.

Our host at our next stop had fought against the Shoan army at Sagale forty-three years before, and he described to us the last desperate resistance before Negus Mikael, fighting sword in hand, was captured at last.

The Bashilo rose near his village, at the foot of cliffs so sheer that a dropped stone would fall clear for hundreds of feet. As we passed there in the morning, large numbers of griffon vultures, lammergeyer and ravens were circling the cliffs, and a peregrine shot by, while rock hyrax sunned themselves on boulders below.

Arriving at Warra-ilu next day, we met the Governor going on

426

his way out; he thereupon turned back and gave me a meal in his house. This was built inside a stockade, on a circular hill dominating the town, with splendid views all round.

Two days later, at Molale, we were on the border of Wollo and I looked across a deep valley into Shoa. It was there, among the gorges and mountains of Manz, that Ababa Aragai, the most redoubtable of the Patriot leaders, had successfully withstood the Italians.

After leaving Molale, we were forced to travel due north for some distance before we could circumvent several gorges descending from the east; after that we turned south along the watershed while chasms, some only a few yards away, yawned on either side. Eventually we found ourselves travelling along the very brink of the great eastern escarpment, on ground carpeted with clumps of flowering thyme, red-hot pokers, yellow and white daisies, blue forget-me-nots, white ranunculus and other flowers unknown to me, white, gold and purple. In the distance, when it was clear, Lake Hertale down in the Danakil desert could be seen, but cloud often obscured the view; there had been a thunderstorm that morning, and hail still lay on the ground. Reaching a small village eight hours after leaving Molale, we camped in a house, and made ourselves snug with a blazing fire of giant heath. Outside was a blustering and stormy night with driving mist.

Next morning however was fine, sunny and clear: I could make out the Arussi mountains and the Chercher range a hundred and fifty miles away across the Danakil desert, as well as Lake Hertale and Mount Ayelu. Most of that day we continued along the very edge of the escarpment. On every shelf were villages and every possible foot of ground had been cultivated, sometimes on slopes so steep that the digging must have been by hand. In the foothills were more villages and cultivation, with bush country beyond. We stopped after six hours at Mazazo, a large, scattered village; ahead I could see the pass of Termaber, where the road from Dessie climbed back up on to the escarpment. Near here some of Walda Hanna's relations had a farm, and in the morning we stopped with them for breakfast before going on for another four hours to spend the night at a police post on the main road. By now Mabratu was exhausted, so I put him on a passing bus and sent him ahead to Addis Ababa.

427

I was anxious to see Ankober, which had been Menelik's residence before he founded Addis Ababa. We therefore made a detour to the east. On our way we passed Tora Mask where in 1916 Ras Lul Seged's troops had been wiped out by Negus Mikael. The battle had been fought where Lul Seged had been camped, on the plateau above Ankober; I was shown where his tent had stood, where he had received his wound, and where he had died. There were stones set up to mark the spots where notable men had fallen, but other-wise on that bare hillside there was nothing to show where the battle had taken place. It had been a slaughter: fewer than two hundred men from Ras Lul Seged's army of eight thousand had survived it.

We went down a long steep slope into a valley, then climbed to the ridge beyond, where Gorobela, the town that had replaced Ankober, was situated; it was in fact little more than a large village. Below us was a small, steep, isolated hill on which Menelik's *gibbi*, of which almost nothing now survived, had stood. It was now over-grown with bushes and going there in the morning I was astonished at how restricted was the area of its summit, but there was a clear view of the approach to Ankober from the lowlands. Menelik, I was told, used to sit under a tree outside his palace and with his tele-scope watch his cattle watering down below.

That night heavy rain fell and as we set off next day on our way back to the plateau it was cold and drizzly weather. But it cleared later and we did ten hours that day; three more hours next morning brought us to the battlefield of Sagale. With us was a village head-man, who had been here as a boy at the time of the battle. Though my Amharic was indifferent I could follow his description of the fighting.

Two small hills eight hundred yards apart rose above the sur-rounding plain. The southern, some fifty feet high, had been occupied by Ras Tafari, the future Haile Selassie, and his personal troops; Fitaurari Habta Giorgis with the bulk of the Shoan Army was on Ras Tafari's right, Ras Kassa with levies from Sagale on his left. In front, and to the right of the smaller hill, a spring flowed into boggy ground. On the day of the battle the Wollo army attempted a surprise attack before dawn, but when some of their cavalry got bogged down here the noise and confusion alerted the Shoans. The battle then began with heavy firing on both sides, but soon the two armies closed and grappled in furious hand-to-hand fighting. For a time it seemed that Negus Mikael's army, led by Ras Ali, would win;

only when Ras Ali was captured did the Wollo forces start to give way.

I had never forgotten how, as a child, I had watched spellbound the triumphant return of the Shoan army to Addis Ababa, decked with the bloodstained clothes they had taken from the dead. Now, standing on Ras Tafari's little hill, I found it easy to picture the battle surging to and fro for hours on the plain below. Our guide said he had been to the battlefield the day after the battle: he described how the ground, especially near the spring, was littered with corpses, many stripped of their clothes. Even now, when I inspected the smaller hill where Negus Mikael had made his final stand, I found the clefts and crannies in the rock still filled with bones and skulls.

There beside the spring, before we left for Addis Ababa, I drank my coffee and ate my scrambled eggs, and sitting there I reflected what would have happened if Negus Mikael had won the battle, as he might so easily have done. Ras Tafari and the other Shoan leaders, if they had not been killed in the battle, would certainly have been executed. The Wollo army would have poured into Addis Ababa and pillaged the town. A bloodthirsty and vindictive Lij Yasu would have been restored as Emperor. As for what would have happened to us, with my father sheltering Ras Tafari's son in the Legation, I could only wonder. The whole future of Abyssinia, deprived of Ras Tafari's dedication to reform and his inflexible purpose, would have turned out very differently.

Two days later, after twenty hours on the road, we arrived in Addis Ababa. Sir Denis and Lady Wright kindly put me up at the British Embassy; I slept in the very room which Brian and I had shared as children.

Looking back on my recent journey, I wished I had been able to include Tigre in the itinerary. I regretted not seeing the giant monoliths at Aksum, and not travelling in the mountains of the Tembien, where the armies of Ras Kassa and Ras Seyum had so valiantly resisted the Italians. I had, however, been back to Lalibela and Imrahanna Krestos, and visited many places I had longed to see: Lake Tana, Simien, Gondar, Sokota, Ankober, the battlefield of Sagale and, above all, Magdala.

Some months later, on 14 December 1960, while I was in England, the Imperial Bodyguard attempted to overthrow the Emperor while he was abroad on a State Visit to Brazil. The revolt was instigated and directed by Germame Neway, who had been educated at a university in the United States and had for a time been Governor of Sidamo. His elder brother, General Mengistu, commanded the Imperial Bodyguard, and they both owed everything to the Emperor's favour. Some other officers in the palace, whom the Emperor trusted, were also involved.

During the night the rebels rounded up various ministers and councillors and held them in the palace. Some, however, escaped arrest, including Asrata Kassa, Ras Kassa's surviving son. He hurried with word of the revolt to Denis Wright, who arranged for the news to be flashed to the Emperor in Brazil.

Meanwhile in Addis Ababa the rebels compelled the Crown Prince, Asfa Wossen, to read a proclamation on the wireless saying that he deplored how 'a few people, depending on their birth and material wealth, had been exploiting the people for personal benefit', and declaring that 'today the will of the Ethiopian people has come to realization'. He was declared Head of a 'People's Government'. Though the university students came out in support of the revolution, the Abuna pronounced a solemn anathema on all who did so, and the regular army under General Merid Mangasha, together with the air force, remained loyal. The army surrounded the palace and there was fierce fighting, with many casualties.

Hurrying back instantly, the Emperor landed first in Asmara, then flew on to Addis Ababa. Arriving there on 17 December he received a tumultuous reception from the people. The country had remained quiet, as had the capital except in the vicinity of the palace. The rebel leaders lined up the ministers they were holding and machine-gunned them; eighteen were killed and several others wounded. Among the dead were Ras Seyum and Ras Ababa Aragai, close associates of the Emperor.

Germame and Mengistu then succeeded in escaping from the palace, but during the ensuing round-up of rebels they were recognized. When they were on the point of capture, Germame shot his brother, but failed to kill him, and then shot himself dead. Mengistu was given a fair trial, and then hanged in the market place; two other rebels tried with him were sentenced to life imprisonment. The Crown Prince told his father that he had only read the rebels' proclamation under duress, and the Emperor accepted the explanation.

CHAPTER 31

Last Days of a Civilization

A s a change from Abyssinia I went at the end of 1960 to Nairobi in Kenya. My destination was not the 'white highlands' then farmed by Europeans, but the Northern Province that borders Somalia, Abyssinia, the Sudan and Uganda. Owing to difficulties of climate and communications, and in some areas the risk of raids from across the frontier, this Province was closed to visitors unless they had a special pass. Fortunately, George Webb, whom I had met in 1959 on the frontier at Moyale, had been transferred to Nairobi with responsibilities relating to the Northern Province, and he obtained from the Governor the necessary permission for me to travel there; some very long journeys on foot were the result.

North from the glaciers and forests on Mount Kenya and from the country's highland areas, the terrain falls away in altitude and becomes increasingly sun-scorched and barren as the traveller approaches the lava fields around what was Lake Rudolf – known today as Lake Turkana. As a boy I had read exciting books by men who had visited or administered the nomadic tribes in this vast and desolate northern region, and I had always wanted to travel there. Now I did so. I lived in a tent, used camels for transport, mainly to carry water, and with a retinue of a dozen tribesmen travelled for months on end. That part of Kenya teemed with wild animals, including herds of elephant and many rhino. By now I had given up all shooting unless it was to get an occasional buck or bird for the pot. Every morning I woke to another marvellous day.

I spent many months in the two years 1961 and 1962 among these tribes, which included the Boran, the Turkana, who were as naked as the Nuer, and the Samburu, an offshoot of the famous Masai. Then in 1963 I crossed over into Tanganyika, where I travelled with donkeys among those Masai who lived on that side of the border, from the Ngorongoro crater as far south as their range extended. Except that they were now pacified, the Masai remained largely unchanged from the days when the earliest explorers met them.

431

Their handsome, arrogant warriors, with their red-pigmented hair and red cloth draped negligently over a shoulder, still carried long-bladed spears and distinctive heraldic shields, and guarded great herds of cattle.

I returned to Kenya in 1968 and during the last eighteen years have spent much of my time in that attractive country. There are few areas in the north where I have not travelled. For several years, as an honorary game warden, I carried out foot patrols with a dozen scouts, most of them Turkana, searching for poachers.

Kenya has changed greatly since I first went there. Tourists now swarm on the once-empty beaches and drive all over the game parks, and much of the country's wildlife today is sadly depleted. But what takes me back to Kenya, rather than elsewhere, is my affection for certain Samburu and Turkana. All my life I have felt the need of human company, and wherever possible have avoided solitude. Even when I could not speak their language I have enjoyed having other people with me on my journeys. I have, however, been most content when I have established a close friendship with individuals, as with Idris on my journey to Tibesti, with bin Kabina and bin Ghabaisha in Arabia, or with Amara and Sabaiti in the Marshes of Iraq. Strangely, I have found this comradeship most easily among races other than my own. Perhaps this trait could be traced back to the hurtful rejection I suffered from my contemporaries at preparatory school when I was a small boy freshly arrived from Abyssinia in an alien English world.

In Kenya Lawi Leboyare has been with me for the past fifteen years, ever since he left his village school at the age of ten, and is as dear to me as a son. Though intensely proud to be a Samburu, he has successfully adapted himself to a changing world. When I once deplored his partiality for cars, transistors and pop music, he laughed and said, 'Of course, the truth of the matter is that you are Old Stone Age, and I am modern man.' Three years ago when he spent a month with me in England I was amused to hear someone say to him quite seriously in the Travellers' Club, 'You were obviously educated in England; which school were you at?' Each year I spend a few months in London in my Chelsea flat overlooking the river, but Lawi's tin-roofed, mud-walled house which we built together at Maralal for him and his family has been my real base in recent years.

In this age of change, revolution and instability, I am always thankful for my home in Kenya, which is one country that since its independence in 1963 has experienced no disruption. Even when Jomo Kenyatta died, the transfer of power to his successor was peaceful. Only in Kenya, of all the countries in Africa, indeed of most countries of the world, can a visitor go anywhere without ever being stopped and questioned by the police as to who he is, what he is doing, or where he is going. Had the abortive coup by the Kenya air force in 1982 succeeded, it would have been very different. Kenya might then have been plagued with the succession of disturbances, revolutions and civil wars that have afflicted so many African countries since independence. As for Abyssinia, that once proud and independent country with its historic monarchy has now been degraded into a Marxist state.

I went back to Abyssinia in 1966 to attend the celebrations of the twenty-fifth anniversary of Haile Selassie's return to Addis Ababa; it was an occasion that marked once again his special friendship with Britain. During his State Visit here in 1954, the Queen had installed him as a Knight of the Garter at Windsor Castle. In 1965, when the Queen and Prince Philip had paid a return visit to Abyssinia, she appointed him a Field-Marshal of the British Army. Now, in May 1966, the Emperor had invited the surviving officers and sergeants who had served with Wingate in the Gojjam campaign to be his guests in Addis Ababa.

General Sir Geoffrey Baker represented the British Army, while Wingate's posthumous son, then a Royal Artillery lieutenant, represented his father. Dan Sandford was already in Abyssinia; the rest of us arrived by air. I was delighted to see them again: Hugh Boustead was there, and Chapman-Andrews, Clifford Drew, Donald Nott, the former Sergeant-Major Grey, now a Lieutenant-Colonel, Laurens van der Post, Neil McLean, W. E. D. Allen, Akavia and others whom I had not previously met. We were installed in a comfortable modern hotel with cars at our disposal and army officers to escort us.

However the luggage of one of the sergeants had been lost in transit, and when we were received by the Emperor on the evening of our arrival, the sergeant, dressed in his travelling clothes, had to apologize to the Emperor for his informal appearance. Haile Selassie smilingly held up his hand to stop him and said, 'I have already heard of your misfortune. Please don't let it worry you.' When the sergeant returned to the hotel he found a dark suit, evening clothes, shirts, underclothes, a razor, toothbrush, in fact everything that he required, laid out on his bed. It was typical of Haile Selassie to concern himself personally with such a detail, during the crowded and eventful celebrations, so as to ease the embarrassment of a minor guest.

During the following three days we attended a faultless parade of armoured and mechanized army units, headed by a jeep carrying a full-grown lion, an impressive regimental mascot. We watched an air force fly-past, and saw parachutists dropping on to a 'target', and massed schoolboys performing Swedish drill in perfect unison. We attended a State banquet in Menelik's great *gibbi*; we visited the University; we were entertained in their club by impeccably dressed army officers speaking excellent English.

All this was interesting to observe, of course, and I could recognize its necessity; but I could feel no enthusiasm about the adaptation to the modern world of this unique and fascinating country. What I now saw was all so different from the Abyssinia of just fifty years before when, as Ras Tafari, Haile Selassie had paraded past the Empress Zauditu after the battle of Sagale, with his victorious Shoan army, a host as colourful and barbaric as those that had fought in the previous century against the Dervishes at Galabat and the Italians at Adua.

Haile Selassie was thirteen when his father, Menelik's right-hand man, the renowned Ras Makonnen, died; from then on, as his son, he had to contend with conspiracies and intrigues that could easily have cost him his life. Inevitably, he grew up to rely solely on himself, and as he acquired power he became increasingly autocratic. Another man, faced with such repeated resistance to his aims, might have developed into a ruthless and brutal tyrant, as did Theodore in similar circumstances. Haile Selassie, however, had an abiding horror of cruelty and executions. He himself never sentenced anyone to 'death, and he never ratified a death sentence except for murder, and then only with personal distress.

From the time he was appointed Regent in 1916, Haile Selassie did his best to introduce the reforms on which he had set his heart. He met with general opposition, not least from the traditionally minded associates of Empress Zauditu. In external affairs, however, he did successfully secure Abyssinia's admission to the League of Nations in 1923. But not until he succeeded to the throne as Emperor in 1930 did he have the necessary authority to start curbing the power of the great feudal Rases, centralizing the country's administration, tackling slavery and overcoming the problems of education, medicine and communications.

By then, time was running short. Five years after his coronation, the Italians invaded and occupied Abyssinia. Among their other atrocities, they systematically hunted down and executed the generation of young men the Emperor had been at pains to educate and on whom he had counted for the future. When the Emperor returned to Addis Ababa in 1941, he was faced with the formidable task of reconstructing his government and reasserting his authority over the country, large areas of which were still much disturbed after having been in perpetual revolt against the Italians. The metalled roads the Italians had built were of assistance to him, but the innumerable weapons captured by the Patriots constituted a serious threat to security; indeed there was soon a rebellion by the Azebu Galla in the north, but it was quickly suppressed.

Haile Selassie always showed great restraint. Many people including Ras Hailu and his own son-in-law, Dedjazmatch Haile Selassie Gugsa, who had defected to the Italians when they invaded, now after his return owed their lives to his clemency. He was deeply religious, and believed that as the Elect of God it was his unremitting duty to serve his country; he worked tirelessly to this end, and his foremost preoccupation was always his people's welfare. Helped by European advisers, he modernized the army and remodelled the administratiopn, especially the legal, financial, medical and educational services. What was displayed to us during those three days in May 1966 was evidence of his great achievement over the previous twenty-five years.

Haile Selassie was devoted to his family, and had an endearing abilility to win the confidence of small children. His wife, the Empress Menen, and his eldest daughter, Tananya Work, were his trusted confidantes. Sadly, his altruistic younger daughter, Princess Tsahai, who had trained as a nurse at Guy's Hospital and later worked dedicatedly for the medical service in Addis Ababa, died in

1942, and his favourite son, Prince Makonnen of Harar, was killed in a car crash in 1957. The Empress herself died in 1962 and their youngest son, Sahla Selassie, in 1963, and the Crown Prince, Asfa Wossen, after suffering a stroke in 1973, was flown for treatment to London where, semi-paralysed, he still lives today.

Certainly with the passing years the Emperor became increasingly lonely and isolated. He had never found it easy to delegate authority, and in the early years of his reign could only achieve results by dealing with each question himself. Moreover, most of the officials he appointed were reluctant to assume responsibility, and always tended to refer any important decisions back to him. This can be partly explained by the traditional deference to superior rank, but partly also by their fear of losing a lucrative post through making a wrong decision. Many Abyssinian officials were corrupt, avaricious and self-seeking.

Ironically, the very ease with which the attempted coup of 1960 had been suppressed led Haile Selassie to underestimate the mounting impatience, on the part of the educated class he had himself largely created, to participate at a high level in the administration of their country. In his old age he came increasingly to occupy himself with foreign policy, and left the running of the country to a government of ageing men. He paid many State Visits, including some to communist and Third World countries; in Africa's newly independent countries he acquired great prestige, with the result that Addis Ababa was selected for the permanent headquarters of the Organization of African Unity.

In January 1972 Dan Sandford died. The Emperor happened to be flying back to Addis Ababa from a State Visit to Nigeria when he heard the news. He immediately sent a radio message asking the Sandford family to delay the funeral so that he could attend it. For fifty years Sandford had devoted himself to Abyssinia: now, on his death, his many friends, including myself, sensed an era had ended.

Next year a drought in northern Ethiopia was followed by famine in Wollo. However, this was not disclosed to the rest of the world by Haile Selassie's Government, until Jonathan Dimbleby toured the area with a camera crew and took some horrifying pictures. He showed these on television, interspersed with others of a banquet at the palace in Addis Ababa. He thereby implied that Haile Selassie feasted while his people starved, but actually the banquet he photographed was on the occasion of a State Visit by the President of the Sudan. Dimbleby's television programme caused much loss of sympathy with Haile Selassie in Europe, and corresponding resentment in Addis Ababa. In fact, as all who were acquainted with him knew, Haile Selassie was personally very abstemious. I remember Princess Ruth, while dining with the Mansfields, remarking, 'It's a pleasant change to have a meal like this. You don't know how simple and monotonous our food is in the palace.'

The drought in northern Ethiopia coincided with a steep rise in the cost of living in Addis Ababa, attributable to the oil crisis after the October 1973 war between Egypt and Israel. This led to the hoarding of food, a strike by taxi drivers, and widespread mutinies by the army.

In February 1974 Haile Selassie appointed a new Government. Its Prime Minister, Endelkatchew Makonnen, was a youngish man who, like several of his colleagues, had been educated at Oxford. His was the most talented government Ethiopia had known, and it augured well for the future. Nevertheless, the Derg, a committee formed by young army officers who had instigated the mutinies, were now determined to seize power. They arrested Endelkatchew and, as a first step, replaced him as Prime Minister by Mikael Imru, Ras Imru's liberally minded son. They were now virtually in control of the country and they took systematic steps to deprive the Emperor of his authority and privileges. They even arrested his family: Princess Tananya Work, with Princess Ruth and others of the Emperor's grandchildren are still in prison in Addis Ababa.

Haile Selassie now was isolated in his palace. One by one, his closest associates withdrew or were arrested, until he was left with merely a handful of servants. Clamorous mobs, made up largely of students, demonstrated outside the palace, howling for his abdication on the grounds of accusations by the Derg, widely publicized, that he had misappropriated vast sums of money. Next, in September 1974, the Derg charged the Emperor with transferring millions of dollars to private accounts in Swiss banks, and formally deposed him. In fact, avarice had no place whatever in Haile Selassie's nature, and it has since been conclusively proved that he had invested no funds abroad.

Haile Selassie was collected from his palace by two officers, and taken in a Volkswagen to the Menelik *gibbi*, where he was accommodated in a small hut. As he left his palace, he remarked to one of the officers, 'If this revolution is for the good of the country then I am in favour of the revolution.' Knowing Haile Selassie as I did, I am sure he meant it.

Having deposed the Emperor, the Derg offered the crown to Asfa Wossen, who was undergoing treatment in London. He was deeply concerned about his father's safety and refused to be involved. At this juncture, if General Aman Andom, a popular and highly esteemed figure, had been able to establish his authority, he might have succeeded in setting up some form of representative Government, perhaps under a constitutional monarch. However, he was confronted by Colonel Mengistu Haile Mariam, an utterly ruthless and intensely ambitious communist. In November 1974 Mengistu attacked Aman Andom's residence with tanks; in the fight that ensued, Aman Andom was killed. On 27 November, Bloody Saturday as it came to be called, Mengistu executed some sixty members of the aristocracy, including Endelkatchew Makonnen and Asrata Kassa, without any form of trial: he had them shot out of hand. This was the start of the 'Red Terror'. In March 1975 the Derg formally abolished the monarchy and declared the country a communist state.

I later asked Sir Willie Morris, who had been our Ambassador in Addis Ababa at the time of the revolution, if it had been Russian or Chinese agents who had introduced communism into Ethiopia. He answered, 'There was no need. The revolution was largely brought about by British and American communist school teachers and university lecturers.'

Haile Selassie had to undergo a prostate operation in May 1975, but for a man of eighty-three made a remarkable recovery. With the undoubted intention of humiliating him, he was put in a public hospital ward, but crowds of people came daily to visit him. Perhaps this evidence of the popular regard that was still felt for Haile Selassie alarmed Mengistu, who on 27 August went with two soldiers to the hut where Haile Selassie was once again confined, and murdered him. It is generally believed that Mengistu personally suffocated him with a pillow. When the death was announced it was

438

attributed to heart failure. However, Haile Selassie had been in good health before his death, and now no doctor saw the body. It was secretly removed, and buried in some place unknown.

Meanwhile, for two years a Brigadier Tafari Benti was Ethiopia's Head of State, until he in turn was murdered by Mengistu, who then proclaimed himself Secretary-General of the Ethiopian Communist Party. In March 1978 Mengistu also murdered Colonel Atnafu, who had been his right-hand man; he justified this act by asserting on the radio that Atnafu had placed a higher value on the wellbeing of the people than on the scientific application of socialism, so had to die.

On 22 March 1978 *The Times* published a lengthy article by Hans Eerik, then resident in Addis Ababa, describing the prevailing conditions in the city. Addis Ababa had been divided into three hundred sub-districts, each with a prison and eight to ten guards 'entitled to take revolutionary measures'. There were thus some three thousand licensed killers in Addis Ababa, as well as officially appointed murder squads. In addition to these sub-district lock-ups, there were the large Government prisons, now largely filled with the victims of malicious denunciations. A hundred to a hundred and fifty people were being taken out daily and shot in the streets. There were posters and leaflets proclaiming 'The Red Terror shall flourish', while on the radio all were enjoined to denounce any neighbour who, as anarchist, feudalist or exploiter of the people, opposed the Revolution. It was generally believed that Mengistu's Russian advisers had impressed on him that only by Red Terror could the will of the people be broken. There was a department of secret security, now controlled by an East German general.

Among other horrors, the report describes how one of the murder squads had entered the house of the Imam of the Great Mosque, and without any explanation abducted the Imam's fourteen-year-old son. Four hours later they had dumped the boy's body outside the house; it had been disfigured by torture, extensively burnt by electric shocks, and the eyes had been gouged out. The Imam, moreover, was ordered to leave his son's body lying there on public display. After some hours it was taken away and thrown into a mass grave. Children were also picked up in the streets, and told to point out their parents' houses. They were then taken inside and shot in front of their parents, who were forbidden to hold the traditional mourning ceremonies.

The failure of the rains in northern Ethiopia since the spring of 1984 has now caused a famine far more catastrophic than that which contributed to the Emperor's overthrow and Mengistu's establishment in power. With worldwide publicity from a television film taken by Mohammed Amin, Ethiopia has received assistance from abroad on a vast scale. The fact that Tigre and Eritrea are in revolt has been the excuse for restricted distribution, but I am convinced that Mengistu, with his utter disregard for human suffering, is anyway using this opportune famine not only against the Tigrean secessionists, but to help him to destroy the historic individualism of all the northern provinces, so as to facilitate the spread of communism. His forcible transfer of their inhabitants, ostensibly on humanitarian grounds, must have this object in view. French 'Médecins sans Frontières', working in Ethiopia on famine relief, estimate that a hundred thousand people died during these transfers. Meanwhile, in 1984 the Ethiopian Government spent a sum variously estimated at between fifty and a hundred million pounds to celebrate the tenth anniversary of the official establishment of the Marxist State.

Writing this on 18 May 1986, I saw on the front of the *Sunday Times* for that day a headline: 'Thousands flee Ethiopian regime'. A long article, written by Peter Godwin at a refugee camp at Tug-Wajale in north-western Somalia, described how up to a thousand Oromo or Galla tribesmen from Arussi and parts of southern Ethiopia were arriving daily in the camp to escape the horrors of the Government's new 'villagization' policy. This plan, to assemble the peasants and herdsmen into guarded villages, was launched in early 1986 and was distinct from 'the forcible resettlement ... which has already led to thousands of deaths'. The government in Addis Ababa had apparently announced the intention of moving millions of people in this way over a nine-year period. Godwin added that the present operation was accompanied by wholesale rape, by religious persecution, and by confiscation of property. The tribesmen were being told that everything, even wives and daughters, had to be shared in accordance with socialist principles.

Ethiopia, with its ancient civilization, its early Christian Church and its proud tradition of independence, is now no more than a wretched Russian satellite. Its communist Government, widely

detested by its subjects on whom it is imposing its ideology, is propped in power by Russian advisers, East German security personnel and Cuban troops. Many of its present inhabitants must look back on Haile Selassie's long reign as on a golden age, and remember their former monarch with the appreciation he deserved. It is my hope that in time historians will assess at its true worth all he did for his country. I was privileged to have known that great man.

EPILOGUE

LOOKING BACK, I realize that my exciting and happy childhood in Abyssinia, far removed from direct contact with the Western world, implanted in me a life-long craving for adventure among untamed tribes in unknown lands.

I knew Abyssinia in all its traditional splendour, with its age-old ceremonies and a pattern of life that had not changed in centuries. As a young man, I achieved a boyhood dream of hunting dangerous animals in the wilds of Africa. Then and later, I travelled in unexplored regions, and spent years among tribesmen who had no conception of any world other than their own. Yet I might so easily have been too late.

One year after my exploration of the Danakil desert in 1934, the Italians invaded Abyssinia, and in the course of their operations occupied Aussa. In 1939, the very year after my journey to the mountains of Tibesti, across deserts where no car had ever penetrated, war was declared; in the course of it motorized Free French forces were assembled there, at Faya, to drive north into Tripolitania. Then, in 1950, even as I was leaving Arabia after exploring the Empty Quarter for five years with my Bedu companions, the oil companies were already negotiating to prospect the hinterland of Oman; there, as elsewhere in Arabia, their industrial activities destroyed for ever the immemorial life of the desert Arab. In 1977, when I briefly returned to Oman and Abu Dhabi, I saw at once that present-day Arabia, with its prodigious wealth, had nothing whatever left to offer me.

Much of the world, including many of the countries where I have spent years of my life, is now in chaos. The Sudan has been torn apart by chronic civil war between North and South, and is now devastated by drought in the western area, where the Zaghawa, Maidob, Bani Husain and other tribes, among whom I lived and served so happily, are dying in thousands of starvation. Over in Tibesti the Tedda, now equipped with automatic weapons and supported by Gadhafi's Libyan troops, are engaged in yet another

442

civil war. Meanwhile, Iraqi and Iranian armies are fighting desperately in the Marshes of Iraq; while in the mountains of Nuristan, as elsewhere in Afghanistan, the tribesmen, who abominate their communist puppet government and are courageously resisting it, are being mercilessly attacked by Russian troops and helicopter gunships. For me, however, the crowning tragedy is the fate of Abyssinia.

In July 1969 I happened to be in Kenya, on the shore of Lake Rudolf, when I heard with incredulity from a naked Turkana fisherman that the 'Wazungu' – as he called Europeans, including Americans – had landed on the moon. He had heard the news at a distant mission station. To him this achievement, being incomprehensible, was without significance; it filled me, however, with a sense of desecration, and of despair at the deadly technical ingenuity of modern man. Even as a boy I recognized that motor transport and aeroplanes must increasingly shrink the world and irrevocably destroy its fascinating diversity. My forebodings have been amply fulfilled. Package tours now invade the privacy of the remotest villages; the transistor, blaring pop music, has usurped the place of the tribal bard. While I was in the desert with the Rashid, they would light a fire by striking a dagger blade against a piece of flint: now they hear the world's news on their radio, or watch it on their television set. Twenty-five years ago, their concern was on account of tribal raiding: now, it is on account of superpower dissension over arms control, and 'Star Wars' of the future. The Rashid today, like the rest of us, know they face the possibility of nuclear annihilation.

In any case, if we survive, the future of serious geographical exploration must be in outer space or in the ocean depths. Moreover, the means to carry it forward can only be attained by modern technology, and at enormous expense; the participants in each venture will inevitably be limited to the selected few. The surface of the globe, having now, thanks to the internal combustion engine, been thoroughly explored, no longer affords scope for the adventurous individual in search of the unknown.

Journeying at walking pace under conditions of some hardship, I was perhaps the last explorer in the tradition of the past. I was happiest when I had no communication with the outside world, when I was utterly dependent on my tribal companions. My

443

achievement was to win their confidence. Among my many rewards was, in Abyssinia, to have been the first European to explore the Sultanate of Aussa; in Arabia, to have reached the oasis of Liwa, and to have found the fabled quicksands of Umm al Sammim; and, in so many of my travels, to have been there just in time.

GLOSSARY

Abuna   archbishop, correctly *Abun* in Amharic
Agawid (Arabic)   elder, often in religious sense
'Allah Karim' (Arabic)   'God is merciful' – exclamation often used in token of
   resignation
amba (Amharic)   steep-sided, flat-topped mountain in Northern Abyssinia
ambach (*Aeschynomene elaphroxylon*)   a tree with a soft, light wood
Ansar (Arabic)   followers of the Mahdi
askari (Arabic and Swahili)   soldier
assegai   stabbing-spear, introduced by Chaka as the weapon of the Zulu
   armies
assida (Arabic)   stiff millet porridge
ayah (Hindi)   nursemaid

'Balak' (Arabic)   'Look out!' 'Mind yourselves!'
Balambaras (Amharic)   junior military rank
banda (Amharic)   local levies used by Italians
bandar log (as in Kipling's *Jungle Book*)   monkey-people
baobab (*Adansonia digitata*)   tropical African bombacaceous tree with
   gourd-like fruit
Bashi-Bazouke (Turkish)   irregular cavalry
Bimbashi (Turkish)   lowest British commissioned rank in the Sudan Defence
   Force; originally equivalent to Colonel in the Egyptian Army

chapli (Urdu)   strap-on sandal
charpoy (Urdu)   bedstead of woven webbing or hemp stretched on a
   wooden frame of four legs
circonscription (French)   district

debtara (Amharic)   precentor, *cantor*, scribe
Dedjazmatch (Amharic)   rank equivalent to senior general

Efendi (Turkish)   a civilian designation approximate to 'Mr'
Etchege (Amharic)   prior of Debra Libanos monastery and senior monk of
   the Abyssinian Empire

faqih (Arabic)   religious teacher
Fitaurari (Amharic)   'commander of the spearhead', an official rank
fula (Arabic)   pond

geber (Amharic)   raw meat feast
gibbi (Amharic)   palace
goumier (French; Arabic)   colonial mounted soldier, North Africa

hagenia (*Hagenia abyssinica*)   a tree, of the family *Rosaceae*
haraz (*Acacia albida*)   a tree, of the family *Mimosaceae*
haskanit (*Cenchaus biflorus*) (Arabic)   tall grass with clinging seeds

Ikhwan (Arabic)   fanatical religious brotherhood of the Wahabis
Imam (Arabic)   term of widely varying meaning in the Middle East: priest,
   saint, successor to the Prophet, religious/political leader

jabal (Arabic)   hill, mountain
jibba (Arabic)   long shirt; when patched with bright colours, was used as the
   uniform of the Mahdist armies

kalpak (Turkish)   large, black brimless hat
kasbah (Arabic)   citadel of a North African city
kavas (Greek)   doorkeeper
Kenyazmatch (Amharic)   'Commander of the Right', title of intermediate
   seniority
Khalifa (Arabic)   successor – a religious term, hence Caliphs, successors of
   the Prophet Muhammad
Khedive (Turkish)   Viceroy of Egypt under Ottoman suzerainty
khor (Arabic)   water-course, usually dry
kororak (Arabic)   exultant pursuit, a term used by Baggara Arabs

machan (Hindi)   raised platform used in tiger hunting with beaters
Magdum (Arabic)   Sultan of Darfur's representative in Northern Darfur
Mahdiya (Arabic)   period when the Mahdi, and his successor the Khalifa,
   ruled the Sudan
Malik (Arabic)   king, in Darfur often used of a tribal chief
Mamur (Arabic)   senior native official in the Sudan Political Service
mansaf (Arabic)   mutton stew with boiled wheat
méhariste (French)   soldier of the French Camel Corps (i.e., mounted on a
   méhari, a camel)
mousse (French)   cabin-boy, ship-boy
muezzin (Arabic)   officer of the mosque who calls the faithful to prayer five
   times a day from the minaret
Mullah (Arabic)   Muslim teacher or religious leader
mullah (Arabic)   sauce eaten with porridge (*assida*) in the Sudan

nahas (Arabic)   large copper war drum
negadi (Amharic)   muleteer

Negus (Amharic)   king
Negusa Nagast   King of Kings, Emperor

praepostor (Latin)   Eton term for a sixth-form boy in attendance on the Head
or Lower Master

Qadi (Arabic)   Islamic judge

Ras (Amharic)   most senior rank or title, often equated with that of Duke

shamma (Amharic)   white cotton toga-like garment
shash (Amharic)   black, shiny gauze
shelegai (Arabic)   broad-bladed, long-hafted Baggara spear
shifta (Amharic)   brigand
Sudd (Arabic)   marsh, vast swamp area of the Upper Nile, Sudan
sufragi (Arabic)   butler
suq (Arabic)   market
syce (Hindustani; Arabic)   groom

tabot (Amharic)   sanctified slab of wood representing the Ark of the
Covenant
talla (Amharic)   Abyssinian beer
teff (Amharic)   small grass cultivated in Northern Abyssinia; flour, paste
therefrom
tej (Amharic)   intoxicating honey mead
tirailleur (French)   skirmisher, sharpshooter; hence soldier, infantryman
tobe (Arabic)   cotton sheet worn round body
tukul (derivation not known)   thatched native hut in Abyssinia

wadi (Arabic)   river bed, water-course
wazir (Turkish; Arabic)   vizier, Sultan's chief official
Wagshum (Amharic)   ruler of Wag in Northern Abyssinia
wat (Amharic)   highly seasoned sauce or meat dish

zabanya (Amharic)   guard
zar (Amharic)   demon, or spirit of divination, which may temporarily
possess an individual
zariba (Arabic)   thorn fence

447

INDEX

Ababa Aragai, Ras, 313, 348, 427; killed, 430
Ababdah tribe, 373
Ababu (muleteer), 412, 419, 425
.Abadabia (Libya), 376
Abakaboro (Abyssinia), 137–8
Abashum, Dedjazmatch, 124
Abaya, Lake, 407
Abba Island (Sudan), 176, 182
Abbai (Blue Nile), 412, 414–15
Abbi Addi (Abyssinia), 227–8
Abd al Marim, 83–4, 258
Abd al-Qadir, Amir, 365–6
Abdallah, Yusbashi, 315
Abdi (Somali), 130, 149, 152, 168
Abdullah Efendi, 197, 246
Abdullahi (gunbearer), 111–14, 117, 129–30, 149, 151, 155, 157, 162–4, 168
Abdullahi ibn al Sayyid Muhammad, Khalifa, 176, 179–82
Abhebad, 147, 153, 155–7
Abu Anja, Amir, 179
Abu Dhabi, 432
Abu Simbel, 175
Abuna Yosef mountain (Abyssinia), 405, 422
Abyssinia: antiquity and history, 31–41; Christian church in, 32, 35–7; Turkish Muslims invade, 35–6; 1895 war with Italy, 41; Italy occupies (1935), 42, 172–3, 192–3, 215, 217, 223–38; revolution and fighting in World War I, 51–7; influenza epidemic, 63; WT hunts in, 94–6; war with Sudan (1887–9), 179; conduct of war with Italy (1935–6), 220, 223–34; poison gas used in, 227, 229, 231–2, 236; under Italian occupation, 236, 241; WT's early wartime visit to, 305–6; Patriots' actions in, 313–15, 327–8, 331–2, 335–7, 344–8; British campaign in, 313, 317, 323–54;

Haile Selassie returns to, 329; refrains from reprisals against Italians, 341–2; liberated, 350–3; British administration in, 352; WT returns to civil duties in, 390, 393–5; WT's later visits and travels in, 401–11, 412–29; missionaries in, 407–8, 418; as Marxist state (and 'Red Terror'), 433, 438–41; under Haile Selassie, 433–4; admitted to League of Nations, 434; drought and famine in, 436–7, 440; 1974 government and revolution, 437
Acland, Peter, 324, 338
Adam (Furawi cook), 207
Adam (Galla cook), 129
Adam Nater-Mi, 283
addax, 212–13
Addis Ababa: founded, 24; described, 43–4, 90–1; in Abyssinian war, 228, 231; Italian massacre in, 236; British recapture, 341; Haile Selassie enters, 344; WT returns to, 428–9; OAU headquarters in, 436; under revolutionary administration, 439
Adi Faro Matal, 154
Adigrat (Abyssinia), 223
Adobada, or the White Water (Abyssinia), 150
Adou – 'the place of thirst' (Abyssinia), 137
Adua: Battle of (1896), 25, 41–2, 172, 219; Italians occupy (1935), 223
Adulis (Abyssinia), 32
Afdam (Abyssinia), 95
Afdub, Mount (Abyssinia), 95, 130
Afghanistan, 401, 443
Afilas, 32
Afleodam (Danakil chief), 125–6
Agaw people, 33
Ageremariam (Abyssinia), 410
Agheila, 377–8
Agibar (Abyssinia; later Debra Sina), 347, 414

Ahamado (Danakil headman), 129–30, 137–8, 148, 160
Ahamado of the Bogale, 136
Ahmad (Somali camelman), 116, 129
Ahmad (brother of Kalol), 210, 242
Ahmad al Aggad, 176
Ahmad Ibrahim (Ahmad Granj), 35–6, 165, 404, 416, 423
Ain Diyar (Syria), 389
Ain Galakka (Tibesti), 282
Ain Qura (Sudan), 207
Airlie, David Ogilvy, 12th Earl of, 89–90, 94
Akavia, Abraham (Wingate's companion), 332–3, 337, 344, 433
Aksum, 31–3
al-Gatrun (Tibesti), 287
al-Hakim (Fatimid ruler), 359
al-Liri jabals (Sudan), 301
Alamayahu, son of Emperor Theodore, 39
Alamein, Battle of (1942), 373, 376
Alaqa Dessi (Abyssinian headman), 425–6
Aleppo, 367
Alexander III, Pope, 34
Alexander, King of Serbia, 28
Alexander, General Harold, 375
Ali, Ras, 428–9
Ali Bakhit, 278, 283–4, 286, 291
Ali Dinar, Sultan of Darfur, 246, 293
Ali Imam (Abyssinian balambaras), 426
Ali Taum, 198–9
Ali Wad Hilu, 181
Ali Wali, 126–7, 129, 131–4, 137–9, 148, 152, 160
Alington, C. A., 73
Alisabiet (Abyssinia), 160
Allen, W. E. D., 433
Allenby, Field-Marshal Edmund Henry Hynman, 1st Viscount, 97, 320
Alston, Lieut. Gordon, 377–83
Aluli valley (Abyssinia), 162
Alvares, Francisco: visits Lalibela, 404; A true relation of the lands of the Prester John, 34–5
Aman Andom, General, 438
Amara (Iraqi companion), 432
Amara Saint (Abyssinia), 415
Amba Alagi (Abyssinia), 341–2, 344, 355

Amba Aradom, Battle of, 1936, 228–9
Amba Farit mountain (Abyssinia), 414–15
Amhara people, 43–4
Anderson, Kenneth, 330
Anga, Abu, 40
Anka wells (Sudan), 200
Ankober (Abyssinia), 428
Antoniali, Sergeant, 159
Aosta, Amedeo, Duke of, 341–2, 344
Aouzou (Tibesti), 287–8
Arab Legion, 240, 355
Arabia, 396–8; see also Empty Quarter
Archer, Geoffrey, 58
Archey (Sudan), 293
Arkell, Tony, 184–5
Armstrong, C. L. ('Stuffy'), 305
Arslan, Amir, 239
Arussi mountains, 112, 118
Arussi people, 114–16, 409
Asassibabifero hills (Abyssinia), 136
Aseila, 158–60
Ashangi, Lake (Abyssinia), 36
Asmara (Eritrea), 41, 341, 355
Asrata Kassa, 430, 438
Assab (Abyssinia), 225
Assal, Lake, 161–2
Astley, Kathleen Mary WT's mother) see Thesiger, Kathleen Mary
Astley, Reginald, 100, 102; death, 393
Aswan (Egypt), 175
Ataturk, Kemal, 366, 389
Athanasius, Patriarch of Alexandria, 3.
Athlit, 386–7, 388–90
Atkinson, C. T., 81
Atnafu, Colonel, 439
Ato Shona (escort commander), 130, 135, 148, 151, 160
Auchinleck, General Claude, 372, 374
Audas, Major R. J., 185, 190, 191–2
Aussa, 119–20, 128–31, 137–40, 144–5, 149–50, 152, 154, 432, 434; see also Mohammed Yaio
Awash river, 119–20, 136–7, 140, 147, 149–57
Ayalew Birru, Dedjazmatch, 224
Ayalou Makonnen, Fitaurari, 325–6, 345–6, 348
Ayelu, Mount, 131–2
Azraq, 240

Badi (camelman), 129

Badoglio, General Pietro, 224, 227–31, 233–4, 236
Bagariya (Sudan), 218
Bagnold, Ralph, 245, 397
Bahdu, 119–20, 124–7, 129, 131–4
Bahr al Arab (Sudan), 263
Bahr al Ghazal (Sudan), 263
Bahr al Jabal – the White Nile (Sudan), 263
Bahr dar Giorgis (Abyssinia), 331, 342
Baisac, Chapon, 168
Balayia (Abyssinia), 323, 329
Bale (Abyssinia), 116
Baker, General Sir Geoffrey, 433
Baker, Samuel, 102, 304
Balcha, Dedjazmatch, 24–6, 49–50, 53–4, 88, 95
Baldwin, Stanley, 222, 225–6
Bani Amir people, 373
Baratieri, General Oreste, 41
Bardage (Tibesti), 287
Bardai, 286–9
Baring, Sir Evelyn, 178
Barker, Pongo, 183, 212
Baro river (Sudan), 305
Barton, Sir Sidney, 90, 94, 103, 128, 232
Beachley, near Chepstow, 45
Beanley Moor, 29
Bedi (camelman), 168
Bedo (Tibesti), 290
Bedu, 397–9
Begember (Abyssinia), 36, 89, 91
Beirut (Lebanon), 239
Belai Zeleka, 338–9, 342
Bell, Gawain, 362
Bell, John, 38
Bentinck, Arthur, 26, 79–80
Berbera, 58–9
Bernard, Capitaine, 160–1
Bevan, C. O., 72
Bilen (Abyssinia), 94, 119–23
bin Ghabaisha, Salim, 432
bin Kabina, Salim, 432
Bir Natrun, 210–13, 215, 218–19
Bir Soltan (Tunisia), 382
Bir Zaltin (Libya), 377
Birru (Galla servant), 112, 117, 129, 142, 168
Birru (Patriot leader), 348
Black, Lieut. (of Green Howards), 79
Blue Nile see Abbai
Blue Nile Falls – Tisisat (Abyssinia), 416

Blue Nile Gorge, 342; see also Abbai
Bogale (Amhara servant), 403, 405, 407, 410, 412, 414, 417, 422
Bono, General Emilio de, 223–4, 228
Boran people, 409
Borkou (Sudan), 279
Bosra eski Sham (Syria), 361–2
Bouerat (Libya), 377
Boustead, Colonel Hugh: WT meets, 214; in Abyssinian campaign, 318–19, 321, 332–4, 339, 342, 344, 353; relations with Wingate, 333–4, 353; at Haile Selassie's 1966 celebrations, 433
Bowcock, Philip, 273
Boyle, Major, 335–7
Brazzaville, 282
Bromley, John, 409
Brown, Lieut., 331–2
Bruce, James, 37–8, 56, 328–9, 341
Buchan, John, 97, 101
Buckle, Mary ('Minna'), 46, 60, 65
Bulchi (Abyssinia), 407–8
Buller, Colonel, 362
Burckhardt, John Lewis, 364
Burgage, Co. Carlow, 29–30
Burton, Sir Richard, 96
Burye (Abyssinia), 332, 334–5
Buxton, D. R.: Travels in Ethiopia, 418
Buxton, Ivor, 111
Buxton, Robin, 239

Cairo, 173–4, 369, 372–4
Cameron, Charles, 38–9
Campbell, Gerald, 66
Campbell, Bimbashi, 316
Campbell, Robin, 77, 102
Cecil, Lord Hugh, 232
Chamberlain, Neville, 305
Chance, Ronald, 69
Chapman-Andrews, (Sir) Edwin, 322, 329, 351–3, 411, 433
Chelalo (Abyssinia), 113
Chelmsford, Adria Fanny, Lady (WT's grandmother), 74
Chelmsford, Frances, Viscountess, 60, 103
Chelmsford, Frederic Augustus Thesiger, 2nd Baron (WT's grandfather), 28, 31, 39, 80
Chelmsford, Frederic John Napier Thesiger, 1st Viscount (WT's

uncle), 58–60, 77–8; death, 103
Chenchia (Abyssinia), 407
Chindits, 354, 386, 396
Choke Mountains, 334
Churchill, Winston S., 97, 312, 316;
  The River War, 102, 181
Claudius, Emperor of Abyssinia, 36,
  416–17
Clerk, Sir George, 85
Collard, John, 362
Colli, Count, 47
Collis, Pilot Officer, 329
Conrad, Joseph, 164
Constantine, Emperor, 32
Constantinople, 81, 84–6, 174
Cooper, Sergeant (of SAS), 378–9
Corbett, Jim: *Maneaters of Kumaon*, 208
Cortese, Guido, 236
Coryton, George, 259, 298, 305
Covilham, Pedro da, 34
Cox, Christopher, 196
Cox, Sir Percy, 171–2
Critchley, Captain, 318
crocodiles, 270–1
Cunningham, General Alan G., 316,
  341, 344, 349–50

Dabarak (Abyssinia), 418
Dabat (Abyssinia), 418
Dadi (Tedda boy), 286, 289, 291
Damascus, 239, 365
Danakil country, 102–3, 109–11,
  119–68, 295, 397, 432
Danakil people, 94–5, 119, 122–5,
  130–4, 140, 153, 156, 164–5
Dangela, 331
Daniel, Paul, 306
Darfur, Northern, 182–3, 186–217,
  240–53, 397
Daro river, 117
Daud (father of Idris), 247, 293
Dawson, Geoffrey, 258
de Bunsen, Charles, 198–9
de Burgh, Hussey, 312
de Gaury, Colonel Gerald, 355, 358,
  361–2
Debra Berhan, plain of (Abyssinia),
  52
Debra Damo (Abyssinia), 405
Debra Karbi Giorgis (Abyssinia), 414
Debra Libanos (Abyssinia), 237, 351
Debra Markos (Abyssinia), 334,

336–41, 350; Italians retreat from,
  341–3, 345
Debra Sina, *see* Agibar
Delhi, 59–60
Dembecha (Abyssinia), 334–6
Dembeguina (Abyssinia), 224, 226, 231
Demise (servant), 112
Derra (Abyssinia), 344–5, 414
Dervishes, 40–1, 59, 176–81; Whirling,
  365–7
Desert Locust Research Organization,
  396–8
Dessie (Abyssinia), 393–6
Desta, Ras, 228, 235; shot, 351
Dhaufar (Muscat), 396
Dickinson, General D. P., 316
Dikil, 148–9, 152–4, 161
Dilla (Abyssinia), 411
Dimbleby, Jonathan, 436
Dimi (Tibesti), 292
Dingwall, Reginald, 186–7, 301
Dinka people, 260–2, 265
Dirda Shihai Bogar-Mi, 288
Dire Dawa (Abyssinia), 49
Dodds, Hugh, 26, 50
Domville, Pat, 369, 372
Dongradi (French *adjudant*), 161, 163,
  166
Doon (Sudan), 289
Dosa, Sultan, 190, 247, 249, 278
Doughty, Charles Montagu: *Arabia
  Deserta*, 367, 380
Doughty-Wylie, Brian, *see* Thesiger,
  Brian
Doughty-Wylie, Colonel Charles
  Hotham Montagu, 26, 45, 84
Doughty-Wylie, Lillian Oimara, 101
Draga, Queen of Serbia, 28
Drage, Colonel, 65
Drew, Clifford ('Pansy'), 215, 246,
  326, 336–7, 433
Druze people, 239; wartime service
  with, 355, 348–68; origins and
  history, 359; 1924 rebellion, 359–60;
  WT revisits, 387–8
Dunn, Brigadier Keith, 362
Dupuis, Charles, 182, 184–5, 190–2,
  200, 202, 219, 411
Durazi, 359

Eden, (Sir) Anthony, 220–2, 225–6,
  232, 316

Edimpi, oasis (Tibesti), 287
Eerik, Hans, 439
Egypt, 173–5, 177; see also Cairo
Ehi Ti (Tibesti), 289
Eighth Army, 372, 380–1, 384–5
El Fascia, 378–82
El Obeid (Sudan), 177
elephants, 274–5
Elizabeth II, Queen of Great Britain, 433
Elphinstone, Colonel, 365
Emi Koussi mountain (Sudan), 283
Empty Quarter (Rub al Khali, Arabia), 396–8, 432
Endelkatchew Makonnen, 437–8
Enfidaville (Tunisia), 385
Ennedi massif (Chad), 279
Entoto (Abyssinia), 41
Erbi (Sudan), 288
Erdi (Sudan), 292
Ergay (zabania), 114, 125
Eritrea: Mussolini claims, 172; and Abyssinian war, 223–4; troops from, 228, 233; British invade, 341; revolt in, 440
Ethiopia, see Abyssinia
Eton College, 68–75
Evans-Pritchard, Edward Evan, 262
Ezana, King of Aksum, 32

Fada (Tibesti), 278
Faisal, Amir, 59
Falasha people, 418
Faras Beit (Abyssinia), 334
Faris Shahin (Druze orderly), 358, 360–2, 387–8
Fasher (Sudan), 183–6, 195, 214
Fasiladas, Emperor of Abyssinia, 37, 418
Fata Burnu (Sudan), 187
Fawwaz, Captain (Druze), 358
Faya (Tibesti), 278
Fergusson, Captain Vere, 261–2, 265, 268–9
Fez, 258
Fiche (Abyssinia), 348–9, 414
Flandin, Pierre Etienne, 232
Foley, Lieut. Tim, 338, 373
Forchi (Sudan), 290
Forodone, Lake (Sudan), 292
Fort Lamy (French Equatorial Africa), 282, 383

Freyberg, General Bernard Cyril (later Baron), 384–5
Frumentius, Bishop, 32
Fullerton, Admiral Eric J. A., 90
Furzi (Abyssinia), 142

Gabra Mariam, Dedjazmatch, 425
Gadhafi, Colonel Muammar, 442
Gagada plain (Abyssinia), 161
Galabat: Battle of (1889), 41, 179; WT posted to, 311–12, 314–16; fort lost and retaken, 317–18
Galawdewos (Abyssinia), 415–16
Galla people, 36, 42
Gallefage (Abyssinia), 139, 140–2
Gallefagibad, Lake (Abyssinia), 149
Gama, Christopher da, 36
Gambeila (Abyssinia), 305
Gandhi, Mohandas Karamchand, 98
Garluak (Nuer chief), 269
Gasha (Galla servant), 403, 405, 407, 410
Gatachew, Ras, 233
Gawani (Abyssinia), 135
Gedaref (Sudan), 311
Gelli, Fitaurari, 52–3
George V, King of Great Britain, 45, 87
Germane Neway, 430
Germany: and outbreak of World War II, 305; overruns Western Europe, 312; North African retreat, 376–85
Ghalib (Zaghawa guide), 210
Ghidole (Abyssinia), 408
Gibbon, Edward, 32
Gideon Force (Abyssinia), 331–2, 334; see also Wingate, Col. Orde Charles
Gigantes, Colonel, 383, 386
Gillan, Sir Angus, 172, 182, 218, 248, 297–8, 302, 411
Gillan, Margaret, Lady, 172
Gish Abbai (Abyssinia), 328
Giulietti, Giuseppe Maria, 120
Gladstone, William Ewart, 177–8
Gloucester, Henry William, Duke of, 87, 89–90, 111
Glubb, Sir John (Glubb Pasha), 240–1, 355
Gobad plain (Abyssinia), 158
Godwin, Peter, 440
Gojjam (Abyssinia), 315–16, 318–21,

324–6, 328–9; Wingate's campaign in, 331–3, 342, 349–52
Gondar (Abyssinia), 37–8, 40, 412, 417–18
Goran people, 246–7, 279
Gordon, General Charles George, 176, 178–9, 209
Gordon, George, 77
Gorobela – Ankober (Abyssinia), 428
Goulimime (Morocco), 258
Goumarri mountain (Abyssinia), 119, 150
Gouro (Sudan), 283
Goutama (servant), 111–12, 129, 142, 157, 168
Graziani, General Rodolfo, 227–8, 236, 351
Great Erg Sand Sea, 383
Greece, 84
Greek Sacred Squadron (SAS), 383–4, 386–7
Grenfell, General Sir Francis, 180
Grey, Sergeant Major (later Lieut.-Colonel), 326, 433
Guda, Mount, 164
Guggi people, 410
Gugsa, Dedjazmatch Haile Selassie, 223–4, 435
Gugsa Wale, Ras, of Begemder, 45, 57, 89, 415
Gurumudli (Abyssinia), 145, 149

Habib (WT's camel), 242–3
Habisa (Sudan), 218
Habta, Giorgis, Fitaurari, 46, 52, 57, 428; death, 88
Habta Mariam (cook), 111–12, 116–17, 129
Habta Wold (syce), 62
Haig-Thomas, David, 103, 109, 111–14, 117–18, 168
Haile Selassie (Ras Tafari), Emperor of Abyssinia: state visit to England (1924), 23; dignity, 23; and Lij Yasu, 49, 51, 420; as Regent, 50; victory at Sagale (1916), 53, 55, 428–9; Taitu plots against, 57–8; illness, 64; coronation, 87, 89–93, 397; proclaimed Negus, 89; authorizes WT's Danakil expedition, 103, 120; and Ras Hailu, 109; appeals to League in protest against Italians,

172, 220, 226, 237–8; and British attitude to Abyssinian war, 222, 225; and conduct of Abyssinian war, 223, 226, 230–4; mission to London, 234–5; visits WT's mother, 270; arrives in Khartoum (1940), 313–14, 316; British recognize as ruler, 316; meets Wingate, 319–20; and British campaign in Abyssinia, 322, 323–54; returns to Abyssinia, 329, 350; hangs Belai Zaleka, 339; forbids retribution against Italians, 341–2; enters Addis Ababa, 344; parades Italian prisoners, 351–2; victory celebrations, 351–2, 355; requests WT's return to Abyssinia, 390, 393; receives WT (1958), 402; attempted overthrow (1960), 430, 436; 25th anniversary of return (1966), 433–4; British honours for, 433; reign and character, 434–7, 441; family, 435–6; and Ethiopian famine, 437; deposed, 437–8; murdered, 438–9
Haile Selassie Gugsa, see Gugsa
Haile Yusuf, 334–6
Hailu of Gojjam, Ras, 88–9, 93, 109, 415; in World War II campaign, 327, 337–9; submits to Haile Selassie, 340, 435
Hajj Thami al Glawi, Pasha of Marrakesh, 257, 401
Halfaya Pass (Egypt), 376
Halifax, Edward Frederick Lindley Wood, 1st Earl of, 232
Hall, Julian, 70
Hama (Syria), 367
Hamdo Ouga (Danakil chief), 135–6
Hamid, Sheikh of the Bani Husain, 191, 244
Hamid (Idris's grandfather), 293
Hamilton, John, 172–3, 214, 258
Hanks, Arthur, 311–12, 314, 317
Harar, 35, 50, 95–6, 341
Haro river, 116
Harper (mate on Sorrento), 82
Harris, Captain, 336–7
Hart-Davis, Rupert, 71
Haymanot, Takla, see Takla Haymanot of Gojjam
Henderson, Lieut. Edward, 365, 367–8

Henry VI, King of England, 72–3
Hertale, Lake, 123–4
Hervey, Lord Herbert, 24–6
Hicks, Colonel William (Hicks Pasha), 177
Hindu Kush, 401
hippopotamus, 273–4, 299
Hitler, Adolf, 172, 222
Hoare, Samuel, 193, 222, 225–6
Hodson, Arnold, 26, 67, 268
Homs (Syria), 367
Horder, Thomas Jeeves, 1st Baron, 353–4
Horrocks, General Brian Gwynne, 384
Humr people, 303–4
101 Mission, see Mission 101
Hunza, 401
Husain, Sheikh: shrine, 117
Husain, Sharif, 59
Hylander, Dr Fride, 227

Ibrahim ('Abu Shakwa'), 283, 286
Iceland, 98–100
Idris Daud: as WT's companion in Sudan, 207–9, 216–19, 241–5, 247, 249, 252; in Western Nuer, 258, 266–7, 269; journey to Tibesti, 270, 276, 278, 283–6, 287, 291, 432; hunting and shooting, 272–4; looks after WT when sick, 276; yearning for adventure, 293; pilgrimage to Mecca, 296, 311; rejoins WT at Galabat, 311; leaves WT, 323
Imrahanna (Abyssinia), 405, 422
Imru, Ras, 93, 224, 226–7, 230–1, 235
India: WT visits (1918), 59–61
Ingebara (Abyssinia), 332
Ingleson, Philip, 202, 209, 215, 245, 248, 250, 252, 294, 296
Iran, 443
Iraq: WT visits in wartime, 389–90; Marshes, 399–400; war with Iran, 443; see also Kurdistan
Isa Adam, 279, 282
Ismail, Khedive of Egypt, 176–7
Istanbul, see Constantinople
Italy: occupies Massawa, 40; 1895–6 war with Abyssinia, 41, 172; 1935 invasion of Abyssinia, 42, 172–3, 191, 215, 219, 223; WT visits, 102; conduct of war with Abyssinia, 220, 223–38; League of Nations sanctions against, 225–6; uses poison gas in Abyssinia, 227, 229, 231–2, 236; victory over Abyssinia, 235–6; in occupation, 236–7, 241; early neutrality in World War II, 306, 312; enters war, 313; troops in Abyssinia, 313–14; British campaign against, 314–15, 317–18, 323, 331; retreat from Debra Markos, 341–3, 345; atrocities in Abyssinia, 351, 435; prisoners paraded by Haile Selassie, 351–2

Jabal al Akhdar – Green Mountain (Libya), 376
Jabal Bishagarah (Sudan), 279
Jabal Druze, 239, 355, 358–63
Jabal Guda (French Somaliland), 166
Jabal Maidob (Sudan), 198
Jabal Nafusa (Libya), 382
Jabal Si (Sudan), 186
Jabal Singhar (Iraq), 389
Jackson, Captain (of Sorrento), 83
Jaipur, 60–1
Jallal al Din al Rumi, 366
Janin (Palestine), 387
Jesuits: in Abyssinia, 36–7
Jibuti, 164–6, 168
Jidda, sack of (702), 32
Jig Jigga (Abyssinia), 49
Jira (Abyssinia), 156
John IV, Emperor of Abyssinia, 40–1, 179, 311, 425–6
John II, King of Portugal, 34
John, Prester, 33–4
Johnson, Bimbashi Henry, 342–3, 351
Judith, Queen, 33
Junod, Dr Marcel, 231–2
Justinian, Roman Emperor, 32, 86

Kabada, Azaj, 326–8
Kadabahdu (Abyssinia), 136
Kaffa kingdom (Abyssinia), 43
Kalol (servant), 200, 210, 212, 216–18, 242
Karakorams, 401
Karnak, 174
Kassa, Ras, 45, 52, 57, 62, 93, 109, 415, 428; in Abyssinian war, 224, 228–30, 233, 235, 421; and British Abyssinian campaign, 348

Kassala (Sudan), 315
Kassimi (head *syce*), 111–12, 116–17,
  126, 129, 151, 155, 164, 168
Kathir (Badayi scout), 246–7, 270, 278,
  283–4, 286–9, 291
Kejku (Sudan), 200, 251
Kennett, J. E., 306
Kenya, 431–3
Kenyatta, Jomo, 433
Keren (Eritrea), 41, 341
Kereri (paddle steamer), 258–9, 261–2,
  264–6, 268–71, 276, 298, 300
Khartoum: WT in, 175–6, 183, 218,
  306, 411; Gordon in, 178–9
Khidr Efendi, 197
Kitchener, Field-Marshal Horatio
  Herbert, 1st Earl, 175, 180–1
Kittermaster, Sir Harold, 90
Kohor, crater (Tibesti), 285
Kondoro, the Mountain of Refuge
  (Abyssinia), 96
Konso (Abyssinia), 407
Konso people, 408–9
Konya (Turkey), 366
Koram (Abyssinia), 233
Kosti (Sudan), 258
Krak des Chevaliers (castle), 368
Kulzikuma mountain (Abyssinia),
  141, 149
Kurdistan, 390, 399, 401
Kurds, 389
Kuri (Amah guide), 283–6
Kuri river (Abyssinia), 161
Kurub plain (Abyssinia), 141
Kutum (Sudan), 182–3, 186, 190,
  192–3, 196–7, 219, 241, 245, 249–53,
  302

Laja lava fields (Syria), 368
Lalibela (Abyssinia), 33, 402–5, 412,
  420, 422–4
Lalibela, King, 404, 423
Lang, R. C. V., 67
Lasta mountains (Abyssinia), 403
Latrun (Palestine), 364
Laurie, Ran, 312, 314
Laval, Pierre, 192, 222, 225–6
Lawi Leboyare (Samburu
  companion), 432
Lawrence, Geoffrey (Mr Justice
  Lawrence), 101
Lawrence, T. E., 97, 239–40, 320, 335,

353, 368; reputation, 350; *Seven
  Pillars of Wisdom*, 367
League of Nations: Haile Selassie
  appeals to, 172, 192, 220–2, 237–8;
  condemns Italy, 225–6; and Italian
  use of poison gas, 232; suspends
  sanctions against Italy, 238;
  Abyssinia admitted to, 435
Lean, O. B., 396
Leather, Mark, 250–2
Lebna Dengel, Emperor of Abyssinia,
  34–6
Leclerc, General (le comte Philippe
  François Marie Leclerc de
  Manteclocque), 383
Lettauré, Commandant, 76
Lettow Vorbeck, General Paul von,
  315
Libyan Desert, 201, 209–13; *see also*
  Tibesti; Western Desert
Liddell Hart, Basil H., 381
Lij Faris, Governor of Tanta, 424–6
Lima, Rodrigo de, 34
lions, 193–4, 203–9, 243–4, 247, 269,
  272–3
Liwa Oasis, 398, 434
Locust Research Organization, *see*
  Desert Locust Research
  Organization
Long Range Desert Group (North
  Africa, World War II), 369, 373,
  375, 377, 397
Lul Seged, Ras, 52–3, 55–6, 428
Luxor, 174–5
Lyautey, Marshal Hubert, 257
Lyttelton, George, 71–2

Mabratu (Tigrean muleteer), 414, 417,
  425, 427
MacDonald, Mr and Mrs
  (missionaries), 271
Macdonald, Colin, 338
MacDonald, General Hector
  Archibald, 181
MacDonald, James Ramsay, 98
Macfie, Dr John, 232
McLean, Neil, 433
MacMichael, Harold, 90
McNeile, A. M., 68–71
'Mad Mullah', 48, 59
Madan (Marsh Arabs), 400
Maffey, Sir John, 89, 262

Mafraq (Trans-Jordan), 355
Magdala: 1868 campaign, 28, 31, 39;
    WT visits, 420, 424–6
Magdalen College, Oxford, 78–9;
    WT's honorary Fellowship, 103; see
    also Oxford University
Magenta mountains (Abyssinia), 138,
    141
Mahdi, The (Muhammad Ahmad),
    176–9
Mahdi, al- (Sayyid Muhammad
    al-Senussi), 283
Mahmud, Amir, 180
Mai Timket ford (Abyssinia), 224
Majdal ash Shams (Lebanon), 388
Makalle (Abyssinia), 41, 223
Makonnen, Bitwoded, 239
Makonnen, Ras, 41, 49, 348, 434
Makonnen (syce), 111
Makonnen of Harar, Prince (Haile
    Selassie's son), 394; death, 436
Malakal (Sudan), 258–9, 263, 276, 297,
    305
Malha (Sudan), 199, 251
Malha (Syria), 358–63, 387–8
Malo (Nuer interpreter), 266–7, 272,
    274, 276
Mammo, Lij, 328, 339
Mana river, 117
Mangasha, General Merid, 430
Mangasha Jambore, Dedjazmatch,
    328, 331, 334, 338
Mansfield, Elinor, 402
Mansfield, Philip, 402–3, 422
Manuel Comnenus, Byzantine
    Emperor, 34
Manz, Shoa (Abyssinia), 36, 44
Maraventano, Colonel, 342, 347, 349,
    351
Maravigna, General Pietro, 231
Mareb river, 42
Mareth Line (Tunisia), 382–4
Mariotti, General Oreste, 224
Marrakesh, 257
Martin, C. H. K., 71
Martin, Dr, Governor of Chercher
    Province, 128–9
Martin, Lieut. (Free French SAS
    officer), 381–2
Masai people, 431–2
Mashakazy gorge (Sudan), 284
Massawa (Eritrea), 40, 164, 341, 355

Massey, Vincent, 101
Mattewos, Abuna, 88
Maurice, Lieut.-Colonel G. K., 185,
    190, 192
Mayne, Brigadier Mosley, 317
Mayne, Major Paddy, 379
Mega (Abyssinia), 409–10
Mehan Pass, Battle of (1936), 233–4
Meknes (Egypt), 258
Melly, Dr John, 231
Menelik (supposed son of Solomon
    and Sheba), 33
Menelik, Emperor of Abyssinia, 24–6,
    31, 38, 40–2, 44, 305, 428;
    succession question, 45–6; and Ras
    Makonnen, 49; founds Addis
    Ababa, 90–1; conquers Arussi, 116
Menen, Empress of Haile Selassie,
    435–6
Mengistu Haile Mariam, General,
    430, 438–40
Metemma, 311, 314, 318
Midji, Lake (Sudan), 292
Mikael of Tigre, Ras, 37
Mikael of Wollo, Ras, Negus of the
    North, 44, 50–3, 55, 58, 141, 420,
    424, 426, 428–9
Mikael Imru, 437
Milebrook, The (house), 66, 74–5, 87,
    100, 171–2, 219–20
Minna, see Buckle, Mary
Miriam Muhammad, Hangadaala of
    Bahdu, 126, 129–32, 135–7, 160
Mission, 101, 315, 326–7
Modiunga wells (Tibesti), 284
Modra valley (Tibesti), 286
Mogadishu, 341
Mohammed Amin, 440
Mohammed Yaio, Sultan of Aussa,
    141, 143–4; WT meets, 145–8, 166;
    and WT's journey, 148–9, 152–3
Mojjo (Abyssinia), 112–13
Molale (Abyssinia), 427
Monfreid, Henri de, 159, 167
Monophysite Church, 35, 37, 407
Montagu, Edwin, 60
Montgomery, General Bernard Law,
    377–8, 383–4
Moore, Guy: in Sudan, 183, 186–7,
    192–203, 209, 214–16, 219, 241–6,
    248–9, 251–3, 267, 294, 411; letter to
    WT's mother, 253–4; takes leave, 278

Morocco, 257–8, 401
Morris, Sir Willie, 438
Moussou oasis (Tibesti), 279, 282, 290
Moyale (Abyssinia), 405, 409–10
Muger river, 109
Muhammad (orderly), 323, 325, 332, 334, 345–6
Muhammad Abai-Mi, 283
Muhammadain Adam Sabi, Malik, 190, 215–16, 249–50, 267, 278
Muhammad Ali, Khedive of Egypt, 176
Muhammad Denkali, 116
Mullu (Abyssinia), 109, 412
Mulugeta, Ras, 89, 93, 223–4, 228–30, 235
Munzinger (Swiss mercenary), 120, 139, 157, 165
Musbat (Sudan), 212, 214
Muscat, Sultan of (1945), 396
Mussolini, Benito: invades Abyssinia, 172, 192, 220–2; and Abyssinian campaign, 224; and Hoare-Laval plan, 225–6; authorizes use of poison gas, 227–8; victory in Abyssinia, 235–6; in World War II, 312, 315

Nachtigal, Gustav, 277
Nairobi, 431
Nanamsena gorge (Sudan), 288
Napier, General Sir Robert, 39, 420, 425
Nasibu, Dedjazmatch, 227
Nasir (Sudan), 305
Natale, Colonel, 332
Natural History Museum, London, 103, 110
Negash Kabada, Dedjazmatch, 328, 334, 338
Nesbitt, Ludovico M., 119–20, 122, 139, 141
New Zealand Corps (World War II), 384
Newbold, Douglas, 184, 245, 302, 306, 321–2, 393, 411; death, 321, 393
No, Lake (Sudan), 263
Northern Provinces, Kenya, 431
Nott, Major Donald, 343–4, 351, 433
Nuba mountains, 263
Nuba people, 301, 304, 306–7
Nuer people, 260–8, 271, 275–6,

302–3; initiation ceremony, 299–300
Nuer, Western (province), 250–2, 259–76, 297–305
Nuri al-Shalan, Amir, 376–8
Nuristan, 401, 443
nyala, 111, 113–14

Obock (French Somaliland), 165–6
Ogaden (Abyssinia), 225
Oman, 397–8, 432
Omar (Somali headman): with WT on Danakil expedition, 110–13, 115–17, 119–21, 124–7, 129–30, 135, 137–8, 142–3, 145–8, 151–2, 156, 159–60, 163, 166–8
Omdurman, Battle of (1898), 176, 180–1, 201; WT visits, 216–19
Operational Centres (Abyssinian campaign), 319, 322, 331–2
Organization for African Unity, 436
Ornano, Colonel Colonna d', 282, 291, 292
oryx, 213
Osman Digna, 177
Oudai oasis (Tibesti), 279, 282
Oudigue pool (Tibesti), 290
Oueita oasis (Sudan), 279, 282
Ouma, Lake (Sudan), 292
Ounianga (Tibesti), 292
Ounianga Kebir (Tibesti), 291
Ounianga Saghir (Tibesti), 292
Owen, T. R. H., 295
Oxford University, 76, 77–9, 97–8, 103; see also Magdalen College

Paez, Pedro, 329
Palestine, 239–41
Parker, Captain Dodds, 320
Parsons, Desmond, 69–70
Pasha al-Atrash, Sultan, 359–61
Patrick, St, 32
Peake, Frederick Gerard (Peake Pasha), 240
Periplus of the Erythrean Sea, 31–2
Perry, May and Walter, 175, 183, 218, 248, 258
Petra, 363–4
Petros, Abuna, 55
Philby, H. St J. B., 397
Philip, Prince, Duke of Edinburgh, 433
Phillimore, Harry, 68, 70, 102

Piccolo Abbai (Abyssinia), 331
Pierre (Breton fisherman), 76, 98
Platt, General William, 315–16, 318, 320, 330, 341–2, 355
Plowden, Walter, 38
Plowman, Clifford Henry Fitzherbert, 96
Power, Frank, 177–8

Qamashlia (Syria), 389
Qasr Rhilana (Tunisia), 383–4

Rai Wur (Nuer chief), 272
Raleigh Club, Oxford, 98
Ramsey (Eton Master), 72
Ras Dashan mountain, 419–20
Ras Tafari, see Haile Selassie
Rashid tribe, 397–8, 443
Rassam, Hormuzd, 39
Red Sea Hills, 373
Reeman, Ian, 409–10
Renouf, 215
Riley, Bimbashi, 347–9
Ritchie, General Neil, 372
Roche, Standish, 66
Rogers, C. C. C., 66
Rogers, Guy, 66, 75
Rohlfs, Friedrich Gerhard, 404
Romilly, H. A., 263–4, 266, 268–70, 272, 305
Rommel, General Erwin, 372–3, 377, 381–4
Roosevelt, Franklin Delano, 220
Roseires (Sudan), 323
Rowe, Lieut., 335, 338, 342, 345–6; death, 347
Royal Geographical Society: WT lectures to, 171
Rub al Khali, see Empty Quarter
Rudolf, Lake (now Turkana), 431
Rufinus, 32
Ruth, Princess of Abyssinia, 402, 437

Sabaiti (Iraqi companion), 432
Sade Malka (Abyssinia), 121
Sadler, Michael, 378
Safiya (Sudan), 218
Sagale, Battle of (1916), 53, 420, 425–6, 428–9
Sahara, 397; see also Libyan Desert; Tibesti; Western Desert
Sahla Selassie, Prince (Haile

Selassie's son), 436
Said Boy (Gurage servant), 112, 117, 129, 168
Said Munge (gunbearer), 111, 113, 117, 129, 151, 155, 157, 168
St Aubyn's School, Rottingdean, 65–8
Sakela (Abyssinia), 326, 341
Salah, son of Dirda Shihai, 288
Salala (Arabia), 397
Salih (Fur servant), 298
Salih Ma'z, 362, 387–8
Salim, Sultan, 35
Salkhad (Syria), 360
Samburu people, 431–2
Sanderson, Paul, 204–6
Sandford, Christine, 94, 109, 111, 241, 394, 402, 412, 414
Sandford, Colonel Dan: in Abyssinia, 94, 103, 109–11, 241, 395; in World War II, 315–16, 318–19, 321–2, 326–31, 334, 339; meets Wingate, 329; Wingate resents, 330; WT stays with, 394, 402; and Abyssinian reprisals, 341; and WT's travels, 412, 414; at Haile Selassie's 1966 celebrations, 433; death, 436
Sandford, Dick, Eleanor and Philippa (Sandfords' children), 402
Sayyah, Malik of the Maidob, 191, 198–201, 216–17, 219, 251–2, 267, 322
Sayyid Abd al Rahman, 183
Selous, Frederick Courteney, 315
Sera Bezu, Fitaurari, 58
Seyum of Tigre, Ras, 88–9, 93, 223–4, 227, 230, 233, 235, 421; killed, 430
Shambe (Sudan), 263
Shahin (Faris's father), 361
Shartai Tigani, 190
Shashamana (Abyssinia), 411
Sheba, Queen of, 33
Shoa (Abyssinia), 38
Shoaragad, wife of Ras Mikael of Wollo, 44–5
Sidamo (Abyssinia), 89
Simien mountains, 412, 418–22
Simon, Sir John, 220–2
Simonds, Captain Anthony, 329, 331
Sindia (Sudan), 242, 246
Slim, Brigadier William, 317–18, 386
Smuts, General Jan Christian, 316
Sobouron (Tibesti), 289

Soddu (Abyssinia), 405, 407
Sokota (Abyssinia), 420–2
Solomon, King of Israel, 33
Somali people, 410
Somaliland, French, 159–61
Somaliland, Italian, 172, 341
Sorrento, SS, 82–3, 85–6
Sousse (Tunisia), 385
Spanish Civil War, 173
Special Air Service (SAS), 374–86
Special Operations Executive (SOE), 363, 369
Stanage estate, 75
Steevens, G. W.: *With Kitchener to Khartum*, 180–1
Stewart, Colonel Herbert, 178
Stewart, General, 59
Stirling, David, 374–5, 377–9, 381–2, 386
Stirling, Peter, 374
Stokes (missionary), 418
Stubbs, Miles, 278, 294
Sudan: WT arrives in, 175–6; Mahdist rebellion, 176–9; Kitchener reconquers, 180–2; WT returns to, 241–4; independence, 411; civil war and drought, 422
Sudan Defence Force, 306, 308, 311–22, 355
Sudan Political Service: WT applies for, 101, 102, 171; established, 182; administration, 201; WT's contract agreement with, 248; tolerance, 297
Sudanese Frontier Force, 323, 331, 336
Sudd, 263
Suez Canal, 221
Sugha Guda tribe, 164
Sulaiman (village headman), 200, 251
Sunday Times, 440
Susannah (*ayah*), 45, 48
Susenyos, Emperor of Abyssinia, 37
Suwaidah (Syria), 361
Sykes, Christopher, 350
Symes, Sir Stewart, 90, 183
Syria, 239–40, 355, 389

Tafari, Ras, *see* Haile Selassie
Tafari Benti, Brigadier, 439
Tagabo hills (Sudan), 193
Taisser (Tibesti), 287

Tajura, 147–9, 152–3, 164–6
Takazze river, 419
Takla Haymanot of Gojjam, 40
Talahun (interpreter), 145, 147–8, 152–5
Tana, Lake, 412, 416–17
Tananya Work (Haile Selassie's daughter), 435, 437
Tanganyika, 431
Tanta (Abyssinia), 424–6
Taroudant (Morocco), 257
Tarso Toon (Tibesti), 287
Tarso Tousside (Tibesti), 289
Tasamma, Ras, 26, 45
Tedda people, 277–8, 285–8, 294, 442
Tehegam wadi (Tibesti), 290
Teho (Abyssinia), 138
Tel el Kebir, Battle of (1882), 177
Telouet (Morocco), 257
Teltale (Abyssinia), 409
Tembien, Battle of (1935), 227, 229
Tendaho (Abyssinia), 141; *waidellas*, 144
Theodore II, Emperor of Abyssinia, 31, 38–40, 420, 425
Thesiger, Brian (*later* Doughty-Wylie; WT's brother): born, 46; and Abyssinian fighting, 52–5; in Aden, 59; in India, 60; life in Abyssinia, 62; schooling, 65–8, 73; in Britain, 65–6; stays with Chelmsford in Northumberland, 78; boxing, 79–80; army career, 101; changes name, 101; gives gun to WT, 183
Thesiger, Dermot (WT's brother): born, 47–8; Spanish influenza, 63; killed in World War II, 73, 101, 393; at Eton, 73; riding, 75; at Oxford, 101; meets Moore, 253
Thesiger, Kathleen Mary (*née* Vigors; *later* Mrs Reginald Astley; WT's mother): in Abyssinia, 24–5, 28, 30, 75; appearance, 28; family background, 29–30; widowhood, 65, 75; inheritance, 74; shooting, 75; qualities, 75; marries Astley, 100; travels with WT, 257–8; Haile Selassie visits, 270; London flat, 393
Thesiger, Percy (WT's uncle), 68
Thesiger, Roderic (WT's brother): born, 48; at Eton, 73; at Oxford, 101; introductions for WT in Morocco,

257; in World War II, 385

Thesiger, Hon. Wilfred (WT's father):
as British Minister in Abyssinia,
24–8, 43, 47; birth and background,
27–9; outdoor sports, 28–9, 61, 111;
poetry, 29; accompanies Ras Kassa
mission to England, 45; 1913
mission to Nairobi, 47; World War I
service, 47–8; on Lij Yasu, 48–51;
and Haile Selassie, 51; defends
Legation, 51–2; and Abyssinian
fighting (1916–18), 53–4, 58;
1917–18 leave in India, 58–61;
relations with WT, 62–3; leaves
Abyssinia, 64; death, 65; schooling,
68

Thesiger, Wilfred Patrick: born, 25;
childhood, 45–6, 62; and 1916
Abyssinian fighting, 52–5; visits
India (1918), 59–61; early reading,
62, 186; Spanish influenza, 63;
returns to England, 65; schooling,
65–73; boxing, 70, 79–80, 98;
shooting and hunting, 75, 93–6,
114–15, 183, 198–200, 203–8, 212,
252, 267, 272–5, 400; at Oxford,
75–81, 97–8; in France, 76; fishing,
78; romantic view of history,
80–1; works passage to
Constantinople and Black Sea,
81–6; attends Haile Selassie's
coronation, 87, 89–93; works on
fishing trawler, 98–9; applies for
Sudan Political Service, 101–2, 171;
Danakil expedition, 103, 109–18,
119–68; Magdalen honorary
Fellowship, 103; relations with
servants and companions, 167, 432;
writes for The Times, 171, 258;
lectures to Royal Geographical
Society, 171–2; learns Arabic, 171,
194, 248, 251; acquires riding
camels, 190, 193, 197–8; pet lions,
193–4; works as Assistant District
Commissioner, 193–7; shoots lions,
203–9, 243–4, 247, 269, 272–3; mixes
with locals, 216; 1936 leave, 218–19;
travels in Syria and Palestine,
239–40; returns to Sudan, 241–51;
on contract with Sudan Political
Service, 248; transfer to Western
Nuer, 251–3, 259–76; 1937 leave,

252, 257; Nuer name, 266; malaria,
276; report on Tibesti trip, 295–7;
food and drink, 295–6; return to
Western Nuer, 297–305; religious
attitudes, 300; return to Kutum,
302; 1939 leave, 304–5; in Sudan
Defence Force, 306, 308, 311–22; in
Abyssinian campaign, 323, 331–52;
loses diary, 343; awarded DSO,
349; on explosives course, 363–5; in
wartime Cairo, 369–74; in SAS,
374–86; on parachute course, 387;
wartime leave in northern Syria,
389; returns to civil duties in Dessie
(Abyssinia), 390, 393–6; with Locust
Research Organization, 396–8; in
Empty Quarter, 397–9; in Iraqi
Marshes, 399–400; Asian travels,
401; 1958 visit to Abyssinia, 401–3;
trip to Lalibela, 402–5; journey to
Kenya border, 405–11; later travels
in Northern Abyssinia, 412–29; at
Haile Selassie's 1966 celebrations,
433–4; *Arabian Sands*, 398–9; *Desert,
Marsh and Mountain*, 401; *The Marsh
Arabs*, 399

Thomas, Bertram, 397

Thompson, J. M., 80

Tibesti ('Tu'), 247, 270, 276–96, 397,
432; art, 289; WT's report on, 295–7

Tieroko (Sudan), 286

Tigiu (Tibesti), 290

Tigre (Abyssinia), 36, 38, 41, 57, 89,
91, 225, 440

Tigrean people, 43–4

Tilho, Colonel, 277

Times, The, 171–2, 258, 439

Tini (Sudan), 242, 247, 278

Tirenno pass (Sudan), 288

Tisisat, *see* Blue Nile Falls

Titley, Radnorshire, 65

Tobruk, 372, 376

Tolodi (Sudan), 301

Tora Mask, Battle of (1916), 428

Torelli, Colonel, 331

Toski, Battle of (1889), 180

Tousside (Tibesti), 289

Tripoli (Libya), 383

Tsahai, Princess (Haile Selassie's
daughter), 435

Tu, *see* Tibesti

Tunisia, 385

Turkana people, 431–2
Turner, Myles, 270

Uccialli, Treaty of (1889), 41
Ugualtiena (Abyssinia), 424
Umar Mukhtar, 376
Umm Buru (Sudan), 215, 249
Umm Idla (Abyssinia), 323, 329
Umm al Sammim: quicksands, 398, 434
Uthman, Sheikh al Din, 181

Van (Asia Minor), 27
van der Post, Laurens, 433
Vansittart, Sir Robert, 222, 226
Victoria, Queen, 38–9
Villa Cipressi, Lake Como, 102
Vincent's (Oxford club), 98

Wad al Nijumi, Amir, 175, 177, 180, 209
Wadi Halfa (Sudan), 175
Wadi Hawar, 212–12
Wag province (Abyssinia), 421
Wagerat people, 138
Wagidi (Abyssinia), 345–7, 352, 414
Waito people, 417
Wakeman, Dr, 24
Walda Hanna (Amhara cook), 412, 417, 420, 422, 425, 427
Waldia (Abyssinia), 403
Walega (Abyssinia), 91
Walkait (Abyssinia), 57
Walwal: fighting at, 172, 220
Warieu Pass (Abyssinia), 228
Warra-ilu (Abyssinia), 426
Waugh, Evelyn, 91–2, 237
Wavell, General Sir Archibald, 97, 316; and Wingate, 319–20, 352
Webb, George, 409–10, 431
Webb, Jo, 410
Webi Shebeli (Abyssinia), 115–16
Wedderburn-Maxwell, H. G., 259–61, 263–6, 268–72, 275–6, 298–300, 303–5
Western Desert: fighting in, 372–86; explored, 397
White Nile – Bahr al Jabal, 263
Whitmore, Corporal T., 326
Wienholt, Arnold, 315–16
Wilson, General Henry Maitland, 355
Wingate, Lieut.-Colonel Orde

Charles: in Sudan, 316, 318–22, 327–8; behaviour and character, 319–20, 330, 332–3, 336, 349–50; accompanies Haile Selassie into Abyssinia, 329–30; promoted, 330; campaign in Gojjam, 331–3, 335–9, 341–52; background, 333; and Boustead, 333–4; and burn victims, 337; takes Haile Selassie to Addis Ababa, 344, 350; reputation, 350; writes report on Gojjam operations, 352; leaves Abyssinia, 352–3; mistrusts British administration in Abyssinia, 353; attempted suicide, 353; with Chindits in Burma, 354, 386, 396
Wingate, Lieut. Orde Jonathan, 433
Wingate, Sir Reginald, 58, 182
Wodaje, Dedjazmatch, 229
Wogara (Abyssinia), 57
Wojju (Abyssinia), 57
Wollo province (Abyssinia), 394–5, 428–9; famine, 436
Wolseley, General Sir Garnet, 177–8
Wossen, Asfa, Crown Prince of Abyssinia (Haile Selassie's son), 23, 51, 93, 351; WT appointed adviser to, 393–5; and WT's visit to Lalibela, 402–3; and 1960 plot against father, 430; suffers stroke, 436; offered crown, 438
Wren, P. C.: Beau Geste, 257
Wright, Sir Denis, 429–30
Wright, Iona, Lady, 429
Wright, Michael, 316

Yaio (father of Mohammed Yaio), 141
Yaio, Kenyazmatch, wazir of Aussa, 142–55
Yakub (brother of Khalifa), 181
Yasu, Lij (grandson of Emperor Menelik): WT's father meets, 26–7; proclaimed heir, 44–5; in succession struggle, 46–9, 327, 429; deposed, 50–1, 420; fights on, 57–8; detained, 109, 420; death, 110, 415; son, 166
Yavello (Abyssinia), 410
Yazidi people, 389
Yekuno Amlak, 33
Yemer, Ras, 57–8, 141, 425
Yoa, Lake (Sudan), 292
Yusuf Efendi, 197, 245–6

Yusuf German, 112, 130
Yusuf Nico, 112

Zalingi (Sudan), 214
Zauditu, Waizero, Empress of
    Abyssinia, 45, 54–5, 57–8, 88–9,
    425, 435

Zebit, Battle of (1930), 89
Zorchi (Sudan), 290
Zoscales, King of Aksum, 32
Zouar (Sudan), 277, 290
Zourmorie, 287
Zubair Rahmah, 176